Strategic Management of e-Business

Second edition

Reviews of the first edition

"Stephen Chen's book provides great in depth and up-to-date analysis of the strategic management issues that face business organizations as they embrace the Internet revolution. Sucinctly describing the main shifts in business economics and the opportunities and threats the digital world presents, *Strategic Management of e-Business* is the most comprehensive strategic guide to success in the online world this side of the millennium. Business leaders, economists, MBA students and e-commerce consultants alike should all read this book."

Peter Spark, CEO, Ecsponent

"As an e-business strategist in an interactive consultancy I am very aware that most books on the subject of e-business either make the error of being too simplistic or get buried in a narrow topic or specific technology. Steve Chen's book is the first I've seen that succeeds in providing a comprehensive coverage of the whole field whilst introducing enough of the technologies and challenges so that readers who get involved in e-business initiatives appreciate what is really involved. Additionally, Dr Chen has selected for us the most insightful pieces of current research and theory to achieve a balance of the pragmatic and the intellectually rigorous, making this a unique asset in understanding this fast-changing and critically important field of contemporary business."

Alan Warr, e-Business Strategy Consultant, Rubus

"As well as giving a valuable overview for newcomers to e-business strategy, Stephen Chen's book combines a powerful synthesis of academic thinking over many years with contemporary illustrations of strategic management issues in e-business. It is both thought-provoking and comprehensive, highlighting the importance of understanding the economic levers and collaboration in developing strategies for the digital economy."

Dr Katrina Delargy, E. Consulting, EDS

Strategic Management of e-Business

Second edition

Stephen Chen

Australian National University

John Wiley & Sons, Ltd

Other Wiley Editorial Offices

John Wiley & Sons Inc., 111 River Street, Hoboken, NJ 07030, USA

Jossey-Bass, 989 Market Street, San Francisco, CA 94103-1741, USA

Wiley-VCH Verlag GmbH, Boschstr. 12, D-69469 Weinheim, Germany

John Wiley & Sons Australia Ltd, 33 Park Road, Milton, Queensland 4064, Australia

John Wiley & Sons (Asia) Pte Ltd, 2 Clementi Loop #02-01, Jin Xing Distripark, Singapore
129809

John Wiley & Sons (Canada) Ltd, 22 Worcester Road, Etobicoke, Ontario M9W 1L1

Library of Congress Cataloging-in-Publication Data

Chen, Stephen.
Strategic management of e-business / Stephen Chan. — 2nd ed.
Includes bibliographical references and indexes.
ISBN 0-470-87073-7 (pbk. : alk. paper)
1. Electronic commerce – Management.   I. Title: Strategic management of
ebusiness.   II. Title.
HF5548.32.C473 2004
658.8′72 – dc22   2004007924

British Library Cataloguing in Publication Data

A catalogue record for this book is available from the British Library

ISBN-10: 0-470-87073-7 (pbk)
ISBN-13: 978-0470-87073-0 (pbk)

Project management by Originator, Gt Yarmouth, Norfolk (typeset in 10/12pt Goudy)
Printed and bound in Great Britain by Biddles Ltd, King's Lynn, Norfolk
This book is printed on acid-free paper responsibly manufactured from sustainable forestry,
in which at least two trees are planted for each one used for paper production.

Contents

CONTENTS

CONTENTS

PREFACE TO THE SECOND EDITION

Since the first edition was published, there have been several developments in the e-business world. First and foremost, the "dot.com crash" has claimed many victims, including many prominent and promising e-business start-ups. Second, as widely predicted, e-business markets have continued to expand at a fast pace, most notably in Asia, South America and Africa. Third, new Internet-related technologies have been developed, most notably for mobile devices. Fourth, much more research on e-businesses has been conducted and published, and much more is now known about e-business management. I am gratified that the book still fills a gap in the market despite all these developments. However, given the pace of developments in the sector, it was clear that a second edition of the book was warranted. Finally, it has been very gratifying that the book has been used in courses and well received by readers in several countries worldwide. However, judging from the feedback from some readers and from my personal experiences, having taught in the USA and Australia, in the meantime it was clear to me that some of the material in the book needed to be adapted for a worldwide audience.

The main changes in the second edition reflect these developments in e-business and the feedback received on the first edition. First, all cases have been updated. Several of the companies that were cited in the first edition failed to survive the dot.com crash and, consequently, have been replaced by other companies in the book. Second, all market data have been updated. More reference is made in the book to markets and companies in Asia, the area of the world that is currently expected to show the fastest growth. Third, the chapter on technology has been updated to reflect the latest developments, such as WiFi. Fourth, all chapters have been updated with the latest research studies to reflect the latest academic thinking and industry practice. Last, more examples from around the world have been added and issues related to less developed e-business markets have been included. However, it should be noted that the aim was not to provide a comprehensive review of the literature or the sector. Inevitably, it has been necessary to be selective and many notable authors and companies will have been excluded. Examples and references have simply been chosen that best illustrate or support the point made in the text. The presence or absence of a mention is, therefore, no indication of implied importance.

These changes have resulted in an almost completely updated Chapter 3, expanded Chapters 2, 7 and 8 and a largely rewritten Chapter 10. As a result some chapters now will require more than one session to cover, which was the original concept in the first edition. After much thought, it was felt that it was preferable to maintain the original structure of the book than to compromise its coherence by introducing new chapters that do not sit well with the others. It is hoped that readers will be able to make their own judgements about what can be covered adequately in each teaching or reading session.

New questions have also been added to the end of each chapter, and some questions have been amended or deleted to reflect changes since the first edition. For teachers and students using the book as a course textbook, the list of cases and other teaching material on the accompanying website have also been updated.

I would like to thank all those who provided useful feedback on the first edition, those who made useful suggestions for the second edition, particularly Edgar Lim who provided most helpful advice on the cover design and layout of the book, and Professor Chong Ju Choi, Executive Director of the National Graduate School of Management at ANU for his support of my publication endeavours.

Stephen Chen
Canberra, August 2004
mail@stephen-chen.com

PREFACE TO THE FIRST EDITION

Like any emerging field, e-business is changing fast and so is the thinking behind it. At present it is probably true to say that practice in the field is developing faster than research and teaching in business schools. There is currently no agreement on what should be taught in an e-business course and how. Many different approaches have been taken by teachers in different schools, and even within the same school. Therefore, it is important to say at the outset that this book is written unashamedly from a strategic management perspective of e-business, although it touches on related areas, such as Internet marketing and information systems. It also aims to achieve a balance between academic theory and practice of strategic management as applied to e-business; this may well be different from the approach adopted by other instructors or schools and by other authors.

This approach has been driven by two needs – one very practical and external in origin, the other more aesthetic and personal. First, the idea for this book came from a very practical need. Having agreed to develop a course on e-commerce for the MBA programme at Manchester Business School, I initially conducted an extensive search for suitable textbooks through the shelves of various bookstores and the catalogues of online bookstores. With a varied commercial and academic background in information systems, marketing and strategy, I felt it was important for the course to place e-business in the wider context of business strategy and for it to be based on sound academic research. At the same time, having studied for an MBA myself at Cranfield School of Management and INSEAD, I was aware that the textbook had to be of practical relevance in the field and not just be purely academic in order to be of interest and value to MBA students. I was disappointed to find no book that met all these requirements. While there were many books that dealt with the technical aspects of e-commerce and many guides of the type "how to build a website in a week", there were few books that dealt with the subject from a strategic perspective and that were supported by sound academic research. Those few books that did attempt to do so only examined a narrow aspect of the subject, such as the phenomenon of increasing returns and the effects of disintermediation.

Second, I felt there was something missing in the treatment given in many texts, which give the impression that the Internet and e-business are new inventions of the late 1990s. Having seen ideas such as electronic commerce, the information superhighway and the information economy evolve from pipedreams to reality over the course of my PhD research on the multimedia industry at Imperial College (1992–6) and post-doctoral research at City University Business School (1996–7), I felt it was important to show the events leading up to the e-business revolution and place e-business in its proper historical context. Furthermore, there were no texts that brought out the important links between the disparate areas related to e-business, such as business strategy, marketing, information systems, economics and law, which I had encountered in my various teaching and research activities.

It soon became apparent to me that I was unlikely to find a book that met all my needs. In order to cover the topics I wished to cover in my courses, I was forced to rely on a mixture of readings from a variety of sources, supplemented by lecture notes prepared by myself. In hindsight, although it has meant a great deal more work, this has been of benefit as it forced me to look at all the various subjects from a fresh perspective and try to link the various concepts together coherently so they can be taught in a single course. It has also encouraged me to try out various ideas in class that I would not otherwise have done. As the old adage says, "The best way to learn is to teach" and I have found it particularly true in this case. The discipline of having to give a lecture a week on a new topic but at the same time relate it to previous lectures was initially challenging, but has been extremely valuable in developing my own thinking about e-business and its various aspects.

The result has been a text that is broader in coverage than most texts on e-commerce and probably unconventional in its approach. However, it is one that has been tested in a variety of course formats with a variety of students and which has benefited from feedback from practical use over a period of 2 years. Various versions of the text or parts of it have been used as the basis for courses ranging from conventional MBA-level courses given once a week over a term, 4-day block courses and courses run over two weekends to executive development courses run over 1 day or half a day; these have been given to an international mix of students on the Manchester MBA programme, Turkish students in Istanbul Bilgi university, students on company programmes from Arthur Andersen and IBM as well as executive students from Brazil, Turkey and the UK. Most of the courses have involved a mixture of lectures and case study discussions. Seeing how students responded to and applied the ideas I presented has not only helped me to see which ideas from academic research are of most value in practice but also how best to present them and relate the academic theory to practice. Despite its undoubted shortcomings at least the text can be said to have passed the test of practical use in a class.

How to use this book

Advice for teachers

Each chapter in the book corresponds more or less to a topic that can be covered in one or two teaching sessions of 3 hours. However, depending on the students' previous experience, instructors may wish to spend more time on some topics. For example, the material presented in Chapter 2 on e-business technologies may be overwhelming if presented in one session for students with little experience in IT. Instructors may wish to spread this over more than one session or cover some material in conjunction with other topics. For example, useful links can be drawn between converging technologies and industry structures or between search engines and transaction cost theory.

Although all the chapters are linked to each other conceptually and cover a coherent set of ideas, it is also possible to change the order or cover one or more chapters in isolation if it is so wished. I have, for example, used Chapter 4 on its own as the basis for a short course on Internet marketing and Chapters 1 and 2 for an introductory course on e-commerce.

I have generally used the material in conjunction with a related case study, in addition to the mini-case studies, which I use to illustrate points in the lecture. This can be done, for example, by giving a lecture introducing the ideas and frameworks and asking students to apply the ideas to the case, either individually or in groups. Alternatively, students can discuss the case in the class followed by a lecture and discussion in which the ideas and frameworks are related to the case. Discussion questions are provided at the end of each chapter, which can be used to stimulate class debate or which can be set as essays. I have found it useful in stimulating discussion to relate the topic to some event in the news relating to e-business or to ask students to think of examples. There should be plenty to choose from at this time.

Due to the speed at which cases go out of date and new cases are being written, cases have not been listed. However, some cases that work well with the topic are listed by chapter on the website accompanying the book and will be updated as required. Additional material available on the website include PowerPoint slides for lectures, a more comprehensive reading list and links to useful websites; these can be used to prepare courses tailored as required. For example, an alternative to a case study discussion is the use of computer-based exercises, such as researching examples of new technologies and conducting market research using a Web.

Advice for students

This book can be used in a number of ways, depending on the course and the student's needs. In a taught course, teachers may either wish to assign chapters as pre-reading or as follow-up reading to accompany lectures. The book contains quite a number of frameworks that can be used in practical cases, but it is recommended that you first understand the principal ideas in each chapter. These are fewer in number and once understood will make the frameworks easier to remember and apply. A list of key concepts and questions for self-test are provided at the end of each chapter to enable you to check understanding.

For those students who are reading the book independently, it is recommended that you skim the book to get an idea of key concepts and links first before reading each chapter in detail. More detailed explanations can be obtained by consulting the articles or books listed at the end of each chapter. Mini-cases have been provided in the text to illustrate certain points and reinforce learning. As noted several times throughout the text, this field is changing rapidly and many of these cases will undoubtedly soon be out of date, but the basic principles should still apply and there should be plenty of fresh examples for you to find. The same applies to further reading listed at the end of each chapter. For updated cases and readings it is recommended that you consult the website accompanying the book.

Having written the book, I am painfully aware that there are still many weaknesses in the text and that by the time it is printed some of the material will be out of date or overtaken by events in the field. During the period when this book was being written e-businesses have experienced a roller coaster ride in the stockmarkets with valuations reaching astronomical heights and then plummeting just as quickly. As I write this preface, there has been talk in the press and other media about adjusting expectations of e-business to more realistic levels, echoing warnings made in Chapter 7 of the book about checking valuations of companies. However, the concepts introduced in the book should still be useful whatever the state of the e-economy and I hope readers will be able to take away something of value after reading it whatever their interest in e-business. Any suggestions or corrections will be gratefully received, either directly or via the publisher.

Stephen Chen
Manchester, January 2001

ABOUT THE AUTHOR

Stephen Chen is Director of the Masters in International Management in Mandarin Programme at the National Graduate School of Management – Australian National University. Previously, he has lectured at Manchester Business School, City University Business School, Henley Management College and Open Business School in the UK and has been a Visiting Associate Professor at the Anderson School of Management at UCLA in the USA.

His original interests and studies were in Natural Sciences before he switched to business and management. His career since has spanned both the practical and academic sides of business; this includes practical experience in IT, marketing and strategy in industry, MBA studies at Cranfield School of Management and INSEAD and a PhD at Imperial College, London on the multimedia industry. His current interests include the management of strategic change brought about by e-business in industries and firms, new e-business models, e-business entrepreneurship and development of e-business in emerging economies.

INTRODUCTION TO E-BUSINESS

We are on the verge of a revolution that is just as profound as the change in the economy that came with the industrial revolution. Soon electronic networks will allow people to transcend the barriers of time and distance and take advantage of global markets and business opportunities not even imaginable today, opening up a new world of economic possibility and progress.

US Vice President Albert Gore, Jr, 1997

Introduction

The beginning of the second millennium will almost certainly be remembered by business historians as a time of unprecedented change in the business world. In the space of a few years entire industries have been radically transformed, hundreds of thousands of new businesses have been spawned and fortunes made and lost by entrepreneurs and investors, all as a result of digital technologies. New technologies, such as the Internet, digital television, mobile telephones and intelligent home appliances, have all reached critical mass at the same time and are poised to revolutionize businesses in a way not seen since the Industrial Revolution. Many people have already named this the E-Business (electronic business) Revolution, an idea that has caught the imagination of many businesses, governments and individuals around the world.

This chapter provides a brief background to the Electronic Business Revolution, outlining some of the political initiatives around the world that have led to the global interest in electronic commerce. (Some of the technological developments will be described in Chapter 2.) It also assesses the economic and business impact of e-business and introduces some of the themes that will be explored in more detail in later chapters, such as electronic marketing methods and impacts on particular industries.

Defining and classifying e-businesses

To begin, it is useful to describe what is meant by electronic business or electronic commerce. There are various definitions of an electronic business or "e-business". Some define it as:

> the conduct of business on the Internet, not only buying and selling but also servicing customers and collaborating with business partners.
>
> *whatis.com*

Others include businesses using any electronic network to conduct buying and selling as well as other activities.

E-businesses can be classified into four main types according to the type of buyer and seller in the transaction (Figure 1.1):

- Business-to-consumer (B2C). These have been the most highly publicized of e-businesses and are online stores or shopping sites. Examples include online retailers, such as Amazon (*www.amazon.com*), and direct sales companies, such as Dell (*www.dell.com*).
- Business-to-business (B2B). Examples include Cisco (*www.cisco.com*) and Intel (*www.intel.com*), both of which offer online procurement and customer support.
- Consumer-to-consumer (C2C). This has been one of the fastest growing sectors and one where the Internet provides significant advantages over conventional channels. Examples include classified advertisement sites, such as Loot (*www.loot.com*), which allow individuals to post notices of items for sale, as well as auction sites, such as e-Bay (*www.ebay.com*), which allow individuals to put items up for auction.
- Consumer-to-business (C2B). This category includes individuals offering their services

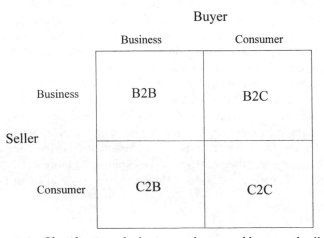

Figure 1.1   Classification of e-businesses by type of buyer and seller.

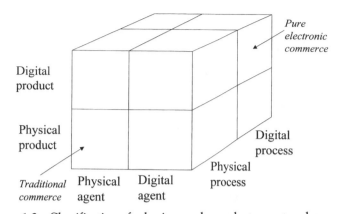

Figure 1.2 Classification of e-businesses by product, agent and process
(from Choi et al., 1997, reproduced with permission from Macmillan).

to businesses (e.g., accountants and lawyers) and sites that allow individuals to offer items for sale to businesses.

An alternative classification (Figure 1.2) is according to the type of product, process and delivery agent (Choi et al., 1997).

A product can be physical or digital, an agent can be physical or digital and the process can be physical or digital; this creates eight possible types of business, ranging from businesses that are purely physical (physical product, physical agent and physical process) to purely digital (digital product, digital agent and digital process). An example of the former is the traditional high street store while an example of the latter might be the music software site Real Jukebox, where the product, agent, delivery and payment are all digital. In this categorization, Amazon.com would not be a pure e-business since its products and part of its processes are still physical in nature.

There are many definitions of electronic commerce. Some people include all financial and commercial transactions that take place electronically, including electronic data interchange (EDI), electronic funds transfer (EFT) and all credit/debit card activity. Others limit electronic commerce to retail sales to consumers for which the transaction and payment take place on open networks, like the Internet. Others distinguish between electronic commerce (e-commerce) and electronic business (e-business), limiting the former to buying and selling activities, not including other business activities, such as servicing customers, collaborating with partners and communicating within the organization, which are encompassed by the latter.

Scope of book

At its most basic, electronic commerce involves the electronic exchange of information or "digital content" between two or more parties, which results in a monetary exchange (Figure 1.3).

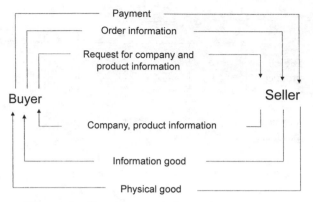

Figure 1.3 Components of electronic commerce.

The basic components required to operate such a system are for the seller:

- Content production.
- Digitization of content (conversion of content into digital format).
- Storage of digitized content.
- Link to electronic network.
- Link to electronic payment system.
- Link to physical manufacturing and delivery systems (where there is an exchange of physical goods).

For the buyer:

- Link to electronic network.
- Search and locate content on network.
- Retrieve information from network.
- Display information.
- Place order.
- Link to electronic payment system.

Although such a system seems relatively simple in principle, in order to allow "any information anywhere" several disparate technologies are required to work together. Examples of various technologies and devices to perform each of the above steps are:

- Content production – word processors, video cameras and editing software, music synthesizers.
- Digitization – digital cameras, scanners, dictation software, "ripper" software for music.
- Storage – a variety of storage is now available for digitized material, including hard disk drives, floppy diskettes, CD-ROMs and tapes.

- Network communications – dedicated lines, telephone, cable, mobile phone, electricity cables.
- Network connections – PC and modem, television and set-top box.
- Information search and retrieval mechanisms – search engines and directories.
- Display devices – PC, TV, mobile phone.

EDI and EFT

Although it discusses traditional e-commerce systems, such as EDI and EFT, this book focuses specifically on business that is conducted over networks that use non-proprietary protocols, such as the Internet. This includes internal networks (e.g., intranets) and networks that extend to a limited number of participants (e.g., extranets). It also includes communications and broadcasting networks, such as telephone, satellite and cable networks.

The focus on networks that use non-proprietary protocols, which are a relatively new phenomenon, is important for a number of reasons. First, earlier forms of e-commerce required expensive and complex custom software, dedicated communication links and, in many cases, strictly compatible equipment. Consequently, usage of early e-commerce systems, such as EDI and EFT, was mainly limited to large businesses and their first-tier suppliers. In contrast, one of the main drivers of growth of Internet systems is that they can exploit the existing information and communication infrastructure, allowing businesses of all sizes and even individuals to utilize a vast global network with minimal investment; this has led to a massive explosion in the adoption of electronic commerce. In 1999, traffic on the Internet was estimated to be doubling every hundred days. To put this in perspective, the Internet took 4 years to reach 50 million users compared with 16 years for PCs, 13 years for TV and 38 years for radio (Figure 1.4).

Some of the technological developments that have contributed to the present explosion in electronic commerce will be dealt with in more detail in Chapter 2. However, apart from the lower cost and ease of use of the technology, one of the

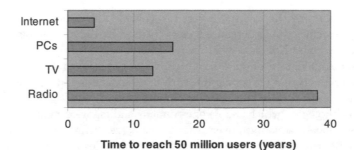

Figure 1.4   Comparison of adoption rates for Internet, PCs, TV and radio.

INDUSTRIES AFFECTED

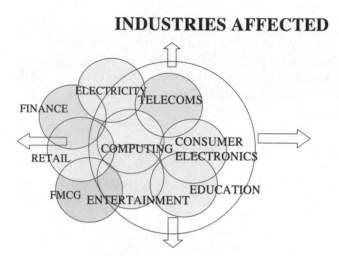

Figure 1.5 Colliding industries
(FMCG = fast moving consumer goods. Reproduced with permission from Paul Kampas).

significant characteristics of the new technology is that the open standards, accompanied by widespread deregulation of the industries, allow telephone systems, computer systems and cable TV systems to be easily interconnected. The phrase "digital convergence" has been widely used to describe the resulting convergence in technologies and industries. The industries most immediately affected were the communications, electronics, computing and information/entertainment sectors (Figure 1.5), although this is now spreading to other sectors, such as manufacturing and retail.

However, as Kampas (2000) shows (Figure 1.6), convergence is also occurring at the infrastructure, appliance and application levels across a range of industries, and the list is ever-increasing. Most, if not all, industries can now be included in the list of industries that are connected in the Internet.

This new information infrastructure provides several advantages for users and extends its usage and coverage well beyond the scope of previous e-commerce systems, such as EDI and EFT. Some of the reasons include the following:

- The cost of accessing the Internet is very low compared with networks that adhere to proprietary systems; this has reduced users' fears that the technology may quickly become obsolete and has encouraged many users to adopt it.
- The widespread adoption of these standards has in turn encouraged firms to invest in developing products that are compatible with these standards and to extend their use to a wide range of data, including voice, audio and video.
- The new technologies, which enable one-to-many and many-to-many communication, present a significant advantage over other e-commerce technologies, such as EDI, TV and telephone; this will have a significant impact on industries that currently rely on these technologies and will create many new business opportunities.

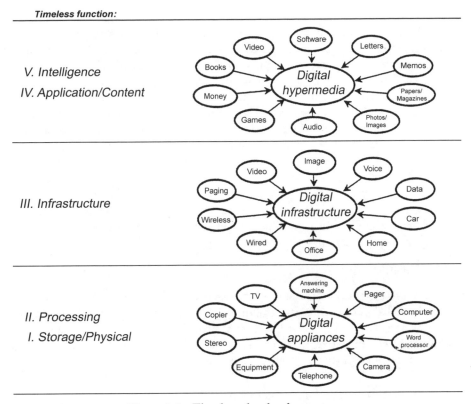

Figure 1.6   The three levels of convergence
(reproduced with permission from Paul Kampas).

Political initiatives

Apart from the technological drivers, another factor driving the phenomenal growth of electronic commerce is that, unlike previous attempts at electronic commerce, the current standards have national and international backing at government level. Although the technological possibility to create a global digital information network had been mooted for many years, the first practical plan to create such a network was first suggested in the draft of the High Performance Computing Act (HPCA) of 1991 by Al Gore, then a US senator. However, this was initially just a plan to link together supercomputing research centres in the USA in a high-speed "information superhighway" and support other work in high-performance computing. When the Democrats later won the Presidential election in the USA, the notion of building an information superhighway to stimulate the US economy became a key component of the Administration's economic reconstruction policy, and the information superhighway has become politically and economically significant.

At the start of 1993 the CEOs of 13 major US computer companies lobbied for legislation that would extend the government's existing high-performance computing and communications programme beyond the realm of government and university laboratories into offices and homes across the USA; this was followed in April 1993 by a proposal from Congressman Boucher to amend the 1991 HPCA to join all schools, libraries and local government offices to the Internet. Later in September 1993, US Vice President Al Gore and Secretary of Commerce Ron Brown announced the National Information Infrastructure (NII) initiative, a public–private partnership to construct "a seamless web of communications networks, computers, databases, and consumer electronics" (Information Infrastructure Task Force, 1993). This infrastructure would "make it easy and affordable to connect people with each other, with computers, and with a vast array of services and information resources" (from Information Infrastructure Executive Order, 1993). Other countries soon launched similar initiatives (e.g., members of the EU, Malaysia, Singapore, China, Japan and Korea).

European initiatives

It was always recognized that, to take full advantage of the technology, the NII had to form part of a global information infrastructure (GII) and similar initiatives have followed in other countries. For example, the UK Department of Trade and Industry launched an Information Society Initiative in 1996. This was followed in 1997 by the European Initiative in Electronic Commerce, which aimed to:

- Promote the technology and infrastructure needed to ensure the competitiveness of the European electronic commerce industry, and put in place structures that will provide efficient access systems for existing and potential users.
- Capitalize on the Single Market by ensuring a coherent regulatory framework for electronic commerce in Europe and in wider global markets.
- Foster a favourable business environment for electronic commerce by promoting adequate skills and by making consumers and industry aware of the opportunities offered by electronic commerce.
- Work toward global consensus from a common European position to ensure effective participation in current international co-operation and negotiation.

Malaysia

In Malaysia a significant programme to harness the new technology for economic growth was initiated in 1998; this proposed a three-phase plan to become a fully developed, mature and knowledge-rich society by the year 2020:

- Phase I – in this phase, which has already begun, Malaysia has created a Multimedia Super Corridor, a corridor 15 km wide and 50 km long, that starts from the Kuala Lumpur City Centre (KLCC) and extends south to the Kuala Lumpur International

Airport, housing high-technology companies, R&D centres, a university and two "intelligent cities", Cyberjaya and Putrajaya.

- Phase II – in this phase, the Multimedia Super Corridor will be linked to other cybercities in Malaysia and the world. The government will also set global standards in flagship applications, champion cyberlaws within the global society and establish a number of intelligent globally linked cities.
- Phase III – the aim is that, by this final phase, Malaysia will be transformed into a knowledge-based society. It will have a cluster of intelligent cities linked to the global information superhighway, be the Asian base for a number of leading multimedia companies and become the platform for the International Cybercourt of Justice.

Singapore

In 1998 the Singapore government launched an Electronic Commerce Plan to stimulate the widespread adoption of electronic commerce in Singapore and to strengthen Singapore's position as an international e-commerce hub; this includes infrastructure building, public awareness campaigns, PR to attract foreign and local businesses, and harmonization of cross-border laws for electronic commerce. The target was to have S$4 billion worth of products and services transacted electronically through Singapore and 50% of businesses using some form of e-commerce by the year 2003.

China

In 1993, Hu Qili, Minister for the Electronics Industry, proposed the idea of the "Three Golden" projects, China's version of the information superhighway. The Golden Bridge project aimed to build an infrastructure for the use of information technology in the national economy, also known as the China National Economic Information Network, incorporating both satellite and landline networks. Golden Gate (Golden Customs) was a foreign trade information network linking the Ministry of Foreign Trade and Economic Co-operation and the Customs Bureau. Golden Card was a credit card verification scheme designed to promote the use and dissemination of credit cards. A fourth "secret" Golden Sea project was aimed at building a security and administration network for leaders of the government, providing them with immediate access to reference data from other institutions, organizations and offices under the direct jurisdiction of the Communist Party Central Committee.

Japan

The Japanese Ministry of International Trade and Industry (MITI) has been active in electronic commerce since 1995, when a supplementary budget of JPY 32 billion was allocated for the promotion of electronic commerce. In addition, pilot projects to accelerate the practical use of electronic commerce were implemented in the supplementary budget for 1998 (over JPY 40 billion). However, the main initiatives have come from industry. For example, the Telecom Service Association (TELESA) has carried out international interconnection tests between Japan and Singapore and between Japan and Korea.

Korea

In Korea the government established the first Master Plan for Informatization Promotion in 1996, a series of 10 key projects aimed at the realization of an advanced information society by 2010, including the building of high-speed information networks; this was followed in 1999 by Cyber Korea 21, a plan to transform the Korean economy into a knowledge-based one for the 21st century, and in 2002 by e-Korea Vision 2006, a 4-year plan to develop Korea as a global player in information technology.

International initiatives

Several initiatives have also been launched at the international level. In 1996 the USA, Canada and Australia jointly produced a discussion paper entitled "Implications of the Communications Revolution for Tax Policy and Administration". In July 1997, US President Bill Clinton and Vice President Al Gore released their proposal for "A framework for global electronic commerce". In 1998, OECD hosted a *Ministerial Conference on Electronic Commerce* to discuss international policy on electronic commerce, which was followed by a second conference in 2000.

Economic benefits

One of the factors behind the initiatives by many governments around the world has been the promise of significant gains in economic productivity from electronic commerce. The Internet economy in the USA is estimated to have grown by 62% from $322 billion in 1998 to $830 billion in 2000 (Internet Economy Indicators *http://www.internetindicators. com*); this includes companies directly generating all or some part of their revenues from Internet or Internet-related products and services. These can be divided into four layers:

- Layer 1 – the Internet Infrastructure Indicator. The gross revenues and attributed employees from companies that manufacture or provide products and services that make up the Internet network infrastructure (e.g., telecommunications and fibre backbones, "last mile" access, Internet dial-up access and end-user networking equipment). It also includes PC and server manufacturers, modem manufacturers and other manufacturers of the hardware necessary for the Internet to function.
- Layer 2 – the Internet Applications Indicator. The gross revenues and attributed employees from companies that provide products and services in this layer that build on the network infrastructure and make it technologically possible to perform business activities online; these include electronic commerce application providers (e.g., Netscape, IBM, Microsoft), Internet consulting services, multimedia applications, development software, search engine software, Web-enabled databases and online training services.

- Layer 3 – the Internet Intermediary Indicator. The gross revenues and attributed employees from companies that increase the efficiency of electronic markets as Internet middlemen by facilitating the meeting and interaction of buyers and sellers via the World Wide Web and Internet. This layer includes online brokerages, Internet ad brokers (e.g., Doubleclick, 24/7 Media), portals/content providers (e.g., Yahoo, Excite, Geocities), market makers in vertical industries (e.g., VerticalNet, PCOrder), content aggregators (e.g., CNET, ZDnet, Broadcast.com) and online travel agencies.
- Layer 4 – the Internet Commerce Indicator. The gross revenues and attributed employees from companies that generate product and service sales to consumers or businesses over the World Wide Web and Internet. This layer includes online retailing, pay-to-use content and other business-to-business and business-to-consumer transactions conducted on the World Wide Web and Internet.

At the same time as the Internet economy has grown, according to the US Department of Commerce, the US economy as a whole has shown a remarkable increase in productivity. Productivity growth doubled from an average of 1.4% between 1973 and 1995 to a 2.8% rate from 1995 to 1999 (Figure 1.7).

Evidence is increasing that this is not mere coincidence and represents real growth in economic productivity as a result of investment in computing and communications technologies. Advances in technology have produced sharp declines in the prices of computer processing, data storage and retrieval, and communications, which are in turn driving both the increase in Internet activity and the increases in business investment in IT hardware and software.

At the same time the IT industries have shown extraordinary growth, increasing their share of the economy from 6.3% in 1994 to a peak of 8.9% in 2000 (Figure 1.8). In contrast, between 1990 and 1994 the average annual growth was only 0.5%. Pre-packaged software and computer services had the highest growth rate, increasing their output at an average annual rate of 17% from 1995 to 2000. Over the same period, the computer

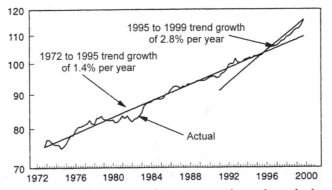

Figure 1.7 The trend rate of non-farm productivity growth accelerated after 1995 (Index 1992 = 100, log scale)

(from US Department of Commerce, 2000).

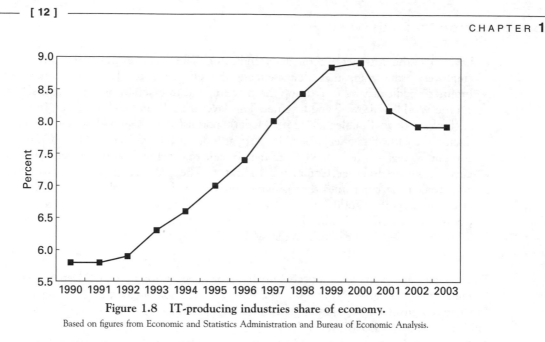

Figure 1.8   IT-producing industries share of economy.
Based on figures from Economic and Statistics Administration and Bureau of Economic Analysis.

hardware and communications equipment industries increased their output at a 9% annual rate, and output in the communications services sector rose at a 7% annual pace.

The contribution to real economic growth is even more striking. IT industries produce less than 10% of total US output. Nevertheless, between 1995 and 2003, they accounted for an average 30% of total real US economic growth (Figure 1.9) and nearly 100% during 2001 when the rest of the economy was stagnant.

One reason for the extraordinary pattern of productivity appears to have been a

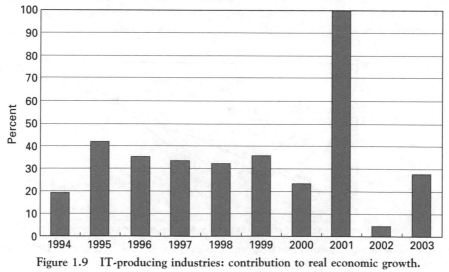

Figure 1.9   IT-producing industries: contribution to real economic growth.
Source: Digital Economy 2003, US Economics and Statistics Administration.

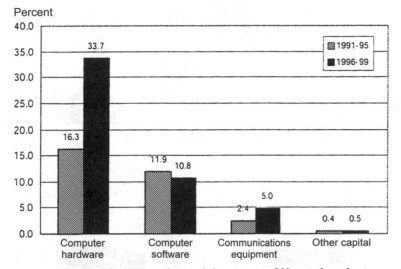

Figure 1.10   Average annual rates of capital deepening in US non-farm business sector
(from Oliner and Sichel, 2000, tables 1 and 2, pp. 24–25).

significant shift from use of labour to IT in the economy shown by a significant IT "capital deepening", beginning in 1991 and accelerating sharply after 1995. The ratio of the capital stock of computer hardware to hours worked increased, on average, by 16.3% per year over the period 1991–1995 and 33.7% per year during 1996–1999 (Figure 1.10). In contrast, over the same period, the rate of capital deepening for all other forms of capital averaged only about 0.5% per year.

According to one study, the adoption of Internet business solutions has already yielded cumulative cost savings of $155.2 billion to US organizations and an increase in revenues of $444 billion. Once all current solutions have been fully implemented, firms expect to realize cost savings of $528 billion and revenue increases of $1,552 billion; this equates to cost savings of 4.3% of GDP over the period 2001 to 2010 or 0.43 percentage points of the future increase in annual US productivity from 2001 to 2011 (Net Impact Study, 2002).

The same study estimates Internet business solutions have already resulted in cost savings of EUR9.0 billion (USD8.3 billion) and revenue increases of EUR86.4 billion (USD79 billion) in the UK, France and Germany combined. Once fully implemented, cost savings of EUR88 billion and revenue increases of EUR230 billion are expected; this equates to cost savings of 1.1% GDP over the period 2001 to 2010 or a 0.11% increase in annual productivity.

The new economy

Some commentators (e.g., Tapscott, 1996) have suggested that a "new economy" is emerging in many developed countries, one that is dominated by knowledge industries

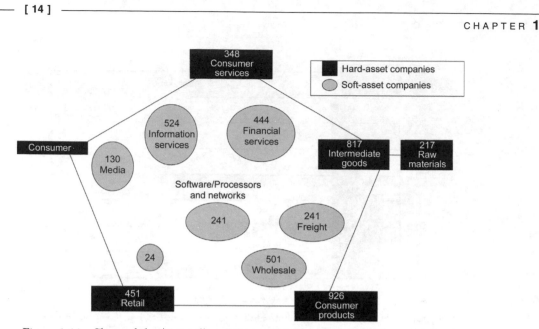

Figure 1.11   Share of the $4.9 trillion US virtual value chain (in billions of dollars)
(from Aldrich, 1999, p. 89. Reproduced with permission from John Wiley & Sons).

and driven by information technologies. For example, "soft" or information-based companies contributed 43% of the total value of the US economy in 1997; these include financial services, media, advertising, freight, software and telecommunications (Figure 1.11). This compares with only 37% in 1987 and 22% in 1957 (Aldrich, 1999, p. 89).

Similar effects are occurring in other developed economies, especially the northern European countries (Finland, Sweden, Norway, the Netherlands and the United Kingdom) (Figure 1.12). In Finland the ICT sector's share of value added nearly doubled from 7.8% in 1995 to over 15% in 2000 and the ICT sector accounts for almost 22% of total manufacturing value added (OECD, 2000).

The ICT sector is also a major source of employment growth in the developed economies (Figure 1.13). Employment in the ICT sector within the OECD grew on average by over 4% annually over the period 1995–2000, almost three times the rate of overall business sector employment. Most of this growth is derived from the ICT services sector except in Finland and Mexico where ICT manufacturing employment grew by over 9% annually, and Canada, the Czech Republic, the Nordic countries, Spain and the United Kingdom, where it grew between 3% and 5% annually.

Impact on businesses and competitive strategy

At this stage of development of electronic commerce, everything that constitutes a market – products, industrial structures, trade and competition rules, regulations and

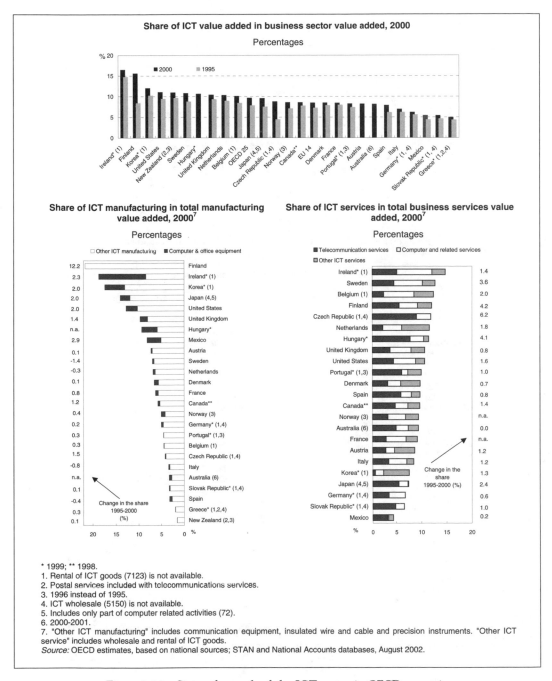

Figure 1.12 Size and growth of the ICT sector in OECD countries

7123 and 5150 are ISIC (International Standard Classification of Activities) numbers; STAN = the OECD Structural Analysis Database
(*source*: 'Measuring the Information Economy 2002', OECD copyright, 2002).

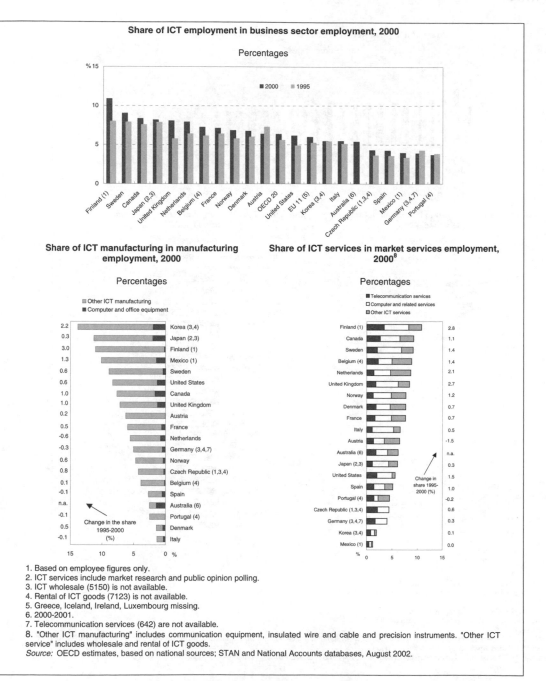

Figure 1.13 The contribution of the ICT sector to employment growth

7123 and 5150 are ISIC (International Standard Classification of Activities) numbers; STAN = the OECD Structural Analysis Database

(*source*: 'Measuring the Information Economy 2002', OECD copyright, 2002)

laws – is in the process of being redefined; this raises numerous new issues for businesses. For example, how will the new networks affect industries and the economy at large, how should firms compete in the new electronic marketplaces that are developing, how can firms utilize the networks for marketing products and services, how can firms integrate the network into existing business operations and how should they manage the new organization? This makes it important for business strategy, marketing, operations, finance and legal specialists as well as IT specialists to understand the networks and their business implications.

New marketing and distribution channels

The most straightforward and obvious impact on many businesses will be the addition of a new channel for marketing and distributing products. The Internet provides a ready-made distribution channel for information or digitized products and a shop window to display products that can be seen worldwide.

Efficiency gains

One of the advantages of using an electronic channel is the efficiency gain. Aldrich (1999) argues that one of the most significant business advantages of electronic networks is the ability to create a seamlessly integrated value chain linking primary sources of goods to consumers (Figure 1.14); this can generate tremendous efficiencies

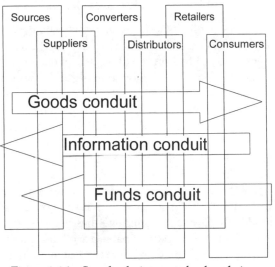

Figure 1.14 Seamlessly integrated value chain
(reproduced with permission from John Wiley & Sons).

through reduced transaction costs, faster throughput and better information to all members of the chain. As will be seen in Chapter 6 this can also lead to radical restructuring of industries and firms (e.g., by creating alternative channels and intermediaries, or substituting existing channels and bypassing existing intermediaries).

Death of distance

Another significant effect of using global networks is what Cairncross (1997) terms the "death of distance", meaning that distance becomes less important. Because a webpage is accessible to anyone with access to the Internet, electronic commerce greatly extends the market reach of firms, vastly expanding opportunities and creating new demand. For example, some Amazon Indian tribes are using the Internet as a means to reach customers for their products around the world, something not previously possible (*www.amazoncoop.org*).

The global reach of e-commerce combined with a reduction in transaction costs also enables an aggregation of demand, creating a market that can sustain new niche products; in the past, the small market potential would have been economically unfeasible. Examples include HotHotHot (*www.hothothot.com*), a US company that specializes in the sale of chilli peppers and sauces to chilli enthusiasts, and Jack Scaife (*www.jackscaife. co.uk*), a family butcher in England that markets home-made, traditional Yorkshire sausages around the world.

Mini-case study: Jack Scaife

Smoked bacon is not the most obvious product that would be associated with the Internet (Figure 1.15). However, Chris Battle, a Yorkshire butcher says, "I've had to eat my words. When my daughters suggested we sell smoked bacon on the Internet I thought they were daft. But now we sell more than three tonnes per week to customers as far afield as Peru, Japan and South Africa."

In 1994, the family-owned shop in Keighley, Yorkshire had annual sales of £90,000 for traditional-style British bacon, made by smoking it over fires fuelled with oak shavings. Initially, business grew through word of mouth and press coverage, generating growing mail order sales for the business. In 1997, urged on by his daughters Joanne and Angela, Battle spent £1,000 to set up a website. "Spending £1,000 setting up a website sounded like a total waste of money," Battle says. At first, he seemed to be proved right as there was no response for several weeks. But then the business suddenly took off and turnover has risen to over £750,000. Initially, the sales came from British expatriates unable to obtain traditional British bacon abroad but, as word has spread, now an increasing amount is sold to the domestic market.

Figure 1.15   Jack Scaife (*www.jackscaife.co.uk*)
(reproduced with permission from Jack Scaife).

Internet-based electronic commerce is also creating new opportunities for trade by creating new delivery channels for digitized products and services. For example, many software firms now use the Internet to distribute software. Other services, from financial services to education to medical services to others yet to be devised, also have the potential to become more globally traded.

The Internet can remove many of the distribution and marketing barriers that can prevent firms from gaining access to foreign markets. For example, many small- and medium-sized firms (SMEs) are using the Internet as a business-to-business tool to open and/or maintain a presence in foreign markets. Electronic commerce lowers the information and transaction costs of operating in overseas markets and provides a cheap and efficient way to strengthen customer–supplier relations (e.g., through email, remote online databases and video links).

In traditional markets, firms seeking to compete globally will usually start by testing their products and building brand recognition and reputation in a small geographic market. The existence of geographical and time barriers allows the local development of multiple players. In addition, these barriers limit players' ability to exploit economies of scale. In contrast, as markets on the Internet have no geographical boundaries, a new entrant cannot, in principle, take advantage of a geographical niche or use a neighbouring geographic market as a springboard. The only neighbouring markets that can serve as a springboard are product markets. For example, Internet retailer Amazon has added music, electronics and other retail activities to book publishing; this is why the current trend is for existing network players to extend their market and globalize their offer. The characteristics of information networks and the related technologies enable these firms to capture markets to an extent not before possible.

Death of time

Equally as important as distance in most business transactions is the factor of time – time to reach the shop, time to search for the required good, time to deliver it, etc.; and just as electronic networks have led to the "death of distance", electronic networks can lead to a "death of time" in some businesses or at least a change in the time factors. One of the most obvious effects of using electronic networks is that it allows instantaneous responses and, in the case of digital products, instantaneous delivery online. Instead of waiting days for a letter or a package by mail, it is possible to place an order and receive the good or service immediately. In some cases this has led to improvements in existing services (e.g., online software delivery).

In other cases it has created entirely new markets. Online auctions, such as those used by airlines to sell unsold seats at the last minute, are one example of using e-commerce to aggregate demand, creating a new market that delivers value to the consumer (inexpensive flights) and revenue to the producer. Another example is lastminute.com, a UK Internet firm, which has built a business around the buying and selling of goods and services at the last minute, creating a new market for unsold airplane and theatre tickets.

Mini-case study: Lastminute.com

Lastminute.com (*www.lastminute.com*) (Figure 1.16) is probably the UK's best known pure Internet business. Whereas some businesses use the Web as an adjunct to what they already offer "offline", Lastminute.com uses the power of the Internet to offer services that traditional offline companies simply cannot provide. The idea behind Lastminute.com is a simple one: to use the Internet to provide last-minute bargains for items such as theatre tickets, flights and hotel rooms to cash-rich, time-poor customers.

The company was launched in November 1998, although co-founder Brent Hoberman says, "I'd had the idea years before. I'd written things down about it over the years about how I could get this thing off the ground, but I thought I wasn't ready and the industry wasn't ready." That all changed as the Internet took off and Hoberman formed a company together with co-founder Martha Lane Fox to develop the idea in April 1998. Prior to forming Lastminute.com, Hoberman had spent 5 years in strategy consulting before moving to LineOne, the UK Internet service provider (ISP) now owned by British Telecom, and subsequently helping to found an online auction business. Martha Lane Fox had also worked in strategic consultancy at

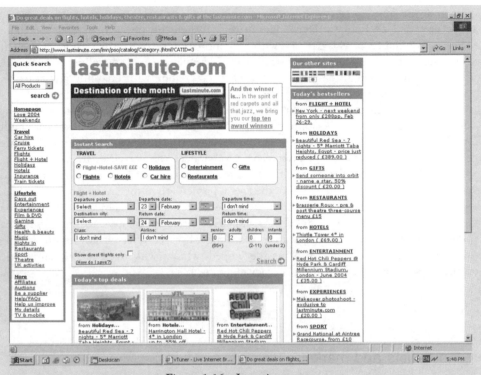

Figure 1.16 Lastminute.com

(© Last Minute Network Limited 2004, reprinted with its permission).

Spectrum Strategy Consultants, where she and Hoberman met, and then at Carlton Digital Channels, where she was responsible for generating and analysing new channel and interactive concepts.

The company was formed with £600,000 of funding to cover start-up costs, and the site went live in November 1998. An additional £6.6 million worth of funding was secured in June 1999 from an investor group led by Global Retail Partners which included Intel Corporation, T-Venture, Amadeus Capital Partners and Harvey Goldsmith, as well as seed investors Arts Alliance, Innovacom and NewMedia Investors.

The company floated on the London Stock Exchange in 2000 amid much fanfare and controversy over a last-minute increase in offer price. It immediately entered the FTSE-100 list of top 100 companies by capitalization, while the founders were featured in an exhibition at the National Gallery in London. Since then, in line with other Internet businesses, share prices have not fared so well and have dropped to below the offer price. Despite this setback, the company is continuing to expand its operations. Following the success of the UK site, local sites have been set up in France, Germany, Sweden and Australia.

Apart from the speed of response, another benefit of electronic commerce is that services can be provided 24 hours a day, 7 days a week. Where no physical product, agent or process is required (e.g., as is the case with an information service), the system can be left to run automatically. Where a physical agent is required (e.g., to deliver a package), instructions can be left to be acted on the next day. Along with enabling global reach, this enables businesses to serve customers around the world anywhere, anytime.

Other technologies can save time not only through faster communication but also by undertaking many of the tasks currently performed by humans. Many businesses are built around saving time for customers (e.g., travel agencies, insurance brokers and estate agents). While it is possible for most people to conduct the activities themselves (e.g., to book flights, accommodation and tours for their own holidays), many people prefer to leave the arrangements in the hands of the agent, particularly if they have a busy schedule. Electronic commerce can radically alter the value of such businesses by reducing the time taken to conduct those same activities. As will be seen in later chapters, technology is now available which will allow easy search and comparison of offers from various online businesses, and technology is being developed which will even allow automatic ordering of services based on the customer requirements.

New products and markets

Apart from creating new marketing and distribution channels, the greatest future economic impact of electronic commerce is also likely to come from the creation of new products or the radical transformation of existing ones and the consequent creation of new markets; these are likely to be of three types.

Radically redefining existing products/services

Many old products are being radically transformed by the addition of intangible digital improvements that continue to erode the distinction between a good and a service. An example is email; this is seen as a substitute for physical mail, but it can be sent securely to many recipients across the globe, with verification, in a few hours. In addition to text, it can contain links to other documents and include audio and video clips and multiple attachments. With traditional mail, this would be either impossible or very difficult. This new functionality and interactivity is an aspect of electronic commerce that is likely to transform old products and thus generate new demand. The same is true of service businesses. The example of Amazon.com, the online bookstore, shows how information technology can transform the traditional book retail experience by providing a selection of millions of books, chats with authors and reviews by critics and customers.

Personalized products

Another benefit that use of IT systems provides is the ability to track customer buying patterns more closely. Businesses can use the information gained in this way to use product suggestions and personalized interfaces as marketing tools. Amazon.com, for example, uses filtering tools to profile customers and determine their purchasing patterns. On the basis of information gleaned from this database, Amazon suggests other books that might interest customers, based on the purchasing patterns of those who have bought similar books.

Marketing "free" products

The lower transaction costs, interactivity and ability to market on a one-to-one basis make it possible to market items using e-commerce which previously could not economically be bought or sold and existed as non-market transactions. Two examples are advertising and private information.

In the past, the only monetary benefit a consumer could have gained from reading an advertisement would be a coupon or rebate for a price reduction when buying the product or possibly an in-kind benefit, such as frequent flyer miles. With pay-per-view advertising, electronic commerce now enables advertisers to pay consumers to read an advertisement. Similarly, in the past, private information about individuals collected by businesses for marketing purposes, such as name, address, and demographic and financial information, was often acquired from individuals without any direct compensation. With e-commerce, it is possible to establish a market for this information, and businesses can buy this "product" from owners just as they compensate workers for their labour.

Another example is the creation of spot markets for products for which the market was too diverse and scattered, but which electronic commerce makes feasible. Using the breadth and instantaneous communications offered by the Internet, DRAMeXchange provides a neutral e-worldwide marketplace for professional dynamic random access memory (DRAM) buyers and sellers.

Mini-case study: DRAMeXchange

Like many other electronic marketplaces, DRAMeXchange was founded on the insight that manufacturers with temporary surpluses or shortages were unable to find and trade with one another without revealing competitive information. Companies with surplus inventory can post anonymous sell orders on the DRAMeXchange website where they are matched with incoming buy orders. Once a deal is struck, DRAMeXchange's logistics and payment system ensures that members can trade anonymously. In addition to the transaction service, DRAMeXchange provides daily and historical spot price, product specification, analyses, news collection to assist in decision making, a members' forum for informal news and a bulletin to publish their news.

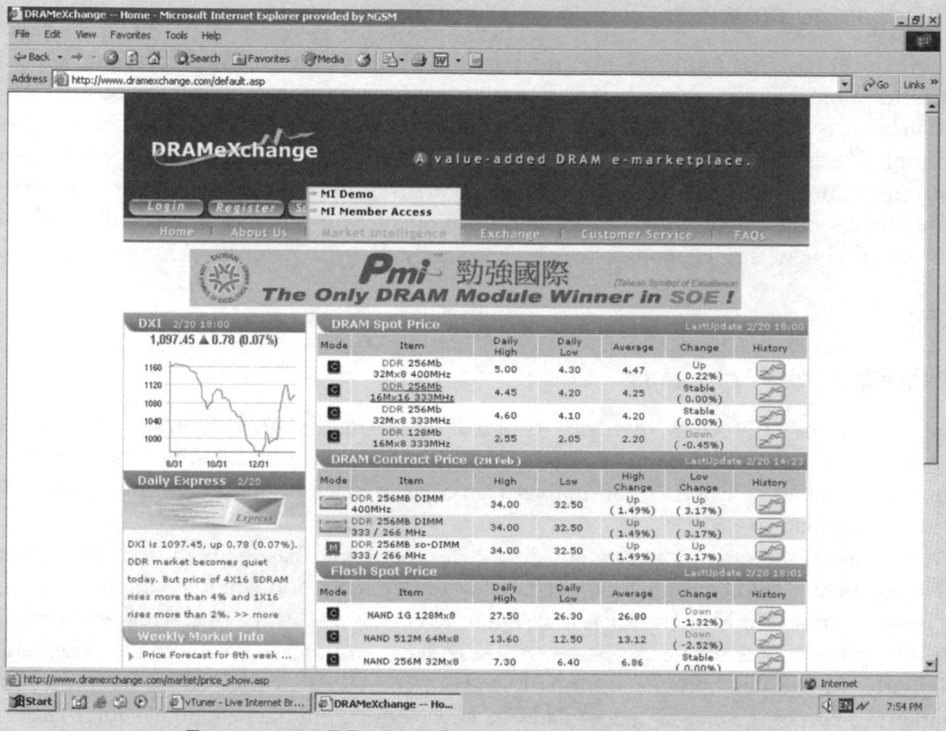

Figure 1.17 DRAMeXchange (*www.dramexchange.com*)
(reproduced with permission from DRAMeXchange.com).

Substitution of existing products and channels

Some of the industries most significantly affected by electronic commerce include the following.

Letter delivery

Email is one of the most popular Internet applications and, while much of this mail consists of small, spontaneous messages that complement existing letter mail, some substitution is inevitable. The Universal Postal Union (UPU) estimates that the share of physical mail in the overall communication market (including mail, fax, phone, email) in Western Europe and North America will drop from about 28% in 1995 to less than 20% by 2005. At the same time the share of email is expected to double from 12% to 24%. The biggest impact is expected in business-to-business mail, where email is expected to capture an additional 12% of the market by 2005; in the business-to-consumer segment, email is expected to capture 4–5%.

Telephony, fax, videoconferencing and the Internet

The Internet provides a standard technology for a wide variety of communications that may lead to substitution of previous systems (e.g., fixed-line, circuit telephone service, fax transmission and broadcasting). However, the quality and reliability of some of these services may be less than current norms where broadband is not available. Therefore, some observers estimate that the immediate impact will be larger on communication services that are not time-dependent (fax, voicemail and pagers) and that only about 5% of the voice market will shift to the Internet in the near future, owing to sensitivity to losses in quality.

In addition, the use of telephony and fax services may change as electronic commerce technology develops. With the development of Internet telephony, most e-commerce sites in the near future will have a telephone link to a customer service representative who could maintain the role of the telephone in the sales process. While this will not have a demonstrable impact on the telephone system itself, it could affect the size and number of call centres as fewer operators are needed as processing transactions becomes more efficient.

Publishing

Many publishers have gone online, but the impact of e-commerce varies according to the product. The majority of online newspapers are free and provide unrestricted access to their websites. However, some impose access restrictions by requiring the reader to register. Others allow free access to part of the paper while requiring a subscription for other parts. Others even offer two separate online versions, one free and one subscription-based. A second category of online publications that has shown a very high rate of growth is that of scholarly journals. As of 2000 it was estimated that there were 20,840 journals available online. Like newspapers, many journal publishers offer both print and electronic versions. In some cases the electronic versions are full-text versions, in others only the abstract is available online. Some publishers bundle the electronic version with print subscription, while others charge separately for the print version and electronic access. The third largest category of publications is that of books. The most significant development in this market has been the development of electronic books or e-books; these are digital files that can be read by various devices, such as computers, personal digital assistants and special hand-held devices. Although a large number of e-books have been published it is difficult to estimate the sales volumes. A relatively new format "print on demand" (POD) allows a book to be stored as an electronic copy, but limits printing to the number of copies paid for. The benefits of these digital technologies for publishers include reducing the cost of printing, warehousing and distribution.

Entertainment

Electronic commerce over the Internet may lead to substitution of some entertainment services. During peak evening viewing periods, the number of people logged on to the

Internet has been increasing at the expense of television. In addition, new products, such as multimedia programmes, are likely to compete with traditional entertainment, such as TV, radio, videos and video game playing. Several TV and radio broadcasters are already offering broadcast services via the Internet. Despite its relatively poor quality, video transmission over the Internet can also be used for conference calls, security and surveillance.

Education

Although distance learning via the Internet is likely to complement rather than substitute most existing schools and universities, some substitution may occur in certain areas of education, such as vocational training and continuing education programmes, where the flexibility of distance learning via the Internet is an advantage. Although distance learning has existed for some time, the Internet makes it possible to combine text with audio/video and allows interaction in real time via email and discussion groups; this could lead to substitution where the advantages of tuition over the Internet outweigh those offered by local institutions. For example, some universities in the USA now provide tuition to foreign students over the Internet.

Health services

Health services could be affected by electronic commerce in two ways. One use of the Internet is to streamline the capturing, storing and processing of information, such as patients' records, physicians' notes, test results and insurance claims information. The second use of the Internet is for telemedicine; this can consist of at least three different services: teleradiology (transmission and diagnosis of X-rays, ultrasound images or magnetic resonance images), telepathology (real-time transmission and diagnosis of information to a pathology lab during an operation) and virtual reality (the use of computer simulation techniques to train and instruct). While it is unlikely that surgery will be performed at a distance or that computer diagnosis will replace human diagnosis, a number of trials have shown that a wide variety of simple procedures, monitoring and preventive medicine can be conducted by telemedicine.

Financial services

Financial services, including banking, stock trading, insurance and provision of financial information, have been significant users of IT in the past and have already been significantly affected by e-commerce. For example, online banking and share-trading services have proved to be some of the most popular services on the Internet. Although there may be some substitution of existing activities, this is likely to be offset by overall increases in the market for these services as prices decline and people make more frequent use of them.

Other professional services

Other professional services that may be affected include those that largely involve the exchange of ideas or advice (e.g., architects, engineers, accountants, lawyers and consultants), especially to acquire and serve clients. It is unlikely that the services will be totally lacking in direct personal contact of some kind, given the personal nature of many problems, so the effects will mainly be in the form of market expansion and greater interaction with clients.

Estimated impact of e-commerce on industries

Forecasting the impact of any new technology is always difficult, as will be seen in Chapter 10. There have been many examples in history where the impact was seriously underestimated (e.g., the telephone and the mainframe computer), as well as examples where the impact was seriously overestimated (e.g., telephone shopping and electric cars). The magnitude of the impact of electronic commerce will probably not be clear for some time, possibly 15–25 years, so any forecasts should be treated with caution. However, Figure 1.18 shows estimates of the size of the impacts of e-commerce on some industries in 2002. Sectors that are forecast to be most affected are those whose products have high price-to-bulk ratio (such as music CDs), commodities (such as routine business flights) and intangible, information products that can be delivered electronically (such as software). It can be seen that impacts range from 60% to 5% of sales. However, it is also important to bear in mind that figures of online revenues are only part of the picture. Even for low-impact industries, electronic commerce may still form an essential part of services. For example, while Internet courses may never totally replace face-to-face courses in the educational sector, they may come to form a small but important part of the overall curriculum.

Structure of book

The rest of this book is structured (Figure 1.19) as a "tour" around various topics and fields of knowledge which it is necessary to understand in the strategic management of an e-business, whether it is part of an existing company or an e-business start-up. Some stages of the tour can be skipped and some topics can be dealt with in a different order. However, in order to gain most from the book, it is recommended that a reader new to the area should follow the order of chapters in the book as each chapter builds on preceding ones.

Chapters 2 to 6 aim to build a foundation in the areas of technology, marketing and economics relevant to e-business. Chapter 2 provides an introduction to the technologies most commonly used in e-business in order to show how they have developed and how

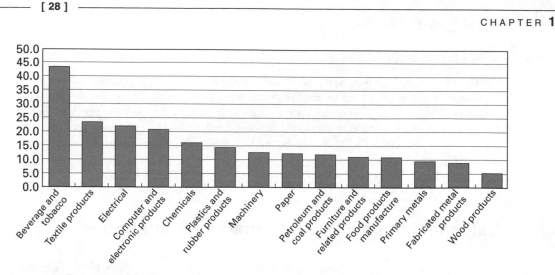

Figure 1.18(a)   Impact of e-commerce on selected industries: manufacturing
(based on figures from US Census Bureau).

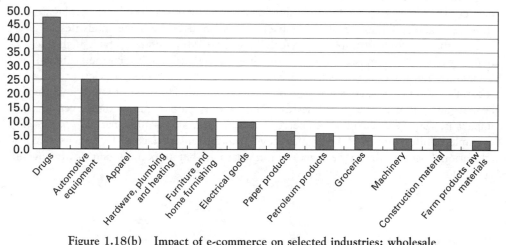

Figure 1.18(b)   Impact of e-commerce on selected industries: wholesale
(based on figures from US Census Bureau).

they are currently used in businesses. Chapters 3 and 4 then build on this base to consider some of the marketing issues that result from using these technologies. Chapter 3 shows the distinctive characteristics of the markets, buyers and sellers, while Chapter 4 discusses some of the new marketing methods that have been made possible using the new technologies. Chapters 5 and 6 examine how the technologies are changing the economic bases of many businesses and leading to radical restructuring of many industries.

Chapters 7 and 8 then build on and integrate the knowledge in the previous chapters in

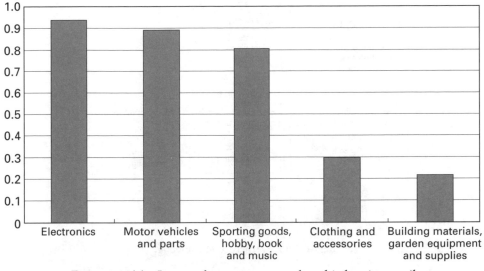

Figure 1.18(c) Impact of e-commerce on selected industries: retail
(based on figures from US Census Bureau).

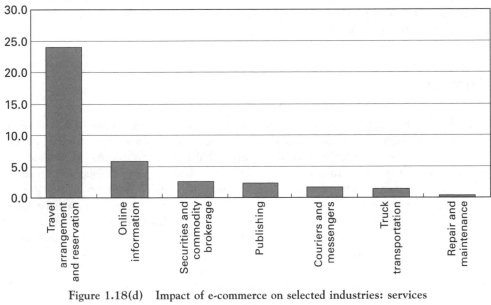

Figure 1.18(d) Impact of e-commerce on selected industries: services
(based on figures from US Census Bureau).

considering the strategic and organizational issues involved in managing an e-business. Chapter 7 examines various strategic frameworks that can be used to analyse e-businesses and develop e-business strategies, while Chapter 8 considers how these strategies can best be implemented and the implications for how the business is organized.

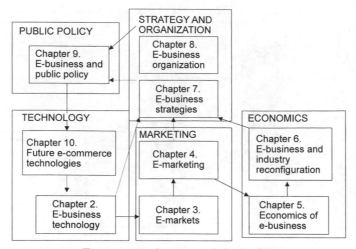

Figure 1.19 Structure of the book.

Chapters 9 and 10 look more broadly at issues that may affect e-business and look forward to the future. Chapter 9 examines some of the public policy issues raised by e-business, while Chapter 10 examines some of the newer technologies that may start a new cycle of change.

Summary

The Internet has brought about a revolution in business in the space of a few years. However, although it may seem that this is a recent phenomenon, the changes are the outcome of political and technological initiatives that have been in progress for a decade or more. Increasing investment in IT is bringing about a shift in many economies, reflected in industry revenues and employment; this will result in some loss of employment from substitution of existing products and services, but this will be more than compensated for by the increased employment resulting from new products and services. Figures from the US Department of Commerce suggest that this has been a major driver of economic growth in the USA, and cost savings of 4.3% GDP are forecast over the period 2001–2010. Many other countries are now instituting similar programmes in order to capitalize on the economic gains to be had from e-business.

References

Aldrich, D.F. (1999). *Mastering the Digital Marketplace*. John Wiley & Sons, Chichester, UK.
Cairncross, F. (1997). *The Death of Distance*. Harvard Business School Press, Boston.

Choi, S., Stahl, D.O., and Whinston, A.B. (1997). *The Economics of Electronic Commerce*. Macmillan, Indianapolis, IN.

Clinton, W.J. and Gore, A. (1997). A framework for global electronic commerce. Available at *http://ww.iitf.nist.gov/eleccomm/ecomm.htm*

Information Infrastructure Task Force (1993). *The National Information Infrastructure: An Agenda for Action*. Department of Commerce, Washington, DC.

Kampas, P.J. (2000). Roadmap to the e-revolution. *Information Systems Management*, **2**(Spring), 8–22.

Net Impact Study (2002). Available at *http://www.netimpactstudy.com/nis_2002.html*

OECD (1998). *The Economic and Social Impacts of Electronic Commerce*. Organization for Economic Co-operation and Development, Paris.

OECD (2002). *Measuring the Information Economy 2002*. Organization for Economic Co-operation and Development, Paris.

Oliner, S.D. and Sichel, D.E. (2000). *The Resurgence of Growth in the late 1990s: Is Information Technology the Story?* Federal Reserve Board, Washington, DC.

Tapscott, D. (1996). *The Digital Economy*. McGraw-Hill, New York.

UNCTAD (2002). Ecommerce and Development Report 2002. Available at *www.unctad.org/ecommerce*

US Department of Commerce (2000). *Digital Economy 2000*. Washington, DC.

Websites

Chinese Information Industry Ministry *www.mii.gov.cn*
European Union *www.ispo.cec.be*
Internet Economy Indicators *www.internetindicators.com*
Korean Ministry of Information and Communication *www.mic.go.kr*
Malaysian Multimedia Corridor *www.mdc.com.my*
OECD *www.oecd.org*
Singapore *www.ec.gov.sg*
UK Department of Trade and Industry *www.dti.gov.uk*
US Dept of Commerce *www.doc.gov*
US E-commerce Initiative *www.ecommerce.gov*

Self-assessment questions

1   Define e-commerce and e-business.
2   Give some examples of different types of e-businesses.
3   Explain what is meant by the NII and the GII.
4   Give examples of various political initiatives for e-business around the world.
5   Explain what is meant by the "new economy".
6   Give examples of some benefits of e-business.
7   List some of the key industry sectors that will be affected by e-business.

Discussion questions

1   How is Internet-based e-commerce different from traditional EDI?

2   Do you agree with Al Gore's statement at the beginning of the chapter that "We are on the verge of a revolution that is just as profound as the change in the economy that came with the industrial revolution."

3   Do you agree that a new economy is emerging or is it simply that the old economy is being transformed?

4   What do you think are the most important implications of e-business?

5   How is e-business affecting your industry or one with which you are familiar?

6   What is the value of government initiatives in e-business?

THE BASICS OF E-BUSINESS TECHNOLOGY

Introduction

Chapter 1 described how the economic revolution has been driven by technological and political initiatives to build a global information infrastructure. This chapter examines in more detail some of the key technologies used in e-commerce: the first two sections ("The pre-Internet era" and "Origins of the Internet") describe how the Internet protocols have become the dominant standards underlying the global information infrastructure; the following three sections ("Components of websites", "Website architectures" and "Intranets and extranets") examine some of the key technologies used on Internet sites; and the remaining sections examine some emerging technologies.

The pre-Internet era

Although the widespread use of the Internet has generated considerable publicity recently, the idea of using electronic networks for conducting business is not new. Electronic networks linking computers within organizations and linking computers in different organizations have been widely used in businesses since the 1980s. With the increasing use of PCs and LANs (local area networks) in the workplace, many organizations took the next step of sharing data with partners in interorganizational systems (IOSs) and exchanging data with other organizations in EDI (electronic data interchange) networks. However, these IOS and EDI networks differ from the present-day Internet in a number of ways.

First, members in an IOS are typically determined in advance as are the type of transactions. Second, EDI transactions have to follow strict formats. According to the International Data Exchange (IDE) Association, EDI is defined as: "the transfer of structured data by agreed message standards from one computer system to another by electronic means." The four essential elements of EDI are:

1. *Structured data*   EDI transactions are composed of codes, values and short pieces of text. Each element has a strictly defined purpose. For example, an order has codes for the customer and product, and such values as quantity ordered.
2. *Agreed message standards*   The EDI transaction has to have a standard format. A standard is not just agreed between the trading partners but is a general standard agreed at national international level.
3. *From one computer system to another*   The EDI message is sent between two computer applications. For example, the message is sent directly between the customer's purchasing system and the supplier's processing system. There is no requirement for people to read the message or to key it into a computer system.
4. *By electronic means*   Usually, this is by means of a data communications network although the physical transfer of magnetic tape or floppy disk would also be within the definition of EDI.

Direct benefits of EDI include:

- *Shorter order time*   Paper orders have to be printed, sealed in envelopes, passed to the postal service, received by the supplier and imported into the supplier's processing system, all of which can take up to 3 days. EDI orders are sent straight to the network, and the only delay is how often the supplier retrieves messages from the system.
- *Cost-cutting*   The use of EDI can cut costs; these include the cost of stationery and postage, of course, but the principal saving from the use of EDI is potentially staff costs. The obvious example of this is that if the orders are directly input into the system there is no need for an order entry clerk. There may also be potential to reduce the number of extra staff needed to deal with peak demand or staff holidays.
- *Elimination of errors*   There is always the potential for errors in keying any information into a computer system. EDI eliminates this source of errors.
- *Faster response*   With paper orders there can be several days before the customer is informed of any supply difficulty, such as the product being out of stock. With EDI the customer can be informed straightaway, giving time for alternative products or suppliers to be used.

EDI standards

Essential to any EDI application is the EDI standard. Computer systems that exchange data need a common format. Without a common format the data are meaningless; this is particularly important where there are several customers or suppliers in the network. The EDI standard provides an agreed standard for data interchange which is independent of the special interests of any party in the network.

The first EDI standards evolved from existing formats used for simple data transfer between computer applications. An early example of EDI in the UK was the bank automated clearing system (BACS). BACS is a consortium of the major banks that provides an automated clearing service for the transfer of money between bank accounts. Many organizations that make a significant number of payments, such as payroll, use this service. Users of the BACS system record the information they would have printed as cheques on a computer file in accordance with the format specified by BACS. The data are then sent to BACS where the payments are processed without the delay, expense and errors associated with paper documents and manual data input. In the early days the computer file was recorded on a magnetic tape and sent to BACS by courier. Nowadays, this is usually done online.

The use of EDI on systems, such as BACS, demonstrated the potential of EDI for the exchange of general business documents, and a number of trade organizations subsequently developed their own EDI formats for use in the sector: for example, ODETTE (Organization for Data Exchange by Tele Transmission in Europe), was an EDI standard developed for use in the European motor industry; and TRADACOMS was developed by the ANA (Article Numbering Association) in the UK and is widely used in the retail and catering trades. Other European countries also developed their own standards for retail and general trade, such as SEDAS in Germany and GENCOD in France. The USA developed different standards in various business sectors. For example, UCS was used in the grocery industry and ORDERNET was used in the pharmaceutical trade. While this allowed firms within a sector to exchange information, the differing standards between sectors led to problems in cross-sector trade and led to the creation of X12 as a national standard within the USA by ANSI (American National Standards Institute).

While national standards did eliminate some problems there were problems using EDI for international trade. This requires a common format for the exchange of standard business forms, such as orders and invoices, sent between organizations in different countries. International trade also requires a great deal of additional documentation, such as shipping, customs and international credit forms. To facilitate this, the United Nations developed the EDIFACT standard in the mid-1980s; this was supported by the EU and effectively became a global standard when the Americans accepted it for international use while retaining their own X12 standard for domestic use in the short term.

Organizations in an EDI network can exchange data directly or, more often nowadays, through specialist value-added network (VAN) or value-added data service (VADS) providers (Figure 2.1). Examples of companies that provide such a service include IBM Network and General Electric Information Services (GEIS). The basic service provided by a VAN or VADS provider is the collection of incoming mail and the forwarding of outgoing mail. For each user of the system there is a postbox where outgoing messages are placed and a mailbox where incoming messages can be picked up.

The final technical element of an EDI system is the EDI software; this can be bought from a specialist provider. The basic functions of EDI software are, first, coding of business transactions into the chosen EDI standard and interfacing with the VADS. Many EDI software suppliers also provide additional functions, such as integrated database of trading

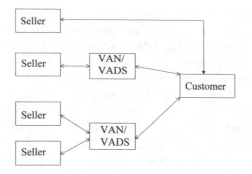

Figure 2.1 Components of an EDI network.

partners; this allows translating of any EDI transaction into the format required by each partner.

Electronic funds transfer (EFT)

Electronic data interchange may be accompanied by EFT; this is defined as "the transfer of funds initiated through an electronic terminal, telephone or computer so as to order or authorize a financial institution to debit or credit an account."

Electronic funds transfer at the point of sale (EFTPOS) is a form of electronic funds transfer where the purchaser is physically present at the point of sale (e.g., at a checkout in the supermarket or in a petrol station); this usually operates using a debit or credit card.

PC modems and bulletin board services (BBSs)

Although EDI networks have been widely used, their use was largely confined to business-to-business communications and electronic networks were not widely available to the general public, mainly owing to the large cost of buying and maintaining such systems. More widespread use of electronic networks by the public did not come until the development of PCs and PC modems in the mid-1980s. Modems work on a similar principle to a facsimile machine. At the transmitting end a modem converts digital signals received from computers into analogue signals to be transmitted over a telephone line (modulation), and a modem at the receiving end converts the analogue signal back to a digital signal (demodulation). The significant advantage PC modems offered was that it was no longer necessary to lease private lines in order to set up a global computer network. It made it possible to link PCs located in different parts of the world using an existing public network, the public telephone network.

Initially, use of this technology was confined to researchers and computer hobbyists. A common application was to exchange information by dialling into a central computer and posting information on a "bulletin board". Others used it to play games with users in other parts of the world. Later on the technology spread to business users, and a number of business information service providers were established. Three notable providers at the time were the Dow Jones News/Retrieval Service, Prodigy and Compuserve. These companies provided services to subscribers which included, among other things, electronic mail, online chat, teleconferencing, bulletin boards, news and access to online databases.

Videotex

The other competing form of electronic network that became available to consumers in the 1980s was videotex. The original idea for videotex came from research at the British Post Office (later British Telecom) on menu-driven systems initiated in the 1960s. In 1973 researchers announced "Viewdata", which was later given the generic name videotex and marketed in the UK as Prestel.

In videotex, a screen and keyboard are connected to a central computer via a telephone line. The need to transmit digital data over an analogue line usually restricts data transmission rates to 1,200 bits per second coming from the database and 75 bps going from the consumer back to the server; this is sufficient to allow a user to access databases containing "pages" of information represented on the screen in text and crude graphics. The idea behind videotex was to create a new market for mass information by combining telephone lines and television sets. Since many homes were already equipped with both television and telephone, all that was needed was to link the two together. However, the system never really caught on in large numbers in the UK, owing to the limited services available and the relatively high cost of the system.

Following the example set in the UK, the French government and France Télécom decided to develop their own videotex service. An important difference was not to follow the British in using televisions as a display device, but to use a dedicated terminal, the Minitel, which would be provided free to all telephone subscribers; this would be paid for by the substitution of the existing paper telephone directories with access to a database containing details of all French telephone subscribers. To keep down unit costs, the terminals would be available on a wide scale. However, after the election of President Mitterrand and the Socialist Party in 1981 the compulsory replacement of the printed directory was abandoned for political reasons and the use of Minitels was optional. Nevertheless, Minitel achieved a penetration rate of 11%, although it was spread very unevenly across the social classes, ranging from 30% among senior managers and the traditional professions to only 6% among senior citizens and 8% among manual workers. Use was similarly divided by age, with the heaviest users in the age range 22 to 49.

One reason why Minitel was more successful in France than Prestel was in the UK lay in the tariff system, which removed the need for prepayment or credit cards. France Télécom records the number of minutes the user is connected to each service and adds a charge to the telephone bill. The service provider does not need a complicated accounting system, nor does it require prepayment by the customer.

Another advantage of the system was that it allowed service providers on Minitel to differentiate themselves: for example, a subscriber can key in the brand name of a product or service, such as "Orangina" or "LeMonde". This is easier to use than the Prestel system of numbered pages (e.g., 10534) and is also easy to advertise in magazines, on products and billboards.

Minitel also provides an easy way to communicate with clients, with suppliers and within firms. Since most firms already had a Minitel and a telephone line, there was no need to buy expensive computers, lease lines, to develop access methods to the public-switched data networks or to acquire telecommunications management skills.

Germany too launched a national videotex service, Bildschirmtext, in 1983, but this was less successful. As in France, a dedicated terminal was chosen because of the strictly defined role of the Deutsche Bundespost. Although it grew steadily, the service ran at an annual deficit of over DM 100 million in the late 1980s. Therefore, in 1994 it was repackaged and marketed as Datex-J, an Internet access service.

Cable television

Another route into the consumer home market has been cable television. Cable television, formerly known as community antenna television, or CATV, started in the mountains of Pennsylvania in the late 1940s. At that time, there were only a few television stations, located mostly in larger cities like Philadelphia, and people living in remote areas were unable to receive television transmissions. Sales of television sets in remote areas were, therefore, poor; this was the problem faced by John Walson, an appliance store owner in the small town of Mahanoy, 90 miles from Philadelphia. His solution was to erect an antenna on top of a nearby mountain to receive the television signals and transport them to his store using co-axial cable.

The idea soon spread, so much so that it became necessary to erect community antennae to provide television signals to several sets in a single apartment block or department store. The first example of a complete urban cable television network came when the entire town of Lansford nearby was wired.

For many years, cable was simply a way to improve reception so people could see network broadcasts. Walson in the early 1950s and later other system owners soon began to experiment with microwave transmission to bring the signals from distant cities. Pennsylvania systems that only had three channels – one for each network – soon had six, seven or more channels as operators imported programmes from independent stations from New York and Philadelphia. Because of the variety it offered to viewers, cable also began to spread to cities.

One of the major events that was responsible for the rapid growth in the cable industry was the development of pay TV. Pay TV was launched in November 1972 when Service Electric offered Home Box Office, or HBO, over its cable system in Wilkes-Barre, Pennsylvania. HBO was only viewed by a few hundred people that first night, but it has gone on to become the world's largest pay cable service with over 11,500,000 viewers; this is due in part to HBO's owner Time, Inc. deciding to later deliver its signals by satellite. HBO was the first programming service to use a satellite to distribute its programming. The television signal is beamed from earth to a satellite in a stationary orbit some 22,300 miles over the Equator and bounces back to receivers on Earth (Figure 2.2). By distributing by satellite, HBO's signal is available to cable operators throughout North America,

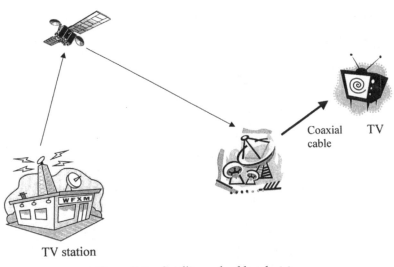

Figure 2.2   Satellite and cable television.

and, because it is so widely available, it has an advantage over Earth-bound, microwave distributed services, such as WOR-TV – the independent station in New York.

Origins of the Internet

The network we now know as the Internet had its origins in a completely different arena. It was first developed as a network for military communications during the Cold War in the 1960s. There was concern at the time within the USA that the defence network of computers was susceptible to attack by a nuclear strike from the USSR; this led in 1964 to the Department of Defense sponsoring Advanced Research Project Agency Network (ARPANET), an experimental project to develop a network capable of withstanding a nuclear attack using packet-switching technology, which had just been developed by the Rand Corporation.

In conventional circuit-switching networks, such as those still used for voice telecommunications, a dedicated link needs to be established and maintained between the caller and receiver for the duration of the call. In contrast, packet-switching technology allows several callers (or computers in the case of computer networks) to share the same network by segmenting the data stream from each caller into packets, each of which contains information identifying the caller and the recipient. Thus, at any given time a link in the network may be carrying data from a number of different sending computers destined for a number of different receiving computers; this obviously has cost advantages in maximizing use of the network resources and sharing costs of the network among a large number of users. Another advantage is that since each data packet contains information identifying the sender and recipient, if a particular link in the network is busy or inoperative, data can be re-routed along another link in the network; this was particularly useful in a military context since the communications network is not dependent on a single computer or link that can be destroyed by the enemy; hence, the interest by the Department of Defense.

TCP/IP

One of the outcomes of ARPANET was the development of a set of protocols or standards for communication between computers, which came to be called TCP/IP (transaction control protocol/Internet protocol). Many of these are still widely used today for communicating on the Internet: for example, SMTP (simple mail transfer protocol), POP (Post Office protocol), MIME (multipart Internet mail extension) and FTP (file transfer protocol).

The first specification of TCP was published as an Internet experiment note in December 1974. TCP/IP was adopted as a standard by the Department of Defense six years later in 1980. By 1985, the Internet was already well established as a technology supporting a large community of researchers and developers, and was beginning to be used by other communities for daily computer communications. However, ARPANET was not the only computer network available at the time. Two other competing networks that deserve to be mentioned are USENET and BITNET.

USENET

USENET was based on the Unix operating system, which was and still is widely used by universities. The idea came from two graduate students at Duke University, Tom Truscott and Jim Ellis, who thought of creating a computer network to link together users in the Unix community. They discussed their idea with other interested students, including Steve Bellovin, who was a graduate student at the neighbouring University of North Carolina at Chapel Hill. Using homemade auto dial modems and the Unix-to-Unix copy program (called UUCP), the Unix shell and the find command, Bellovin wrote some simple shell scripts allowing linked computers to automatically call each other up and search for changes in the date stamps of the files. If there were changes, the changed files were copied from one computer to the other.

Initially, this facility was used to link three computer sites, "duke" at Duke University, "unc" at the University of North Carolina at Chapel Hill and "phs" at the Physiology Department of the Duke Medical School. Several months later, the software was made available for general distribution at the Delaware Summer 1980 Usenix Meeting. The handout distributed at the conference declared, "A goal of USENET has been to give every UNIX system the opportunity to join and benefit from a computer network (a poor man's ARPANET, if you will) . . ."

The idea was to make USENET available to anyone who was interested as long as they had access to the Unix operating system (which in those days was available at a very low cost to the academic and research computer community). USENET was soon being widely used by other universities and was also adopted by some large commercial organizations, like AT&T's Bell Labs and Digital Equipment Corporation (DEC). By 1988 there were some 1,800 articles a day posted at 11,000 sites.

BITNET

BITNET – "Because It's Time NETwork" – was based on IBM's VNET, which the company used for internal communications. At first BITNET just connected Yale University to the City University of New York, but other universities were added throughout the 1980s, reaching thousands of computers in the USA and Mexico. Sister networks, physically part of BITNET but governed by different bodies, were set up in Canada (NetNorth), Europe (EARN, or "European academic and research network"), Japan (AsiaNet) and other countries. Using BITNET, users could exchange electronic mail, files and interactive messages between member institutions. A number of technologies used on the Internet, including LISTSERV mailing lists, originated on BITNET.

However, compared with the Internet, BITNET was not robust and did not have much bandwidth. To reduce costs, network traffic passed between two institutions by just one path. To make up for this lack of redundancy BITNET allow store-and-forward messaging. En route to their destination, data were often relayed through several institutions or nodes. Each node would temporarily store the data before forwarding them to the next. If there was a temporary break in the network, preventing a node from forwarding its traffic, it could hold the data until the network became available again. As the Internet grew and became more affordable, it became apparent that BITNET was obsolete. In 1996, BITNET's managing body, CREN (Corporation for Research and Educational Networking), recommended that its members terminate their use of BITNET by the end of that year. Today, BITNET, in its original form, is largely defunct. However, BITNET II, which uses the Internet as a medium to transfer BITNET protocols, is still in use by some institutions.

Internet

The dominance of the Internet over these other networks was established when it was used by the National Science Foundation (NSF) in its Net initiative in 1986. By 1990 when the ARPANET itself was finally decommissioned, TCP/IP had supplanted most other wide-area computer network protocols worldwide. By 1990, most commercial email carriers in the USA, such as MCI, were linked to the Internet, and many others from around the world followed. Initially, the NSF enforced an "acceptable use policy" (AUP) which prohibited usage of its backbone network service for purposes "not in support of research and education"; this led to the emergence of "private", competitive, long-haul networks, out of various networks, inspired and sponsored by the National Science Foundation: NYSERNet formed Performance Systems International (PSI); UUNET Technologies formed Alternet; IBM, MERIT and MCI formed Advanced Network Systems (ANS); General Atomics, which also runs the San Diego Supercomputer Center, formed CERFNET; and Sprint formed Sprintlink. Similar services were developed in the UK, Sweden and Finland.

The culmination of the NSF's privatization policy was the defunding of the NSFNET backbone in April, 1995 and the redistribution of funds to regional networks to buy national-scale connectivity. On October 24, 1995, the US Federal Networking Council unanimously passed a resolution defining the term Internet: "The Federal Networking Council (FNC) agrees that the following language reflects our definition of the term 'Internet'. 'Internet' refers to the global information system that – (i) is logically linked together by a globally unique address space based on the Internet Protocol (IP) or its subsequent extensions/follow-ons; (ii) is able to support communications using the Transmission Control Protocol/Internet Protocol (TCP/IP) suite or its subsequent extensions/ follow-ons, and/or other IP-compatible protocols; and (iii) provides, uses or makes accessible, either publicly or privately, high level services layered on the communications and related infrastructure described herein."

Accessing the Internet

Most private users access the Internet by registering with an Internet service provider (ISP), such as AOL or BT Net. Some providers, such as AOL, may also act as a "portal" site by providing access to a range of other services, such as news, information and shopping services. Most commonly, a fee is charged for this service. There may be telephone connection charges as well. A study by the OECD (2000) showed that total access costs and the proportions paid to telcos and ISPs vary considerably from country to country (Figure 2.3).

A recent trend is the provision of free Internet access with the ISP getting its revenues from advertisers and the telephone company (e.g., Freeserve) or one-off lifetime fees.

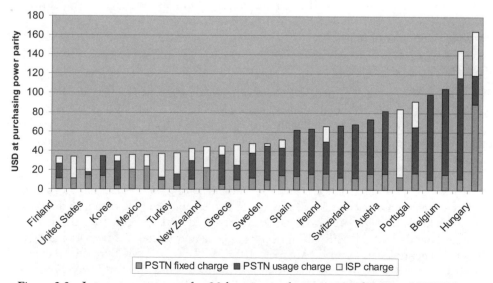

Figure 2.3   **Internet access costs for 20 hours at peak times using discounted PSTN rates**
(based on figures from OECD).

Mini-case study: Freeserve

Prior to 1998 in the UK, users had to pay for Internet access via an Internet service provider, such as Demon, Compuserve and AOL, on top of telephone connection charges; this changed toward the end of 1998 when British Telecom introduced a new pricing tariff enabling service providers to offer low-cost calls. In September, 1998 the electrical retailer Dixons launched the first, mass-market, free-of-charge ISP, Freeserve (Figure 2.4) (*www.freeserve.co.uk*), in collaboration with telecoms group Energis and its portal subsidiary Planet Online. The deal with Energis provided a steady income from interconnect fees paid to Energis from BT, while the portal built by Planet Online provided revenues from advertising and e-commerce. Marketing costs were also low as the Dixons Group was able to advertise the service in its various retailing operations – Dixons, Currys, The Link and PC World.

Freeserve started a revolution in Internet service provision in the UK, and other organizations followed suit in offering free Internet access, such as Toys 'R' US (*www.toysrus.uk*), the *Sun* newspaper (*www.currantbun.co.uk*) and Tesco supermarket (*www.tesco.net*), most of which have now ceased. Freeserve still offers its "free" service although it now also offers a paid service. In December 2000, an offer to acquire Freeserve was made by the Wanadoo Group, France's leading media and online services company, and the acquisition was completed in Spring 2001.

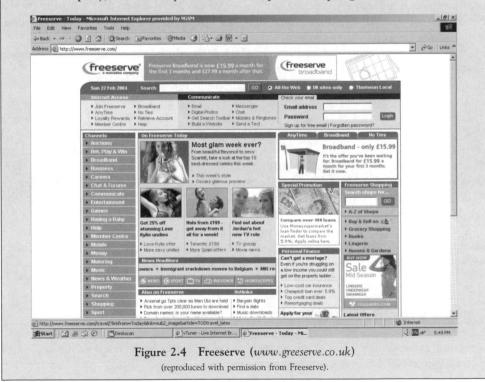

Figure 2.4 Freeserve (*www.greeserve.co.uk*)

(reproduced with permission from Freeserve).

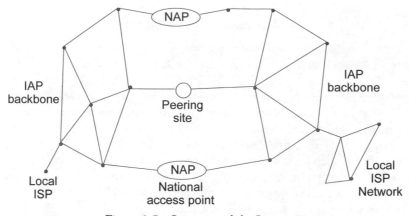

Figure 2.5 Structure of the Internet.

Once registered with an ISP, users can access the Internet by dialling in via a modem and a telephone line to the ISP's server. Users can then connect to other sites on the Internet and exchange information along a series of interconnecting networks (Figure 2.5).

Large Internet access providers (IAPs), such as AT&T, Sprint, UUNET and MCI, own high-speed international networks that form the backbone of the Internet. Commercial organizations that provide Internet access own high-speed lines that connect to the backbone network at locations called "peering sites". In response to concerns about traffic at these peering sites clogging the Internet, private peering exchanges have also been set up by network service providers, such as BBN, MCI, Sprint and PSINet, allowing direct exchange of data between network providers. Smaller ISPs connect their own customers to another Internet provider's backbone Internet network.

No single organization is responsible for the Internet; rather, the Internet is run informally by a number of organizations and bodies. For example, the Internet Society (ISOC) promotes policies and promotes global connectivity of the Internet; the Internet Engineering Task Force (IETF) sets standards focusing on TCP/IP protocol standards issues; the World Wide Web Consortium (W3C), run jointly by the MIT Laboratory for Computer Science, the National Institute for Research in Computer Science & Automation (France) and Keio University (Japan), develops common standards for the World Wide Web.

Inevitably, this lack of a single authority has led to some conflicts over technical standards and legislation, which are only beginning to emerge and to be gradually resolved. We will examine this in more detail in Chapter 9.

Components of websites

Most e-commerce applications currently run on Internet sites rely on a number of common types of hardware and software, the most common being data compression software, browsers, webpages, Java, CGI, intranets, extranets and encryption software.

Data compression

Early uses of the Internet were hampered by the fact that most applications were text-based owing to the much longer times required to transfer graphics files. It was only following the development of data compression techniques, which allowed graphic files to be compressed, that more user-friendly applications developed. Two standards that were significant in allowing transmission of graphics files on the Internet and that are still widely used are GIF and JPEG.

In 1984, while working for Sperry Corporation, Terry Welch modified the Lempel-Ziv 78 (LZ78) compression algorithm for greater efficiency for implementation in high-performance disk controllers; this was incorporated by Compuserve in 1987 in the GIF (graphical interchange format) file format for the storage and online retrieval of graphical data. This typically allows a compression of $2:1$ to $3:1$.

This was followed in 1992 by JPEG (pronounced "jay-peg"), a standard for image compression agreed by the Joint Photographic Experts Group, the original name of the committee that wrote the standard. JPEG typically allows a $10:1$ to $20:1$ compression of either full-colour or greyscale images, allowing a 2-MB full-colour file to be compressed to 100 KB.

World Wide Web

Another critical technological development that led to widespread use of the Internet was the development of what is now known as the "World Wide Web"; this accounts for somewhere between one-third and one-half of the total traffic on the Internet, and many people often use the term World Wide Web synonymously with the term Internet.

The idea goes back as early as 1945, when Vannevar Bush, science adviser to President Roosevelt, described the concept of a memex, a device (based on microfilm) for storing vast amounts of documents in a single desk, with mechanical aids for finding, organizing and adding to the repository. In 1968 Ted Nelson coined the term "hypertext" to describe such a computer system for linking various documents.

The idea was later taken up by researchers at CERN (the European Laboratory for Particle Physics) who faced a common problem among researchers: how to cross-reference and keep track of documents located in different sites worldwide. Collaboration among researchers is common among the physics community around the world, and a system that facilitates the exchange of data and documents is clearly of great value. In 1989, Tim Berners-Lee, then a researcher at CERN, proposed a networked hypertext system for CERN, which he termed the "World Wide Web". In 1990 such a system was purchased for evaluation by CERN, and SLAC, the Stanford Linear Accelerator Center in California, became the first web server in the USA, holding a large database of abstracts of physics papers.

The World Wide Web increased the usefulness of the Internet exponentially by allowing files held on different computers to be linked dynamically using the hypertext transfer protocol (HTTP). For example, a hyperlink, or link between two documents, may be set up such that by clicking on a portion of the text in one document the user can

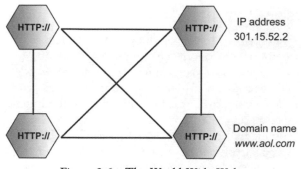

Figure 2.6 The World Wide Web.

automatically retrieve information in a different document. The other document need not necessarily be on the same computer and may be anywhere on the Web. For example, documents held on several different machines (called "clients") in different locations may refer or be linked to a page of one document held on a central machine (the server) in another part of the country or the world (Figure 2.6).

The location of each document on the World Wide Web is specified by its uniform resource locator (URL). Each URL has three basic parts: the protocol, the server machine and the file being requested. The protocol is everything up to the colon and the first two slashes. For a web browser, the most common protocols are *http://*, *ftp://*, *gopher://* and *news://*.

Following the protocol, after the double slashes but before the next single slash, is the name of the server machine on which the document is located; this name can be either the domain name of the machine or the IP address. Just as every document on the Internet has a unique identifier, every machine on the Internet must also. This identifier is a number known as the IP address (e.g., 301.15.52.2). Because names are easier for people to remember than numbers, IP addresses are usually aliased to domain names, such as *www.yahoo.com*; these are mapped onto the IP address by special domain name servers located worldwide. Sometimes the domain name may be followed by a colon and a number, such as *www.yahoo.com:8080*; this indicates that the server is accessed via port 8080 instead of the default port for web servers, which is port 80.

After the protocol and the name of the server machine, the URL contains the name of the file being requested. This name often includes subdirectories on the server machine. If no subdirectories are included, the server looks in the document root, which it believes to be the highest level directory. For example, *www.name.com/faq.html* refers to a file *faq.html* in the document root on the machine called *www.name.com*, and *www.name.com/ customer/bill* refers to a file called "bill" in a subdirectory called "customer". If a file is not specified, the web server automatically looks for a file called *index.html* and returns that file. If *index.html* does not exist, the web server returns a list of files contained in that directory.

Domain names

Domain names also follow a set form. For example, the domain name *www.name.com* locates a host server called *www* at the Internet address for *name.com*. The *com* part of the domain name reflects the purpose of the organization (in this example, "commercial") and is called the top-level domain name.

There are two types of top-level domains: generic and country code. Generic domain names describe the type of organization owning the site:

- .com identifies a commercial organization;
- .edu identifies an educational organization;
- .gov identifies a US governmental body;
- .int identifies an international organization.
- .mil identifies a military body;
- .net identifies a network provider;
- .org identifies a non-profit organization;

The .gov, .mil, .int and .edu domain names are reserved for US government, military, international and educational organizations, respectively, although use of other domain names can be obtained if they have not already been registered (by applying and paying a fee to the relevant authority). Country code domains were created to be used by each individual country as they deemed necessary. Common ones include *.us* (USA), *.uk* (UK), *.fr* (France), *.de* (Germany) and *.jp* (Japan).

The "name" part of the domain name defines the organization or entity and, together with the top level, is called the second-level domain name. The second-level domain name is mapped to the Internet address given on registration and held on various domain name servers around the world. A third level of domain name can also be defined to identify a particular host server at the Internet address. In the above example, *www* is the name of the server that handles Internet requests, but there may be another server called *www2*. A third-level domain name is not required if there is only one server, as the attached server will be assumed by default. Subdomain levels can also be used (e.g., *www.firstname.name.com*).

Registration of IP addresses and domain names is overseen by ICANN (The Internet Corporation for Assigned Names and Numbers) through member organizations in each country. ICANN took over some functions previously performed under US Government contract by IANA (Internet Assigned Number Authority) and other entities. Registrations for .com, .org and .net domain names are done though ICANN-registered organizations worldwide. Country-level domain names (e.g. *.uk*, *.jp*, *.fr*, *.de*) are processed by relevant registration authorities in each country, such as Nominet in the UK, AFNIC in France, DENIC in Germany and Japan NIC in Japan.

HTML

Most of the documents on the Web are written in hypertext markup language (HTML); this is a language adapted from standard generalized markup language (SGML), a language used by book publishers which specifies document types and how to display the various types. It was first adopted for use on the World Wide Web at CERN in 1991 and has since become the accepted standard for World Wide Web documents. The first specification was written in 1992, and since then various extensions have been added. HTML consists of various tags that describe how to display the information contained within the document. An example is the following:

```
<HTML>
<HEAD>
<TITLE>bookhome</TITLE>
</HEAD>

<P>HTML Example</P>
<P>This is the Home page for the book</P>
<B><P>Strategic Management of E-Business</P></B>
<I><P>by Stephen Chen</P></I>
<P>Published by Wiley &amp; Sons, Chichester, UK
<A HREF="http://www.wiley.co.uk/">http://www.wiley.co.uk</A></P>
</BODY>
</HTML>
```

Examples of HTML can be seen by selecting "View Source" from the menu in Internet Explorer or Netscape Navigator. In addition many word-processing packages, such as Word, now offer the facility to convert text files to HTML.

Browsers

HTML documents are displayed using software called a "browser". In 1992 CERN released a simple portable browser as freeware. The Gopher system from the University of Minnesota, simpler to install but with no hypertext links, was also popular. (The name derives from the university's sports teams who are called "the Golden Gophers" but it also aptly describes the activity it performs.) Gopher is an Internet application protocol in which hierarchically organized file structures are maintained on servers that themselves are part of an overall information structure and allows a user to locate and retrieve files from all over the world. Two tools for searching Gopher file hierarchies are Veronica and Jughead. Many of the original Gopher file structures, especially those in universities, still exist and can be accessed through most web browsers (because they also support the Gopher protocol). Although most Gopher browsers and files are text-based, some Gopher browsers, notably HyperGopher, were later developed that displayed graphic images (GIF and JPEG files).

Graphical browsers make it easier to display documents containing images on the Web. They also take some of the work out of surfing the Web by allowing addresses of favourite sites to be stored and automatically translating domain names into IP addresses by sending a request to a designated domain name server. The first graphical browser, Mosaic, was created by the National Center for Supercomputing Applications at the University of Illinois and CERN. Mosaic, was intended to be a general purpose, standard browser that would be made available free to the general public.

However, realizing the commercial potential of the market for browsers, some of the developers of Mosaic formed their own company to create Netscape, an easy-to-use, graphical browser that became available in 1994; this was soon followed by the release of Internet Explorer from Microsoft in 1995. Initially, Netscape established a strong lead by giving away the browser for free, but this lead was soon taken over by Microsoft who bundled their browser with the Windows operating system.

Interactive website technologies

The technologies described above are sufficient for basic passive websites, which simply display information. However, in order to develop websites with interactive capabilities, such as database searching and online ordering, computer programs are required, the most common of which are Java and CGI script programs.

Java

Java is a programming language expressly designed for webpage development and was introduced by Sun Microsystems in 1995; this is based on the C++ language and allows object-oriented programming (OOP). OOP splits systems into "objects", or discrete packages of data and functions that can exchange data among themselves. For example, customer information may be stored in a customer object that contains data about the customer's transactions along with a function that produces the account balance. This information can then be shared with another object, say an object that evaluates applications for loans.

This data-sharing facility makes it particularly useful in a distributed network environment and allows the creation of complete applications that may run on a single computer or that are distributed among servers and clients in a network. For example, in e-commerce sites, Java is often used to build either "applets", small application modules that can be downloaded to a webpage and that enable users to interact with the page, or "servlets", objects that are installed on the web server and that can be called from HTML pages (Figure 2.7).

Both Netscape and Internet Explorer include a Java "virtual machine", software that interprets Java code, and almost all major operating system developers (IBM, Microsoft

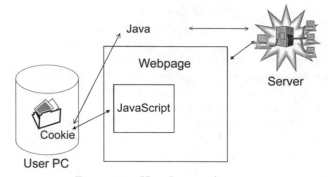

Figure 2.7   How Java works.

and others) now provide Java compilers enabling Java programs to be converted into machine-executable code.

In a further development Netscape has also introduced JavaScript, an interpreted programming or script language allowing program code to be embedded in HTML and interpreted by the web browser. JavaScript generally takes longer to process than compiled Java programs, but is useful for shorter programs that, for example, automatically change a formatted date on a webpage or to display a linked page in a popup window. Java and Java scripts can usually be seen in applications, such as online banking, to encrypt transmissions and provide secure login to the server.

CGI

Apart from Java applets and JavaScript in webpages the third type of program commonly used in e-commerce applications is a CGI script. The common gateway interface, or CGI, is a standard for communicating between web documents, and a CGI script is a program that uses this standard to dynamically interact with web documents, such as HTML documents, text files or image files. CGI programs can be written in almost any language, but commonly used ones include Perl, Basic and C.

When a web browser requests a CGI script from a web server, the server starts running the CGI script and passes the information from the web browser to it. One of the most useful applications is a *search engine*, a program allowing the user to search for information on the Internet. For example, a typical search engine works by executing a CGI script that uses a keyword input by the user in a web browser. Normally, when the CGI script has finished executing, the output is passed back to the web server, which formats an HTTP response header and sends the information to the web browser. (It is also possible for the CGI script to format the HTTP response header and send the data directly to the web browser, an approach that is sometimes used in the case of a heavily used web server.) A *directory* such as Yahoo! works in a similar fashion although it searches for relevant information using an index compiled beforehand.

The main advantage of using CGI scripts is that it allows information in webpages to be

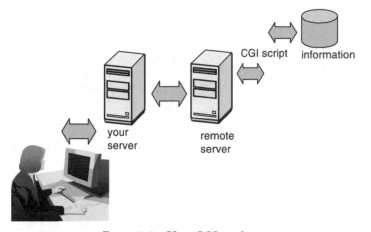

Figure 2.8   How CGI works.

dynamically updated. HTML pages are static, and the information does not change unless the file is edited. However, since CGI scripts are executed when the webpage is accessed they can display real-time information (e.g., time, date and current share prices).

CGI can be interfaced with a database to make dynamic documents. For example, a CGI script can be used to display current inventory in an online ordering application. When a user requests information about a particular item of stock in your database, the CGI script extracts the relevant data and displays it in the browser. It can also be used to allow the user to change the data by adding, deleting or modifying records (e.g., the number of items on order).

CGI scripts also provide a mechanism for making webpages interactive. For example, by using the <FORM> tag in HTML, data can be input by the user from a selection in a menu or by filling in a blank box. All of these data can then be sent to a CGI script that acts upon them (Figure 2.8).

Mini-case: Google

Google is the world's most used search engine. The name is a play on the word "googol", which refers to the number represented by the numeral 1 followed by 100 zeros. It was developed by two Stanford University Computer Science graduate students, Larry Page and Sergey Brin. In 1996 they had begun collaboration on a search engine called BackRub, named for its unique ability to analyse the "back links" pointing to a given website.

Encouraged by the feedback received on Backrub, they developed the idea further and began calling on potential partners who might want to license the technology. In their paper written in 1998, "The anatomy of a large-scale hypertextual web search engine" (available at *http://www-db.stanford.edu/~backrub/google.html*), Brin and Page described the unique features of Google:

The Google search engine has two important features that help it produce high precision results. First, it makes use of the link structure of the Web to calculate a quality ranking for each web page. This ranking is called PageRank and is described in detail in [page 98]. Second, Google utilizes link to improve search results ...

The citation (link) graph of the Web is an important resource that has largely gone unused in existing web search engines. We have created maps containing as many as 518 million of these hyperlinks, a significant sample of the total. These maps allow rapid calculation of a web page's "PageRank", an objective measure of its citation importance that corresponds well with people's subjective idea of importance. Because of this correspondence, PageRank is an excellent way to prioritize the results of web keyword searches ...

The text of links is treated in a special way in our search engine. Most search engines associate the text of a link with the page that the link is on. In addition, we associate it with the page the link points to. This has several advantages. First, anchors often provide more accurate descriptions of web pages than the pages themselves. Second, anchors may exist for documents which cannot be indexed by a text-based search engine, such as images, programs, and databases. This makes it possible to return web pages which have not actually been crawled.

Initially, they had little interest in building a company of their own until Yahoo! founder David Filo suggested that they grow the service themselves by starting a search engine company. Taking his advice, they wrote up a business plan, put their PhD plans on hold and sought out investment. Andy Bechtolsheim, one of the founders of Sun Microsystems, was sufficiently impressed after a brief demonstration to invest $100,000, and ultimately they brought in a total initial investment of almost $1 million.

On September 7, 1998 Google Inc. started operations in the garage of a friend who sublet space to the new corporation's staff of three. Google soon gained in popularity as articles extolling it appeared in *USA Today* and *Le Monde*. In December, 1998, *PC Magazine* named Google one of its top 100 websites and search engines for 1998. By February 1999 the service was answering more than 500,000 queries per day, the staff had grown to eight and the company moved to an office on University Avenue in Palo Alto. The open source software developer Red Hat signed on as its first commercial search customer, and on September 21, 1999 they were sufficiently confident to remove the beta label from the website.

Google continued to grow in popularity and recognition. The Italian portal Virgilio signed on as a client, as did Virgin Net, the UK's leading online entertainment guide. In 1999 the company gained a Technical Excellence Award for Innovation in Web Application Development from *PC Magazine* and inclusion in several "best of" lists, culminating with Google's appearance on *Time Magazine's* top ten best cybertech list for 1999. On June 7, 2000 the company announced that it had secured $25 million from the two leading venture capital firms in Silicon Valley: Sequoia Capital and Kleiner Perkins Caufield & Buyers. On June 26, 2000 Google announced a partnership with Yahoo, and, in the months that followed, other partnership deals were announced, with China's leading portal Netease and the portal Biglobe in Japan both adding Google search to their sites.

Website architectures

The pieces of hardware and software above can be assembled in different ways in a commercial website, but four common architectures are:

1. Website providing static information.
2. Website providing dynamic information.
3. Website with ordering facility.
4. Website fully integrated with ordering, inventory, billing and delivery systems.

Type 1 is the simplest and allows a customer to access information in static HTML documents using a browser. Type 2 adds more functionality by using CGI to generate HTML pages in response to customer requests. The CGI program fetches information from the company's databases and merges this with an HTML template to provide up-to-date information. Type 3 uses Java applets to handle customer transactions, which are encrypted and then processed by Java servlets linked to the ordering system. Orders and credit card authorization are then processed manually. Type 4 further automates the process by linking the ordering system to inventory, credit card authorization and delivery systems. Figure 2.9 shows a typical website setup.

Intranets and extranets

Although the Internet protocols were developed originally for communication between remote sites, a significant boost to their use in businesses has been the increasingly

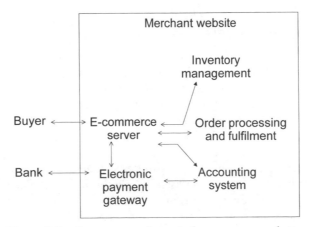

Figure 2.9   Components of a typical e-commerce website.

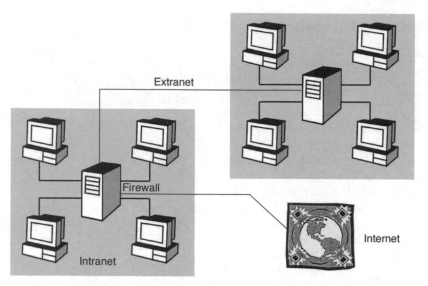

Figure 2.10   Intranets, extranets and the Internet.

widespread use in internal networks, or intranets, substituting or complementing proprietary LAN software, such as Ethernet. For example, employees within a company can use Internet browser software on their PCs to access information on internal websites and to exchange files with each other, whereas previously this may have been done using proprietary LAN applications.

Some companies have also set up "extranets", or networks that use Internet technology to communicate with customers, partners and lenders. For example, customers can use extranets to access supplier databases to check on stock availability, to place orders and to check the status of orders (Figure 2.10).

Firewalls and proxy servers

One major issue of concern with the use of extranets is ensuring security of data held on the company's network; this is usually done using firewalls and proxy servers. A firewall is a set of programs located on a company's network gateway server which prevents unauthorized external users from accessing the company's intranet and controls which external resources its own users can access. One way to prevent unauthorized access is to only accept requests from authorized IP addresses and domain names. Another is to use logon passwords and authentication certificates.

Firewalls are often used in conjunction with a proxy server, which is a server that acts as an intermediary between a user's workstation and the Internet. The proxy server only allows access to authorized sites and only allows access by authorized users. It may also act as a cache server, holding copies of previously accessed webpages; this is of advantage where there are many users or where users frequently access the same pages, since response times can be reduced. In addition some proxy servers run virus detection programs on incoming files, reducing the risk of corrupted data on the user's computer.

Mini-case study: The Love Bug, Sobig and Mydoom

In May, 2000 hundreds of computer systems around the world were temporarily halted as they were infected by a virulent virus named the "The Love Bug" after the subject line of its enticing email which reads "I LOVE YOU". Organizations that were infected included the British House of Commons, the Pentagon, NASA, TWA, Ford, the Jet Propulsion Lab and TicketMaster CitySearch, while hundreds of other companies were forced to shut down their computer systems as a preventive measure.

The Love Bug worm invades computers and servers via email attachments by exploiting a feature of Microsoft Outlook which enables computers to run software automatically and invisibly when users open an attachment. The first thing it does when executed is to save itself to three different locations: in the system directory as MSKernel32.vbs and LOVE-LETTER-FOR-YOU.TXT.vbs, and in the Windows directory as Win32DLL.vbs. Then it creates several start-up commands to execute the programs when the machine restarts. The worm also modifies Internet Explorer's start page to randomly select between four URLs at the domain *www.skyinet.net* that will download a binary called WINBUGSFIX.exe which allows it to change its behaviour any time a new one is downloaded.

In August, 2003 computers around the world were hit again by the Sobig F virus that overwhelmed 1 in 17 emails, even more than the Love Bug which peaked at 1 in 28 emails. As in the case of the Love Bug, the virus is contracted via email file attachments. Sobig also regularly changes its subject line and the name of the attachment in order to fool people. Unlike the Love Bug, the virus carries its own email-sending program and does not use Outlook to despatch infected mail. As well as using Microsoft Outlook address books to send mail to new victims, Sobig F also attempts to implant a background program that turns infected machines into a relay for any messages sent by the virus's creator.

This was followed in January, 2004 by an even faster spreading virus, Mydoom. As in the case of Love Bug and Sobig, Mydoom arrives as an email attachment in a text file which sends itself out to other email addresses if opened. Mydoom peaked at infecting 1 in 12 emails. Like Love Bug and Sobig, Mydoom works by copying email addresses from the infected computer and randomly choosing the next victim from these. The virus was also programmed to flood software vendor SCO with emails from February 1 to 12, prompting suspicions that the virus was released in retaliation for SCO's claim that key parts of the open-source operating system, Linux, are under SCO's copyright.

Virtual private networks

For further security on a public network, some companies also use virtual private networks (VPNs). A VPN is a private data network that makes use of the public telecommunication infrastructure, maintaining privacy by using tunnelling protocol and security procedures. A VPN can be contrasted with a system of owned or leased lines that can only be used by one company. The idea of the VPN is to give the company the same capabilities at much lower cost by using the shared public infrastructure rather than a private one. Telephone companies have provided similar, secure shared resources for voice messages. A VPN makes it possible to have the same secure sharing of public resources for data. Many companies today are looking at using a VPN for both extranets and wide-area intranets.

In a VPN data are encrypted before being sent through the public network and decrypted at the receiving end. An additional level of security involves encrypting not only the data but also the originating and receiving network addresses. Microsoft, 3Com and several other companies have developed the point-to-point tunnelling protocol (PPTP), and Microsoft has extended Windows NT to support it. VPN software is typically installed as part of a company's firewall server.

P2P

A network technology that is rapidly being adopted is P2P, short for peer-to-peer. This refers to a group of public or private users on the Internet sharing similar interests. Each group member has access to the hard disk of every other member of the group. Hence any member of the group can view the files lying on any other computer within the group. One of the best-known P2P networks was Napster (now shut down), which allowed users to download files in MP3 (Mpeg 1 Audio Layer 3) format from the hard disk of some other computer. Although initially opposed to P2P sites, such as Napster, which allowed free downloads, some music companies are now embracing the technology themselves by developing software that will allow users to listen to songs before deciding to buy them; Shaun Fanning, the founder of Napster, is doing likewise. P2P, therefore, seems likely to become a key means of delivery in the music and other entertainment industries in the future.

P2P technology has also been finding uses in the business and the academic community, where P2P networks have proved to be capable of working well under two kinds of situations:

1. At places where files needs to be shared by different users.
2. At places where processing capabilities and free storage space needs to be shared at different locations

---

Mini-case: P2P in outer space

The search for extraterrestrial intelligence (SETI), a project aimed at searching out intelligent life in outer space by trying to receive radio signals from space, has a subprogram called SETI@home, which works over a P2P network. SETI@home allows anyone to be part of the massive search project as a member. SETI sends small parts of the huge amount of data it receives on a regular basis to member computers. Thereupon, all the subsequent processing on that part of data is done on the local computer itself. This way, SETI gets the massive computational power that it needs for the project. For members, these SETI-related computations only happen during free CPU cycles, such as when the computer is idle. So, it does not influence the performance of members' computers. Moreover, members have a chance to be a part of, arguably, the biggest event in humankind's history, just in case the data sent to them from SETI happens to be something from another world.

Security of transactions

A crucial element allowing electronic commerce over the Internet has been the development of software to ensure security of transactions. New software and standards are being developed all the time to improve security of transactions, but the two standards that are most commonly used at present are SSL and SET.

SSL (secure sockets layer) uses a separate program layer between the application and the Internet's TCP/IP layer for transmitting messages in a network via port 443 on the PC. As a further security measure it uses the RSA algorithm developed by Rivest, Shamir and Adelman (1977) to encrypt the message. The algorithm randomly generates a very large prime number to use as a public key and relates this to another very large prime number to use as a private key. This is used as follows. First, the vendor transmits the public key (P) to the customer's web browser. The browser then generates a secret key for the session (S) and encrypts this using the public key (P) it has received. It sends the encrypted key back to the vendor which then decodes it using its private key (P') so now it too has the secret key (S). Further exchanges between the customer's browser and the vendor's server are then encoded and decrypted using the secret key (S) (Figure 2.11).

SSL establishes a secure session between a browser and a server so that messages cannot be read by a third party. However, it does not authenticate the parties who are using the software (i.e., it does not authenticate that the vendor and the customer are who they

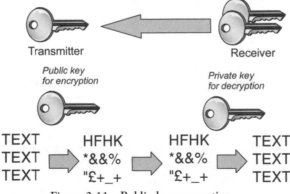

Transmitter

Receiver

Public key
for encryption

Private key
for decryption

TEXT   HFHK   HFHK   TEXT
TEXT   *&&%   *&&%   TEXT
TEXT   "£+_+   "£+_+   TEXT

Figure 2.11   Public key encryption.

claim to be). PKI, or public key infrastructure, is one solution to this problem; this relies on three elements: encryption to make information secure when passing through the Internet, an electronic signature to identify the user and a digital certificate to authenticate the identity of the user. Electronic signatures and digital certificates can be bought from certification bodies, such as the post office, network providers and some banks.

The secure electronic transaction (SET) Internet payment system developed by Visa and Mastercard is a PKI designed for credit card transactions; this relies on the customer and vendor each obtaining:

1. A digital wallet, software that is used to store credit card account information.
2. A digital certificate, proof of the holder's identity.

The customer and vendor each hold a digital certificate within a digital wallet on their respective machines; these function as a signed credit card slip and stamped store receipt, respectively. When a customer makes a purchase using the SET protocol, the digital certificates are exchanged, allowing each party in the transaction to verify each other's identity. The merchant then sends the bank the order information, the customer's payment information and the merchant's certificate. Once the bank verifies the merchant's certificate and the order information, it authorizes payment to the merchant. Furthermore, to ensure integrity of messages between the different parties, when a message is sent via the SET protocol it is encrypted together with a unique number that changes if the message is tampered with.

Communication technologies

Although significant advances have been made in recent years, the ultimate goal of the global information infrastructure (GII) is "any information, anywhere, anytime". Two major technological routes are currently being explored to achieve this goal – wireless and broadband landlines – although both routes will eventually converge (Figure 2.12).

Wireless technologies

The technology that is arousing the most interest at the present time is the mobile communications route, termed by some "m-commerce". Demand is expected to be large owing to the low entry cost for users of purchasing a mobile phone compared with purchasing a networked PC or interactive television system; this new market is being actively targeted by many companies. The user device that most companies in this area are targeting is an enhanced mobile phone, although the idea dates back to earlier ideas of a "thin client" PC promulgated as early as 1990.

The term "thin client" originated in the 1990s to describe a new category of client devices, such as network computers (NCs) and Windows-based terminals (WBTs). Thin

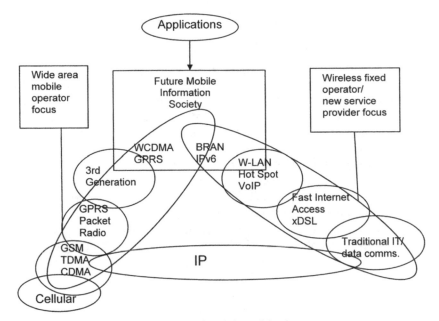

Figure 2.12 Convergence of mobile and land communications.

clients run operating systems locally as opposed to traditional PC operating systems (Win95, NT, etc.). Today "thin client" is the accepted generic term for a network-based approach to information processing which is comprised of both hardware and software elements. In a thin client architecture most of the processing is done by a powerful back end server, thus less hardware and software is required on the client computer. In conventional client–server systems, clients are often desktop personal computers with local storage operating systems and peripherals. These "fat-client" PCs are more expensive to buy and maintain. In fact, much of the software and hardware can be reduced. For example, if the client is used simply to pick up messages, a hard disk is unnecessary. Instead, the files can be stored centrally. By locating all the software centrally, installation and upgrades are easier and software maintenance is reduced. Furthermore, since there is only one central access point to be protected, security should also be easier.

In parallel with a move toward thin-client PCs has been a move toward networking using wireless devices, such as mobile phones and personal digital assistants (PDAs). The latest trend is digital cellular phones. They use the same radio technology as ordinary cellular phones, but convert the analogue signal into digital format and then compress it. This compression allows between 3 and 10 cellphone calls to occupy the space of a single analogue voice call. Using TDMA (time division multiple access) technology each cellular channel is divided into three time slots. TDMA is used by Digital-American Mobile Phone Service (D-AMPS), Global System for Mobile communications (GSM) and Personal Digital Cellular (PDC) Digital Enhanced Cordless Telecommunications

(DECT) standards. However, each of these systems implements TDMA in a somewhat different and incompatible way.

Carrier detection multiple access (CDMA), one of the three wireless telephone transmission technologies, takes an entirely different approach from TDMA. CDMA, after digitizing data, spreads them out over the entire bandwidth it has available. Multiple calls are overlain on top of each other on the channel, with each assigned a unique sequence code. A group called PCS PrimeCo which includes NYNEX, Bell Atlantic, US West and Airtouch Communications has announced plans for PCS (personal communications service) systems that use CDMA in the USA.

Until recently wireless Internet access has been limited by the capabilities of hand-held devices and wireless networks which were designed to handle smaller volumes of data. Internet standards, such as HTML, HTTP and TCP, are inefficient over mobile networks, requiring large amounts of mainly text-based data to be sent. Standard HTML content also cannot be effectively displayed on the small-size screens of pocket-sized mobile phones and pagers. A number of standards have emerged to overcome these constraints.

WAP

Wireless application protocol (WAP) overcomes the constraints of wireless transmission by utilizing a subset of Internet standards optimized for low bandwidth and less stable transmissions. Binary transmission is used for greater compression of data and WAP sessions can cope with intermittent coverage over a wide variety of wireless transports. Instead of HTML, wireless markup language (WML) and wireless markup language script (WMLScript) are used to produce WAP content; these allow displays from two lines of text to a full graphic screen on the latest smart phones and allow screen navigation with one hand. WAP also incorporates a "push capability" as standard which enables information providers such as stockmarket, weather and travel service providers, to automatically provide relevant information to clients. WAP users can access the Internet by dialling in to a WAP gateway linked to the Internet (Figure 2.13).

Some current WAP offerings include:

- Advertising
  Loot *http://wap.loot.com*

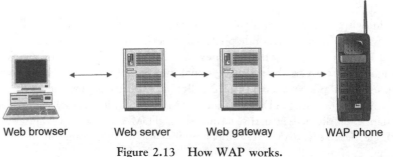

Figure 2.13   How WAP works.

- Auctions
  QXL *http://mobile.qxl.com*
- City guides
  Barcelona *http://artbites.com/bcn.wml*
  Istanbul *http://wap.ismap.com*
  London *http://mmm.e-street.com*
- Late bookings
  Lastminute *http://mobile.lastminute.com/wap*
- Location finder
  Where on Earth *http://www.whereonearth.com*
  Somewherenear *http://www.somewherenear.com*
- Music
  MP3 *http://wap.mp3.com*
  Electrowap *http://www.electrowap.fr.st*
- News
  Guardian Newspaper *http://www.guardian.co.uk/wml*
  El Salvador News *http://wap.elsalvador.com*
- Railway guide
  Danish Railways *http://wap.bane.dk*
- Share information
  TD Waterhouse *http://wdat.com/tdwuk*
  Stock Alerts *http://wap.stock-alerts.com*
- Sports
  Eurosport *http://www.eurosport.com*
  Total Sports *http://wap.totalsports.net*
- Taxi guide
  Wap Cab *http://wapcabwap.com*
- Travel guide
  Australia *http://www.ewap.com.au*
  Brazil *http://wap.brasilwap.com.br*
  Germany *http://wap.travelchannel.de*
  Ireland *http://www.IRLwap.com*

i-Mode

While WAP is the emerging standard in Europe and North America, the leading standard for wireless Internet in Japan is i-mode (Figure 2.14); this was developed jointly by Sun Microsystems and NTT DoCoMo (*www.nttdocomo.com*) and uses a subset of Java, the K virtual machine (KVM), on specially adapted wireless phones using W-CDMA (wideband carrier detection multiple access) radio transmission.

W-CDMA spreads the data over a wide band and allows multiple users to share radio frequencies by allocating a unique spreading code to each user. Because a wider band is used, this reduces the effects of interference, noise and changes in received power,

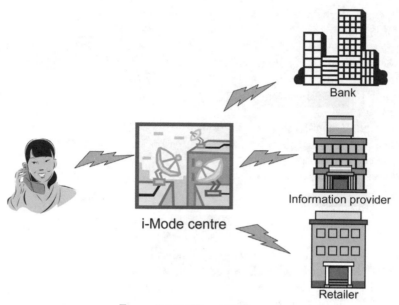

Figure 2.14   How i-Mode works.

compared with standard transmissions. Furthermore, it can be used not only to transmit voice, data and still images but can also handle smooth full-motion video. Field trials have successfully transmitted full-motion video at a speed of 2 Mbps.

Like WAP, i-mode allows display of HTML-based pages, but is slower. Currently, some 6,000 websites are available, including games, financial services, ticket booking, restaurant guides and news. Unlike WAP, however, services are bundled by the mobile operator, so not all services can be accessed.

Both WAP and i-Mode enable new services to be offered on mobile devices by condensing the information that is shown on normal PC screens and so minimizing the data that need to be transmitted. However, many more services will be possible once transmission speeds for mobile networks are improved.

GSM

GSM (Global System for Mobile communication) is the digital mobile telephone standard that is currently used in Europe and in many other parts of the world. GSM uses a variation of TDMA and is the most widely used of the three digital wireless telephone technologies (TDMA, GSM and CDMA). GSM digitizes and compresses data, then sends them down a channel with two other streams of user data, each in its own time slot. It operates at either the 900-MHz or 1,800-MHz frequency band. In the USA, American Personal Communications (APC), a subsidiary of Sprint, is using GSM as the technology for a broadband PCS. However, GSM will soon be replaced by newer standards, allowing greater transmission speeds.

Some carriers are already offering high-speed, circuit-switched data (HSCSD) which achieve higher data rates by combining multiple voice channels. Another development is referred to by some as "direct IP access". The user makes a circuit-switched data call, but rather than switching the call into the public-switched telephone network, the carrier terminates it at a router that is connected to the Internet. From the user perspective, the carrier appears like an ISP offering a dial-up service. This hybrid circuit/packet type of service will also work with HSCSD and is a stepping stone to more advanced packet-switching technologies, such as GPRS.

GPRS

General Packet Radio Service (GPRS) refers to a high-speed packet data technology that makes it possible and cost-effective to remain constantly connected, as well as to send and receive data at much higher speeds than today. It will increase data transmission speeds to over 100 kbps compared with 9.6 kbps with GSM, and it will extend the Internet connection all the way to the mobile PC. The fact that GPRS will operate at much higher speeds than current networks should provide a huge advantage from a software perspective. Today, wireless middleware is often required to allow slow-speed mobile clients to work with fast networks for such applications as email, databases, groupware or Internet access. With GPRS, wireless middleware will often be unnecessary, and thus it should be easier to deploy wireless solutions than ever before. Whereas most wireless applications today tend to be text-oriented, the high speed offered by GPRS will finally make multimedia content, including graphics, voice and video practical. It will be possible, for example, to take part in a videoconference while travelling on a train or waiting for a flight at the airport.

Another advantage of a packet-based approach is that GPRS only uses the network for the duration of time that data are being sent or received; this means that multiple users can share the same radio channel. In contrast, with current circuit-switched connections, users have dedicated connections during their entire call, whether or not they are sending data. With packet data, users only pay for the amount of data they actually send, not the idle time. In fact, with GPRS, users could be "virtually" connected for hours at a time and only incur modest connection charges.

For example, the user could be working on a document without even thinking about being connected and then automatically receive new email. They could then decide to continue working on the document, before reading the email message and replying to it. Throughout this period the user has had a network connection and not once had to dial in to receive or send emails, as in circuit-switched networks. Furthermore, GPRS allows for simultaneous voice and data communication, so the user can still receive incoming calls or make outgoing calls while transferring data.

EDGE

At the same time GSM standards bodies are already looking at defining data networking technologies that go beyond GPRS. One such technology is called enhanced data rate for

GSM evolution (EDGE) which will offer a maximum theoretical rate of 384 kbps, although normal operating speeds will be about half this rate.

UMTS

Beyond EDGE, third-generation cellular systems will eventually offer data rates of 2 Mbps. UMTS (Universal Mobile Telecommunications System) will allow mobile data to be transferred in packets as quickly as via fixed-line networks. Within a small area such as an office or factory, speeds of up to 2 Mbps will be possible and in wider areas speeds of 384 kbps will be possible. Even at 384 kbps the technology will offer high-speed Internet access, fast file transfer and high-quality videos.

BRAN

UMTS will eventually develop to BRAN (broadcast radio access network) technologies; these could provide speeds of up to 11 Mbps. To support these new communication technologies mobile phones will be equipped with voice-activated web browsers, using voice-activated markup language (VML); this will allow users to navigate the Web using verbal commands, eliminating the need for a keyboard or pointer device.

Connectivity

As well as developments allowing transmission of more data on wireless networks, the usefulness of wireless devices has also been increased by new standards allowing greater connectivity between wireless devices and other devices, the most prominent being Jini, Bluetooth and Symbian.

Jini

Jini is an architecture that allows different kinds of devices to collaborate with such PCs, PDAs and mobile phones in an "intelligent" network. Unlike standard architectures that assume devices are fixed in the network, Jini allows devices to be added dynamically by allowing devices to sense other devices in the network using JavaTones, similar to the dial tone on a telephone. When a device is plugged into a Jini network, it is immediately recognized by the directory service layer as a member of the network. Its necessary program objects are then placed in a JavaSpace layer, so that other members of the network can download them when required. Unlike traditional networks, devices are not controlled by a central network manager and other devices in the network can directly call on any registered device; this is done as and when required using Jini's remote method invocation (RMI). This releases users from the task of system administration and allows devices to be easily added or removed from the network. It will no longer be necessary to make sure that the correct device driver is present or added to the operating system in order to use the resource. The operating system will be able to access the required information through the network registry.

Jini enables manufacturers to make devices that can attach to a network independently of an operating system like Windows 95: for example, a printer could be shared by users with different operating systems, such as Windows, Macintosh and UNIX. Mobile devices can easily be transported to another network and plugged in: for example, a digital camera can be added to the network by registering the services it provides with the look-up service and periodically renewing this registration. When it is no longer required it can be removed and used elsewhere.

Bluetooth

Bluetooth (*http://www.bluetooth.com*) is conceptually similar to Jini in that it allows devices in a network to sense other devices, but is particularly useful for mobile devices as it does away with the need for a wire connection. Instead, devices sense when they come in range of each other and communicate with each other using 2.4-GHz, short-range radio transmissions. Using Bluetooth, users of cellular phones, pagers and PDAs will be able to use the device to perform a range of functions in different networks. For example, a PDA may be used to download data from a PC in the office when it comes within range of the radio transmissions, then used to read the data in the car and to print out the data on a printer at home, all without the need for wires.

Bluetooth works using a microchip transceiver that transmits and receives in the previously unused frequency band of 2.45 GHz; this will allow the device to exchange data within a range of 10 m at a rate of 1 Mbps. In addition, three voice channels are available. To ensure security, Bluetooth has integrated encryption and authentication functions allowing secure transactions, and "hops" between different frequencies in transmission making it difficult for unauthorized users to access the transmission (Figure 2.15).

EPOC

A complementary technology standard, which will work with Bluetooth, is the EPOC mobile operating system for use in mobile phones and PDAs. EPOC is being developed by Symbian (*www.symbian.com*), a joint venture owned by Ericsson, Matsushita, Motorola, Nokia and Psion, and has been designed for the specific requirements of portable, battery-powered, wireless information devices. The primary requirements are effective use of battery power, small ROM and RAM footprint, effective power management during normal operation, robust response to low-power conditions and instant access to user data during a power failure. EPOC will also include features designed to make it easy to transfer data between devices, such as inter-machine clipboard transfer, and infrared data exchange between devices.

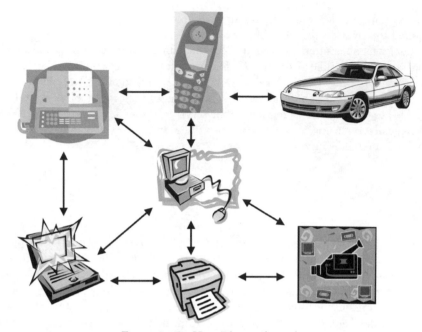

Figure 2.15 How Bluetooth works.

Wi-Fi networks

One of the fastest growing means of accessing the mobile Internet is through Wi-Fi networks. "Wi-Fi" is a shorthand name for a communications system that transmits computer data over short distances using radio waves. All Wi-Fi systems follow a set of standards known as 802.11, created by the Institute of Electrical and Electronics Engineers (IEEE). The most commonly used standard is 802.11b, which allows for the transmission of data at 11 Mbps over a range of 100–1,000 feet. A Wi-Fi network operates just like a wired network, but without the cumbersome need for wires, and provides easy connections to the Internet and business networks while travelling. Thousands of Wi-Fi networks have now been implemented in many public spaces, such as airports, cafes and petrol stations, around the world. Many wireless access points around the world are listed on HotSpotList.com. The Wi-Fi Alliance has also made available a WAP-based application that will let anyone with a WAP-enabled cellphone or PDA find hot spots listed in the Alliance's Wi-Fi zone database (*http://wap.wi-fizone.org*).

Mini-case study: Some wireless hotspots

- Coffee chain Starbucks launched an international campaign to put wireless access with T1 speeds (up to 1.54 Mbps) in some 2,000 of its US and European stores by the end of 2003.

- Fast-food chain McDonald's has opened hot spots in New York, San Francisco and Seattle (and many other places in the USA), in all of its restaurants in Guangzhou, China and throughout Hong Kong.
- Chicago-based Coastal Hotel Group, which owns 14 luxury hotels in Washington, California, Arizona, Florida, Kentucky and Illinois, is going to be adding Wi-Fi for guests.
- Starwood Hotels & Resorts now offers wireless networking in common areas in its W hotels. The chain's flagship, the W Times Square in New York, is wireless throughout the entire hotel. The company says that Wi-Fi would be available in guestrooms in all of its US hotels by the end of 2005.
- Pittsburgh's Telerama Internet, which runs for-fee hot spots all over the city, has signed a deal with the non-profit Pittsburgh Cultural Trust to put Wi-Fi access throughout the 14-square-mile downtown area called the Cultural District.
- Statoil Detaljhandel AS, co-owned by Norwegian oil company Statoil and the ICA supermarket chain from Sweden, is providing hot spots in its service stations in Norway.
- The Blood tribe Indian reservation in Alberta, Canada uses a Wi-Fi network to provide Internet and network access to all the town residents.
- The Kasetsart University in Bangkok, Thailand has one of the largest academic wireless nets in all of South-East Asia, covering 43 buildings on the Bangkhen Campus.
- The Queensland State Government, Australia is offering Wi-Fi in a 12-month trial in 20 public locations, such as railway stations, sports venues and courtrooms, along the Gold Coast and in Brisbane.

Broadband technologies

The other major technology route that is being explored apart from mobile devices is broadband communication using fixed devices, the major transmission channels being telephone, cable and satellite networks. Which route is preferred for Internet connection varies according to country (Beardsley et al., 2000). In the USA, 70% of households already subscribe to cable, whereas in Western Europe only 28% of households do. However, penetration of mobile phones is higher in Europe than the USA: 41% in Western Europe generally and over 60% in Sweden and Finland, compared with 31% in the USA. It is likely, therefore, that the terrestrial route will be adopted faster in the USA, whereas the mobile route will be adopted faster in Europe (Kehoe, 2000). Rate of adoption of mobile Internet connections is also expected to be higher than terrestrial connections in less developed countries, the price of a mobile phone being much less than that of a PC and modem.

BISDN

ISDN (integrated services digital network) standards for sending voice video data or packets over the public-switched telephone network were first published in the mid-1980s and have been used in the corporate environment for several years. It is now increasingly being marketed for home use as well. The advantage of ISDN is that it works over existing networks using copper wiring, but allows much greater transmission speeds (up to 14.4 kbps for basic-rate ISDN and 1.54 Mbps for premium-rate ISDN). However, even as ISDN is being marketed to new users, it is already being eclipsed by BISDN (broadband integrated services digital network), a set of standards for integrating digital services using a broadband network of fibre optic and radio media. BISDN will encompass a number of technologies, the key ones being DSL, frame relay, ATM and SONET.

Digital subscriber loop technology

DSL technology was first introduced by Bell Corporation in 1989 as a way to send video and television signals from the telephone central office to end-users over standard copper wire. There are many types of DSL technology (Table 2.1); the most widely available is asymmetric digital subscriber loop, or ADSL. As the name suggests ADSL is asymmetric in that the line operates at different speeds away and toward the customer. Large-sized files, such as video, are sent downstream at a fast speed whereas information from the customer is sent upstream at lower speed (typically upstream at a speed of 176–640 kbps and downstream at 1.5–6.14 Mbps). Unlike normal telephone connections, this provides 24-h continuous connection at low cost.

Frame relay

Frame relay is a data transmission technology that allows multiple organizations to share the same private network, with the management of the network being left to the network

Table 2.1 Varieties of DSL technology

Service	Upstream rate (kbps)	Downstream rate (kbps)	Maximum distance from central office (km)
ADSL	176	54,000	6
	640	6,140	4
HDSL	1,540	1,540	4
VDSL	640	13,000	1.5
	23,000	52,000	0.3
RADSL	176	1,540	6
	640	6,140	4
	128	600	7
IDSL	128	128	6

provider. However, another added benefit is that since each organization performs its own error checking, faster speeds are achievable on the network. It is most commonly used in conjunction with ATM transmission technology.

ATM

ATM, or asynchronous transfer mode, is a high-speed switching service capable of carrying voice data video and multimedia images. Speeds on ATM networks can reach up to 10 Gbps. ATM is fast for a number of reasons. First, ATM packages the data it switches into fixed size cells of 53 bytes instead of variable size cells; this saves time since the network does not have to look for a sign telling it when the cell ends. Another reason is that the cell's are switched in the hardware instead of looking at each cell's address in software. An ATM switch sets up a route through the network when it reads the first cell of a transmission and stores this information in the hardware. The next time it sees a cell with the same header it is routed down the previously established path. A third way ATM increases speed of transmission is by switching asynchronously. In synchronous switching each of the multiple terminals that may be on the line is allocated a time slot even if it has nothing to send. With ATM, time slots are allocated according to the information in the cell header so that, for example, voice and video are allocated more slots than email messages since they require fewer delays and a faster overall speed of transmission.

SONET

The synchronous optical network (SONET) is a standard way to interconnect high-speed traffic from multiple vendors. Whereas ATM achieves speed by switching and multi-plexing, SONET achieves speed by using fibre optic cabling; this enables speeds of up to 10,000 Mbps. SONET will probably become more widely used in the future as data loads increase, but at present is not widely available owing to the high costs of establishing an optical fibre network. To date, the most common uses are for emergency services, such as the fire service, police and armed forces.

Broadband satellite communications

Satellite communication has been available since the 1960s, and satellites have been widely used to carry international telephone calls and international television broadcasts since that time. In addition both business and home users have been able to use satellites for communication using VSAT networks. VSAT (very small aperture terminal) is a satellite communications system that serves home and business users. A transceiver receives or sends a signal to a satellite transponder in space. In turn the satellite sends and receives signals from an Earth station computer that acts as a hub for the system. For one end-user to communicate with another, each transmission has to first go to the hub station, which retransmits it via the satellite to the other end-user's VSAT. VSAT offers a number of advantages over terrestrial alternatives. For private applications, companies can have total control of their own communication system without dependence on other companies. Business and home users can also get higher speed reception than by using an ordinary telephone service or ISDN.

Another type of satellite that is expected to expand the market for satellite network access is the low earth-orbiting satellite (LEOS). Traditional geosynchronous satellites orbit the Earth at 22,300 miles above the Earth's surface. This height allows them to beam signals to a wide area. However, it also causes delay problems with data transmission. LEOSs on the other hand are positioned from 435 to 1,000 miles above the Earth's surface; this provides less coverage, but reduces the delay and promises easy access to the Internet for people living in remote regions where there is no telephone or cable network.

There are four market segments that broadband satellites are ideally placed to serve (Evans et al., 1998):

- *Dedicated point-to-point connectivity* A significant market for satellites is expected to be the provision of temporary communication links, such as links over large distances, links in countries that have poorly developed terrestrial network and links for special events.
- *Shared connectivity* Broadband satellites can also be used to supply companies with short-term links on demand for transaction-based data, such as credit card validation or for point-of-sale updates across a large network.
- *Transport* Broadband satellites could be used to carry telecommunications traffic from one part of the country to another in countries where the telecommunications infrastructure is poor and developing a terrestrial network would be too expensive.
- *Fixed telephony* As LEOSs spend much of their time over countries where demand for more sophisticated services is weak, they could also be usefully employed to carry basic, low-margin telephone traffic.

As well as the four segments described above, broadband satellite systems could also be used to provide an "Internet in the sky." Although it may not be possible to provide a full Internet service cost-effectively, satellites could be used to distribute broadcast and multicast content: for example, information could easily be distributed by satellite, downloads from such sites as Adobe could be done in the background while news providers, such as CNN, could broadcast top pages at intervals. Although the service would not be truly interactive each user would only receive the information requested, giving the appearance of interactivity.

Multimedia data

The importance of the GIF and JPEG compression standards in making the Internet more useful and popularizing the use of the Internet was discussed earlier. Similar standards are helping to extend the usefulness of the Web even further by allowing audio and video files to be easily exchanged.

XML

As described earlier, most webpages are written in HTML. However, this can sometimes be limiting. For example, a buyer may wish to extract the current list of prices from the webpage of a supplier on a regular basis. In order to do this in HTML, the buyer must examine the structure of the HTML document to find where the prices are listed and write a program that parses the document to extract the relevant items from the page (a procedure called web scraping). To display this information in their web browser, the buyer must then reconvert this information back into HTML. If the supplier changes the format of the page, the program will no longer work correctly since the information will be located in a different place.

This problem could be solved using SGML which allows arbitrarily structured documents, but SGML is complicated to use and would be too difficult to implement on a web browser. So, XML (extensible markup language) was created. Like HTML, XML makes use of tags and attributes (of the form name = "value"), but while HTML specifies what each tag and attribute means, XML uses the tags only to delimit pieces of data and leaves the interpretation of the data completely to the application that reads it. As well as text and graphics, these include vector graphics, e-commerce transactions, mathematical equations and many other kinds of structured information.

An early application was chartware, software that uses XML to describe medical charts so that doctors can share information. However, XML is now finding commercial applications. For example, the credit card company Visa has developed a standard based on XML for completely automating the payments process in e-commerce. The problem is that different information is required by different countries for tax-accounting purposes and, with conventional EDI standards, systems from different countries may not be compatible. The solution is an invoice structure based on XML that is flexible enough to accommodate any type of information that might be required anywhere in the world.

Book publishers are also using XML to create books that can be displayed on a variety of compatible devices. The Open eBook standard (*www.openebook.org*) allows books to be downloaded to portable electronic books, notebook PCs or palmtops.

VRML

Although HTML allows the creation of document-style webpages that can incorporate raster graphics images (such as GIF or JPEG files), it has serious limitations both in terms of its information structuring and its interaction capabilities. The virtual reality markup language (VRML) enables the next level of interaction, by moving beyond the document-based webpages to 3-D virtual worlds based on interactive computer graphics. VRML is a file format that not only describes the shape of 3-D objects it also describes the interactive behaviours to be applied when a user interacts with them. These objects can range from simple geometric objects, such as cubes and spheres, to complex objects, such as humanoids. Applications of VRML range from business graphics to manufacturing, scientific, entertainment and educational applications, and virtual worlds and communities.

VRML standards were initially agreed informally by a small group of researchers working on VR, but there is now a formal group called the Web3D Consortium which is responsible for administering the standard, and VRML is now an official ISO standard (ISO 14772). In order to view VRML files a special VRML browser is required, such as Blaxxun's Contact and ParallelGraphics Cortona.

MP3

MP3 stands for Mpeg 1 Audio Layer 3 and is a compression algorithm based on a complicated psychoacoustic model. Based on the fact that the human hearing range is between 20 Hz and 20 kHz and is most sensitive between 2 and 4 kHz, MP3 eliminates the frequencies that the human ear is unable to hear and leaves intact all the frequencies that can be heard in the data. Different levels of compression can be set with a 12 : 1 compression ratio being common; this allows, for example, a 4-min-long song (40 MB) to be compressed to less than 4 MB, a size that can be easily transmitted over the Internet.

In order to listen to an MP3 file it is necessary to load an MP3 player, such as WinAmp, onto the PC. Small portable players are also available and can be plugged into the PC's parallel port to download songs. To convert songs from a CD to MP3, it is necessary to use ripper and encoder software. The ripper copies the song from the CD to the PC, while the encoder compresses the song into the MP3 format. MP3 files can also be written to CD using some encoders and a plug-in (if using WinAmp). It is, of course, illegal to copy music from a CD without permission of the copyright owner as highlighted by recent court cases against sites, such as MP3.com and Napster.com, which enable users to share MP3 files.

Streaming audio and video

Even with compression very large multimedia files can still take a long time to download and view. An alternative is to stream it. Streaming video is a sequence of "moving images" that are sent in compressed form over the Internet and displayed by the viewer as they arrive. Streaming media is streaming video with sound. With streaming video or streaming media, a user does not have to wait to download a large file before seeing the video or hearing the sound; instead, the media is sent in a continuous stream and is played as it arrives. A streaming media player is required to decompress and send video data to the display and audio data to speakers. A player can be either an integral part of a browser or downloaded from the software maker's website.

The three major video-streaming technologies currently in use are RealMedia, QuickTime and Windows Media. Each of the three streaming technologies have their own proprietary server and types of media files that they use. QuickTime, RealMedia and Windows Media each have their own corresponding server designed to stream files in their respective formats. Each technology also has its own media player, a plug-in component for web browsers. Users need the player installed on their computer to view or listen to streaming media designed for that player. The third component common to each streaming technology is file creation and encoding; this relates to the way media files are created for a particular streaming format. Each of the three technologies has its own proprietary way of encoding media files for playback from a streaming server.

Microsoft's technology offers streaming audio at up to 96 kbps and streaming video at up to 8 Mbps (for the NetShow theater server). However, for most web users, streaming video will be limited to the data rates of the connection (e.g., up to 128 kbps with an ISDN connection). Streaming video is usually sent from pre-recorded video files, but can be distributed as part of a live broadcast "feed". In a live broadcast, the video signal is converted into a compressed digital signal and transmitted from a special web server that is able to do multicasting, sending the same file to multiple users at the same time.

Widespread availability of media-streaming software and webcams has created a whole new mini-industry producing short films online, such as AtomFilms and Ifilm. The pornographic film industry has been a heavy user of streaming video, but streaming video has also become increasingly popular for news broadcasts on the Internet.

Digital television

An alternative to both mobile phone and telephone networks which is starting to be more fully exploited for data transmission is the television network; this has many advantages including an existing industry infrastructure for delivering the service and consumer familiarity with the technology. The limitation until recently has been that the technology is analogue and so is not suitable for digital data transmission. However, with the development of digital television (DTV), the television network has become a viable alternative.

One of the primary drivers for the development of DTV is high-definition television, or HDTV. Development of HDTV started in the mid-1980s when the major Japanese consumer electronics firms developed a new standard for television transmission. HDTV transmissions contain up to six times more data than conventional television signals and at least twice the picture resolution. HDTV images have a 16:9 aspect ratio (the ratio of width to height), providing a wider image than the 4:3 ratio that has been used in television since 1941. In addition HDTV offers five discrete channels of CD-quality audio.

However, DTV offers many benefits other than those offered by HDTV. As it uses a digital signal, unlike previous HDTV standards, DTV enables broadcasters to offer a variety of new services. Instead of sending an HDTV signal of 19.4 Mbps, for example, a broadcast station can send as many as five digital "standard definition television" (SDTV) signals, each of which might consist of 4 to 5 Mbps. Although SDTV images are not as sharp as HDTV, they are superior to existing television images. This new capacity, known as "multicasting" or "multiplexing", will allow broadcasters to compete with other multichannel media, such as cable and direct broadcast satellite systems. Moreover, as new advances in compression technology occur in the years ahead, broadcast stations are expected to fit even more SDTV signals into the same spectrum allotment.

Another DTV capability is the ability to provide new kinds of video and data services, such as subscription television programming, computer software distribution, data transmissions, teletext, interactive services, "zoned" news reports, advertising targeted at specific television sets, "time-shifted" video programming and closed circuit television services.

Broadcasters have the flexibility to shift back and forth between different DTV modes during the day. For example, a station might show four SDTV channels in the morning and afternoon and switch to a single HDTV programme, such as a widescreen movie or sports programme in the evening. A broadcaster is also able to mix and match video programming with data services. The latter is particularly interesting given the anticipated convergence of personal computer and television technologies. For example, broadcast television may develop new services in alliance with other telecommunications media or with information providers. Although the merger of Time-Warner and AOL announced in January 2000 has proved less successful than anticipated, it could be only one of many alliances that will develop between media, telecommunications and computing firms.

Java TV

An example of the anticipated convergence between television and computing technologies is Java TV. Developed by Sun Microsystems in conjunction with key companies involved in the digital television industry including Hongkong Telecom, LG Electronics, Matsushita, Motorola, OpenTV, Philips, Sony and Toshiba, the Java TV application programming interface (API) enables the secure delivery of interactive television content and services via the Java platform. A set-top box or digital television that supports the Java TV API offers consumers interactive television content, such as enhanced television, video on demand (VOD), electronic programming guides (EPGs) and interactive, multi-camera-angle sporting events. In addition, the Java TV API provides an independent software platform to access the hardware features that are unique to televisions, such as tuner control for channel changing and on-screen graphics, while maintaining portability across operating systems and microprocessors.

Java TV enables broadcasters to deliver value-added services to a diverse array of Java technology-enabled devices in their networks, regardless of the underlying microprocessor or operating system on those devices. Conversely, users will be able to access interactive TV and other services from a range of different devices, making it possible, for example, to switch from TV to PC to PDA as befits the occasion.

Summary

Internet-based systems offer significant advantages over traditional EDI networks, such as lower cost and a global reach. However, the Internet was not initially designed for commercial or public use and the technologies that enable it to be used so widely have developed piecemeal. Some critical technological innovations that have made it accessible for commercial and public use are:

- PC modems.
- World Wide Web.
- Browsers.
- Java.
- CGI.

Internet technologies are now being used for internal networks within the organization (intranets) and for external networks with partners (extranets). The Internet protocols have also been adapted to link mobile phones and other devices, such as digital television to the Internet: the aim is "any information, anywhere, anytime".

References

Beardsley, S.C., Ragunath, R. and Wilshire, M.J. (2000). The emergence of broadband in Europe. *McKinsey Quarterly*, **2**, 39–42.

Evans, A.L., Rose, J.S. and Venkateraman (1998). The future of satellite communications. *McKinsey Quarterly*, **2**, 6–17.

Kehoe, C.F. (2000). M-commerce: Advantage Europe. *McKinsey Quarterly*, **2**, 43–5.

OECD (2000). *Local Access Pricing and E-commerce*. Organization for Economic Co-operation and Development, Paris.

Rivest, R.L., Shamir, A. and Adelman, L. (1977). *On Digital Signatures and Public Key Crypto-systems* (MIT Laboratory for Computer Science Technical Memorandum No. 82). MIT Press, Cambridge, MA.

Further reading

The following books provide useful introductions to key technologies used in e-business:

Giaglis, G. (2004). *Mobile Business Technologies, Applications and Markets*. Butterworth-Heinemann, Oxford, UK.

Van Slyke, C. and Belanger, F. (2002). *E-business Technologies: Supporting the Net-enhanced Organization*. John Wiley & Sons, New York.

Sharma, C. and Nakamura, Y. (2003). *Wireless Data Services: Technologies, Business Models and Global Markets*. Cambridge University Press, Cambridge, UK.

Websites

The following websites provide practical advice on setting up a website:

www.geocities.com
www.webmonkey.com

The following site provides simple explanations of the key Internet technologies:

www.whatis.com

Key concepts

- ADSL
- Applets
- Audio streaming
- BISDN
- Bluetooth
- BRAN
- Broadband
  technologies
- Browser
- CGI
- Data compression
- Domain name
- DSL
- DTV
- EDI
- EPOC
- Extranet
- Firewall
- Frame relay
- GIF
- GSM
- GPRS
- HTML
- HTTP
- I-Mode
- Intranet
- IOS
- ISDN
- ISP
- Java
- JPEG
- LAN
- LEOS
- Modem
- MP3
- Portal
- Proxy server
- Search engine
- Servlets
- SET
- SONET
- SSL
- Symbian
- TCP/IP
- UMTS
- URL
- Video streaming
- VPN
- VRML
- VSAT
- WAN
- WAP
- WiFi
- XML

Self-assessment questions

1 What is the difference between EDI networks and the Internet?
2 Describe the physical structure of the Internet.
3 What is TCP/IP?
4 What is the difference between an ISP, a portal, a search engine and a directory?
5 What is a domain name?

6 List the hardware and software needed to operate a simple website.

7 What is the difference between an intranet, an extranet and the Internet?

8 What is the role of a firewall in a network?

9 What is PKI?

10 How does video- and audio-streaming work?

11 What are the different standards for the mobile Internet?

12 What are emerging broadband technologies?

13 Explain the difference between HDTV and DTV.

Discussion questions

1 What are the problems and deficiencies with the existing Internet technology and how would you change things if you could?

2 What are the key strategic groups in the "portal industry" and which portals are likely to win out in the battle for customers?

3 What should be done to improve security on the Internet?

4 Which of the emerging platforms for the Internet – PC, TV and mobile – is likely to dominate?

5 How are the mobile Internet and digital television different from PC-based Internet access?

6 What will be the likely impact of the next generation of communication technologies?

THE MARKETS FOR
ELECTRONIC COMMERCE

3

Introduction

The previous chapters showed how the Internet started off as a very obscure technology used by a small group of researchers to become the basis of a global information network that is the basis for growth of a new global economy. What has been most remarkable is just how quickly the Internet has been commercialized and how quickly the Internet technologies have been adopted. Of course, the two go hand in hand as whole new markets have developed using the technology. As might be expected given the origins of the technology and the initial user base, the markets that have developed around the technology show some distinctive, "path-dependent" features. This chapter examines some of the distinctive features of the markets and characteristics of the buyers and sellers in these markets. First, some general market trends are examined and, then, the markets are examined in more detail applying classical marketing segmentation methods. The consumer markets are segmented according to geographic, demographic, psychographic and behavioural variables, while the business markets are segmented by industry and geography.

Size and growth of the market

Figure 3.1 shows the growth in the number of websites, while Figure 3.2 shows the growth in the number of Internet domain names. The use of the Internet and related e-commerce technologies is growing so rapidly that statistics rapidly become out of date. Nevertheless, some general trends can be identified. Although the growth in Internet domain names shows a slight flattening off, the growth in the number of websites appears to fit quite well with "Metcalfe's law", originally coined by Stan Metcalfe, founder of the local network provider 3 Com, who noticed a similar trend in growth of telecommunication networks. This "law" states that the utility to the user increases exponentially with the number of users in the network (Figure 3.3); this is because the number of other users who can be contacted increases exponentially as more users join the network.

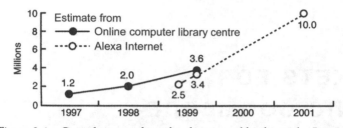

Figure 3.1 Growth in number of websites worldwide on the Internet.

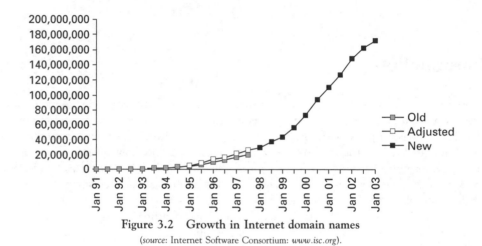

Figure 3.2 Growth in Internet domain names
(*source*: Internet Software Consortium: *www.isc.org*).

Consumer market segmentation

Although Figures 3.1–3.3 in the previous section are useful in confirming the global market potential of e-commerce, for marketing purposes it is necessary to break these down into more detail as the total figures mask some significant differences between different market segments. As will be seen in Chapter 4 there is an argument that segmenting markets is becoming less relevant with the Internet which allows more customized marketing to meet the needs of a particular customer or buying organization. However, at present, cases of truly customized marketing are still rare and the Internet has not fully spread to all market segments, so this exercise is still of use.

There are many bases on which the market could be meaningfully segmented, but the classical consumer marketing variables are by geographic, demographic, psychographic and behavioural variables (Kotler and Armstrong, 2004, chap. 8). Significant differences can be found in each of these segments for electronic consumer markets.

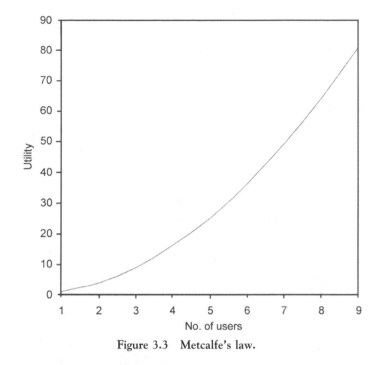

Figure 3.3 Metcalfe's law.

Demographic segmentation

Demographic variables are one of the most popular bases for consumer market segmentation owing to the ease of measurement. They include such variables as gender, age, income, education, etc. Demographic segmentation shows that significant differences in Internet adoption can be found between different segments in the Internet population; these can be largely explained by the innovation diffusion theory first proposed by Rogers (1962). Based on a study of over 500 new product innovations this predicts that new products typically diffuse through groups in a population in the following sequence (Figure 3.4):

- The first 2.5% of consumers to purchase a new product (innovators) tend to be risk takers, are eager to try new products and have higher educational levels and income. They are usually self-reliant and prefer to rely on information from experts and the press rather than from peers.
- The next 13.5% of consumers (early adopters) are also eager to try new products, but are more community-minded than innovators. They tend to communicate with others about new products and are often opinion leaders in a community.
- The next 34% (early majority) tend to collect information first, perhaps from opinion leaders, before trying new products. They purchase only after thoughtful consideration and watching other people.

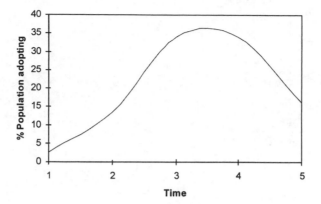

Figure 3.4   Innovation diffusion curve.

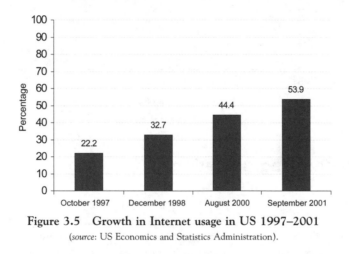

Figure 3.5   Growth in Internet usage in US 1997–2001
(*source*: US Economics and Statistics Administration).

- The next 34% (late majority) are more sceptical and only purchase out of a need to conform. These people usually rely on word of mouth rather than advertising.
- The final 16% (laggards) are very traditional and usually of lower socio-economic status. These people may adopt a product when newer ones have already been introduced.

It should be noted that Internet adoption has increased rapidly in the developed markets. Figure 3.5 shows the number of adults online in the USA since 1995. However, there are still significant differences between users and non-users (Table 3.1).

Income

Income too is related to occupation and education and so, as we would expect, Internet usage is highest among those in the higher income brackets (Table 3.2). What is perhaps less predictable is the usage by income.

Table 3.1   Internet users compared with non-users

	Users (%)	Non-users (%)	All Americans (%)
Men	50	46	48
Women	50	54	52
Whites	77	71	75
Blacks	8	14	11
Hispanics	9	10	10
18–29	29	14	23
30–49	47	32	42
50–64	18	22	20
65+	4	28	15
Less than $30,000 yearly household income	18	41	28
$30,000–$49,999	23	17	21
$50,000–$75,000	18	9	14
More than $75,000 yearly household income	26	6	18
Not high school graduate	5	25	14
High school graduate	23	41	35
Some college	34	21	25
College and graduate school degree	37	11	26
Rural community	21	31	26
Suburban	52	42	28
Urban	26	26	26

Note: This table reports the share of the Internet population that comes from each group. Base: 3,553, March–May 2002.
Source: Pew Internet & American Life Project.

Table 3.2   US Internet users by household income August, 2003 (home, work and university users)

	Internet users	Average usage (time per month, h)	Average pages (viewed per month)
$15,000–$24,999	11,422,000	23.3	2,292
$25,000–$39,999	18,144,000	26.4	2,526
$40,000–$59,999	37,719,000	26.4	2,670
$60,000–$74,999	23,206,000	26.4	2,577
$75,000–$99,999	24,654,000	27.5	2,636
$100,000 or more	25,793,000	27.6	2,964
Total Internet users	148,811,000	26.5	2,648

Source: comScore Media Metrix.

Table 3.3   Internet users by gender (at home users)

Country	Per cent male	Per cent female
Germany	63.40	36.60
France	61.88	38.12
Italy	60.91	39.09
Spain	60.88	39.12
Belgium	60.60	39.40
Netherlands	59.81	40.19
Brazil	59.71	40.29
Switzerland	58.69	41.31
Japan	58.39	41.43
Austria	58.13	41.87
Norway	57.95	42.05
UK	57.17	42.83
Israel	57.10	42.90
Hong Kong	56.61	43.39
Singapore	56.51	43.49
Denmark	55.86	44.14
Taiwan	55.80	44.20
Ireland	54.78	45.22
Sweden	54.76	45.24
South Korea	54.35	45.65
Mexico	54.00	46.00
Finland	53.94	46.06
New Zealand	52.52	47.48
Australia	51.57	48.43
Canada	49.00	51.00
United States	47.28	52.18

Source: Nielsen/NetRatings, 2001.

Gender

As expected given the traditional bias toward males in technology subjects and the historical origins of Internet usage, initially among scientists and computer hobbyists, it is not surprising perhaps that there has been a bias toward males in the Internet population. However, latest figures from the USA show the gap has narrowed and in fact there are slightly more women than men on the Internet. Outside the USA, however, there is still a strong bias toward males (Table 3.3).

Age

As would be expected of a technology that had its origins in academic research before spreading to computer hobbyists and business, the bulk of Internet users are adults aged

Table 3.4 Activities on the Web. What teens have done online: the percentage of youths with Internet access aged 12 through 17 who have done the following activities online.

	%
Send or read email	92
Surf the Web for fun	84
Visit an entertainment site	83
Send an instant message	74
Look for info on hobbies	69
Get news	68
Play or download a game	66
Research a product or service before buying it	66
Listen to music online	59
Visit a chat room	55
Download music files	53
Check sports scores	47
Visit a site for a club or team that they are a member of	39
Go to a website where they can express opinions about something	38
Buy something online	31
Visit sites for trading or selling things	31
Look for health-related information	26
Create a web page	24
Look for info on a topic that is hard to talk about	18

Source: Pew Internet & American Life Project Teens and Parents Survey, November–December 2000. Margin of error is ±4%.

30–49 (Table 3.1). However, the numbers in the older and younger age groups are growing rapidly. One of the most attractive markets has been that of teens, most of whom spend a lot of time on the Internet and spend a large proportion of their income on the Internet. The most popular uses are email, research, playing games, chat rooms and downloading music (Table 3.4).

Geographic segmentation

Geographic segmentation variables include nations, states, regions, counties, cities, etc. Although these may seem to be of less interest with such a global medium such as the Internet, it should be remembered that not many firms are global in reach and even these may need to adapt their offerings to local markets, which can differ considerably in other ways.

Table 3.5 Distribution of Internet users worldwide

#	Country or region	Population (est. 2003)	Internet users, latest date	Growth (2000–2003) (%)	Population (penetration) (%)	Users (%)
1	USA	291,639,900	184,447,987	93.4	63.2	27.0
2	China	1,311,863,500	68,000,000	202.2	5.2	10.0
3	Japan	127,708,000	59,203,896	25.8	46.4	8.7
4	Germany	81,904,100	44,139,071	83.9	53.9	6.5
5	UK	59,040,300	34,387,246	123.3	58.2	5.0
6	South Korea	46,852,300	26,270,000	38.0	56.1	3.8
7	France	59,303,800	22,039,401	159.3	37.2	3.2
8	Italy	56,209,900	19,250,000	45.8	34.2	2.8
9	Canada	31,720,400	16,841,811	32.6	53.1	2.5
10	India	1,067,421,100	16,580,000	231.6	1.6	2.4
11	Brazil	179,712,500	14,322,367	186.4	8.0	2.1
12	Spain	41,547,400	13,986,724	159.6	33.7	2.0
13	Australia	19,978,100	12,823,848	94.3	64.2	1.9
14	Taiwan	23,614,200	11,602,523	85.3	49.1	1.7
15	Netherlands	16,258,300	10,351,064	165.4	63.7	1.5
16	Malaysia	24,014,200	7,800,000	110.8	32.5	1.1
17	Sweden	8,872,600	6,726,808	66.2	75.8	1.0
18	Russia	141,364,200	6,000,000	93.5	4.2	0.9
19	Turkey	73,197,200	4,900,000	145.0	6.7	0.7
20	Thailand	63,393,600	4,800,000	108.7	7.6	0.7
21	Mexico	101,457,200	4,663,400	71.9	4.6	0.7
22	Hong Kong	6,827,000	4,571,936	100.3	67.0	0.7
23	Switzerland	7,376,000	4,319,289	102.4	58.6	0.6
24	Argentina	36,993,000	4,100,000	64.0	11.1	0.6
25	Indonesia	217,825,400	4,000,000	100.0	1.8	0.6
	Top 25 in users	4,096,094,200	606,127,392	91.4	14.8	88.8
	Next 208 countries	2,259,449,610	76,292,120	72.3	3.4	11.2
	Total world (users)	*6,355,543,810*	*682,419,512*	*89.1*	*10.7*	*100.0*

Source: InternetWorldStats.com, accessed January 12, 2004 (available at *http://www.InternetWorld Stats.com*).

Although the number of Internet users around the world is rapidly growing, the growth is highly skewed toward more developed nations (Table 3.5). The top 12 countries account for 76% of worldwide Internet users (including business, educational and home Internet users). The USA has an overwhelming lead in Internet use with more than 184 million users, which represents 27% of the total 682 million worldwide Internet users. Although they have low Internet penetration China, Brazil and India are also among the top 12 owing to their large populations.

Table 3.6 Internet penetration by country

#	Country or region	Population (est. 2003)	Internet users latest data	Population (penetration) (%)
1	Sweden	8,872,600	6,726,808	75.8
2	Hong Kong	6,827,000	4,571,936	67.0
3	Australia	19,978,100	12,823,869	64.2
4	Netherlands	16,258,300	10,351,064	63.7
5	USA	291,639,900	184,447,987	63.2
6	Denmark	5,387,300	3,375,850	62.7
7	Iceland	294,300	175,000	59.5
8	Switzerland	7,376,000	4,319,289	58.6
9	UK	59,040,300	34,387,246	58.2
10	South Korea	46,852,300	26,270,000	56.1
11	Singapore	4,225,000	2,308,296	54.6
12	New Zealand	3,785,600	2,063,831	54.5
13	Germany	81,904,100	44,139,071	53.9
14	Canada	31,720,400	16,841,811	53.1
15	Finland	5,215,100	2,650,000	50.8
16	Norway	4,551,100	2,300,000	50.5
17	Taiwan	23,614,200	11,602,523	49.1
18	Bermuda	64,500	30,000	46.5
19	Japan	127,708,000	59,203,896	46.4
20	Estonia	1,268,300	560,000	44.2
21	Austria	8,037,400	3,340,000	41.6
22	Slovenia	1,951,500	800,000	41.0
23	Belgium	10,339,300	3,769,123	36.5
24	Luxembourg	451,700	165,000	36.5
25	Portugal	10,366,900	3,700,000	35.7
	Top 25 in penetration	777,729,200	440,922,600	56.7
	Next 208 countries	5,577,814,610	241,496,912	4.3
	Total world (users)	6,355,543,810	682,419,512	10.7

Source: InternetWorldStats.com, accessed January 12, 2004 (available at *http://www.InternetWorld Stats.com*).

In terms of penetration per head of population it is Sweden, Hong Kong and Australia that lead (Table 3.6). All are countries in which the government and industry have made significant investments in the Internet. The populations are also relatively prosperous, so gaining Internet access is not a significant barrier. In the case of Sweden and Australia, another possible explanation is that the sparseness of populations in these countries makes the Internet particularly useful for communication and access to information outside the local community.

Table 3.7   Internet growth and penetration by region

World regions	Population (est. 2003)	Usage (year 2000)	Internet usage, latest data	Growth (2000–2003) (%)	Population (penetration) (%)	Table (%)
Africa	879,855,500	4,514,400	8,073,500	78.8	0.9	1.2
America	864,854,400	126,164,800	232,212,333	84.1	26.8	34.3
Asia	3,590,196,700	114,303,000	210,902,251	84.5	5.9	31.1
Europe	722,509,070	103,075,900	198,729,311	92.8	27.5	29.4
Middle East	259,318,000	5,272,300	12,019,600	128.0	4.6	1.8
Oceania	31,528,887	7,619,500	15,090,079	98.0	47.9	2.2
World total	*6,348,262,557*	*360,949,900*	*677,027,074*	*87.6*	*10.7*	*100.0*

Source: InternetWorldStats.com, accessed January 12, 2004 (available at *http://www.InternetWorld Stats.com*).

However, in terms of regional distribution it is Oceania that shows the highest rates of penetration at 47.9% while the Middle East has shown the highest rate of growth over the period 2000–2003 (Table 3.7).

Language

Since the Internet is global and allows geographic barriers to be overcome to some extent, perhaps more useful than geographic segmentation is segmentation by language. The latest estimates are that native-English speakers account for about 35.6% of Internet users worldwide (Figure 3.6), with Chinese speakers the second largest group

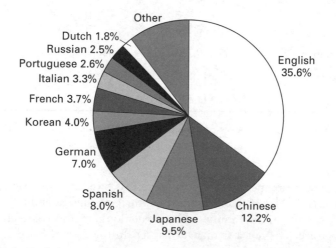

Figure 3.6   Distribution of users by language. Online language populations (total 680,000,000, as of September, 2003)

(*source*: Globalreach).

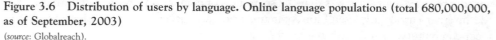

at 12.2%; this compares with only 5% for numbers of native English speakers worldwide and reflects the relative dominance of English-speaking countries in the adoption of Internet technology, although this is likely to change, particularly as more Chinese users come online.

Psychographic segmentation

Apart from demographic variables, lifestyle or psychographic variables are some of the most commonly used factors in consumer market segmentation. Kotler and Armstrong (2004) defines lifestyles as "a person's pattern of living as expressed in his or her activities, interests and opinions." Consumers' different lifestyles mean they have different values, which usually influences various marketing implications. For example, the increase in home shopping can be linked to increasing value being placed on convenience and time saving.

Many advertising and market research agencies have now developed their own systems for segmenting various markets, but one of the most popular methods is the VALS typology developed by SRI International (*www.future.sri.com*).

VALS

VALS is based largely on the research of psychologist Arnold Mitchell (1983), who in turn based his research on the theories of Abraham Maslow. Using the results from a survey on 2,000 consumers in the USA, Mitchell divided the US population into nine categories based on Maslow's hierarchy of "needs growth". Maslow believed that most human behaviour is based on certain internal drives or needs, and that personal development consists of stages of maturity marked by fulfilment of these needs. Until the needs of one stage are satisfied, an individual cannot progress to the next level of maturity.

In 1978 the consultancy SRI International formed the VALS (values and lifestyles) typology from Mitchell's study. The VALS typology was revised in 1989 to focus more explicitly on explaining and understanding consumer behaviour. VALS2 (Figure 3.7) classifies all US adults into eight consumer groups based on their answers to attitudinal and demographic measures. The main dimensions of VALS2 are self-orientation (horizontal) and resources (vertical). "Resources" include income, education, self-confidence, intelligence, eagerness to buy and energy level. "Self-orientation" refers to three ways to reach the group characterized by low self-realization and few means: principle, status and action. "Principle" describes a functional and practical disposition, attaching importance to confidence and security. "Status" describes individuals who attach importance to hard work, achievement and career. "Action" describes individuals who enjoy doing things themselves and getting experience.

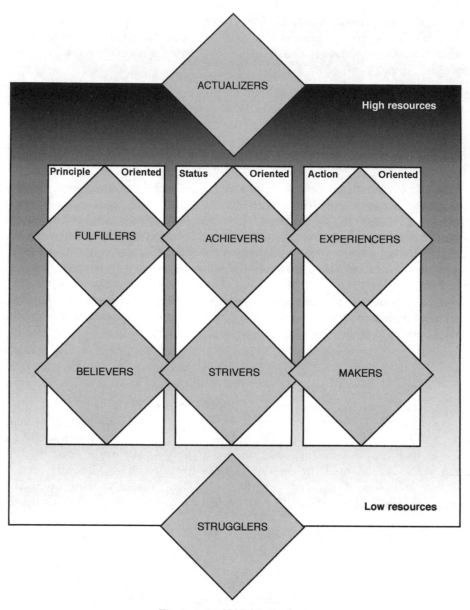

Figure 3.7   VALS2 typology.

According to a study by Hoffman et al. (1995), actualizers represented 50% of the web population in 1995. The other 50% is predominantly made up of what SRI refers to as "strivers" and "experiencers" in the VALS2 typology. These findings are consistent with Roger's theory of innovation diffusion.

Behavioural segmentation

Behavioural segmentation divides buyers into groups based on their knowledge, attitudes, uses or responses to a product and is often the best predictor of buying behaviour. Bellman et al. (1999) in their test of consumer buying behaviour in a virtual market found that demographics had some influence on whether a person is online in the first place compared with the general population, but only a small influence on whether or not they buy (1.2%). Once a person is online, psychographic characteristics, such as whether they like being online and how much time they have for shopping, are a better predictor of whether they buy online and how much they spend; these explain 55% of buying versus not buying and 28% of annual online spending. However, that still leaves unexplained some 44% of buying versus non-buying and 72% of online spending. Bellman et al. concluded that better predictions would be obtained by examining past buying behaviour.

However, behavioural variables are also often the most difficult to measure. What little research there is suggests that online buying behaviour is not only different from offline buying behaviour but also that they are not straight substitutes for each other. For example, according to a study from the Poynter Institute and Stanford University (*http://www.poynter.org/eyetrack2000*), online news-reading patterns differ greatly from newspaper and magazine-reading patterns. Some of the findings included the following. People reading news on Internet sites tend to focus on the article text first, looking at photos and graphics afterwards. Those who read newspapers and magazines do the opposite. They look at illustrations first then read the text.

Internet users who read news online read 75% of each article, whereas newspaper and magazine readers read less than 30% of each article. Online news readers visit six news sites per reading session and focus on gathering information. They dislike personalized news sites as they were afraid they might miss some news they felt they ought to know about.

Surfers visiting news sites viewed a surprisingly high 45% of banner advertisements for 1 s, which is long enough to perceive an online advertisement fully, and 64% of photos and 22% of other images were viewed for this length of time.

Local newspaper sites were a popular starting point for online news readers: 45% of those studied visited these sites first; 28% went to a national news site first; 8% started reading at a speciality site; and 9% began their news browsing at a portal.

The different uses made of online and offline information suggests that different factors may be involved in the decisions to purchase online and offline. Other research suggests that several factors are taken into account by consumers in deciding which products to buy from which channels, including such factors as branding of the good. For example, Balabanis and Vassileou (1999) found that:

1. Past Internet shopping experience did not have any effect on shoppers' intentions to buy from a website.

2. However, experience of home shopping through non-Internet modes and attitudes toward a website have a direct positive effect on consumers' intentions to buy through that website.

3. Income directly affects shoppers' intentions to buy through a website, but only for strong brands.

4. Involvement with a product category has a negative effect on buying through a retailer's website, but only for retailers with weak brands.

5. Similarly, previous experience with a retailer's branded products has a positive effect on the intentions to buy through a retailer's website, but only for retailers with weak brands.

Similarly, Phau and Poon (2000) in their study of Singaporean Internet buyers found that, generally, products and services that have low outlay are frequently purchased, have intangible value, are relatively high on differentiation and are more likely to be purchased via the Internet.

Several behavioural segmentation methods have been developed by various consultancies and researchers.

Ebates dot-shoppers

- *Clicks and mortar* Females who browse online but buy offline (23%).
- *Ebivalent newbies* Internet newcomers who rarely spend online (5%).
- *Hooked online and single* Internet veterans – young, affluent and male – who bank, play and shop online (16%).
- *Hunter-gatherers* Married baby boomers with children, who use the Internet like a consumer magazine to compare prices and products (20%).
- *Time-sensitive materialists* Cyber-shoppers who regard the Internet as a convenience tool for buying music, books and computer software (17%).
- *Brand loyalists* Web fans who regularly visit favourite merchants and spend the most money online (19%).

Pew Internet users

- *Newcomers* Online less than a year and log on for games and messaging (13 million).
- *Experimenters* Online for 1 to 2 years and have begun to venture into more serious activities, such as comparing products, trading stocks and getting news (27 million).
- *Utilitarians* Online for 3 or more years and use the Net as a tool for work-related research (30 million).
- *Netizens* The earliest Internet adopters who go online for work and play, to bank, trade stocks, pursue their hobbies and connect to their friends.

Prizm segments

- *Country squires*   The wealthiest small-town lifestyle Internet users, 85% of whom have online access and regularly patronize travel and financial sites (1% of US households).
- *Boomers and babies*   Young, white-collar suburban families who frequently go online for entertainment and automotive information.
- *Upward bound*   Mostly young, upscale families in mid-size cities, tend to devour online news and sport information.
- *New ecotopia*   Rural mix of blue- and white-collar families have an online access of 79% and typically visit shopping and sweepstakes sites.

Technographics segments

- *Fast forwards*   Affluent and career-focused early adopters of online technologies (10% of North Americans).
- *New age nurturers*   Upscale, family-oriented consumers who are particularly fond of educational software and websites (7%).
- *Mouse potatoes*   An entertainment-focused cluster whose wealthy consumers rank high in online usage and interactive games (8%).
- *Techno-strivers*   Students and entry-level employees who use the Internet for work research and career advancement (8%).
- *Digital hopefuls*   A low-income, family-oriented group with a passion for technology and the Net (8%).
- *Gadget grabbers*   Low-income consumers who regularly frequent entertainment-oriented websites (9%).
- *Handshakers*   Successful professionals with an aversion for all things technological (7%).
- *Traditionalists*   A high-income, family-oriented group with little technology beyond VCRs (8%).
- *Media junkies*   Upscale, entertainment-oriented consumers who love TVs, not computers (5%).
- *Sidelined citizens*   Super-cluster filled with downscale technophobes who have only recently started to log onto the Internet (30%).

TDS Shopper Clusters Onliners Group

- *Cyber chic*   Young, high-income couples who are twice as likely as the average American to buy online (1.5% of all Americans).
- *Clicks and bricks*   Older, affluent baby boomers who frequent both online and brick and mortar retailers at high rates (1.1%).
- *E-generation*   Upscale singles and couples who devote the greatest portion of their total expenditures to online purchases (3.5%).

B2B

Although much of the early interest in e-commerce has focused on B2C (business-to-consumer) markets, in fact B2B (business-to-business) represents a much larger market. B2C accounted for 7% of e-commerce in the US in 2002 compared with 93% for B2B (US Department of Commerce, 2004).

As discussed in Chapter 2, EDI (electronic data interchange) systems have been in use by firms for decades, and early predictions for the growth of electronic commerce were that growth would take place initially in the business market. One of the best known was the prediction outlined by Malone et al. (1987) that EDI systems would evolve into electronic markets for two reasons: first, widespread use of information technology would decrease the costs of co-ordination involved in tasks such as selecting suppliers, scheduling activities and budgeting resources; and, second, the relative complexity of products and the specificity of assets required to produce them, factors which normally favour the use of hierarchies. As information technology develops, products and services that were previously considered complex would become lower in complexity relative to the technology available to process them. At the same time, flexible manufacturing technology would allow rapid changeover of production lines and decrease the specificity of firms' assets. These changes also favour market transactions over hierarchies.

Malone et al. hypothesized that a typical development path for electronic networks would begin with a biased market in which suppliers, often the providers of the co-ordinating technology, would attempt to push customers toward their product or service. The next stage would be an unbiased market where systems provide equal access to all vendors. However, as customers now have more supplier and product information than they can handle, this would lead to the third stage of a personalized market, supported by decision support systems that allow customers to select products and services that closely match their individual requirements from the many available.

In fact, electronic markets have not developed entirely as Malone et al. predicted, and early attempts to establish electronic markets failed. See, for example, Been et al. (1995) on an attempt in the air cargo industry. However, with the widespread use of the Internet for business, recent market research suggests that the markets of the form Malone et al. predicted may develop in some areas. Currently, most B2B transactions are still carried out using EDI, but the Internet B2B market is widely expected to overtake conventional EDI in terms of size, growth and profitability. The IT consultancy Gartner expects the total worldwide value of goods and services purchased by businesses online to increase from a figure of $433 billion in 2000 to $8.5 trillion by 2005 (Figure 3.8). According to another consultancy, IDC, the USA will remain the largest market for B2B commerce, with a compound annual growth rate (CAGR) of 68% during this period. Western Europe will experience a CAGR of up to 91% from 2001 to 2005, while Asia Pacific will see the most growth with a compound annual rate of 109%.

Even though EDI is a mature technology that has been in use for over 20 years, the market will continue to grow in Europe at more than 15% over the next 5 years, amounting to €809.9 billion in 2006. The total value of goods purchased by EDI

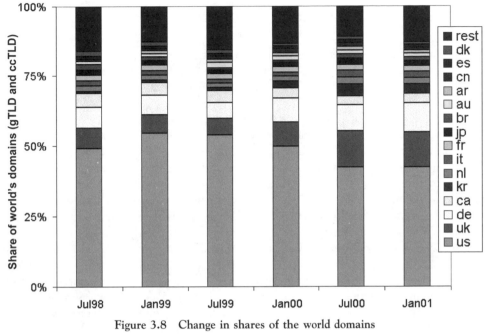

Figure 3.8 Change in shares of the world domains

(© 2001 Matthew Zook; gTLD = generic top-level domain; ccTLD = country code top-level domain).

commerce in Europe in 2002 will amount to €712 billion, according to a recent study by IDC. Traditional EDI will remain a steady driver of EDI commerce value, growing from €599.9 billion in 2001 to €809.9 billion in 2006. However, the requirement to leverage existing investments will result in Internet EDI becoming the preferred business interaction method for small- and medium-size enterprises (SMEs) because of relatively low cost and high reliability.

Meanwhile, Forrester Research predicts that the EU's online trade will surge from the 2001 figure of €77 billion to €2,2 trillion in 2006 – increasing from less than 1% of total business trade to 22%. Europe's three major markets – the UK, Germany and France – will transact at least 23% of sales online, and their combined trade volumes will represent a whopping 64% of the EU total online trade. IT investments will be a key influence among each country's online trade figures. Forrester finds that Scandinavia will charge ahead, powered by high IT spending, and Europe's "big three" of France, Germany and the UK will bring volume online, while Southern Europe will fail to take off.

A recent development has been the development of private trading networks (PTNs). According to a survey by Jupiter, 61% of B2B executives cited closer supplier relationships as a key function of PTNs. A key benefit of such networks is the ability to add collaborative applications, including inventory-level monitoring and product design. Other information-sharing uses included collaborative planning, forecasting and replenishment, and product design. Commodities buying and procurement management were the only transactional applications identified in the survey.

International dominance of the Internet

As the Internet has become more widely adopted, this has been reflected in the relative shares of some countries. Although US sites still constitute the largest percentage of the world's domain names, their share has steadily declined as other nations have more widely adopted the Internet (Figure 3.8).

The World Economic Forum uses the networked readiness index (NRI) to measure "the degree of preparation of a nation or community to participate in and benefit from information communication technology (ICT) developments." The NRI is composed of three component indexes which assess: the environment for ICT offered by a given country or community; the readiness of the community's key stakeholders (individuals, businesses and governments); and the usage of ICT among these stakeholders. The ranks for 2003 are shown in Table 3.8. The USA still leads, but is closely followed by Singapore, Finland, Sweden and Denmark.

The Economist Intelligence Unit (EIU) similarly uses nearly 100 quantitative and qualitative criteria, organized into six distinct categories: connectivity and technology infrastructure (25%); business environment (20%); consumer and business adoption (20%); social and cultural environment (15%); legal and policy environment (15%); and supporting e-services (5%). The EIU ranking of countries is broadly similar, although they rank Sweden, Denmark and the Netherlands ahead of the USA.

Compared with B2C e-commerce, B2B e-commerce is larger, growing faster and has less unequal geographical distribution globally. However, there are considerable differences in the leading sectors in each region (Figure 3.9), reflecting national competitive advantages as well as infrastructure constraints.

Kshetri and Dholakia (2002) found that factors that determine the share of global B2B e-commerce in a country include income and population size, the availability of credit, venture capital, and telecom and logistical infrastructure, tax and other incentives, tariff/non-tariff barriers, government emphasis on the development of human capital, regulations to influence firms' investment in R&D, organization level politics, language and the activities of international agencies.

Summary

There are many distinct market segments for e-business, each with their own characteristics. Despite the promise of global marketplace offered by the Internet, there are significant regional and national differences between markets, and the market is currently heavily skewed toward the developed countries of the West, in particular English-speaking countries. However, this is changing rapidly as adoption in other countries increases. Markets in Asia, South America and Africa have shown the greatest growth over the last 3 years and are predicted to continue to do so.

The top 12 countries account for 76% of worldwide Internet users. The USA accounts for 27% of the total 682 million worldwide Internet users. Although they have low

Table 3.8   Country NRI rankings

NRI rank	Country	Score	NRI rank	Country	Score
1	USA	5.50	52	Trinidad and Tobago	3.37
2	Singapore	5.40	53	Jamaica	3.36
3	Finland	5.23	54	Uruguay	3.35
4	Sweden	5.20	55	Botswana	3.34
5	Denmark	5.19	56	Turkey	3.32
6	Canada	5.07	57	Dominican Republic	3.32
7	Switzerland	5.06	58	Panama	3.31
8	Norway	5.03	59	Namibia	3.28
9	Australia	4.88	60	Colombia	3.28
10	Iceland	4.88	61	Romania	3.26
11	Germany	4.85	62	El Salvador	3.22
12	Japan	4.80	63	Russian Federation	3.19
13	Netherlands	4.79	64	Morocco	3.19
14	Luxembourg	4.76	65	Egypt	3.19
15	UK	4.68	66	Sri Lanka	3.15
16	Israel	4.64	67	Bulgaria	3.15
17	Taiwan	4.62	68	Vietnam	3.13
18	Hong Kong (SAR)	4.61	69	Philippines	3.10
19	France	4.60	70	Peru	3.09
20	Korea	4.60	71	Tanzania	3.09
21	Austria	4.56	72	Venezuela	3.09
22	Ireland	4.55	73	Indonesia	3.06
23	New Zealand	4.48	74	Ghana	3.06
24	Belgium	4.43	75	Macedonia (FYR)	3.05
25	Estonia	4.25	76	Pakistan	3.03
26	Malaysia	4.19	77	Serbia	2.98
27	Malta	4.15	78	Ukraine	2.96
28	Italy	4.07	79	Nigeria	2.92
29	Spain	4.01	80	Uganda	2.90
30	Slovenia	3.99	81	Senegal	2.90
31	Portugal	3.94	82	Gambia	2.85
32	Chile	3.94	83	Cameroon	2.82
33	Czech Republic	3.80	84	Kenya	2.81
34	Greece	3.76	85	Zambia	2.80
35	Latvia	3.74	86	Guatemala	2.76
36	Hungary	3.74	87	Algeria	2.75
37	South Africa	3.72	88	Malawi	2.71
38	Thailand	3.72	89	Ecuador	2.68
39	Brazil	3.67	90	Bolivia	2.66
40	Tunisia	3.67	91	Paraguay	2.62
41	Slovak Republic	3.66	92	Madagascar	2.60
42	Lithuania	3.63	93	Bangladesh	2.57
43	Mauritius	3.62	94	Nicaragua	2.56

continued

Table 3.8 (*cont.*)

NRI rank	Country	Score	NRI rank	Country	Score
44	Mexico	3.57	95	Zimbabwe	2.53
45	India	3.54	96	Mali	2.52
46	Jordan	3.53	97	Mozambique	2.51
47	Poland	3.51	98	Honduras	2.41
48	Croatia	3.48	99	Angola	2.32
49	Costa Rica	3.46	100	Haiti	2.27
50	Argentina	3.45	101	Ethiopia	2.13
51	China	3.38	102	Chad	2.09

Source: World Economic Forum Global Information Technology Report 2003–4 (Dutta et al., 2004). SAR = self-administrative region. FYR = former Yugoslav republic.

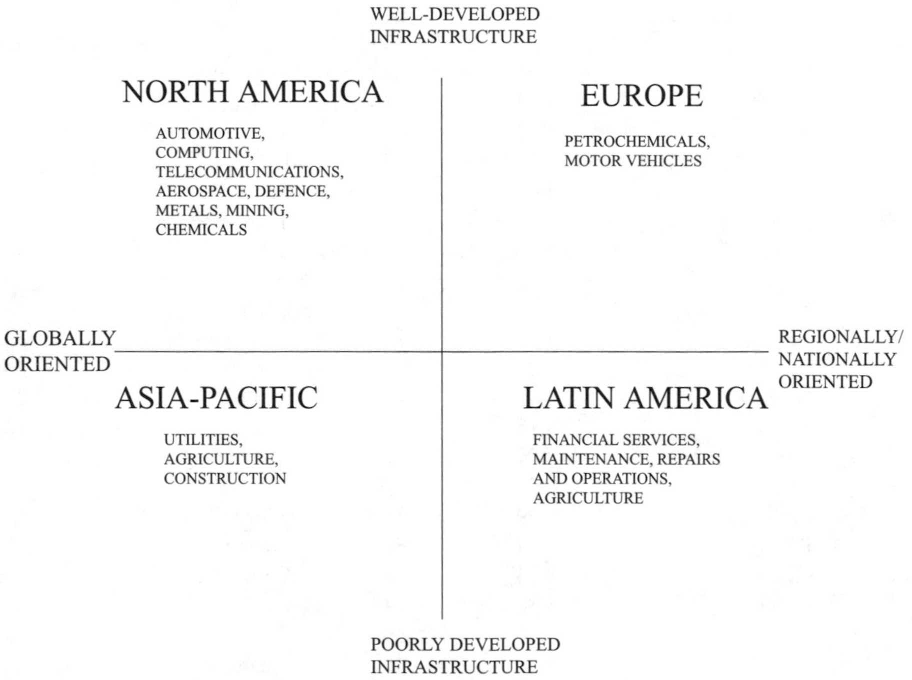

WELL-DEVELOPED
INFRASTRUCTURE

NORTH AMERICA

AUTOMOTIVE,
COMPUTING,
TELECOMMUNICATIONS,
AEROSPACE, DEFENCE,
METALS, MINING,
CHEMICALS

EUROPE

PETROCHEMICALS,
MOTOR VEHICLES

GLOBALLY
ORIENTED

REGIONALLY/
NATIONALLY
ORIENTED

ASIA-PACIFIC

UTILITIES,
AGRICULTURE,
CONSTRUCTION

LATIN AMERICA

FINANCIAL SERVICES,
MAINTENANCE, REPAIRS
AND OPERATIONS,
AGRICULTURE

POORLY DEVELOPED
INFRASTRUCTURE

Figure 3.9 Global B2B distribution: leading sectors by region.

Internet penetration China, Brazil and India are also among the top 12 owing to their large populations.

Within each population the profile of online buyers is still quite distinct from that of the general population, demographically, psychographically and behaviourally. However, this is changing rapidly as use of the Internet spreads to other segments of the population.

Within the subpopulation of Internet users, several distinct segments of Internet users can also be identified.

References

Balabanis, G. and Vassileou, S. (1999). Some attitudinal predictors of home shopping through the Internet. *Journal of Marketing Management*, **15**, 361–85.

Been, J., Christiaanse, E., O'Callaghan, R. and van Diepen, T. (1995). Electronic markets in the air cargo community. Paper given at *Third European Conference on Information Systems*, Athens.

Bellman, S., Lohse G.L. and Johnson, E.J. (1999). Predictors of online buying. *Communications of the ACM*, **42**(12), 32–8.

Dutta, S., Lanvin, B. and Paua, F. (2004). *World Economic Forum Global IT Report*. Oxford University Press, New York.

Hoffman, D.L., Novak, T.P. and Chatterjee, P. (1995). Commercial scenarios for the Web: Opportunities and challenges. *Journal of Computer-mediated Communication on the Web Quarterly*, December.

Kotler, P and Armstrong, G. (2004). *Principles of Marketing: Activebook 2.0*. Prentice Hall, Upper Saddle River, NJ.

Kshetri, N. and Dholakia, N. (2002). Determinants of the global diffusion of B2B e-commerce. *Electronic Markets*, **12**(2), 120–129.

Malone, T., Yates, J. and Benjamin, R. (1987). Electronic markets and electronic hierarchies. *Communications of the ACM*, **30**(6), 484–97.

Mitchell, A. (1983). *Nine American Lifestyles: Who We Are and Where We Are Going*. Macmillan, New York.

Phau, I. and Poon, S.M. (2000). Factors influencing the types of products and services purchased over the Internet. *Internet Research*, **10**(2), 102–13.

Rogers, E. (1962). *Diffusion of Innovations*. Free Press, New York.

Maslow, A. (1943) A theory of human motivation. *Psychological Review*, **50**, 370–96.

U.S. Department of Commerce (2004). 2002 E-commerce multi-sector report. Available at *www.census.gov/estats*.

Useful market research websites

comScore Media Matrix *www.comscore.com*
Cyberatlas *www.cyberatlas.com*
E-marketer *www.e-land.com*
Forrester Research *www.forrester.com*
Gartner *www.gartner.com*
Harris Interactive *www.harrisinteractive.com*
IDC *www.idc.com*
InternetWorldstats.com *www.internetworldstats.com*
Jupiter *www.jupiterresearch.com*

Nielsen//NetRatings (2001) *www.nielsen-netratings.com*
NUA *www.nua.net*
Pew Internet and American Life Project *www.pewinternet.org*
Poynter Institute and Stanford University *www.poynter.org/eyetrack2000*
PricewaterhouseCoopers (2000) *www.pwcglobal.com*
SRI International *www.future.sri.com*
World Economic Forum *www.weforum.com*

Key concepts

- Behavioural segmentation.
- Demographic segmentation.
- e-Marketplaces.
- Geographic segmentation.
- Innovation diffusion curve.
- Metcalfe's law.
- Psychographic segmentation.

Self-assessment questions

1 How can the exponential growth in Internet hosts and websites be explained?
2 What is the innovation diffusion curve?
3 What are the key demographic variables that need to be considered in segmenting Internet markets?
4 What is psychographic segmentation, and why is it useful for understanding Internet users?
5 What are the factors that determine the suitability of products for electronic shopping?
6 What is an electronic marketplace?
7 Explain the reasons that Malone and his colleagues predicted the increase in electronic markets.

Discussion questions

1 What are the likely problems in applying the innovation diffusion curve to emerging Internet markets?
2 Is market segmentation a valid exercise given the increased ability to personalize one-to-one transactions on the Internet?
3 What are the possible weaknesses in Malone's electronic markets hypothesis?

E-MARKETING

4

Introduction

In Chapter 2 some of the technologies used in electronic commerce were outlined and examples of some applications were given. This chapter discusses the distinctive features that applying these technologies brings to e-marketing.

Kalyanam and McIntyre (2002) identified more than 30 e-marketing tools and terms currently in use from their review of the marketing literature. The applications can be grouped into five categories according to the type of customer benefits that e-business technologies make possible (Table 4.1). First, as with previous information technologies, by integrating and accelerating business processes, e-business technologies make it possible to speed up response and delivery times. Second, electronic networks create new business opportunities for exploiting information-based products and services, opportunities some people have referred to as the virtual marketspace. Third, websites can be integrated with customer databases, making it possible to more fully exploit customer information and more fully identify customer needs. Fourth, the interactive nature of computer-based systems allows marketers to interact with customers in a two-way dialogue online and not only speed up response but also more fully address requests. Finally, the Internet is distinctive in that it allows customers not only to communicate directly with suppliers but also among themselves. Some of the companies that have been most successful in Internet marketing have been ones that have been able to exploit these communities. To simplify the discussion each of these applications is discussed separately, although in practice a business will probably apply the various technologies in more than one way.

Accelerated marketing

A key benefit that e-business offers is the ability to accelerate all the processes involved – buying, selling, manufacturing and distribution. These trends have been occurring in businesses for several years, and many firms have undertaken business process

Table 4.1   E-marketing tools

Accelerated marketing	Virtual market	Personalization	Interactive marketing	Community marketing
Build to order	Information	Customization	Wireless	Email lists
Distribution to order	Communication	Individualization	DTV	Net pager
Billing	Distribution	Rules-based system		Groupware
NPD	Transaction	Collaborative filtering		Games and simulations
				Viral marketing

re-engineering projects designed to streamline business processes. However, the emergence of IP networks enabling easy and cost-effective linking of processes within companies, between companies, and between companies and customers has enabled major transformations of business processes that were not possible with earlier networks; these include transformation and linking of processes in manufacturing, distribution, billing and new product development.

Build to order

Improving manufacturing efficiency through better co-ordination of activities has been practised for many years by manufacturing companies, one of the best known techniques of which is JIT (just-in-time), or lean production. JIT aims to eliminate sources of manufacturing waste by producing the right part in the right place at the right time. Waste results from any activity that adds cost without adding value, such as transportation and storage of inventory. JIT aims to reduce inventory levels (increasing the inventory turnover rate), reduce production and delivery lead times, and reduce other associated costs such as machine set-up and equipment breakdown. Instead of buffer inventories, a JIT system uses underutilized (excess) capacity to hedge against problems that may arise. The general idea is to establish flow processes (even when the facility uses a jobbing or batch process layout) by linking work centres so that there is an even, balanced flow of materials throughout the entire production process, similar to that found in an assembly line.

Although JIT has been practised for several years in business-to-business (B2B) relationships, with a few notable exceptions it has been less widely used for consumer items. However, it requires expensive communication networks and systems to integrate customers and suppliers. The widespread use of the Internet allows similar principles to be easily applied to consumer markets.

Mini-case study: Dell Computers

One of the pioneers of build to order using the Internet is Dell Computers (Figure 4.1). Using the Internet to sell PCs directly to customers, Dell increased its sales from 360

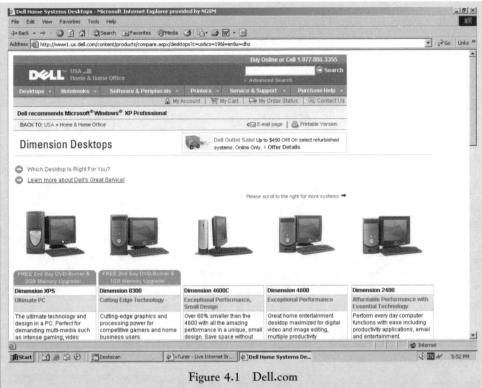

Figure 4.1   Dell.com

(reproduced with permission from Dell).

million in 1990 to 12 billion by 1998. The secret of Dell's success is a build-to-order system that makes it possible for the company to receive an order over the Internet, assemble the PC to the required specification and ship the assembled PC to the customer in just 4 hours. Not only does the system provide benefits to the customer of a quick and personalized service but, since PCs are built or rather assembled to order, it also enables Dell to significantly reduce its inventories; this not only saves warehousing costs but is a significant advantage in an industry where technical obsolescence can reduce the value of stock by 1% a week.

Distribution to order

Build to order is only one stage toward real-time marketing. Oliver et al. (1998) argue that as well as direct sales and build to order, direct distribution is essential if the manufacturer wants to move to "real-time marketing". They define this as a system where "personally customized goods or services continuously update themselves to continuously track changing customer needs without intervention by corporate personnel often without conscious or overt input from customer." Very few companies have yet implemented distribution to order, at least with physical products, the main problem being the difficulties of establishing a flexible and cost-effective distribution network that is capable of adapting to customer demands. It could be argued that Fedex with its online tracking system for packages is moving in this direction although the service does not currently allow online adjustments to delivery times.

Mini-case study: Cemex

One company that has developed an innovative distribution system that allows JIT delivery is the Mexican company Cemex, the third largest cement producer in the world (Figure 4.2). Concrete is mixed en route to the construction site and must be delivered within a certain time or it will be unusable. Rather than waiting for orders, preparing delivery schedules and sending out deliveries as most companies do, Cemex has trucks fitted with automatic satellite positioning systems patrolling the road at all times, waiting for orders; this allows the company to guarantee delivery within 20 min of the agreed time. Real-time data on each truck's position are available not only to company managers but also to clients and suppliers, enabling them to plan their schedules to fit in with the next available truck.

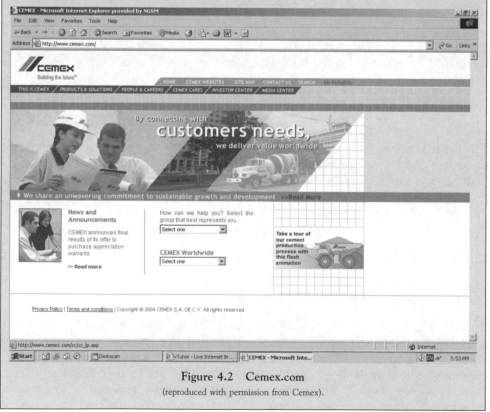

Figure 4.2   Cemex.com

(reproduced with permission from Cemex).

> ### Mini-case: Shiseido
>
> The Japanese cosmetics maker Shiseido (Figure 4.3) often misjudged demand for its cosmetics, leaving warehouses full of unsold stock. To reduce the wasted inventory, the company has invested in a $55 million network linking factories and sales outlets; this allows Shiseido beauty consultants at sales counters to download sales information and upload data on hot-selling products via their mobile phones. The result has been that inventory was cut by 30% in 2002.
>
>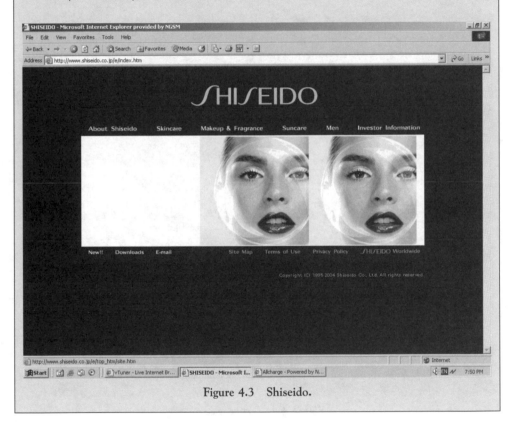
>
> Figure 4.3   Shiseido.

Real-time billing

Probably the simplest process to accelerate is billing; this has already been done for some time with smart cards that automatically debit the card after the service has been used (e.g., for telephone calls). However, some telephone companies are now providing other services in real time, such as reviewing statements and payment online.

> ### *Mini-case study: Teligent*
>
> Teligent (Figure 4.4) is a local exchange carrier in the USA which uses microwave networks to connect to customers. Its e-magine service enables customers to examine their account details in real time, to download data used to calculate the bill and to pay their bills online. As well as simplifying and speeding up payment, this provides additional benefits to customers, such as monitoring call usage, showing patterns of calls and direct data input into the accounting system.
>
>
>
> **Figure 4.4   Teligent.com**
> (reproduced with permission from Teligent).

New product development

Some companies have taken the concept of real-time marketing even further by using an "information acceleration system" at the new product development stage. An information acceleration system uses digital technologies to create virtual worlds that capture several of the most important aspects of the new product purchase decision; this allows the behaviour of consumers to be studied in a test environment that simulates what consumers will face at the time they make the purchase decision. For example, a study on future consumer purchases of electric cars involved simulation of virtual showroom visits, advertising, review articles and word of mouth. Architects are already commonly using computer simulations to show how new buildings will look from different perspectives.

The benefits of using information acceleration systems are that if marketers can create realistic systems that measure consumer demand of artificial products and services they can replace expensive prototypes and dramatically reduce design time. A much larger number of possible products can be tried and valuable new features can be identified and designed into the next generation of products. The use and benefits of information acceleration systems are likely to increase as virtual reality technology improves.

Virtual marketspace

The new virtual business opportunities created by e-commerce can be categorized into four "virtual marketspaces" using the information communication distribution transaction (ICDT) model (Angehrn, 1997): a virtual information space, a virtual communications space, a virtual distribution space and a virtual transaction space (Figure 4.5).

Virtual information space

The virtual information space consists of new Internet-based channels through which economic agents can display information about themselves and the products and services they offer; these include sites providing information, such as brochureware sites where companies publish catalogues of their products and services, information services providing financial information and bulletin boards advertising employment opportunities. In addition to creating new opportunities in virtual information, the Internet

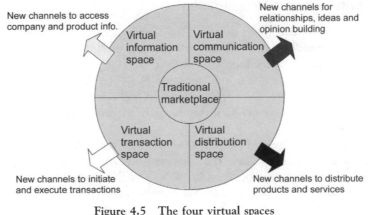

Figure 4.5   The four virtual spaces
(reprinted from Anghern, 1997).

may also create new opportunities to offer related services, such as Internet marketing and advertising, consulting services and information search, gathering and filtering agents, etc.

Virtual communications space

The virtual communications space includes new opportunities in which economic agents can exchange ideas and experiences, influence opinions or negotiate. Examples are bulletin boards (already mentioned above), chat rooms and videoconferencing. These opportunities deserve a special mention as a number of new marketing practices have developed using the Internet; these are discussed more fully later in the sections on real-time, interactive and community marketing.

Virtual distribution space

The virtual distribution space consists of new distribution channels for a variety of products and services. The first category of products includes those products that can be efficiently distributed by means of the Internet. These are products that can be digitized and transmitted through computer networks, such as text, pictures, digital music and video, software and computer games. The second category includes such services as text, voice or video-based consulting and training.

Virtual transaction space

The virtual transaction space consists of new Internet-based channels through which economic agents can exchange formal business transactions, such as orders, invoices and payments; this can range from simple email and online order forms to online ordering using a credit or debit card and online accounts (e.g., for share dealing).

Virtual marketspace competencies

An e-business may utilize more than one of these virtual marketspaces, and "pure" Internet companies will typically utilize all four, using the Internet to provide company and product information, communicate with customers, make the transaction and distribute the product or service to the customer. However, Angehrn suggests that each marketspace requires specific competencies and that it may be useful to plot the extent of company's activities in each marketspace in order to determine the required mix of competencies (Figure 4.6).

For example, establishing presence in the virtual information space or virtual communication space will directly affect the company's front office operations; this requires competencies in the design of appropriate webpages, the harmonization of the virtual information space (VIS) presence with the current marketing and PR strategy of the company, and knowledge of the regulations on direct marketing on the Internet. Establishing virtual communication space (VCS) presence requires, in addition, training of

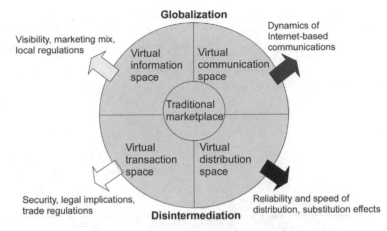

Figure 4.6   Generic issues/competencies.

company employees in how to use the Internet effectively as a communication medium and how to establish electronic relationships with customers. On the other hand, strategies aimed at establishing a presence in the virtual distribution space or virtual transaction space will more directly affect the company's back office operations and require competencies in distribution, managing unwanted substitution effects as well as technical, legal and trade regulations.

In turn, the new competencies acquired can lead the company into the development of a new generation of Internet-based services. For instance, a company that has developed a new way of distributing digital products might offer the same possibilities to other companies, becoming their distribution partner. An example is Interactive Investor International, a financial information site in the UK, which has used its experience in setting up its own site to provide consultancy services to other companies wishing to establish an Internet site.

Virtual marketing activities

It is possible to run a completely virtual business where all the normal marketing activities are done online. Some of the marketing activities that can now be done virtually include advertising, retailing, distribution and payment.

Online advertising

The most popular form of web advertising is the banner ad or display advertising. This is the advertisement often found on webpages at the top of the browser window. Banner ads remain the most popular form of web advertising, accounting for 22% of all online ads in 2003, although this is down considerably from 32% in 2002 (Interactive Advertising Bureau) (Table 4.2).

Table 4.2   Percentages of different types of Internet adverts

	Second quarter, 2003 (%)	Second quarter, 2002 (%)
Display advertising (formerly "banners")	22	32
Sponsorships	11	24
Classifieds	18	15
Keyword search	31	9
Slotting fees	4	8
Interstitial	3	3
Email	4	4
Rich media	6	3
Referral	1	2

Source: Interactive Advertising Bureau.

However, there are signs that use of banner ads is waning as the "click-through" rates (rates of customers clicking on the advertisement to access the sponsor) fall. When the first banner advertisement was used on HotWire in 1994 the click-through rate was nearly 10%. However, over time, as banner ads have become commonplace, web surfers have become more discriminating and the click-through rate on banner ads slid to less than 1% in 2003.

The biggest problem with banner ads arises for brand advertisers. A company with a well-known brand, such as Coca-Cola, gains little from advertising on the Web which will help build the brand. A Coke banner does not allow the user to buy Coca-Cola online, at least at present. All it can do is link the user to a website that provides information on the company and the product.

There is another difference between direct-response advertisements and branding campaigns. Offline branding campaigns usually require media saturation to have a significant impact (e.g., regular showings on television over a sustained period). Although this is possible to achieve with a passive medium, such as television, where the user can switch off or engage in other activities, such as talk or making a coffee, it is more difficult to achieve online without irritating users.

Advertisers have tried to counter the trend by making banner advertisements more active, some of which are shown in Table 4.3.

An increasingly popular technique is the use of "interstitial" advertisements, a separate window of advertising that pops up spontaneously, blocking the site behind it, or "superstitial" advertisements, a window that appears during dead time (e.g., while the home page is loading). The aim is to grab the consumer's attention for the second or so it takes to close the window.

Another popular technique is rich media expanding banners – banners that have some functionality and product identity built into them. This provides immediate benefits for customers, rather than simply forcing them to link to another site. For example, using rich-media techniques, some banner ads now give customers information and let them

Table 4.3   Types of banner advertisements

Type of banner	Features
Animated GIF	Multi-layer banner allowing primitive animation (usually, up to 12 different frames in the same GIF)
Action click-through	Banner prompts user to enter a query into an input box and, once completed, the user is taken to another website where the input is used to entice the user
Action remain	Similar to action click-through, but user stays at site
Rotating banners	User will experience several different banners each time a page is visited
Targeted banners	Banner advert targeted to a specific, user-related factor (e.g., query related, location related, demographically related)

order products and perform other tasks right on the banner. This model allows more targeted responses. For example, a company, such as Timberland, which wishes to market its fashion footwear for city use while continuing to reach its traditional outdoors market could set up different advertisements on different types of sites. The banner could play a short promotional video clip, take down consumers' details and refer them to the nearest store without directing them to a different page. The Internet advertising agency DoubleClick reported an increase in the use of rich media, with rich media increasing from 17.3% of all ads in the first quarter of 2002 to 37% of ads in the third quarter of 2003. Click-through rates for rich media at 1.57% are more than five times higher than those for non-rich media at 0.29%.

Online retail

In online retailing the most common method used on websites is to mimic aspects of the real store (Table 4.4).

Where there is a real store as well as a website a webcam can be used to provide live video images of the store and the staff. A webcam can also become an added value service in itself. For example, *beachheads.co.uk*, a surfing equipment retailer in the UK, and *longbeachsurfcam.com*, a surfing retailer in Long Beach, NY, both provide live webcams of local beaches, allowing surfers to see the conditions before setting out.

Online distribution

The Internet is ideally suited for distribution of digital products and services, and, as was discussed in Chapter 2, information and news service providers have been providing online distribution ever since the beginning of commercial consumer networks, even pre-dating the popularization of the Internet. There are now thousands of news and

Table 4.4 Retail store activities and Internet retail equivalents

"Real" store activity	Internet retail equivalent
Salesclerk service	Product descriptions, information pages, gift services, search function, sales clerk on the phone/email
Store promotion	Special offers, online games and lotteries, links to other sites of interest, appetiser information
Store window displays	Home page
Store atmosphere	Interface consistency, store organization, interface and graphics quality
Aisle products	Featured products on hierarchical levels of the store
Store layout	Screen depth, browse and search functions, indices, image maps
Store location	Website links
Checkout cashier	Online shopping basket and/or order form
Look and touch of the merchandise	Limited to image quality and description, potential for sound and video applications

Adapted from Lohse and Spiller (1999).

information sites available offering live news reports, stock prices and even the latest prices for fish in markets.

What has been made possible or more cost-efficient as the technology has improved is the use of the Internet for other products, such as software and games, and other services, such as live entertainment. Many software companies are now using the Internet for software distribution, particularly for updates. For example, Microsoft allows PowerPoint users to download clip art from a library of several hundred on its site, while Norton allows users of its antivirus software to download updates of fixes for new viruses. The online distribution of software has also led to a wealth of sites offering freeware (free software) and shareware (software that is meant to be paid for after a trial period), in addition to pay software. Well-known sites include Tucows.com, simtel.net and download.com.

Increasingly, more and more entertainment products are also being distributed this way; this has happened to a large extent in music, following the development of the MP3 (Mpeg 1 Audio Layer 3) format, which allows music tracks to be distributed online. As the speed and volume of data that can be carried on the Internet improve similar prospects are likely for other forms of entertainment. Live pop concerts are already being broadcast on the Internet as well as "adult entertainment" using live webcams. As new data compression techniques are developed or broadband transmission becomes commonplace, it is conceivable for entire feature length films to be easily downloaded.

Online payment

The most common method of payment online is by credit cards (as described in Chapter 2). However, in countries where credit cards are not commonly available other methods are also being tried. For example, in China, customers can come into a store and buy online credits which can be used to buy online products. Other companies are bypassing the credit card system altogether. For example, B2B sites usually offer a credit facility for businesses. Some companies offer specialist electronic bill payment services (e.g., paymybills.com, checkfree.com). Cable & Wireless also offer the facility for users to have online bills from websites added to their telephone bill using special software from eCharge.

Personalized marketing

Whereas virtual marketing involves the use of the Internet to provide new products and services based on information, database marketing uses data collected and held in customer databases to better serve the customer. Computer databases have been used in marketing for many years now, pre-dating commercial use of the Internet. For example, marketing information systems to store and analyse customer details or market research data have been popular since the 1980s, while more recently many companies have implemented customer relationship management systems that track customer orders and help identify profitable customers (Groman, 1999).

Customer relationship management

CRM represents a shift in marketing perspective from "making sales of products" to "gaining and retaining clients". McKenna (1993) describes the key elements of this approach as:

- Dominating a specific market segment by developing highly appropriate products and services.
- Building a deep relationship with customers in order to develop appropriate products and services.
- Responding flexibly to market needs by continual monitoring, analysis and feedback.
- Developing relationships with suppliers and vendors in order to maintain an edge in the market.

Similarly, Peppers and Rogers (1997) recommend the five Is:

- *Identification* Learn as much about the customers as possible in order to establish a dialogue.

- *Individualization* Tailor the approach to each customer by offering a benefit based on the customer needs.
- *Interaction* Continue to learn more about the customer through continued interaction with the customer.
- *Integration* Extend the relationship with the customer thoughout all parts of the organization.
- *Integrity* Maintain the trust of the customer.

Customer relationships on the internet

Although CRM pre-dates e-commerce on the Internet, the relationship marketing approach can be equally well applied to the Internet. However, there are some differences. First, marketing may be two-way. On the Internet, customers may be active market players that play an important role in marketing tasks, such as informing other customers. Second, in traditional CRM only dyadic relationships are considered, typically that between customer and supplier. The Internet makes possible a wider range of relationships, such as relationships between supplier communities, customer communities and other parties. Wang et al. (2000) suggest that the process occurs in three distinct stages:

1. *Initial investigation* During this first stage, the relationship between market participants does not yet exist and the main activity is information gathering. Communication is primarily one-way, either from vendor to consumer or from consumer to vendor and most likely initiated through normal "interruption marketing" (Godin, 1999).
2. *Full-range communication* This stage is characterized by transaction-oriented, full-range interaction in which consumers "sample" competitive products or services without established confidence or trust. Database marketing and interaction marketing are both used in this stage (by both marketers and consumers). Permission marketing (Godin, 1999) may be used to target consumers.
3. *Relationship network building* In this stage, the information is relationship-centred. Market experience and perceptions become more important than hard data, such as price. Market participants are ready to make decisions based on established relationships. Permission marketing will be at its highest levels, such as the brand trust level and the situational level.

Relationship building has taken on an increased importance in many organizations with the increasing use of the Internet, since technology is readily available which allows the searching and buying transactions of online customers to be tracked.

Cookies

One of the commonest ways that customer visits to a website can be tracked is by using "cookies" (Figure 4.7); these are small data files that are written to the user's hard disk (usually in the "cookies" subdirectory in Windows) when a user browses a website or fills

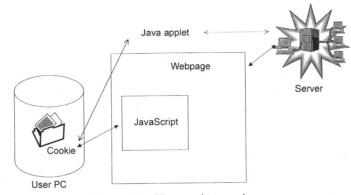

Figure 4.7   How cookies work.

in a registration form. Cookies store the user's identification and possibly references to pages visited or items ordered. Once stored it can be reaccessed the next time the user visits the relevant website (e.g., to show previous orders or the last page visited).

One possible sequence is as follows. The user visits a website, such as Amazon, registers and places an order for some books. The server sends a request to the user's browser to write a cookie file to the user's hard disk, such as the user "ID". The next time the user visits the site, the server issues a request to the browser to open the cookie file and sends back the user ID from the file. The user ID is then used to look up the user's name in the user's file and the previous orders in the orders file; this allows the company, for example, to greet the user by name and recommend a list of new books by the authors of the books ordered last time or books on a related topic. Alternatively, the company may use the data in the cookie to balance the demand in its customer processing. Software is now available from a number of companies which allows companies to use data in the cookie (e.g., to direct frequent, high-spending customers to faster machines, while directing customers who are just browsing to slower ones).

Cookies can also be written from websites the user has not visited; this can occur when a page containing advertisements is downloaded. For example, Amazon may send a page with a placeholder for an advertisement, but without the advertisement itself; instead, the page contains code that requests the advertisement directly from an advertising agency. The advertising agency delivers the advertisement, which is merged with the webpage from Amazon, and issues a request to write a cookie to the user's hard disk. The user now, without knowing it, has a cookie file from the advertising agency. The next time the user visits another site served by the advertising agency, the information from the cookie file can be retrieved and used (e.g., to produce personalized advertisements). The advantage for the user is that hopefully the advertising will be of interest, but there have been some understandable concerns over data privacy; this has led to suggestions that legislation should be put in place requiring sites to request permission before writing cookies. At the time of writing, however, this is not in place.

Mini-case: DoubleClick

DoubleClick (*www.doubleclick.com*) (Figure 4.8) is an online advertising agency that monitors users browsing the websites of their clients. By inspecting Internet addresses of the visitors to these companies' websites and matching them against a database of about 100,000 Internet domain names, it may be able to identify the visitor. Even if it cannot, by using a cookie file stored on the user's hard disk it can check whether the user has visited any of the participating sites previously. As the user searches the site, intelligent software records their activities, such as sites visited, purchases, etc. The next time the user visits a participating site, the customer ID is retrieved from the cookie file and the corresponding customer dossier is used to prepare a targeted advertisement.

Using their DART targeting technology the company is able to target users according to the following criteria:

- *Content targeting* Allows placement of advertising message on a particular interest site or within an entire interest category, such as:

  ○ Automotive.

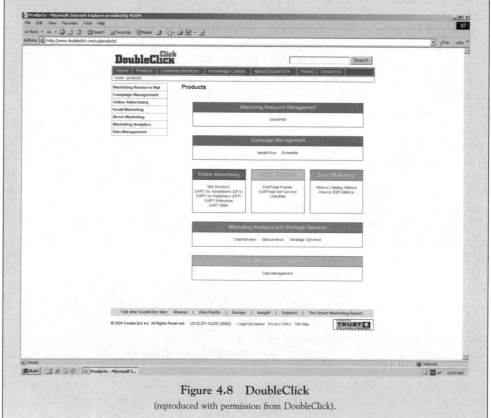

Figure 4.8 DoubleClick
(reproduced with permission from DoubleClick).

- o Business and finance.
- o Entertainment.
- o Health.
- o News, information and culture.
- o Search, directories and ISPs (Internet service providers).
- o Sports.
- o Technology.
- o Travel.
- o Women and family.
- *Behavioural targeting* An audience can be targeted according to how they use the Web. For example, advertisers can select business users by delivering advertisements on Monday to Friday between 9 a.m. and 5 p.m. or leisure users by targeting messages in the evening hours. Behavioural targeting includes the psychographic aspects of advertising. For example, it has been shown that the impact of advertisements tends to decline after they have been viewed three or four times. It is possible through DoubleClick to save money on the total number of ad impressions by showing an advertisement to an individual up to a maximum number of times.
- *User targeting* This enables advertisements to be placed according to the specific characteristics of the audience, such as their geographic location (based on country or zip code), domain type, business size or type according to standard industry classification (SIC) code.

Mailing lists and push technology

While cookies allow targeted but unsolicited advertising, another way of targeting advertisements to users is by request; this can be done using mailing lists and "push" software. The simplest method is to place one's name on a computer mailing list in the same way as offline lists. The Internet utility LISTSERV then allows copies of email messages to be sent to all users on the list.

A more sophisticated method is to use the push software that is already on both the client and server; this allows messages to be to sent to users according to more complex criteria, which can be matched against details held on a customer database (Figure 4.9). For example, messages can be targeted at users who live in a particular locality *and* are married *or* divorced *and* have children *and* earning more than $100,000 *and* have an interest in new cars. An early pioneer was PointCast (acquired by Entrypoint, *www.entrypoint.com*, in 1999). First, any Internet user could download its software to get access to free news, sports results, and stock quotes and advertisements. Second, using the PointCast interface, a user could define an interest profile or "filter". Third, the software would install a screen saver routine. When the machine was connected to the Internet, a persistent connection was established between the client (user's PC) and the PointCast server. Along this "channel" information was pushed. When the PC was disconnected,

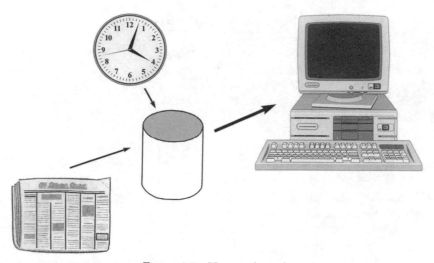

Figure 4.9   How push works.

the screen saver would display downloaded information from the PC's cache. Although PointCast proved popular with users, a problem with early versions was the volume of data transferred. The persistent connection means that the client's PC or server is connected to PointCast and information flows continuously. Eventually, many networks became clogged up with the volume of information.

However, as push technology has matured, it is becoming popular once again, particularly in the B2B marketplace. Microsoft and Netscape Communications have now also integrated push technology into their browsers. As well as applications for targeted advertising, push technology can be used within organizations to replace printed memos or updates to policy and procedures manuals by electronic versions. It is also possible to link a news story to a client profile resident on an internal proprietary database. A salesperson seeing a news story about a major expansion plan announced by a client, for example, can then call the customer to enquire about new equipment requirements.

Mini-case: Albertson's Inc.

US supermarket Albertsons Inc. (Figure 4.10) uses Marimba Inc.'s desktop and server management software throughout the 2,300 food and drug retail stores it operates in 31 states. Albertson's began deploying the software in March for tracking IT assets and making automated software changes to tens of thousands of devices, including servers, desktop and laptop PCs, and point-of-sale terminals. Albertsons will also use Marimba's software to automate the deployment and management of antivirus software and security patches.

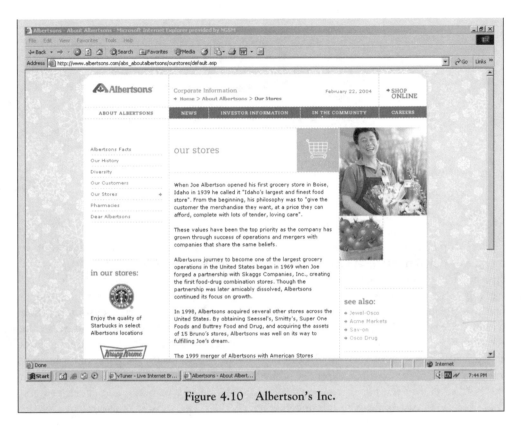

Figure 4.10   Albertson's Inc.

As Internet advertising becomes more widespread, there has been a shift from advertising toward "Permission marketing", a term coined by Seth Godin, head of direct marketing at Yahoo! (Sealey, 1999). Instead of forcing advertisements on large numbers of people many of whom are not interested in the product, termed "interruption marketing" by Godin, there is a shift toward asking permission before initiating a dialogue with consumers. Permission marketing can work in many media, but is particularly well suited to the Internet which allows cheap, fast, targeted, interactive communications (Godin, 1999). Sealey goes further and argues that not only does the Internet facilitate communication with customers it also gives customers unprecedented control over the marketing process. Instead of just being passive consumers of information, as they become proficient at using the Internet they will increasingly actively solicit information from marketers.

Profitable personalization

Despite the high degrees of personalization using customer databases, Peppers and Rogers (1993) have stressed the importance of considering customer lifetime value in deciding the degree of personalization that is appropriate. Figure 4.11 shows their view of the

Figure 4.11 Personalization matrix.

relationship between personalization and customer profitability. The horizontal dimension represents differentiation of customer needs. When customer needs are uniform almost all customers consume the same basic product and there is little value in differentiation. This situation occurs when there is a high similarity of expected and augmented product features throughout the customer base. As we move right in the figure customers differ widely in needs. Although they may need the same core product, important differences in some features of the expected and augmented product appear. The vertical dimension of the matrix shows differences in the lifetime value of the customer. Lifetime customer value is the total discounted expected profit from a new customer over their lifetime. At the bottom end of the figure customers show similar lifetime values, while at the top end there is a wide distribution of lifetime customer values. Let us now consider each of the four quadrants in detail:

- *Quadrant 1*   In quadrant 1 there are uniform consumer needs and few differences in profitability. Examples are basic products like gasoline and electricity. The main challenge for firms selling these products is competitive switching and mass-marketing methods that are commonly used to get customers to use their brand product when the purchase occasion occurs. Personalization is not very useful for products and services in quadrant 1.
- *Quadrant 2*   In quadrant 2, although customers may not differ much in their profitability, they have a wide variety of needs that are met by a wide variety of products. Examples include products that cater to different lifestyles, such as pensions, or individual tastes, such as house purchases and furniture. The key marketing challenge in quadrant 2 is helping customers find the best purchase choice and a personalization system that creates effective choice which may conceivably add value for customers.
- *Quadrant 3*   In quadrant 3 the important features of the product do not vary much across customers, although the intensity of use may vary a great deal. Examples are airline travel, hotels, rental cars and share trading. The major marketing challenge in quadrant 3 is identifying, acquiring and retaining highly profitable customers. One of

the most common approaches to accomplish this is the use of frequency marketing and continuity programmes. Examples include frequent flyer programmes of airlines, gold service plans of hotels and rental car agencies, and discounts for shopping at supermarkets. A personalization system for tracking customer use may be very profitable if it allows lifetime-profitable customers to be identified. In B2B marketing this information may be used to identify key accounts that get special attention from sales staff. Some companies (e.g., computer suppliers and consultants) may even keep some dedicated sales and support staff at the key accountant site, so they are available when needed. Customer retention is a fundamental concern, so online services that support and inform key accounts is also highly valuable. For example, extranets may be used to provide confidential or expensive material that is not appropriate for the general public.

- *Quadrant 4* In quadrant 4 there is a wide variety in customer needs and customer lifetime valuation, so each account needs to be treated separately, with the customers being rewarded for increasing the business and being supported in their use of the product. The greatest opportunities for personalization are available in this quadrant. As customer tastes vary widely, uncertainty and confusion about the best product to choose may appear. There may be a need to collaborate and design personalized products as well as possibilities for personal after-sales support.

Personalization systems

Different personalization systems can be used depending on customer needs and product attributes. Products with a few simple attributes compete primarily on price and value, so a good personalization system is one that allows customers to find the best deal that meets their requirements. On the other hand, products with complex and qualitative attributes compete primarily through branding, so a good personalization system will need to take into account other factors, such as customer lifestyle and perceptions. Figure 4.12 highlights the main online personalization systems and situations where they can best be used.

Rule-based systems use information that the company develops about its customer base to make educated guesses about special offers, promotions and information that the company provides to visitors. The systems are capable of representing specialized information to each new customer. Because rule-based systems rely on observing behaviour to predict preferences, they are best used where the product space is not too complicated and where attributes are quantifiable. Examples include the activity tracking and push software mentioned earlier.

Computer-assisted, self-explication systems work by asking visitors a series of questions about what they like in order to narrow down the choices. An example is the Hotels.com website that helps users select appropriate hotel accommodation by city, location, budget, etc. (Figure 4.13). Endorsement systems are used when the product needs of consumers do not differ greatly and quantifying attributes of available products is difficult. Examples include book recommendations (Amazon.com) and computer games (Jungle.com).

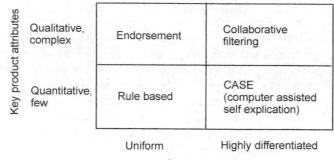

Figure 4.12   Personalization systems.

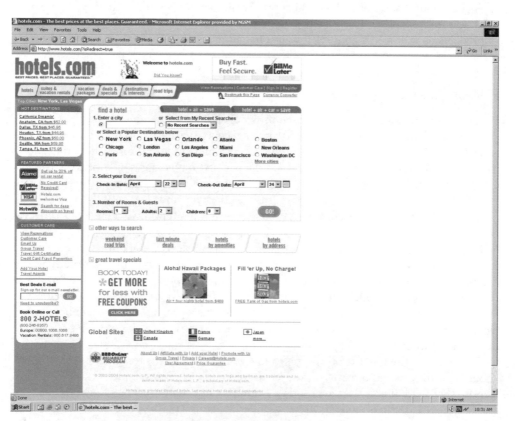

Figure 4.13   Hotels.com

(reproduced with permission from Hotels.com).

Collaborative filtering

Collaborative filtering is used when the product space is complicated and preferences are highly subjective, qualitative and complex. The system works by matching different users who seem to have similar profiles on the basis that people who share similar tastes in one area are likely to share similar tastes in another. (This is similar to the lifestyles segmentation discussed in the previous chapter and can be usefully combined with market research data on user lifestyles.) Amazon identifies cross-selling opportunities by deploying highly sophisticated CRM technologies that track and record every single customer click.

Collaborative filtering relies on statistical methods that are based on correlation between user preferences to develop recommendations for other users with similar personal profiles. Collaborative filtering has three parts: first, to query the user about various items; second, to develop user profiles; and, third, to rank and present new items. The query process can be explicit or implicit. Explicit queries require that the user respond with a score, rank, verbal or other classification of the item. Implicit queries are performed by agents that monitor the user's behaviour; this can be accomplished by examining bookmarks, cookie files, history files or by tracking browsing characteristics, such as time spent on sites, repeat use, save and print operations.

User profiles are developed using responses about user preferences. Both positive and negative responses are used since a strong dislike about something helps in classifying new items. Different algorithms have been proposed to develop user profiles. New items are evaluated by selected users, who are asked to rate each item. The software combines the ranks of items from users fitting a certain profile and presents them to other users fitting the same profile.

The concept of collaborative filtering can be extended in individualized filtering, where the individual is monitored to develop a profile that is used in future to guide searches for useful information. For example, Page Minder software works with Notes Navigator, Notes' built-in web browser, and automatically checks frequently accessed webpages and determines if there are any significant changes in these pages. You have the option to check several times a day, daily or weekly, and you can be notified by a summary of the new page or by actually having the whole page emailed to you. Another filtering software product is Autonomy. Autonomy's software builds up a profile of users' interests or employee expertise by extracting key ideas from the information a user reads. It then builds a profile that can be used for personalizing information or serve targeted advertising messages. Because these services are based on users' actual interests, they do not require users to fill out lengthy questionnaires or rate their likes and dislikes. These profiles can be kept completely anonymous and do not require the user to provide any private demographic information, although profiles can be combined with any known demographic information to further personalize the services provided.

Mini-case study: Ski Matcher

Ski Matcher (Figure 4.14) is a customized version of the TripMatcher^{TM} recommendation engine developed by TripleHop Technologies Inc. The engine uses filtering

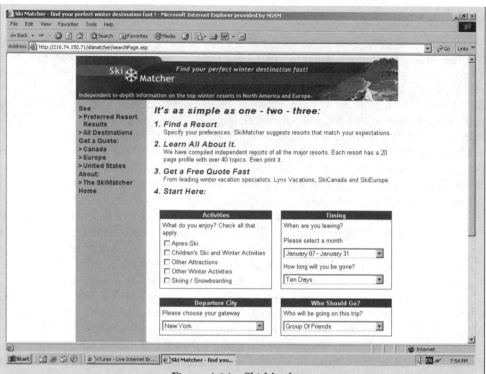

Figure 4.14   Ski Matcher.

technology based on 6 years of research conducted at the Nagoya Institute of Technology in Japan. The system combines four levels of filtering: content-based filtering, event-based filtering, attribute-based collaborative filtering and context-based filtering. In this way, Ski Matcher understands user requirements and preferences, and then provides recommendations that closely match those expectations. Ski Matcher also explains why it recommends one thing over another, so users can make better informed decisions.

Recommendations are based on information provided by a team of more than 40 travel writers and researchers who spend considerable time and effort researching the best North American and European ski resorts. Each writer is responsible for writing an extensive destination report narrative that captures the atmosphere and flavour of each locale. In addition, the researchers are responsible for evaluating a list of over 60 activities and characteristics. All ratings are loaded into a database and used to match what users say they like with what Ski Matcher knows about a given destination. Three more levels of filtering involve the prediction of a complex set of preferences through correlation with other users, click stream analysis and other contextual information. The system also takes into account weather conditions, hotel rates and airfares throughout the year. Statistical tools are also used to estimate average weather conditions for each week of the year in a specific destination, so Ski Matcher tries to match users with a destination that offers the climate they prefer at the time of year they travel.

Interactive marketing

Perhaps the most important characteristic of electronic networks which makes them such powerful marketing tools is the potential for interactive communication. Many sites start off with static webpages or "brochureware", a straight copy of an offline brochure. However, in order to fully utilize the capabilities of e-commerce technology, interactivity needs to be added. Unlike other media, such as television, radio or print, which are consumed passively, the Internet offers the opportunity to actively engage consumers in a dialogue. Many consumers switch on the television or radio as background noise without paying much attention to the content. Similarly, many newspaper readers skim through the newspaper only reading in detail items that interest them. However, most research seems to indicate that most people use the Internet more actively, searching for particular information or for a specific purpose, pay more attention to what is presented and are not easily distracted.

For example, the Stanford-Poynter Eyetracking Project (*www.poynter.org/eyetrack2000*) tracked users' behaviour on news sites, using eyetracking equipment that recorded where the eyes stopped to absorb information. Some of the findings were:

- Users' eyes fixated initially not on photos or graphics, as expected, but on text. The eyes of online news readers then come back to the photos and graphics, but sometimes not until they have returned to the first page after clicking through a full article.
- Also, contrary to much current belief, banner ads do catch online readers' attention. Of the 45% of banner ads looked at, readers' eyes fixated on them for an average 1 s. Graphics other than banners were looked at 22% of the time and received about 1-s eye fixation, while 64% of photos were looked at on average for about 1.25 s.
- Online news readers tended to read shallowly but widely, while at the same time pursuing selected topics in depth.

One characteristic of the Internet noted by many observers is the ability to sustain the interest of the user such that in many cases they lose track of time. Hoffman and Novak (1996) call this a state of "flow". They define flow as a state that is (1) characterized by a seamless sequence of responses facilitated by machine interactivity, (2) intrinsically enjoyable, (3) accompanied by a loss of self-consciousness and (4) self-reinforcing. In the flow state, consumers are so actively involved that nothing else seems to matter.

Based on various psychological theories, Hoffman and Novak have proposed a model that describes consumer navigation in websites (Figure 4.15). Two primary antecedents must be present for flow to occur: first, consumers must focus their attention on the

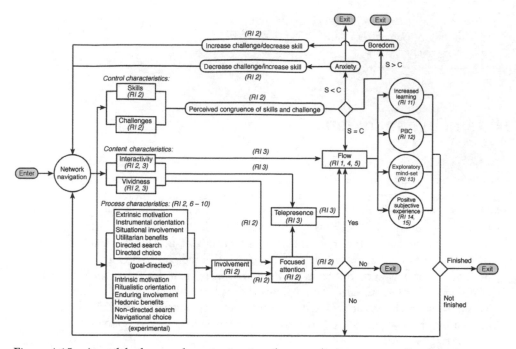

Figure 4.15   A model of network navigation in a hypermedia computer-mediated environment (CME). R = research issue; S = skills; C = challenge
(*source*: Hoffman and Novak, 1996).

interaction so that irrelevant thoughts are filtered out, and, second, they must perceive a balance between their skills and the challenges of the interaction. If the challenges significantly exceed their skills, they may give up through frustration, while if their skills significantly exceed the challenges, they may give up through boredom.

In addition to the primary antecedents, two secondary antecedents enhance flow: interactivity and telepresence. These secondary antecedents increase the subjective intensity of the flow state, although they are not sufficient in themselves to induce flow. A strong sense of telepresence (i.e., the computer-mediated perception of an environment) is induced by interactivity and vividness as well as focused attention.

Focused attention in turn depends on whether the activity is goal-directed (i.e., the goal is most important) or experiential (i.e., the process is more important). For example, a corporate executive who uses the Web to identify suppliers of a machine component is more likely to engage in goal-directed behaviour, getting satisfaction from the outcome of the search. On the other hand, a teenager who is surfing the Web in order to find the most interesting sites is more likely to engage in experiential behaviour, getting pleasure from the act itself.

Hoffman and Novak also suggest that consumers differ in their ability to experience flow, a personality trait termed "autotelic" in the literature and which may be learned, developed through practice or have a neurological basis. The implication is that the relative likelihood that a person will experience flow is an important marketing segmentation variable in a computer-mediated environment.

Site "stickiness"

Understanding users' behaviour is particularly important in the design of the website itself. Sometimes referred to as site "stickiness", the length of time a user spends on site is very dependent on how the site is designed. Figure 4.16 shows the importance of understanding how users will use a site. The figure shows the length of time spent on the Xerox company website, although the pattern is typical for many sites. The horizontal axis shows the length of user visit to a site measured in the number of pages viewed. The vertical axis shows the cumulative percentage of visitors with that number of views or less. The graph shows several features that are interesting from a marketing perspective. First, there is strong bias toward visits of 4 pages or less, which account for nearly 70% of visits. On the other hand, a few visitors make extensive visits, the maximum for the Xerox site being 110 pages. Huberman et al. (1998) suggest that this pattern can be explained by a simple model in which the user is constantly making judgements about the value of continuing or stopping a visit to a website, depending on the value of the current page and uncertainty about the value of pages not yet seen. If there is a chance that future pages might be of high quality, the user will continue the visit, otherwise the user will leave. Huberman et al. that the observed results can be explained by an upward-sloping curve, such that the value of the current page increases as the number of pages visited increases (Figure 4.17).

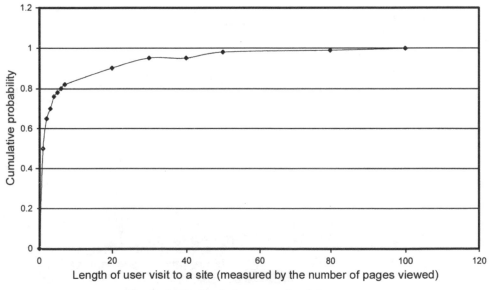

Figure 4.16 Typical pattern of website usage.

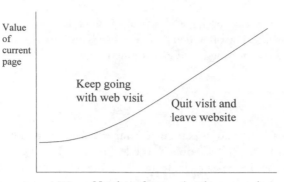

Figure 4.17   Model of website usage.

In other words, early on in a visit the value of the page need only be low for a visitor to continue, but as the visit continues the threshold rises and the page must be of increasing value for the visit to continue.

One obvious implication is that the higher the value of a site, the longer the duration of visits. A second implication is that it is important to guide visitors to the relevant pages quickly, otherwise they will leave. Third, pages must be of increasing value in order for visits to continue; this also emphasizes the importance of marketers engaging in discussions early on with website designers. Although customers may be willing to wander around a supermarket in order to locate an item of grocery, they may not be willing to do so on a website.

Some methods that can be used to encourage users to stay longer include:

- Sponsorship of an event, team or personality.
- Regularly updated information.
- Monthly product discount.
- Competitions.
- Quizzes.

Some methods that can be used to encourage repeat visits include:

- Regular newsletters.
- Regular promotions.
- Discounts or special deals.
- Rewards or loyalty schemes.

Mini-case study: Clickrewards.com

Clickrewards (Figure 4.18) offer its members the opportunity to earn currency (in a similar way to acquisition of air miles) by shopping at partner websites. Companies participating in this loyalty scheme include Adidas, Dell, Gap and Microsoft. Points

Figure 4.18   Clickrewards
(reproduced with permission from Clickrewards).

can be redeemed for airline miles or for merchandise from their *Rewards Catalogue*, including gift certificates, toys, jewellery, electronics, office supplies and more.

Reibstein (2002) found that the highest incidence of repeat buying was for small-ticket items, such as music and books. As the frequency of buying increases, the average number of items per order also increases. This finding contrasts with that of Fader and Hardy (2001), who found that within a cohort the purchase rates decrease. By "cohort" they mean customers who made their first purchase in the same time period. As they observe their purchases over time, each cohort's purchase amount and rate diminish. This frequency rate also differs significantly by product category. For example, the entertainment category, which has such products as music and books, has numerous repeat buyers, while apparel sales might be significantly less frequent. For categories in which there are multiple purchases within the category over time, it is essential for these customers to be retained at that site. The margins from each purchase rarely justify the individual acquisition costs.

Interacting with wireless devices

As noted in Chapter 2, wireless technology and applications are becoming increasingly common. However, the present devices have certain limitations. For example, wireless devices tend to have limited facilities for viewing content – often as small as 14×7 characters. Wireless devices also tend to be monochromatic, there are no mice and the keyboards are difficult to use. The most common navigational technique on wireless devices is a list with drill-down capabilities. Because of the constraints of using a wireless device and the relative inconvenience of performing any but the most straightforward, time-critical of tasks, it is unlikely that wireless users will want to "surf the Web" in the traditional sense. It is more likely that they will want to use their devices to execute small, specific tasks, such as looking up the train timetable, purchasing a CD and looking up sports scores or stock prices, etc. Sites will, therefore, need to be designed to allow drilling down through the site from general information to detailed information and without the use of a mouse.

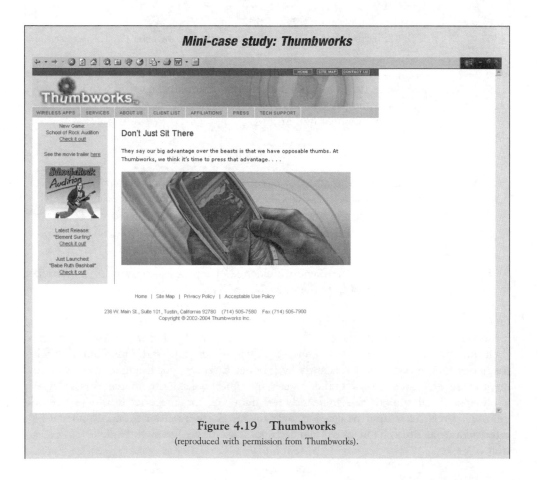

Figure 4.19   Thumbworks
(reproduced with permission from Thumbworks).

> Suzuki's target market for its motocross bikes is 18- to 24-year-olds. However, these are notoriously difficult to reach as they are often quick to dismiss advertising efforts as condescending and intrusive, so companies like Suzuki have traditionally relied on other means, such as sponsorships of motocross events and riders to market its motocross bikes. A new channel that it is trying is through the mobile handsets that most young people own. In conjunction with wireless publisher Thumbworks (Figure 4.19) it has developed a branded motocross game for mobile handsets. Suzuki Motocross Challenge generated over 650,000 downloads during its first 12 months. Each player saw the logo a minimum of five times, and most probably saw it more, each time the game was played. Since Suzuki Motocross Challenge was released, Jeep and Honda both signed up with Thumbworks to sponsor mobile games of their own.

Interacting with DTV

Digital television (DTV) introduces new opportunities in integrating advertising content within traditional programme content and in integrating this with the World Wide Web. DTV will allow much more direct response to advertisements; this is particularly important in marketing terms because the likelihood for responding to a persuasive appeal diminishes with time. The capacity to respond immediately and with minimal effort creates new opportunities for prospective advertisers.

An example given by Microsoft founder, Bill Gates, is this:

> You are watching an episode of Seinfeld on TV and you like the jacket he is wearing. You click on it with your remote control. The show pauses and a Windows-style drop-down menu appears at the top of the screen, asking if you want to buy it. You click on "yes." The next menu offers you a choice of colors; you click on black. Another menu lists your credit cards asking which one you'll use for this purchase. Click on MasterCard or whatever. Which address should the jacket go to, your office or your home or your cabin? Click on an address and you're done – the menus disappear and Seinfeld picks up where it left off.
>
> *Lee and Lee (1995)*

Another example might be to enable audiences to order ingredients directly while watching a cookery show. Similarly, audiences seeing an advertisement for fast food, for example, could simply click their remote control to have that food delivered to them within minutes – with tracking available to report on the status of the order until it is delivered.

Digital compression will allow much greater volumes of data to be transferred along with programmes. Personal video recorders (PVRs) are already in production through such firms as Replay Networks and TiVo which can store as much as 30 h of programming. A wide range of media can be stored (music, pictures, text, etc.), so the type of content stored can be diverse and varied. Likewise, the decoder boxes used in pay TV solutions already contain memory allowing services, such as weather and programme guides, to be downloaded and available for immediate access on demand. The ability to time-shift programmes by storing them and playing them later enables new types of broadcasting services. For example, viewers will be able to spend more time viewing an advertisement without missing out on their programmes. Alternatively, viewers could subscribe to a range of services delivered overnight and available for viewing at a convenient time. The storage capacity of digital media could also allow broadcasters to sell advertisements based on specific users rather than programmes.

In a similar way to push technology on PCs, audiences could themselves specify the types of advertisement they would like to receive, and software would select the appropriate version of an advertisement to appear in a particular household.

Community marketing

Another characteristic of the Internet that makes it different from other media is the ability for many-to-many communication. As discussed in Chapter 2 the Internet was used initially by groups of researchers and hobbyists around the world to communicate with each other, and online communities continue to be some of the most heavily visited websites.

The number and size of virtual communities continue to grow as Internet technology improves and costs of access continue to fall. Groupware has been available and used for a number of years now in companies; this allows collaborative working, such as joint document creation, audio- and videoconferencing.

However, such software was designed to run on private networks and has not been widely used by the general public. The Internet enables similar groups to be set up worldwide very easily and at low cost, enabling groups with millions of members.

Like communities in the real world, virtual communities often form around shared interests, but allow the normal constraints of distance found in communities in the real world to be transcended. An example is webmarriages.com, a website that allows people to find suitable marriage partners from similar communities around the world.

Some virtual communities have formed from real communities. For example, many villages, towns and cities around the world now have websites that provide community information and that allow people in the community to interact. Examples include mymanchester.com (UK), concordma.com (USA) and aboriginalhunter.com (Australia). Particularly in the case of remote and isolated communities, such as the Orkney Islands and Shetland Islands north of Scotland, the Internet is often the only way for people to share information and gain access to resources other communities take for granted, such as museums and libraries.

In other cases a real community has formed from a virtual one. A particularly striking example and one that might never have been able to form without the Internet is the XPS (Xeroderma Pigmentosum Society), an organization dedicated to helping young children who suffer from a rare genetic disorder that makes them allergic to sunlight. The Internet has allowed families whose children suffer from the disorder from all around the world to form a self-help group, where they can exchange information and provide mutual support.

The virtual community has been so successful that some families have now set up a permanent year-long camp where the children can go and enjoy themselves in a specially organized regime. Yet, others have taken the opposite route and completely abandoned the link with the real one, allowing people to inhabit virtual worlds with new personalities (*www.virtualworldsreview.com*).

Many businesses are now trying to build similar, stable communities of interest related to their products.

Mini-case: iVillage.com

iVillage.com (Figure 4.20) is the leading site in the USA which provides practical advice and support for women. The site is organized into channels and communities

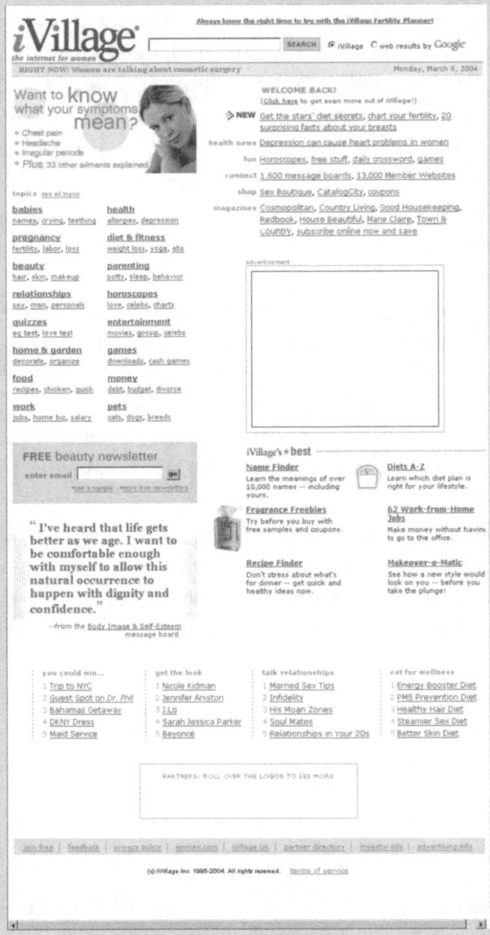

Figure 4.20   iVillage.com
(reproduced with permission from iVillage).

across multiple topics of high importance to women and offers interactive services, peer support, content and online access to experts and tailored shopping opportunities. The major content areas include babies, beauty, diet and fitness, entertainment, food, health, home and garden, horoscopes, money, parenting, pets, pregnancy, quizzes, relationships and work. The site hosts over 3,000 individual communities, led by community leaders who control the message boards.

Types of virtual community

Communities can be categorized according to the technologies used, the two main categories (Table 4.5) being communication rings and content trees (Hanson, 2000).

Communication rings send messages directly between individuals, and everybody in the ring gets all the messages. Tools for doing this include email lists, web pagers, groupware and multi-user games and simulations. The simplest is a shared email list that allows messages to be copied to all the people on the list. Web pagers provide instant notification when other members come online and allow impromptu direct chats between users. More sophisticated pagers also allow multiple lists and rings, stored by topic of interest. Groupware is software that allows members of a group to share files and exchange ideas. Multi-user games and simulations allow several users to take part in a game or simulation and exchange ideas and experiences.

Unlike communication rings, content trees send messages indirectly through a central point, such as a bulletin board; this allows larger scale communication and more structured discussion. Tools used include Usenet discussion groups, bulletin boards, chat rooms and websites that publish member content.

Kozinets (1999) suggests that virtual communities can also be categorized according to their social structure and group focus (Figure 4.21). Each category tends to attract different types of members. Multi-user "dungeons" originally referred to computer-generated environments where several players could act out fantasy games such as "dungeons and dragons", although the term is now used for any structured game. Dungeons tend to have a tight social structure and focus on social interaction; these are populated by "insiders" who have strong social ties and personal ties to the activity, "minglers" who

Table 4.5 Types of community technologies

Communication rings	Content trees
Email lists	Usenet
Net pager	Bulletin boards
Groupware	Chat rooms
Games and simulations	Virtual worlds Websites

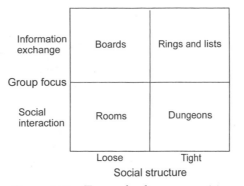

Figure 4.21   Types of online community.

have strong social ties but only a secondary interest in the activity and a few "visitors" who lack strong ties to the community and only a passing interest in the activity. Like dungeons, rooms are computer-mediated environments where people can meet, but without the structured format of a game. They also focus on social interaction, but since they have a looser social structure they tend to be populated by minglers and visitors.

Whereas dungeons and rooms focus on recreation and social interaction, the other two categories focus on information exchange. Rings and lists provide structured information exchange centred around such themes as nuclear disarmament and politics. They are particularly attractive for marketing since they contain a high proportion of insiders and "devotees", people who have a strong interest in the activity, but only weak ties to the group. However, since they tend to be more closely knit communities, it can be difficult to gain access. The final category of virtual community is bulletin boards; these are also attractive for marketing since they are organized around shared interests, such as music, wine, etc., and since they tend to contain a mixture of insiders, devotees and a few minglers. Since many bulletin boards are public they are generally easier to access than rings or lists.

Dynamics of community formation

The significance of virtual communities for firms is that they have led to a significant shift of power from lenders of goods and services to the customers and increases the importance of understanding the dynamics of how such communities form.

Hagel and Armstrong (1997) described four critical cycles that stimulate and sustain the growth of virtual communities (Figure 4.22). The first two, content attractiveness and member loyalty, provide increasing benefits to new and current members by building up the content and member base. Interesting content attracts more members and more members generate more content.

Member profiles and transaction offerings are cycles that are of particular interest to commerce as they are closely connected to the profitability of the online community. An

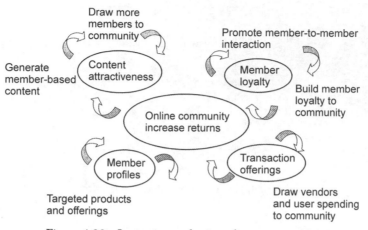

Figure 4.22 Increasing cycles in online communities
(reproduced with permission from Harvard Business School Press).

attractive membership profile enables vendors to target specific offerings that will appeal to members, while attractive offerings in turn attract new members and other vendors. Like the boom towns of the Gold Rush in the USA, the presence of customers with money to spend attracts vendors wishing to capitalize on the opportunity and in turn the presence of a thriving trading community attracts more people to join the community. Let us look at the four cycles in detail:

1. *Content attractiveness* The content attractiveness cycle shows how content that is extensive and interesting encourages current customers to spend more time reading and reacting; this in turn encourages more member-to-member interaction and more member-generated content. Increased content in turn makes the site more attractive to new members who initiate more interaction and more content. Methods that site owners can use to encourage this interaction include the use of discussion boards and chat rooms. Attractive content in turn helps reduce member churn and feeds back into increased loyalty.
2. *Member loyalty* Increased member loyalty normally leads to increased number of hours online and a lowered churn rate. Each of these in turn creates the continuity and commitment among the members that lead to trust and collaboration. The more members are committed to each other, the more connected they are to the community and the more interactions they have with the community.
3. *Transaction offerings* A stable and active community in turn attracts vendors to the site. If their offerings are valuable to members, then this in turn can attract more members or increase member loyalty. Since most online communities rely on advertising from vendors, this is an important cycle to get right.
4. *Member profiles* The fourth cycle links site content to transaction offerings. Increasing community-generated information enables more relevant advertisements and higher

advertising revenue. It also enables targeted transaction offerings, which increases transaction volumes.

Balancing the four cycles is the challenge for owners of virtual community sites. While attractive content and member loyalty are necessary in the first place to attract and retain members without some churn and the introduction of new members the site may not generate much new content and will stagnate; without advertising the site may not survive. On the other hand, excessive advertising will deter members, particularly if the community was originally set up for non-commercial reasons. Another is how to manage the community as it grows. As the community expands it may be necessary, for example, to establish more formal structures or subgroups.

Eventware

As well as permanent or long-standing communities, another feature of groups on the Internet is the presence of transient communities, or communities that form for a limited time. Examples are live pop concerts or other public events. Up to now this has mainly consisted of video broadcast on the Internet, but future developments could include "eventware", or software that allows real-time collaboration in synchronized events worldwide. Such software has been used mainly for educational purposes (e.g., to allow hundreds of students worldwide to participate in a lecture and discussion at the same time). However, there clearly is potential for non-educational use. For example, eventware could be used to hold professional forums and conferences enabling professionals, such as doctors, lawyers and academic researchers, to exchange ideas and information worldwide. Other companies have set up virtual trade shows that enable manufacturers to display new products without the expenses normally associated with a trade show, such as brochures, accommodation, displays, etc. Other benefits include a broader reach, flexible opening times and easier access to information.

Viral marketing

Another Internet marketing method that makes use of community contacts, real or virtual, is viral marketing. "Viral marketing" is the term coined by venture capital firm Draper Fisher Jurvetson (*www.drapervc.com*) to describe the exponential growth of Internet companies resulting from customer referrals. DFJ was an investor in such companies as Hotmail, NetZero, Third Voice and Homestead (Hotmail is often cited as one of the early pioneers of viral marketing for the Internet). Established in 1996, Hotmail provides a free email service and grew to over 40 million subscribers in 3 years. Whenever a customer sent an email, a message was inserted at the bottom of every email:

Get Your Private, Free Email at *http://www.hotmail.com*

The low price (free) and referral of their service combined with inertia for a person to change email addresses allowed Hotmail to spread and grow quickly.

Two types of viral marketing can be distinguished (Zien, 1999). The first is "frictionless viral marketing" which is exemplified by Hotmail. The customer spreads word of the service merely by using the service. Others learn about the service by contact through an existing customer or subscriber. Another example is Blue Mountain Arts, a site that allows you to send an electronic greetings card to someone. An email is sent to the recipient notifying them of a greeting cards and the card is then "picked up" by visiting Blue Mountain Arts' website.

The second type of viral marketing is "active viral marketing" which requires the active participation of a customer in recruiting new customers. An example is ICQ, the popular chat program that allows people to communicate with each other only if they already are running the ICQ chat software; this means that customers must actively convince their friends, relatives or co-workers to also use ICQ in order to communicate with them. Another example is Amazon.com's associates program. In exchange for directing a customer to a site, the associate is paid for the referral or given other incentives.

Combining techniques

In order to simplify discussion, the previous sections have discussed different e-marketing techniques in turn. Of course, websites often use more than one technique in reality. For example, Watson et al. (1998) distinguish websites that combine differing degrees of interaction and customization (Figure 4.23).

A company may also decide to use different techniques for different target customer groups and for different marketing objectives.

Breitenbach and Van Doren (1998) suggest that the various marketing techniques used should be tailored to the type of user as shown in Table 4.6, while Kiani (1998) suggests in Table 4.7 the different methods are suitable at different stages of customer purchase.

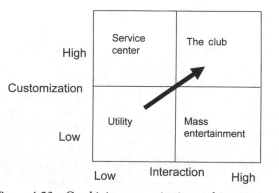

Figure 4.23 Combining customization and interaction

(© 1988. The Regents of the University of California, reprinted from Watson et al., 1998 by permission of The Regents).

Table 4.6 Marketing techniques for different types of user

Internet user type	Directed information seeker	Undirected information seeker	Bargain hunter	Entertainment seeker	Directed buyer
Product/Company information	×	×	×	×	×
Open communication	×	×	×	×	×
Real-time browsing/ transactions					×
Demonstration	×				
Club membership	×		×		
Giveaways			×		
Entertainment		×	×	×	
Virtual tour		×	×	×	
Instruction	×				×
Complementary services	×	×	×	×	×

Reproduced by permission of Emerald.

Table 4.7 Marketing objectives and supporting features

Objectives	Examples of supportive features
Awareness	Announcement through letterheads, business cards, brochures, packages, newspapers, magazines, TV; mnemonicness of address: similarity to company name
Attraction	Hyperlinks from other sites: search engines addressing the site, searchable indexes addressing the site, hotlinks from other sites; content length of document: the higher content the less speed to be downloaded; bandwidth of connection speed
Visit/Engage	Information: about products and company; facilities: Java, search engines, sound, video and animation
Purchase	Order facilities: ordering form, mail, fax, cellphone and email; payment facilities: cash/cheque, credit card and direct account; delivery/booking facilities: mail, fax, cellphone and email
Repurchase	Freshness: communities/clubs/user-to-user communication, what's new, FAQs; hyperlink to other sites; customization: collecting user information, demographic information, customer needs, optional menu and diagnostic requiring user input

Reproduced by permission of Emerald.

A typical pattern for e-commerce sites has been to begin with simple techniques, such as brochureware providing company and product information, and progress to online transactions and online communities, before tackling more complex applications, such as real-time multimedia and integrated business processes.

E-marketers need to integrate a variety of marketing channels and media (Figure 4.24). As Schultz (1996) argued, marketing integration is inevitable for two main reasons. First,

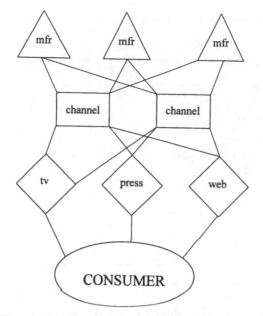

Figure 4.24   Integrated advertising and marketing
(reprinted from Schultz, 1996, with permission from Elsevier).

there is the increasing availability of feedback loops measuring the behaviour of consumers in the real world, in some cases in real time, and linking previously disconnected activities, such as advertising and distribution. The market research data demonstrate that consumers respond to the compound effect of many things, such as advertising, price promotions, PR, etc., and increase the need to manage all the various marketing channels as a holistic system. Second, there is a technological shift of control of the market from manufacturers to consumers. In this scenario the task of marketing managers will be to manage all the various information sources and resources that might influence a consumer and to respond to customer requests whatever the inter-mediating channel.

Mini-case study: 3 Suisses

3 Suisses (Figure 4.25) is the second largest mail order company in France with a turnover of $1.2 billion. It has succeeded in combining new and traditional channels to provide the best of both old and new for customers. The company sells mainly through a 1,000-page mail order catalogue, but it has continually leveraged technology to find new ways to interact with customers. It started first with telephone orders and then, in 1982, launched a site on Minitel. It started to sell via the Web in 1997 (*www.3suisses.fr*), and today its website is fully integrated with the company's other systems. 3 Suisses has placed most of its catalogue online and updates

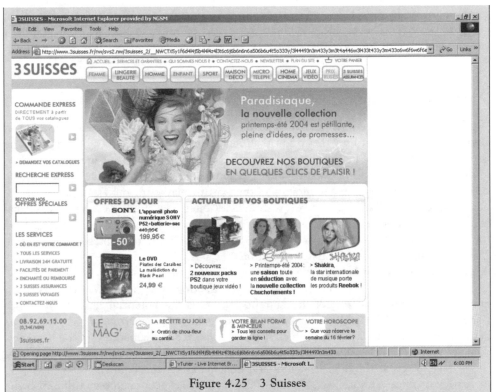

Figure 4.25   3 Suisses
(reproduced with permission from 3 Suisses).

the site regularly with information about stock availability. Customers can ring for advice prior to purchase, book training and receive after-sales support.

The Internet service is backed up by a bricks-and-mortar network of 28 of its own boutiques and 4,000 affiliates, such as bookshops and florists. The boutiques offer a number of services, such as order pickup (within 24 hours) at no extra cost, free returns, order taking and credit card applications, while the affiliates focus solely on pickups and returns.

Although there has been a trend toward allowing customers to initiate transactions on the Internet, some other authors have criticized the move in some companies toward self-service as being too extreme. For example, Moon and Frei (2000) argue that while it is relatively easy to search for flights if the exact dates and times are known and price is not an object, it is usually necessary to perform several searches if the itinerary is flexible and the aim is to find the cheapest flight. In contrast, by calling a call centre, an experienced sales agent can take into account complex preferences and will undertake the task of searching through the airline databases in order to find the best match. Moon and Frei suggest a better approach to e-commerce is co-production, where the company performs some of the tasks now being undertaken by the customer, in other words a return to customer service. The problem for marketers is to identify areas where the company can provide a better service which outweighs the benefits customers will gain elsewhere.

Impact on existing marketing mix

While the previous sections have focused on the new marketing approaches used in e-commerce, this is not to say that traditional marketing concepts cannot be applied. The conventional four Ps of marketing, product, price, promotion and place, are as relevant to online businesses as offline ones. However, e-commerce brings new issues that must be considered and may require a rethinking of the existing marketing mix. Of the four Ps, we have already seen that e-commerce technologies offer new products/services ("Virtual marketspace" section) and new placing options ("Personalized marketing" section). In the next chapter we will see how e-commerce offers new pricing strategies ("Targeting customers and market segmentation" section). However, one of the biggest effects has been on promotion (or branding).

For example, one of the key cornerstones of marketing over the last 50 years has been brand management and one of the current debates is the potential impact on brands (Chen, 2001). In the real world, brands serve to identify a particular product or its manufacturer and are usually protected by a registered trademark. On the Internet, domain names serve a similar purpose and, as will be seen later, a number of legal issues have arisen as the domain names and trademarks systems conflict.

However, some authors (e.g., Sealey, 1999) argue that e-commerce will diminish the role of brands altogether. Greater access to information coupled with more sophisticated search and comparison software will make it easier for consumers to compare different offerings and so reduce the need for brands.

Maklan and Knox (1998) argue that brand management is not only inefficient it also misses opportunities to add real value for customers. They argue that the previous marketing approach of launching a large number of brands and products only adds complexity and stress for the consumer. It is better instead, they argue, to focus internally on adapting company processes to meet customer needs. Instead of focusing on the "unique selling proposition", companies should focus on the "unique organization value proposition". An example is Virgin Group which has been successful at selling the Virgin brand across a range of industries, such as air travel, financial services and soft drinks. Maklan and Knox attribute Virgin's success to identifying industries that have a complex range of activities which add little value for consumers, and applying processes that work across a range of industries, such as price transparency, integrity and service. Could such an approach work with e-commerce? Sealey suggests it could. For example, the customer now has a huge choice of ways to connect to the Internet, such as the telephone, mobile phone and cable television. There is an opportunity for a company to provide a single connectivity service allowing customers to access the Internet by whichever means they choose and have it charged to one bill. Similarly, there is now a vast array of financial products available on the Web and we can imagine customers might be confused about the different offerings so that they choose to rely instead on a single, trusted provider, such as Charles Schwab or Yahoo.

Summary

This chapter has described some of the new marketing practices arising from the ability of e-business technologies to provide key customer benefits:

- Faster processing.
- Virtual products and services.
- Personalization.
- Interactivity.
- Many-to-many communication.

As firms experiment and the technology improves, other methods will undoubtedly arise.

However, as e-business technology has become more widespread and has been adopted by mainstream organizations, the key question is now less about whether or how marketing can be done electronically, but more about – a recurring question since computers were first invented – which marketing activities can best be done by humans and which activities are best undertaken by computers.

References

Angehrn, A. (1997). Designing mature Internet business strategies: The ICDT model. *European Management Journal*, **15**(4), 361–9.

Breitenbach, C.S. and Van Doren, D.C. (1998). Value-added marketing in the digital domain: Enhancing the utiltity of the Internet. *Journal of Consumer Marketing*, **15**(6), 558–75.

Chen, S. (2001). Assessing the impact of the Internet on brands. *Journal of Brand Management*, **8**(4/5), 288–302.

Fader, P. and Hardy, B. (2001). Forecasting repeat sales at CDNOW: A case study. *Interfaces*, **31**(May–June): S94–S107.

Godin, S. (1999). *Permission Marketing*. Simon & Schuster, New York.

Groman, J. (1999), Value gap marketing: Customer value optimisation using database marketing. *Interactive Marketing*, October/December, **1**(2), 149–55.

Hagel, J. and Armstrong, A. (1997). *Net Gain: Expanding Markets through Virtual Communities*. Harvard Business School Press, Cambridge, MA.

Hanson, W. (2000). *Internet Marketing*. South Western College Publishing, Cincinnati, OH.

Hoffman, D. and Novak, T. (1996). Marketing in hypermedia computer-mediated environments: Conceptual foundations. *Journal of Marketing*, **60**(July), 50–68.

Huberman, B.A., Pirolli, P.L.T., Pitkow, J.E. and Lukose, R.M. (1998). Strong regularities in World Wide Web surfing. *Science*, **280**, 95–7.

Kalyanam, K. and McIntyre, S. (2002). The e-marketing mix: A contribution of the e-tailing wars. *Academy of Marketing Science Journal*, **30**(4), 487–500.

Kiani, G.R. (1998). Marketing opportunities in the digital world. *Internet Research*, **8**(2), 85–194.

Kozinets, R.V. (1999). E-tribalized marketing?: The strategic implications of virtual communities of consumption. *European Management Journal*, **17**(3), 252–264.

Lee, B. and Lee, R.S. (1995). How and why people watch TV: Implications for the future of interactive television. *Journal of Advertising Research*, November/December.

Lohse, G.L. and Spiller, P. (1998). Electronic shopping. *Communications of the ACM*, **41**(7), 81–6.

Maklan, S. and Knox, S. (1998). *Competing on Value*. Pitman Publishing, Washington, DC.

McKenna, R. (1993). *Relationship Marketing*. Addison-Wesley, Reading, MA.

Moon, Y. and Frei, F.X. (2000). Exploding the self-service myth. *Harvard Business Review*, May/June, 26–7.

Oliver, R., Rust, R., and Varki, S. (1998). Real time marketing. *Marketing Management*, Fall/Winter, 29–36.

Peppers, D. and Rogers, M. (1993). *The One to One Future*. Doubleday, New York.

Peppers, D. and Rogers, M. (1997). *Enterprise One to One*. Doubleday, New York.

Reibstein, D.J. (2002). What attracts customers to online stores, and what keeps them coming back? *Academy of Marketing Science Journal*, **30**(4), 465–74.

Schultz, D.E. (1996). The inevitability of integrated communications. *Journal of Business Research*, **37**, 139–46.

Sealey, P. (1999). How E-commerce will trump brand management. *Harvard Business Review*, July/August, 171–6.

Wang, F., Head, M. and Archer, N. (2000). A relationship-building model for the Web retail marketplace. *Internet Research*, **10**(5), 374–84.

Watson, R.T., Akelsen, S. and Pitt, L. (1998). Attractors: Building mountains in the flat landscape of the World Wide Web. *California Management Review*, **40**(2), 36–56.

Zien, J. (1999). Viral marketing for Internet websites. Available at *http://internet.about.com/industry/internet/library/weekly/1999/aa092799.htm*

Useful websites

Ad Resource *http://adres.internet.com*
DoubleClick *http://www.doubleclick.com*
Interactive Advertising Bureau *www.iab.net*
Online Advertising Hypermart *http://onlineadvertising.hypermart.net/index.html*

Key concepts

- Accelerated marketing
- Banner ads
- Build to order
- Bulletin boards
- Click-through rates
- Collaborative filtering
- Community marketing
- Computer-assisted self-explication

- Cookies
- Customer relationship marketing
- Database marketing
- Digital marketing cycle
- Distribution to order
- Endorsement systems
- Flow state
- ICDT model
- Information acceleration
- Interactive marketing
- Interstitial advertisements
- Multi-user dungeons
- Personalization matrix
- Push technology
- Real-time billing
- Rings and lists
- Rule-based systems
- Superstitial advertisements
- Viral marketing
- Virtual marketing
- Virtual marketspaces
- Website stickiness

Self-assessment questions

1 Describe the four virtual marketspaces created by e-commerce.
2 List the various forms of online advertisements.
3 Describe the stages of the digital marketing cycle.
4 Explain how cookies can be used to target website advertisements.
5 Explain how push technology works.
6 Explain the difference between the various types of personalization systems.
7 Explain how the Internet can be used in new product development, build to order, distribution to order and real-time billing.
8 Explain the concept of flow in websites and how this can be used in website design and advertising.
9 Explain what is meant by community marketing and how this is different from marketing to an individual.
10 Explain what is meant by viral marketing.

Discussion questions

1 Is there a future for brands on the Internet?
2 Has the Internet shifted power to consumers?
3 Will personal service still be important in marketing on the Internet?
4 Which emerging technologies are likely to have the greatest impact on marketing?
5 Discuss the possible problems in implementing an integrated marketing campaign.
6 How should we assess the effectiveness of a website?

THE ECONOMICS OF
E-BUSINESS

Introduction

In earlier chapters we looked at some of the technologies used in e-business and the benefits that they offer to businesses and customers, such as:

- More information.
- Lower production and distribution costs.
- Lower costs for buying and selling.
- More precise targeting of customers.
- Benefits from virtual communities.

In this chapter we will examine in more detail the economic implications of these changes for businesses and some specific characteristics of digital products and services.

More perfect information

Economists describe an efficient market as one that clears or leaves no excess supply or demand. In reality, most markets fail to match supply with demand at least temporarily, leaving some sellers with excess inventories and some buyers without desired products or services. Reasons for market failure include the following: simultaneous participation of all sellers and buyers may be prevented by geographical distance, lack of information or the failure for a market to be co-ordinated. Still other reasons that prevent efficient market clearing include high transaction costs – even if all buyers and sellers are in the market and have perfect information, the costs of the transaction may outweigh the benefits to each party. Transaction costs will be discussed in more detail later, but in this section we will examine how e-business can overcome some of the other causes of market failure.

An electronic market not only offers a cheaper, more cost-effective way to transact business it also brings about a more efficient market-clearing mechanism, because it is not constrained by geographical distance or time. A typical market, such as the London Commodities Exchange, consists of buyers and sellers, a commodity and a price discovery mechanism, such as a simultaneous ascending price auction or a sealed bid auction. An electronic market operates in a similar fashion, but is not limited by the need for buyers and sellers to be physically present. Such electronic exchanges are now commonplace for the trading of stocks and shares and are now starting to be used for the trading of other products. For example, the Japanese company Aucnet (*www.aucnet.co.jp*) offers a clearing market among used car dealers, while General Motors in the USA has figured out that online auctions are a good way to sell off used cars when they come off lease.

In some cases, an electronic market may open a new opportunity to trade a product that may not have been possible otherwise. One of the key benefits of the Internet is access to more information; this has allowed the creation of new markets that did not exist or were not possible previously. For example, if sellers are not aware that there are potential buyers for their product and vice versa, this market would never be created. Economists describe this as a "missing market". However, to an entrepreneur this represents an opportunity to make profits, and many new businesses have been set up by astute entrepreneurs who have identified the benefits of utilizing the Internet to provide better, more timely information. Examples are some of the business-to-consumer (B2C) and consumer-to-consumer (C2C) auctions or business-to-business (B2B) exchanges discussed earlier which bring together buyers and sellers and allow better information exchange.

Mini-case study: Pan-European Fish Auction

One of the oldest and most traditional of European markets is being transformed by the Internet. The Pan-European Fish Auction (PEFA) (Figure 5.1), located in Brussels, allows buyers from all over Europe to buy direct from fish markets using the Internet. The benefits to fishermen of such an auction is considerable. Owing to the vagaries of customers' demand, fishermen can sometimes arrive in port to find only two or three local buyers. PEFA allows them to find buyers elsewhere in Europe. The scope of the auction means that species unpopular in one part of Europe can be sold in another.

The system includes networked fish markets in the Republic of Ireland (Ardglas), UK (Milford Haven, Lowestoft, Troon and Lochinvar), Belgium (Zeebrugge), Netherlands (Scheveningen, Stellendam and Colijnsplaat), Iceland (Grindavik), Faroe Islands, Denmark (Thyboron, Køge) and Italy (Cattolica) as well as stand-alone auctions in Skibbereen (Ireland), Turballe and Cherbourg (France), and Bermeo (Spain). The auction works with real-time bidding and uses the Dutch auction system in which prices start high and are sold when the price attracts a buyer. Users view each auction bid through an image similar to a clock face, with a hand displaying the countdown in prices, and bid by pressing a button. The system also allows buyers to

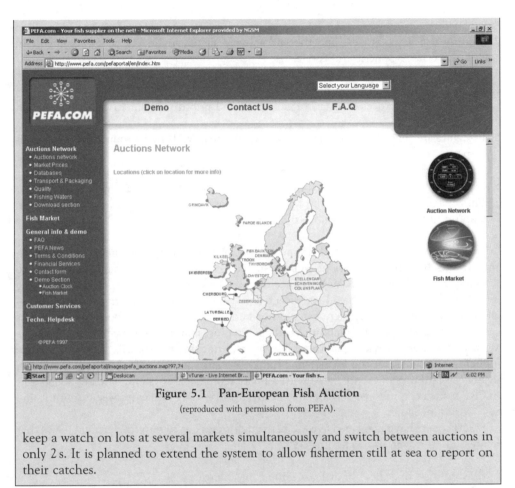

Figure 5.1 Pan-European Fish Auction
(reproduced with permission from PEFA).

keep a watch on lots at several markets simultaneously and switch between auctions in only 2 s. It is planned to extend the system to allow fishermen still at sea to report on their catches.

Production and distribution costs

Another benefit of electronic commerce is the significant reduction in production and distribution costs. Reducing costs in the production and distribution process has been an aim of most IT projects since the development of computers. However, two of the efforts most focused on cost reduction in recent years have been BPR and ERP. Business process re-engineering (BPR) aims to analyse and redesign workflow within and between enterprises. BPR was popularized in the early 1990s when Michael Hammer and James Champy published their best-selling book, "Reengineering the Corporation" (1993); this argued that radical redesign and reorganization of an enterprise was necessary to lower costs and increase quality of service and that information technology was the key enabler for that radical change. Hammer and Champy suggested seven principles of re-engineering to streamline the work process and thereby achieve significant levels of improvement in quality, time management and cost:

1. Organize around outcomes, not tasks.
2. Identify all the processes in an organization and prioritize them in order of redesign urgency.
3. Integrate information processing work into the real work that produces the information.
4. Treat geographically dispersed resources as though they were centralized.
5. Link parallel activities in the workflow instead of just integrating their results.
6. Put the decision point where the work is performed and build control into the process.
7. Capture information once and at the source.

By the mid-1990s, according to Hammer, a lack of sustained management commitment, unrealistic scope and expectations, and resistance to change prompted many companies to abandon the concept of BPR and embrace the next new idea, enterprise resource planning (ERP). ERP refers to the broad set of activities supported by multi-module application software that helps a manufacturer or other business manage the important parts of its business, including product planning, parts purchasing, maintaining inventories, interacting with suppliers, providing customer service and tracking orders. ERP can also include application modules for the finance and human resources aspects of a business. Typically, an ERP system uses or is integrated with a relational database system. The deployment of an ERP system can involve considerable business process analysis, employee retraining and new work procedures.

Practitioners have identified five elements that stand out to form the critical issues that define BPR (Grover and Malhotra, 1997):

1. BPR consists of radical or at least significant change.
2. BPR's unit of analysis is the business process, not the department or functional area.
3. BPR tries to achieve major goals or dramatic performance improvements.
4. IT is a critical enabler of BPR.
5. And organizational changes are a critical enabler of BPR and must be managed accordingly.

Building on the cost savings brought out by BPR and ERP, many businesses have sought to develop applications using Internet technology (Wells, 2000). Reduction in production costs can occur, for example, by streamlining business processes to enable better inventory management, reduce clerical operations and improve utilization of plant and machinery. Distribution costs may also be reduced, for example, by streamlining processes in the supply and distribution chain to enable more cost-efficient shipment of goods and utilization of transport. These cost reductions lower the minimum efficient scale of production and allow customized products to be produced profitably.

A classic example of a company that has masterfully used a combination of electronic

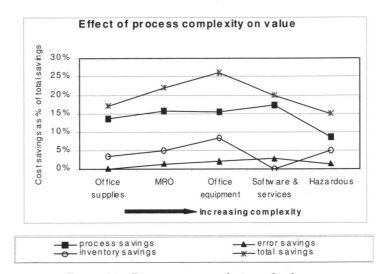

Figure 5.2   Procurement complexity and value

(*source*: Subramaniam and Shaw, 2002, Reproduced with permission of ME Sharpe Inc.).

commerce, BPR and EDI to reduce production and distribution costs is Dell. In 1993 the company achieved $2.6 billion in sales and carried an inventory of $342 million. In 1998, by introducing online ordering of PCs on the Internet integrated with JIT (just-in-time) assembly, the company managed to increase sales to $12.3 billion, while reducing inventory to only $233 million.

In many cases companies have obtained benefits by outsourcing the distribution to a delivery service, such as FedEx, which apart from handling the delivery can also operate the merchant server, picking and packing. As shown in Figure 5.2, Web-enabled B2B has the potential to reduce costs more significantly in moderately complex items (e.g., MRO – maintenance, repair and operating, office equipment and software) than in simple or complex items.

Mini-case study: FedEx Logistics Support Services

FedEx InterNetShip (Figure 5.3) allows customers to use the Internet to request a parcel pickup or find the nearest drop-off point, compute shipping cost, print packing labels, request invoice adjustments and track the status of their deliveries. The website is supported by FedEx's proprietary network, FedEx COSMOS, which allows the company to keep track of every package every step of the way from the point at which a customer requests a parcel pickup to the point at which it reaches its final destination.

FedEx also provides logistics support for other companies, operating warehouses that pick, pack, test and assemble products, as well as handle the delivery, which sometimes involves consolidating products with other shipments and clearing customs. Using an extranet embedded in their own sites Fedex customers can also make use of FedEx's order-tracking system, allowing customers to track deliveries directly.

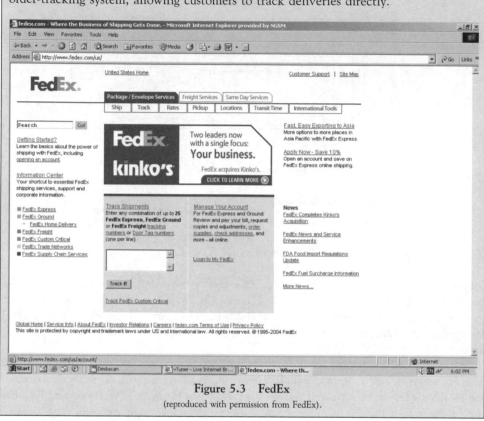

Figure 5.3   FedEx
(reproduced with permission from FedEx).

Transaction cost reductions

Significant as they can be, operational efficiencies, such as lowering the costs and speeding up internal operations, are only some of the benefits of e-business. What makes them more significant is that more recent electronic commerce systems have gone one better in significantly reducing transaction costs between buyer and seller. Transaction costs are incurred at every stage of the buying–selling process, and where e-businesses have scored over traditional businesses in many industries has been the ability to significantly reduce costs in one or more stages of the transaction.

Ronald Coase (1937), then a student at the London School of Economics, discovered the concept of transaction costs while studying American firms during the Great Depression. Given the increasing number of large, integrated corporations in the USA, he wondered why certain firms choose to conduct certain transactions internally rather than via the market. He concluded that firms arise when the costs of performing certain activities are cheaper than purchasing in the market, an insight that contributed to his Nobel Prize over 50 years later. Coase identified six types of transaction cost:

- *Search costs* Buyers and sellers finding each other inside the increasingly broad and disorganized open market.
- *Information costs* For buyers, learning about the products and services of sellers and the basis for their cost, profit margins, and quality. For sellers, learning about the legitimacy, financial condition and need (which may lead to a higher or lower price) of the buyer.
- *Bargaining costs* Buyers and sellers setting the terms of a sale or contract for services, which might include meetings, phone calls, letters, faxes, emails, exchanges of technical data, brochures, entertainment and the legal costs of contract negotiations.
- *Decision costs* For buyers, evaluating both the terms of the seller compared with other potential sellers and the internal processes, such as purchasing approval, designed to ensure that purchases meet the policies of the organization. For sellers, evaluating whether to sell to one buyer instead of another buyer or not at all.
- *Policing costs* Buyers and sellers taking steps to ensure that the goods or services and the terms under which the sale was made, which may be ambiguous or even unstated, are in fact translated into the real goods and services exchanged; this might include inspecting the goods and any negotiations having to do with late or inadequate delivery or payment.
- *Enforcement costs* Buyers and sellers ensuring that unsatisfied terms are remedied; this includes costs, such as agreeing discounts and other penalties and the cost of litigation to settle disputes associated with the transaction.

Reductions in transaction costs are one of the key benefits and drivers of electronic commerce.

Search costs

For example, before a buying–selling transaction can occur, buyers and sellers need to find each other and costs may be incurred in the process of searching for a suitable partner. Buyers need to search for a supplier of the desired good, and sellers need to search out potential buyers of their products. With the ever-increasing choice of products available in an increasingly wide marketplace these costs may be substantial.

This is perhaps the most obvious area where e-businesses have been able to significantly reduce costs. In earlier chapters we looked at how the worldwide reach of the Internet has significantly increased the choice and made it easier to contact a large number of potential suppliers and buyers. The widespread availability of search engines and directories, such as Yahoo!, Excite and Lycos, has also made it easier to locate potential partners.

Another recent phenomenon has been the use of the Internet to search out solutions or new ideas to problems. For example, InnoCentive.com is a website set up by pharmaceutical company Eli Lilly to locate answers to tricky scientific problems. People can submit ideas and then earn rewards if they work. At the same time this reduces Eli Lilly's R&D budget.

Information costs

Once a potential supplier or buyer has been found, further costs are usually incurred before the transaction is completed. For example, buyers may require information about the products and services offered sellers, such as product features, prices and quality, while sellers may wish to learn more about the specific requirements and financial soundness of buyers.

Once again this is an area where e-businesses have been able to significantly reduce transaction costs; this can range from basic product information to online quotes. For example, in the mortgage business most companies now provide information on the company and products on their websites, while some sites, such as Mortgage Express (UK) and Loantownusa.com (USA), provide facilities for online quotes.

One firm that has developed information provision to a high degree is Air Products. One of the world's leading suppliers of chemicals and gases, the Air Products site enables customers to search through the product catalogue, get quotes and place orders online as well as linking into the company's intranet for specialist advice.

Bargaining costs

If the information received is satisfactory, buyers and sellers then enter the next phase of the transaction, bargaining or agreeing terms. Typical costs incurred in this phase include travelling to meetings, telephone calls, letters, faxes, entertainment and the legal costs of contract negotiations. At a basic level, emails can be seen as a cheaper and faster communication medium, but e-commerce goes much further than that. With online auction sites, it is now possible to conduct much, if not all, of the bargaining phase entirely online. In the USA, E-Bay has pioneered the sale of items to consumers by public auction and has since been joined by a host of other sites offering auctions, including Amazon and Yahoo.

Mini-case study: QXL

QXL (Figure 5.4) is Europe's largest pan-European online community. The site combines both B2C and C2C auctions in 12 countries for products ranging from computer hardware and software, consumer electronics, household appliances, collectables to travel-related items and sports equipment. Set up as Quixell in September 1997 by journalist Tim Jackson, the company hosted its first online auction in the UK in November 1997 and set up a German site in October 1998. It was renamed QXL in December 1998 to reflect its European expansion and the launch of C2C auctions. Other sites followed in France (January, 1999), Italy (June, 1999), The Netherlands (October, 1999), Norway (December, 1999), Denmark (January, 2000) and Spain

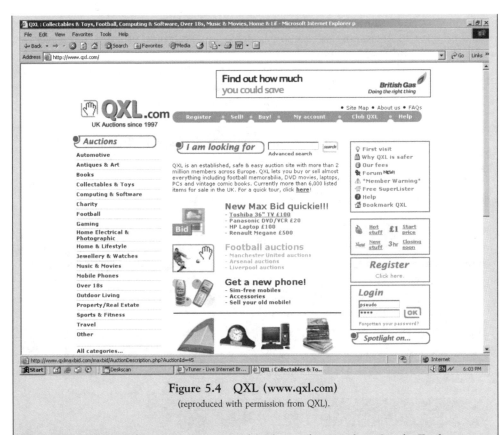

Figure 5.4   QXL (www.qxl.com)
(reproduced with permission from QXL).

(February, 2000). The company was placed on the London Stock Exchange in February, 2000 and raised £40.2 million. Since then the company has continued to expand, including the acquisition of Bidlet, the leading Swedish online auction service and a merger with ricardo.de, a leading German e-commerce and online auction site in 2000, the acquisition of Aucland, a leading French online auction site and an exclusive agreement with *The Times* in 2001 and co-branding agreements with Premium TV (which runs over 80% of official, top English professional football club websites), top English football club Manchester United and Yahoo! Europe in 2002.

Decision costs

Once mutually agreeable terms are reached, further costs may be incurred before a decision is reached. For example, buyers may need to spend time evaluating the terms of the supplier and compare these with offers from other potential suppliers, while suppliers may need to spend time deciding whether to supply one buyer instead of another buyer or not at all. Here too e-businesses have been able to reduce costs by providing software to enable easier comparison of competing offers. Comparison-shopping sites, such as mysimon.com and bizrate.com, enable offerings from multiple suppliers of a wide range of goods and services, including books, music, videos, software, travel and toys, to be accessed with one click and readily compared.

Other transaction costs that were not listed by Coase include the cost of the purchase order itself, invoicing and collections, etc. Here again significant savings are achievable using e-business technologies to reduce paperwork and improve processing times.

Mini-case study: e-procurement at Imperial College

As one of the major colleges of the University of London, Imperial College (Figure 5.5) has 8,000 people working, researching or studying. It spends £100 million a year on goods ranging from stationery to laboratory equipment and kit for scientific research. Over 200,000 purchase orders are processed every year. Most of these are for low-value items, such as stationery, printing and photocopying, and laboratory consumables, which were estimated to represent an annual spend of £34 million. However, owing to the highly devolved nature of the college, there was no mandatory application of the purchasing policy and 83% of the procurement budget was spent outside the formal procurement system. As a result, considerable savings potentially achievable through bulk purchasing were not being achieved.

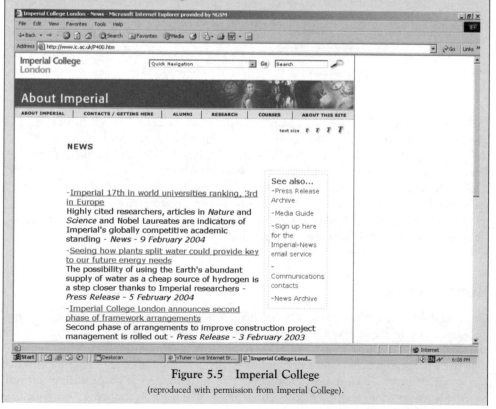

Figure 5.5 Imperial College
(reproduced with permission from Imperial College).

Crucially, it was not only the purchasing department that could see the benefits of e-procurement. Academics complained about the amount of time spent on processing paperwork, all of which takes time out of more productive research work. For a world-class institution like Imperial, this was the key selling point. A cost–benefit study of e-procurement showed that it could save some 70,000 research hours, which equated to £8 million a year. As a result Imperial installed an e-procurement system, one of the most advanced higher education purchasing systems in the world. Its architecture consists of an extranet linked to a central server which provides the bridge via HTTP links to university client and supplier servers. There are four levels of user: account controllers, who are responsible for setting departmental budgets; account holders, who have full visibility of all transactions in their departments; administrators; and end-users. The system is able to check if the user has both the budget and authority to purchase items.

Zeng and Reinartz (2003) make the point that it is important to consider all stages of the buying process in assessing the impact of the Internet on an industry. Their study found that most of the e-commerce activities so far have focused mostly on increasing the effectiveness of online search and paid less attention to facilitating transactions and helping consumers make better decisions. They argue this is why, for example, while 56% of potential mortgage customers in the USA have sought information online, only 1.5% have actually bought online.

Consumer costs and benefits

It is also necessary to consider the additional costs of buying online. Although there may be certain benefits derived by consumers in electronic markets (e.g., lower prices and lower search costs), it also increases the complexity of their decision process by adding another option to consider, beyond retail stores, mail order and so forth. Strader and Shaw (1999) conducted a survey of 400 customers in order to compare their experiences in traditional markets and electronic markets; these were drawn from a population of adults who had purchased sports-trading cards through an e-market in 1996 and so would have experience of electronic commerce. Table 5.1 lists the costs and risks identified, and Table 5.2 summarizes the findings from the survey.

This would suggest that the additional benefits or cost savings in product price, search costs and sales would need to outweigh the higher risk, distribution and market costs in order to encourage consumers to take part in electronic markets.

B2B transactions

Reduction in transaction costs using the Internet have had most impact in the B2B market, which has grown significantly as shown in Chapter 2. There are some economists who argue that widespread use of B2B e-commerce sites, which reduce transaction costs for buyers and sellers on a wide scale, could lead to a so-called "frictionless

Table 5.1 Consumer costs and risks

Product price	The sum of the production costs, co-ordination costs and profits of the value chain that provides the product or service
Search costs	The time, effort and money involved in searching for a seller who has the product demanded at an acceptable price with acceptable features and quality
Risk costs	The costs involved in minimizing transaction risk as well as the costs associated with losing value in a transaction
Distribution costs	The costs associated with physically moving the product from the seller to the buyer
Sales tax	Self-explanatory
Market costs	The costs associated with participating in a market

Adapted from Strader and Shaw (1999) with permission from MCB Publishing.

Table 5.2 Comparison of consumer costs in traditional and electronic markets

	Traditional market	Electronic market
Product price	Higher	Lower
Search costs	Higher	Lower
Risk costs	Lower	Higher
Distribution costs	Lower	Higher (for physical goods)
Sales tax	Higher	Lower
Market costs	Lower	Higher

Adapted from Strader and Shaw (1999) with permission from MCB Publishing.

economy" and result in as much as 5% increase in productivity in the economy (*The Economist*, 2000).

Kaplan and Sawhney (2000) classify B2B sites into four categories according to the type of input and method of purchase (Figure 5.6). Types of input can be either manufacturing inputs or operating inputs. Manufacturing inputs are the raw materials and components that go directly into a product or a process (e.g., chemicals in a plastics company or steel in a car manufacturer). Operating inputs, by contrast, are not parts of finished products. Often called maintenance, repair and operating (MRO) goods, they include things like office supplies, spare parts and airline tickets.

A second way B2B purchases can be distinguished is according to the method of purchase. Companies can either engage in systematic sourcing or in spot sourcing, depending on the product or industry. Systematic sourcing involves negotiated contracts with qualified suppliers, usually ones with whom the firm has established close relationships. In spot sourcing, on the other hand, the buyer's goal is to fulfil an immediate need at the lowest possible cost, usually with little regard to long-term relationships.

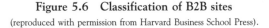

Figure 5.6 Classification of B2B sites
(reproduced with permission from Harvard Business School Press).

In *MRO hubs*, the operating inputs tend to be low-value goods with relatively high transaction costs, so these sites provide value largely by increasing efficiencies in the procurement process. Many of the companies in this arena, including W.W. Grainger, Ariba and Commerce One, started out as providers of "buy-side" e-procurement software to large companies, which used the software on their own intranets. Now, instead of licensing their software to individual companies, they host it on their own servers to provide an open market.

Yield managers add value by allowing firms to liquidate or acquire resources at short notice; this is useful in situations with a high degree of price and demand volatility, such as the electricity and utilities markets, or with huge fixed cost assets that cannot be liquidated or acquired quickly, such as manpower and manufacturing capacity. Examples of yield managers include Youtilities (for utilities), eLance (for human resources) and iMark.com (for capital equipment).

Online *exchanges* similarly allow purchasing managers to smooth out variations in demand and supply by rapidly exchanging the commodities or near-commodities needed for production. Examples of exchanges include e-Steel (for the steel industry), PaperExchange.com (for the paper industry) and IMX Exchange (for the home mortgage industry).

Finally, *catalogue hubs* automate the procurement of non-commodity manufacturing inputs, creating value by reducing transaction costs. Like MRO hubs, catalogue hubs bring together many suppliers at one easy-to-use website, but are usually industry-specific. Examples include PlasticsNet.com (in the plastics industry) and SciQuest.com (in the life science industry).

B2B sites create value in two ways: aggregation and matching. Sites that use the aggregation mechanism bring together a large number of buyers and sellers under one virtual roof; this reduces transaction costs by providing one-stop shopping. PlasticsNet.

com, for example, allows plastics processors to issue a single purchase order for hundreds of plastics products, sourced from a diverse set of suppliers. Aggregation works best in the following settings:

- The cost of processing a purchase order is high relative to the cost of items procured.
- Products are specialized, not commodities.
- The number of individual products is extremely large.
- The supplier universe is highly fragmented.
- Buyers are not sophisticated enough to understand dynamic pricing mechanisms.
- Purchasing is done through pre-negotiated contracts.
- A meta-catalogue of products carried by a large number of suppliers can be created.

Unlike aggregation, which is static, matching involves bringing buyers and sellers together to negotiate prices dynamically and in real time. For example, Youtilities matches utility industry suppliers with excess supply to buyers at short notice. Matching works best in the following settings:

- Products are commodities or near-commodities and can be traded sight unseen.
- Trading volumes are massive relative to transaction costs.
- Buyers and sellers are sophisticated enough to deal with dynamic pricing.
- Companies use spot purchasing to smooth the peaks and valleys of supply and demand.
- Logistics and fulfilment can be conducted by third parties, often without revealing the identity of the buyer or seller.
- Demand and prices are volatile.

Targeting customers and market segmentation

More accurate targeting of customers was discussed in Chapter 2 on e-marketing, but the important point to reiterate here is the impact on costs. Not only is it possible to more accurately identify and reach specific customer groups, but it is also possible to do this much more cheaply using e-business technologies. To give some indication of the costs, Internet advertising consultants DoubleClick estimates that the base cost of advertising on the Internet is $3.50 per 1,000 impressions compared with $16 via TV, $6 in magazines and $19 in newspapers (*http://onlineadvertising.hypermart.net/onad/Online_Advertising_2.html*).

In earlier chapters the development of various recommender systems was described, such as intelligent agent software that scours the Web and searches out desired information and push software that enables a subscriber to be updated on new products and services. These systems enable much more specific targeting of customers and personalization of products to meet the needs of a specific user.

Price discrimination

Better targeting of customers also enables price discrimination. Discriminatory prices do not reflect the difference in production or transaction costs; this means that different consumers are charged different prices for the same product, based on their own valuations. For example, a consumer with a high income or with an urgent need may be willing to pay a higher price for the same product than another consumer with a lower income or no immediate need. If sellers can distinguish between these consumers, they can charge a higher price for the former and establish a lower price for the latter.

Economists distinguish between three types of price discrimination. Discriminatory pricing based on group identification is called third-degree price discrimination. Examples are student and senior citizen discounts. In the absence of group identifiers, sellers may have to rely on consumers to select themselves. For example, given optimal product choices, consumers will sort themselves out according to product characteristics and a price schedule that reveals their preferences. This pricing scheme based on consumers' voluntary choices is called second-degree price discrimination. The final method, first-degree, or perfect, price discrimination refers to charging individual prices for each buyer, based on the consumer's willingness to pay.

Economically, price discrimination is usually regarded as desirable, since it often increases the efficiency of the economy; this is why it is frequently promoted by governments, either through explicit mandates or through indirect means. On the other hand, price discrimination often arouses strong opposition from the public.

Odlyzko (2003) argues that price discrimination is likely to increase given the wider availability of information and technology on the Internet. On the other hand, other factors may slow the spread. One such factor is arbitrage, in which buyers who secure low prices sell to those who are faced with high prices. Another, even more important factor slowing the spread of price discrimination is that customers do not like being subjected to dynamic pricing; this may encourage the use of new tools for detecting price discrimination. Odlyzko concludes that the result is likely to be that price discrimination will grow, but in a concealed form.

The instantaneous feedback and increased ability to track consumer buying on the Internet has encouraged some sellers to turn to individualized pricing through online price negotiation and auctions. For example, Priceline has reversed the price-setting mechanism common in many industries by organizing auctions where the customers can state the price they are prepared to pay for a product and sellers bid for their custom, while the now-defunct Hagglezone reverted to the age-old method of bargaining between buyer and seller over prices using a software application that did all the negotiating, after taking into consideration such factors as the shopper's bidding history and pattern of negotiation, the availability of inventory and a database of previous sales.

On the other hand, the Internet removes important cues that salespeople can use to determine a consumer's willingness to pay. A salesperson cannot take into account the buyer's clothing, body language, vehicle or accent as signals of the buyer's reservation value or bargaining ability. The last two – vehicle and accent – may be revealed to the salesperson during the course of the negotiation if it takes place over the phone and includes discussion of a trade-in.

However, the dealer clearly has less information about the buyer than would be the case were the buyer in the dealer's showroom.

Mini-case study: do minorities pay more? – Autobytel.com's effect on differential pricing

Autobytel.com is an independent Internet referral service that offers consumers detailed information about individual cars, including current market conditions and invoice pricing. At any point a consumer may submit a free purchase request that is forwarded to one of Autobytel.com's contracting dealers. Consumers provide their name, address, contact information and the type of car they are looking for. A salesperson at the dealership contacts the consumer within 48 hours (often much sooner) with a price. While Autobytel.com strongly encourages its contract dealers to set a fixed price, dealers are free to deviate from the initial price offer in response to consumer negotiation. Communication may occur by email or telephone. In this way consumers may purchase a car without setting foot in the dealership until they pick up the vehicle. Autobytel.com assigns dealers an exclusive territory; any leads generated within that territory are passed on to the dealer in exchange for a dealer subscription fee. Car prices are individually negotiated, so there is opportunity for significant price discrimination in the market. The same car sells for different prices because consumers differ in characteristics.

To test for the effect of Internet usage Scott Morton et al. (2002) used purchase requests submitted by consumers on Autobytel.com during 1999. Autobytel.com forwarded slightly over 2 million referrals to dealers. They found that offline African American and Hispanic consumers pay approximately 2% more than do other consumers; however, 65% of this price premium can be explained by differences in income, education and search costs; this suggests that price discrimination in car buying has a "disparate impact" between minorities and whites, rather than being evidence of a "disparate treatment" of these groups.

The Internet has also allowed other more innovative ways to price products. For example, LetsBuyIt.com has used the power of the Internet to offer group discounts on a wide range of items.

Mini-case study: LetsBuyIt.com

A company that has used the global reach of the Internet to offer group discounts on a wide range of items is LetsBuyIt.com (Figure 5.7). Founded in January, 1999 in Sweden, LetsBuyIt.com is the established European leader in co-operative shopping, or "co-shopping", an Internet service that allows consumers to combine their purchasing power in order to beat down prices. In effect, this allows the individual to buy at

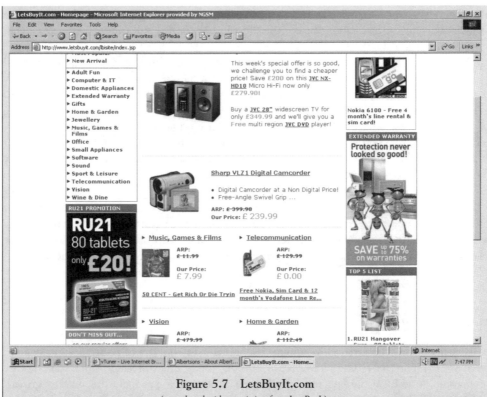

Figure 5.7   LetsBuyIt.com
(reproduced with permission from LetsBuyIt).

wholesale prices without having to purchase a huge quantity of the product. LetsBuyIt.com launched online in April 1999 in Sweden, moving into Denmark, Finland and Norway in August and into Germany and the UK in November. The company expanded into several other European countries at the height of the dot.com boom, but following the dot.com crash, the company has refocused on the UK, Ireland and Germany.

Network externality effects

As we saw in Chapter 4, many new e-businesses have been built up around so-called "virtual communities", or groups of individuals centred around a particular bulletin board or website. Initially, many of these communities may have been, and may be still are, centred around a particular set of interests. For example, AOL and Compuserve originated as networks providing email and newsgroup services that allow people with similar interests to communicate with each other. Many new websites and bulletin boards have also been set up to cater for more specific interests, such as the Motley Fool site (*www.fool.com*) for investment tips or the Elvis Presley online site (*www.elvispresleyonline. com*) for Elvis Presley fans.

Although many of these communities were originally established with non-commercial objectives, the potential of these communities for commercial gain has not been missed by businesses. First, existing communities provide a ready access point for firms that wish to market to specific groups. For example, the potential benefits of sponsoring or advertising on the Jewish.com site for caterers supplying kosher food are obvious. Second, many new e-businesses have actively encouraged communities to form around their site. For example, Amazon.com encourages users of its site to write reviews of books that they have bought. It has recently introduced an online auction facility enabling other users to buy and sell goods among themselves.

Virtual communities as discussed above can also accelerate the uptake of a particular product or service since they act as a reference group which customers use when deciding what to purchase. For example, a purchaser of a scanner who is unsure which one to buy may turn to others in the community who have previously purchased for advice.

Positive and negative feedback

In systems terms, such virtual communities are subject to strong "positive and negative feedback" (Figure 5.8). The more people who buy a particular product, the faster the rate of market growth. When people stop buying a particular product, the market growth diminishes rapidly. Sometimes these effects are also termed a virtuous cycle and a vicious cycle, respectively. (Such effects are not limited of course to electronic markets and can be seen, for example, in the rise and fall of share prices in stockmarkets. Prices of popular shares tend to increase rapidly as demand grows and accelerates, but they can just as quickly fall once investors lose confidence.)

Economists term such effects "externalities". In general, an externality arises when an individual's production or consumption decision directly affects the production or consumption of others other than through market prices. A network externality describes a specific effect that depends on external factors in the networks with which the product is associated, not on the product or service itself. An example of the economic impact of network externalities is "Metcalfe's law", introduced in Chapter 3. Named after Ron Metcalfe, the founder of local area network provider 3-Com, the "law" states that the

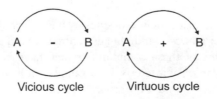

Vicious cycle   Virtuous cycle

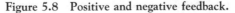

Figure 5.8 Positive and negative feedback.

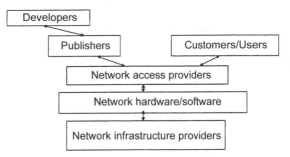

Figure 5.9 Complex system.

utility of a network increases with the square of the number of users. As more users join a network, it becomes more and more attractive for other users to join.

More generally, network externalities are observed in complex systems that exhibit "ensemble" properties (i.e., the behaviour of the whole system is not wholly determined by the properties of the elements); this may arise, for example, from the interaction of elements with each other.

This is often amplified in many e-business systems for two reasons (Chen, 1997): first, on the supply side, as shown in Chapter 2 on electronic technologies, many different technologies need to work together for the system to develop successfully (Figure 5.9); and, second, the ability of the Internet to form virtual communities increases network externalities on the demand side.

This increases the importance of technical standards that allow the transfer of data between different systems. A firm that creates a winning standard has a significant competitive advantage, since other firms must adopt this standard if their systems are to communicate with other systems; this creates high switching costs, leading to "lock-in". Some common types of lock-in and switching costs are:

- Contractual commitments.
- Durable purchases.
- Brand-specific training.
- Information and databases.
- Specialized suppliers.
- Search costs.
- Loyalty programmes.

Standards also increase the importance of complementary products. A user who has purchased one product in a system will be more likely to purchase another product with which it is compatible. For example, a user who has already purchased a word-processing package is more likely to purchase a spreadsheet that allows ready interchange of data with the word-processing package than one that does not. Similarly, a user who has purchased a digital camera is more likely to purchase compatible software that allows manipulation of the images. Complex systems thus tend to amplify positive feedback loops that may arise in user communities. The implications of this feature of e-business will be examined in more detail in Chapter 7 on competitive strategies, but one implication is the increased importance of collaborating with companies that provide complementary products.

Law of increasing returns

The distinctive cost structure and presence of strong positive and negative feedback effects in electronic markets leads to some unusual economic effects (Arthur, 1996). In most manufacturing-based businesses there is a law of diminishing returns to scale (Figure 5.10); that is, as inputs increase, the rate of output gradually diminishes. For example, by employing an additional 40 workers productivity may be increased by 40%, but employing a further 40 workers only increases productivity by 30%. In contrast in many e-businesses, the law of increasing returns applies (Figure 5.11); that is, as inputs increase, the rate of output increases as well.

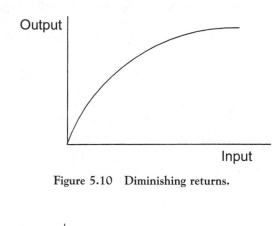

Figure 5.10   Diminishing returns.

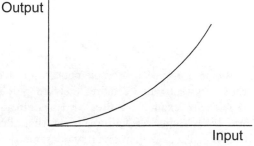

Figure 5.11   Increasing returns.

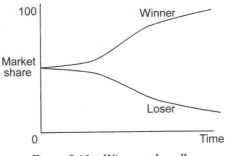

Figure 5.12   Winner takes all.

Arthur (1996) identifies several reasons why increasing returns have become more common in the new economy:

- *High upfront costs*   High-tech products, such as pharmaceuticals, computer hardware and software, and telecommunications equipment, typically have R&D costs that are large relative to their unit production costs. For example, Windows cost Microsoft $50 million to develop, yet each additional copy costs only $3.
- *Network effects*   Many high-tech products need to be compatible with a network of users. So, if much downloadable software on the Internet will soon appear as programs written in Sun Microsystems' Java language, users will need Java on their computers to run them. Java has competitors, but the more it gains prevalence, the more likely it will emerge as a standard.
- *Customer groove-in*   High-tech products are typically difficult to use and so require training. Once users invest in this training, it becomes easier to capture markets for updated products.

Arthur argues that increasing returns account for the tendency toward monopolies in some markets. By increasing "first-mover advantages" where a firm that gains a small lead in a market maintains that lead over competitors, leading ultimately to a situation where the advantage is so complete that the "winner takes all" (Figure 5.12). The market domination by Microsoft in PC operating system software is often cited as an example.

Building critical mass

A major hurdle in this type of competition is building sufficient mass for the market to take off; this can be done, as in the case of PC operating systems, by locking customers in until sufficient mass is achieved. Critical mass can also be built by improving customer retention through, for example, better quality and better service. Some firms, especially start-ups, sometimes attempt to build critical mass by introducing "loss-leaders", products that do not make profit, but encourage customers to purchase and hopefully encourage them to purchase additional products. A practice that is now widespread on the Internet is to give away free software, either for a limited period or with limited functionality, in the hope that customers will purchase additional software from the same firm. An example of a firm that successfully adopted this approach is Netscape, which gained 70% of the market by giving away its Internet browser software free.

This is not to say that all e-businesses enjoy first-mover advantages and that the winner inevitably takes all: first, the initial product or service offered may be imperfect and so never catch on; second, the market may not be ready for the product, however good; third, second-movers may be able to gain an advantage by offering an innovative product or service that outweighs any advantages that the first-mover may have; and, fourth, second-movers may be able to learn from the mistakes of first-movers. This question about sustainability of competitive advantage will be discussed further in Chapter 7.

Open source communities

An increasingly common phenomenon is the growth of open source communities using the Internet for software development (Lerner and Tirole, 2002). Open source describes software whose source code may be freely modified and redistributed with few restrictions. The best known examples are the Linux operating system and the Apache web server. These were developed by loosely organized *ad hoc* communities of programmers from all over the world who have never met face to face, but share code and ideas through the Internet. Since the developers of such software are also key users, such communities benefit from increasing returns on both the supply and demand side.

Mini-case: SquirrelMail

SquirrelMail (Figure 5.13) is an open-source webmail package written in PHP4 which is freely distributed and widely used in many academic institutions. The project grew from the need of the developers to access email and address books from anywhere in the world. After reviewing several open source projects, they realized that they were going to need to do some fairly major customization, so the decision was made to write a new package. The software includes built-in pure support for the Internet Message Access Protocol (IMAP) and Simple Mail Transfer Protocol (SMTP) protocols, and all pages render in pure HTML 4.0 (with no JavaScript required) for maximum compatibility across browsers. It has all the functionality you would want from an email client, including strong Multipurpose Internet Mail Extension (MIME) support, address books and folder manipulation.

Figure 5.13   SquirrelMail

(reproduced with permission from SquirrelMail).

Digital products and services

Although examples of companies, such as Dell and FedEx, which have achieved significant cost savings in physical production and distribution by using e-business are impressive, the potential for cost savings is even more significant in the case of digital products. These types of goods are often characterized by a distinctive cost structure: the cost of producing the first copy is high, but the cost of reproducing subsequent copies is relatively low. For example, a software publisher may spend hundreds of thousands of pounds on the development of the software, but once the first copy of the software has been produced the cost of reproducing another copy is usually only negligible.

Digital product goods also differ from most other products in another way. If worldwide sales of automobiles increase substantially beyond the limit of existing production capacity, Ford and other automobile manufacturers will need to invest heavily in new plant, machinery and people, significantly pushing up the cost of producing an additional unit. This need arises less often with most digital products where the reproduction capacity requirements are lower. Because of this cost structure digital products are particularly susceptible to vast economies of scale: the more you produce, the lower the average cost of production; this is one reason software giant Microsoft with its overwhelming dominance in PC operating systems and business applications enjoys gross profit margins of 92%.

The large proportion of fixed costs is not the only thing distinctive about the cost structure. The fixed costs and the variable costs themselves have unusual characteristics. The fixed costs are also often sunk costs, which are not recoverable if production is halted. Investment costs in an office building, factory or machinery can be partially recovered if the project is cancelled. However, if a software project is cancelled, it is unlikely that the cost of the script or the sets can be recovered.

The unusual cost structure for digital products – high fixed costs, low variable costs and high sunk costs – has implications for competitive strategies. In traditional industries, adopting a cost leadership strategy requires the use of supply chain management, workflow analysis and other tools to cut costs of parts, assembly and distribution. With digital products, unit costs of production are negligible, so such techniques as supply chain management usually do little to reduce initial costs. Since the variable costs are low, information can be used over and over again with little additional cost. For example, popular television shows and films can be repeated for years at little additional cost. Therefore, with digital products the best way to reduce average cost is to increase sales volume. (We shall see later various strategies that can be used to achieve this.)

Apart from the cost structure, digital products also have some other characteristics that are of interest – manipulability, durability and ease of sharing (Choi et al., 1997).

Product differentiation

The ease of manipulating digital data allows different versions of the product to be easily produced to appeal to different types of customers. For example, different versions of software can be readily produced for novice and expert users. The increasingly wide range of digital platforms and formats also enables the same product to be differentiated according to the format (e.g., CD-ROM, DVD, etc.). Shapiro and Varian (1999) identify several ways in which different versions of digital products can be produced, including the following:

- *Features* The most obvious type of personalization is to offer products with different features to different customer groups. For example, different users of software may have different needs and have different price sensitivities, so can be served by different versions. The Dragon dictation software with which this text was written is offered in three versions at three prices: a standard version, an enhanced version and a professional version. A light user who only occasionally requires dictation and who only requires basic word-processing features can purchase the standard version, while heavy users who require more sophisticated features can purchase the enhanced and professional version at higher prices. Dell, which was cited earlier as an example of faster processing, has also used e-commerce to enable a much more personalized offering. Not only are customers to receive their orders more quickly but they are also able to order a PC with specifications tailored to their needs. By only assembling the PC on receiving the customer specifications, Dell is not only able to save on warehousing costs but can also deliver a product that more closely fits customer requirements.

- *User interface*   One common way of differentiating software is by developing different interfaces for different users. For example, Adobe offers software with a simple interface for home users and a version with a complex interface for professional designers.
- *Comprehensiveness*   In other cases, detail and comprehensiveness of information is a crucial dimension. For example, researchers and students at universities may need and wish to have access to the most comprehensive dictionaries, encyclopaedias and databases, while home users may only need abridged versions.
- *Image resolution*   In the case of digital products that include images, different versions can be developed that offer different image resolution. For example, this is quite common with pornographic sites on the Internet, which provide "thumbnail" versions of their photographs for free in order to encourage users to pay for the ability to view and download higher resolution images.
- *Manipulation*   Another important dimension that can form the basis for versioning is the capability for users to store, duplicate, print or otherwise manipulate the information. For example, Adobe makes its Reader freely available from its website, which allows users to read .pdf files, but users who wish to edit .pdf documents must purchase the complete package.
- *Annoyance*   As well as differentiating by adding features, in some cases it may be useful to differentiate by removing certain features. For example, subscribers to Silicon Investor also get an added benefit – the ability to switch off the advertisements posted throughout the site.
- *Delay*   The instantaneous transaction processing possible with e-commerce also allows greater scope for differentiation according to time. Postal and delivery services have for a long time priced differently according to the speed of delivery services. For example, FedEx offers two classes of service, the premium class that promises delivery before 10 a.m. and the next-day service that only promises delivery some time in the next day. The same pricing strategy can be applied to electronic information. For example, a provider of stockmarket information may offer different levels of service depending on how up-to-date the information is. Some customers who require up-to-the-minute information may be willing to pay more than other customers who only require weekly updates. Taking time and price sensitivity to the extreme are last-minute auction sites (e.g., lastminute.com) which offer late bookings for airline tickets, cruises and holidays at highly discounted prices.

- *Convenience* Restricting the time or place at which a customer can access information is another way of differentiating a service. America Online, for example, offers different monthly membership plans based on convenience, ranging from unlimited access for heavy users to 3 h of connection time per month for users who use the service solely for email. Similarly, British Telecom offers different schemes for Internet access ranging from 24-h unlimited access to access only at off-peak times.
- *Support* It may also be possible to differentiate according to the level of support provided. An example is Freeserve which is able to offer free Internet access in the UK partly by not offering helpline support as a standard entitlement of membership, but by charging for this.

Bundling and subscription

The benefits of product differentiation need to be weighed against the benefits of bundling. In the physical world, information products are often bundled and sold by subscription; this is convenient for producers because precise information about consumer demand for each component or between components is not required, simplifying pricing and payment decisions. For example, a newspaper contains a whole range of news and information, only some of which will interest a particular individual, but by bundling together an appropriate mix newspaper publishers are able to appeal to a broad section of the market with one common product.

However, the online world offers consumers additional benefits: interactivity, customization, search, links, and storage and reproduction mechanisms. For example, an online newspaper may be linked to computer programs that input and analyse news items for investment decisions, allow emails to friends and so on. Digital television programmes provide yet more benefits. For example, broadcasters can charge consumers directly for programmes, instead of relying on advertisers as in pay TV channels and pay-per-view services. Furthermore, advertising may be separated from content and sold as a separate product. As a result of the technology allowing usage to be monitored more precisely, it is also possible to unbundle some products and charge individuals only for that part they use, so-called micro-products.

In order to offer micro-products, micro-payment systems may also be required. For example, it is not presently possible using coventional credit cards to pay for items less than 1 cent or 1 penny. In particular, micro-payment systems may be required where there is a need to assure product quality. In the case of a long-term subscription of bundled digital products, the reputation of the seller may be sufficient to guarantee quality. However, reputation needs to be developed after repeated purchases. If sellers know that the market will end soon or they are short-run players, they may find it profitable to cheat by selling low-quality products at high-quality prices. This problem is magnified if buyers are required to commit to a long-term subscription or to pay for a large bundle of unknown quality. Micro-payments would allow shorter subscriptions or smaller items to be paid for, reducing the risk for consumers.

Mini-case: Newgenpay

Newgenpay (Figure 5.14), a spin-off from technology that was developed in the IBM research lab, was founded in December, 2000 and is headquartered in Tel Aviv. It focuses on developing core payment technology that provides the infrastructure for creating an interoperable network of independent payment service providers (PSPs), such as telecommunications companies, mobile operators, banks, credit card companies, ISPs and portals. The company's Valuto System provides an open and extendible platform for developing multiple payment applications, including wireless payments, micro-payments and person-to-person money transfer. It is an implementation of the common markup for micro-payment per-fee-links specification agreed by W3C (World Wide Web Consortium).

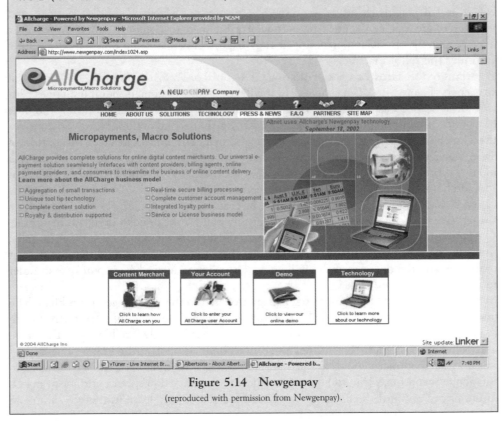

Figure 5.14 Newgenpay
(reproduced with permission from Newgenpay).

Durable goods monopoly

The durability or non-degradability of digital products can lead to the so-called "durable goods monopoly" problem; this was first noted by Ronald Coase, who also developed the idea of transaction costs. Coase published this in a paper over 25 years ago (Coase, 1972),

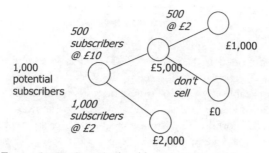

Figure 5.15   Coase's durable monopoly problem.

but it is still highly relevant for today's e-businesses. Where a good is durable and purchasers are not constrained or particularly inclined to purchase immediately, they may be tempted to delay purchasing if they expect prices to come down in the future. Consider the following case.

A music store faces a choice of offering CDs at £10 or £2 in a market of 1,000 potential customers (Figure 5.15). If it charges £10 it will attract 500 customers, but if it charges £2 it will attract 1,000 customers. At first glance it might seem that the first option would be best, since it will bring in £5,000 versus £2,000 for the second option. However, consider the choice after the first 500 customers have joined. The firm then faces the option of charging £2 to attract the remaining customers who were unwilling to pay £10 and so bring in an additional £1,000 or of not reducing charges, thereby losing this income. Logically, it should choose the first option, to maximize profit from the service. The paradox noted by Coase is that since this action is predictable by customers, a customer who does not have a strong reason to join immediately should logically wait for the price to drop before joining.

Many firms face similar problems when introducing a new product or service. Initially, they may need to charge high prices to recoup their costs, but buyers will not purchase at that price and the only way prices will come down is if sufficient buyers purchase in order to allow economies of scale.

A number of possible solutions have been proposed to the durable goods problem. The first is to discount the price heavily initially to pre-empt the possibility of further price reductions. Obviously, the success of this strategy depends on the credibility of the move and belief by customers that further price reductions are not forthcoming. The second solution is to contract to hold back any unsold stock, thereby removing the second stage in the above scenario. A third solution is to allow future price drops, but contract to match future prices. A fourth is effectively not to sell the good but to lease it, thereby taking on the risk of price drops from the customer.

Two other solutions, which may not be so obvious, are to make the good less durable and to destroy any unsold stock. The first solution is quite common among computer software firms, who effectively make goods less durable by bringing out new models and versions on a regular basis. Although old hardware and software can often be used for considerable periods, long after new models have been introduced, they will often not be compatible with the latest systems; this encourages customers to continually buy the latest hardware or software and discourages any waiting since the product will soon be out of date.

The second method has been used often by entertainment companies. For example, Disney will make video versions of its films available for a limited period and take any unsold stock off the market; this also deters waiting, since the product can only be bought by a certain date. An example of an Internet firm that has adopted this strategy is Cahoot, an Internet bank in the UK. It offered preferential deals to new customers, but also limited the number of customers who could sign up. Although this was primarily to prevent overload of the system, it also had a secondary effect such that the bank was overwhelmed by new applications within a few days.

Shared digital products

Apart from the ease of manipulation and durability, another characteristic of digital products is the ease of sharing it with other people. As shown in Chapter 1, one of the earliest functions of the Internet was to allow information sharing; this has a number of consequences for sellers of digital products. For example, a group of consumers may form a club to buy a product if the value of the product exceeds each individual's share of the price and the accompanying transaction costs, such as the waiting time for one's turn. An example of a sharing mechanism is a library that allows consumers who are not willing to pay for a book to still use it.

A library book is known as a club good as opposed to a pure public good or a pure private good. Unlike a pure public good, whose optimum number of users is all consumers in the market, and a pure private good, whose optimum number of users is one, the optimum number of users in club goods is determined by the marginal condition that the benefit of adding a marginal member must be equal to the associated cost. The group's benefit may increase by adding a member (association benefits), the user cost may increase (congestion effects) or the production cost or purchasing price may be lowered (economies of scale).

Association benefits are common in social clubs, and a similar benefit is observed in pure private goods, such as computer software as discussed earlier, also known as a network effect. Congestion effects are evident in the example of library books, where more members create more waiting for a turn to borrow. Economies of scale come into effect by reducing the cost per member of purchasing a book.

Sharing arrangements are common when a product is used only once and the quality of the product is not degraded as in the case of digital goods. However, if a product is used more than once, consumers may prefer to buy it outright, especially if the sharing cost is high enough to justify the purchase price, because the total cost of an alternative to buying includes transaction costs. For instance, casual readers may borrow a book from a library; however, if they plan to read a book more than once, they will often prefer to buy it outright, since borrowing from a library requires waiting and only allows use of the book for a limited time. The sum totals of these transaction costs and the sale price will determine whether the consumer buys or shares. For digital libraries, both of these transaction costs may be negligible unless restrictions for checkout and returns are imposed.

There may be circumstances where the seller prefers to share or rent the product, even where the valuation of the product exceeds the offer price; this is usually in order to control consumer arbitrage. The first-sale doctrine allows consumers to do whatever they want with a product after they buy it, including reselling, renting, leasing or disposing of the product, while copyright protection only applies to copying or reproducing the content of the book, not to selling the original copy. In contrast, renting or leasing does not change the ownership of the book, and the owner of the book (the seller) may specify certain rules regarding its use. For example, software licensing may not only control how many persons can use a program but also how often it is used in a given time period.

Sharing as an alternative to purchase may increase on the Internet, as various software vendors have come up with software to facilitate charging for data that are freely shared; this has been termed "superdistribution". Programs, such as Digital Containers (*www. digitalcontainers.com*) and IBM's Electronic Media Management software, "wrap" around any digital file and control its use. The basic idea is simple. The creator of a digital item makes it widely available online, but each digital item contains a piece of code that both limits access to authorized users and is able to collect charges. Copying is always free, but use results in the collection of the fee. Superdistribution prices may be fixed at the time of distribution or be based on the currently prevailing charge.

Congestion pricing

As the Internet has been transformed from being a club good, primarily for academic researchers, into a public good, one of the growing problems is congestion. Although bandwidth capacity is increasing dramatically, it is still being stripped by growth in demand.

The result could be a "Tragedy of the Commons". This classic scenario from game theory arises when too many users exploit a resource, resulting in its destruction. To see how this might arise consider the case where two shepherds have the right to graze their sheep on a common, which being of poor quality can only support one flock of sheep. The pay-offs to each are shown in Figure 5.16. By not using the common, either shepherd only

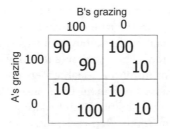

Figure 5.16   Tragedy of the Commons.

gets a return of 10%; this is well below the return each could get by grazing the common alone (100%) and also below what each could get by sharing the common (90%). The best option in this scenario for each shepherd (i.e., one that maximizes their pay-off) is to graze the commons. The result is that eventually the commons will be overgrazed.

Two basic schemes have been proposed to manage the demand: the first is to increase capacity at bottlenecks, such as routers, regional networks, Internet access points, modem banks and local telephone lines; and the second approach is to adopt some sort of pricing scheme to limit demand.

Parallels can be found in non-digital networks (e.g., a highway: Choi et al., 1997). Suppose all drivers make one car journey to work per day, but that some have the option of making the journey at non-congested times. Typically, travel time increases as traffic volume increases and increases at a rapid rate when traffic volume nears the capacity of the highway. In deciding whether to travel during the congested period, a driver compares the incremental benefit of travel with this incremental cost in time and makes the journey if and only if the former exceeds the latter.

From the point of view of the entire community, however, the social cost of travel time is the sum of every driver's private time costs. If a driver decides to make an extra trip, the extra travel time is born by all drivers, not just the driver making the extra trip. In order to maximize the social benefits, ideally only those drivers whose incremental benefit from travelling during the congested period exceeds the incremental social cost should do so and the others should postpone their travel to uncongested periods. One economic solution would be to set the price of highway access during the congested period equal to the incremental social cost, called the optimal congestion toll. One reason such a toll system has not been introduced for physical highways has been the cost of administering such a system. However, with electronic highways, it is possible to compute and assess charges with negligible administrative cost. A number of schemes have been proposed:

- *Static priority pricing* The first scheme is to set socially optimal fixed prices for each service. This scheme aims to maximize user benefits over time by setting prices such that users will voluntarily select the socially optimal priority. These priority prices are "static" in that they do not vary with the dynamic state of the network. There will be times when the network is badly congested and high-priority users will be paying too little.
- *Dynamic optimal pricing* In this scheme, the user would be presented with a menu of options for Internet access, including the monetary cost and (when relevant) expected throughput time for each option. The options would specify a priority class and possibly contingency options, such as "submit the service request when the cost falls below $x." The user would then select the most preferred option. A personalized smart agent could automate the user's decision process based on previously specified user preferences. Frequently updated price and time information would come from the user's access provider. In addition, smart agent software could serve this function, gathering information from posted prices of transport providers and network congestion status reports.

The smart market approach

MacKie-Mason and Varian (1995) have proposed a different approach to implementing optimal congestion pricing. Instead of using econometric methods to estimate the social cost of congestion, they propose a mechanism in which the users have incentives to state their true willingness to pay for faster service; this would be accomplished by a smart market mechanism.

Each person would submit a monetary bid for the right to have their job processed. Submitted bids are ordered from the largest to the smallest, and the jobs are processed in this order. The price paid by every processed job is the bid of the first job not processed during the allotted time interval. If all jobs are processed, the price is zero. It is optimal for every user to bid the true value of the job, no matter what the other users do.

The problem with the smart market solution is that it assumes the following:

- All potential users care only about whether their job is done or when, but not both.
- All potential users are present at the auction.
- And the value of the job is not contingent on any other market.

All these assumptions would rarely be valid in the real world. In theory an accounting system could be devised that overcomes these problems. However, so far this scheme has proved impractical.

Connection-only and flat rate pricing

Because of the problems in implementing the above methods of pricing, the most common forms of pricing on the Internet are a combination of connection-only and flat rate pricing. The connection-only fee is usually based on the bandwidth of the user's connection for a contracted period of time, with discounted rates for longer term contracts.

In addition to these fixed connection fees, some providers charge a variable fee based on active connection time. Online service providers usually charge hourly fees if the user exceeds the maximum hours allowed monthly. In contrast to connection time charging, flat rate pricing consists of a fee for a set bandwidth that does not vary with the level of actual bandwidth usage nor the current state of congestion.

The advantage of connection-only and flat rate pricing is simplicity. However, neither are entirely accurate measures of bandwidth usage. For example, they do not discriminate between transmission of a real-time video session and transmission of an email. Therefore, they may not reflect the true social cost. As yet, pricing of the Internet is still the subject of considerable debate, and a socially optimal solution has yet to be found.

Mini-case study: AltaVista aborts unmetered access in UK

Unlike the USA and some other countries, in the UK Internet surfers are charged per minute for local calls. In March, 2000 the search engine and ISP AltaVista promised to change the way people used the Internet in the UK by launching an unmetered Internet service. Anyone signing up for the deal would pay a low annual or monthly fee for their Internet access and would never have to pay call charges again. The new service was welcomed by Prime Minister Tony Blair and the telecoms regulator Oftel as a key step toward broadening Internet access in the UK. However, just 6 months later in August, despite signing up some 274,000 prospective customers, the company was forced to abort its plan after failing to come to an agreement with BT. In a statement AltaVista said the business model for the service was unsustainable due to BT's delay in providing flat rate circuits.

In turn BT blamed AltaVista for launching a product before agreeing network provider set-up. BT controls the local phone exchanges in Britain and did not offer a wholesale unmetered service to ISPs when AltaVista announced its plan. BT, after pressure from Oftel, has since made available an unmetered access service to ISPs, known as flat rate Internet access call origin, or FRIACO (details available at *www. oftel.gov.uk/ competition/fria500.htm*); this allows ISPs to offer end-user access without a per-minute charge at evenings and weekends. BT's own ISP offers the same service.

Analysts blamed AltaVista for not working out the full cost implications before announcing the service in March. There was a similar response from Oftel, which noted that AltaVista chose to launch before wholesale products were available. David Edmonds, Director General of Oftel is reported to have said, "It is up to AltaVista, as other commercial companies, to make sure that before they launch a product they have a sound business plan to support it."

Summary

This chapter applied some standard microeconomic analyses to e-business in order to undertand how and why e-business has had such a significant economic impact in many industries and in order to lay the foundation for future chapters on creating new business models.

First, it was shown how the Internet and other e-business technologies have altered the behaviour of existing markets or created new markets by:

- Providing better market information.
- Lowering production and distribution costs.
- Lowering transaction costs for buying and selling.
- Allowing more precise targeting of customers.
- Allowing the creation of virtual communities.

Second, it was shown how the characteristics of digital products – manipulability, durability and ease of sharing – not only create particular issues in pricing but also allow new methods of pricing, such as micro-products and micro-payments. Finally, some economic solutions to the problem of congestion on the Internet were discussed.

References

Arthur, W.B. (1996). Increasing returns and the new world of business. *Harvard Business Review*, July/August, 100–9.

Chen, S. (1997). A new paradigm for knowledge-based competition: Building an industry through knowledge sharing. *Technology Analysis and Strategic Management*, **9**(4), 437–52.

Choi, S.Y., Stahl, D.O. and Whinston, A.B. (1997). *The Economics of Electronic Commerce*. Macmillan, Indianapolis, IN.

Coase, R.H. (1931). The nature of the firm. *Economica*, **4**, 386–405

Coase, R. (1972). Durability and monopoly. *Journal of Law and Economics*, **15**, 143–9.

Economist, The (2000). Internet economics: A thinker's guide (April 1, pp. 77–9).

Grover, V. and Malhotra, M. (1997) Business process re-engineering: A tutorial on the concept, evolution, method, technology and application. *Journal of Operations Management*, **15**(3), 193–213.

Hammer, M. and Champy, J. (1993). *Reengineering the Corporation: A Manifesto for Business Revolution*. HarperCollins, London.

Kaplan, S. and Sawhney, M. (2000). E-hubs: The new B2B marketplaces. *Harvard Business Review*, May/June, 97–103.

Lerner, J. and Tirole, J. (2002). The simple economics of open source (NBER Working Paper Series). Available at *http://www.nber.org/papers/w7600*

MacKie-Mason, J. and Varian, H. (1995). Pricing the Internet. In: B. Kahin and J. Keller (eds), *Public Access to the Internet* (pp. 269–314). MIT Press, Cambridge, MA.

Odlyzko, A. (2003). Privacy, economics and price discrimination on the Internet. In: N. Sadeh (ed.), *ICEC2003: Fifth International Conference on Electronic Commerce* (ACM, pp. 355–66). Available at *http://www.dtc.umn.edu/~odlyzko/doc/privacy.economics.pdf*

Scott Morton, F., Zettelmeyer, F. and Silva-Risso, J. (2002). Consumer information and price discrimination: Does the Internet affect the pricing of new cars to women and minorities? Available at *http://papers.ssrn.com/abstract=288527*

Shapiro, C. and Varian, H.R. (1999). *Information Rules: A Strategic Guide to the Network Economy*. Harvard Business School Press, Boston.

Strader, T.J. and Straw, M.J. (1999). Consumer cost differences for traditional and Internet markets, Internet Research: Electronic Networking Applications and Policy, **9**(2), 82–92.

Subramaniam, C. and Shaw, M.J. (2002). A study of the value and impact of B2B e-commerce: The case of Web-based procurement. *International Journal of Electronic Commerce*, **6**(4), 19–40.

Wells, M.G. (2000). Business process re-engineering implementations using Internet technology. *Business Process Management Journal*, **6**(2), 163–85.

Zeng, M. and Reinartz, W. (2003). Beyond online search: The road to profitability. *California Management Review*, **45**(2), 107–30.

Further reading

Vulkan, N. (2003). *The Economics of E-Commerce: A Strategic Guide to Understanding and Designing the Online Marketplace*. Princeton University Press, Princeton, NJ.

Key concepts

- Auction sites
- B2B hubs
- Bid sites
- Bundling of information products
- Business process re-engineering (BPR)
- Club good
- Complementary products
- Critical mass
- Discriminatory pricing
- Durable goods monopoly problem
- Enterprise Resource Planning (ERP)
- First-mover advantages
- Fixed costs
- Law of diminishing returns
- Law of increasing returns
- Micro-payments
- Micro-products
- Operational efficiencies
- Personalized markets
- Positive and negative feedback loops
- Public good
- Private good
- Transaction costs
- Variable costs
- Virtual communities
- Winner takes all

Self-assessment questions

1 Give examples of how e-commerce can reduce the following types of cost:
   - Production.
   - Distribution.
   - Transaction.
2 Which types of cost are likely to be higher for consumers in electronic commerce?
3 Give examples of different types of B2B exchanges.
4 Give examples of how e-commerce enables greater product differentiation.
5 Describe the various types of discriminatory pricing and how these can be achieved in e-commerce.
6 Explain the differences between private, public and club goods and give an example of each in e-commerce.
7 Explain the law of increasing returns.
8 Give examples of different Internet pricing schemes.

Discussion questions

1 How is e-commerce changing costs in your industry?
2 What would be the impact of micro-payments in your industry?
3 Will e-commerce lead to lower consumer prices generally?
4 Should unlimited sharing of digital products, such as software, be allowed?
5 How should Internet access be priced?
6 Does the Internet advantage or disadvantage minorities in purchasing?

ANALYSING THE INDUSTRY
IMPACTS OF E-BUSINESS

Introduction

In the previous chapter we looked at how e-business technologies are changing the fundamental economics of some businesses. In this chapter we will examine in more detail how changing the economics of an industry impacts industry structures.

First, we will examine two effects that have been noted for some time with previous information technologies: changing the balance of power within an industry and better co-ordination of activities within and between firms. Then, we will examine three other effects acting directly on industry value chains which have come to prominence as a result of the significant changes in the economics of business brought about by the Internet: disintermediation, disintegration and digital convergence of the value chain. Although these effects have been observed before, they have become more significant as a result of the specific benefits brought about by global networking.

Changing industry power

One of the best known frameworks for industry analysis is Porter's (1980) five-forces model. Porter identifies five key forces that determine profitability in an industry:

- Threat of new entrants into the sector.
- Threat of a substitute product or service.
- The bargaining power of the buyers.
- The bargaining power of the suppliers.
- Competitive rivalry among existing firms in the industry.

Threat of new entrants

The threat of new entrants relates to the ease with which a new company or a company in a different industry can enter a given industry. Barriers to entry into a particular market include the need for capital, knowledge and skills. For example, in the car-manufacturing sector barriers to entry include the need to design and develop a new model, build a car assembly plant, contract a large number of component suppliers and sign up a dealer network. Gaining entry into the software industry, in contrast, is much easier as there is not the same need for investment in product development or large-scale production facilities. IT systems can also create a barrier to entry. For example, some airlines have in the past created significant barriers to entry in airline ticketing by making substantial investments in computerized reservation systems. This experience and investment can be difficult for a new entrant to match. However, one of the features of the Internet is that it allows new entrants into existing markets without the need to match the large infra-structure investment of the existing players. Therefore, competition from new entrants is likely to increase in many industries. For example, the Internet has allowed online book retailers such as Amazon.com to set up in competition with traditional bookshops without the need to invest in a chain of high street bookstores.

Threat of substitution

In some sectors, e-business has changed the nature of the product sufficiently to be classified as a substitute product. Substitution is a threat to existing players where a new product becomes available that supplies the same function as the existing product or service. Classic examples are the substitution of the horse-drawn carriage by the motor car or the replacement of mechanical adding machines by the computer. To survive, existing players must then either keep their product up to date or else become major players in supplying the substitute product. As seen in previous chapters, many new products and services have been created that could partially, if not completely, replace existing ones (e.g., online music and e-mail).

Bargaining power of buyers

The third major force that needs to be considered is the power of buyers. Where there is an excess of supply over demand or where there are few buyers relative to suppliers, the buyers may be in a stronger bargaining position than the seller. The bargaining power of buyers may increase as the Internet increases the choice of potential suppliers and makes available more information on them. On the other hand, the Internet could also allow firms in the industry to identify more potential buyers, thereby reducing the power of buyers. The outcome will depend on which force is stronger.

Bargaining power of suppliers

Suppliers are in the same position to firms in the industry as firms in the industry are to their buyers. Therefore, the Internet can have similar effects as described above, either increasing or decreasing their power, depending on how the technology is applied.

Competitive rivalry between existing players

The final force is competition between existing players in the market; this is likely to increase as e-business generally increases efficiency in the industry, reducing production, distribution and transaction costs, and increases the efficiency of the supply chain.

Interestingly, Porter himself argues that the Internet will not be disruptive to most existing industries and established companies and that, as all companies embrace Internet technology, the value of Internet technology as a source of advantage will become less and less important (Porter, 2001). This view is challenged by others who argue that the Internet is creating a new economic structure and new ways of competing (Tapscott, 2001).

Mini-case study: Increasing customer power

The British are usually reluctant to complain about bad service; however, that may change with the new Internet sites that give people a public platform to complain about service they have received from companies and other organizations. For example,

Figure 6.1   dooyoo.co.uk

a German company, dooyoo.de, has launched a UK version of their site that allows people to review products and services ranging from holidays to household goods and get rewarded for their contributions. At dooyoo.co.uk (Figure 6.1), reviewers get 250 dooyoo miles for writing an opinion, 50 miles each time a member reads your opinion and 10 miles each time you rate another member's opinion (1,000 dooyoo miles are worth £1 and can be exchanged for cash or vouchers or a charitable donation). Top reviewers are rewarded by being listed in a hall of fame and through dooyoo miles.

Value system analysis

A second model from Porter (1985) which is popularly used to analyse industries is the value chain. Porter's model is essentially concerned with reducing cost and maximizing value added from the internal activities of the company. E-business can assist in this objective in all activities of the value chain.

The three primary activities of a product process are:

- *Inbound logistics* Receiving supplies, storing them and making them available to operations as required.
- *Operations* The production process.
- *Outbound logistics* Taking delivery of the final products of the company, storing them and distributing them to the customer.

To these basic primary activities Porter adds two further primary activities:

- *Marketing and sales* Finding out the requirements of potential customers and informing them of the products and services that can be offered.
- *Service* Any requirement for installation or advice before delivery and, then, after-sales service once the transaction is completed.

To support these primary functions there will be a company infrastructure that performs a number of support activities. Porter classifies these activities as:

- *Procurement* The function of finding suppliers of the materials required as inputs to the operations of the organization. Procurement is responsible for negotiating quality supplies at an acceptable price and with reliable delivery.
- *Technology development* The organization needs to update its production processes, train staff and to manage innovation to ensure that its products and its overall range of goods and services remain competitive.
- *Human resource management* The recruitment, training and personnel management of the people who work for the organization.

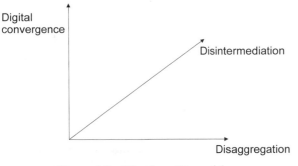

Figure 6.2   The three Ds model.

- *Firm infrastructure*   The overall management of the company, including planning and accountancy.

As seen in previous chapters, e-business can improve the efficiency at all stages within the value chain (e.g., in procurement, logistics, operations, etc.). However, it can also have an even more significant impact external to the value chain. The value chain within a company can be extended to include value chains of other companies in a "value system". The overall competitive advantage of an organization is not just dependent on the efficiency of the company and the quality of its products but also on that of its suppliers, partners, wholesalers and retailers. E-business can affect links the firm may have with these organizations, such as jointly shared information networks, and have a direct impact on the value chains of these organizations.

The three Ds model

There are three main effects of e-business on the value system, which for convenience can be remembered as the "three Ds" (Figure 6.2).

First, as shown in Chapter 3, in many markets intermediaries, or middlemen, are being replaced, or "disintermediated". Second, firms in many industries are finding themselves being unravelled, or radically "disaggregated". Last, as outlined in Chapter 1, "digital convergence" is breaking down barriers between many industries that provide the infrastructure for electronic commerce, such as telecommunications, computing, electronics and entertainment.

Disintermediation/Reintermediation

The first effect on the value system arises from changes in the economics of the supply chain (Figure 6.3). In many industries it is common for manufacturers or suppliers to

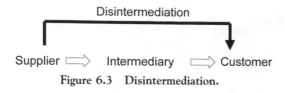

Figure 6.3   **Disintermediation.**

distribute their goods through a middleman or intermediary. There could be many reasons for going through a middleman, but the most common include:

- Lack of financial resources to carry out direct marketing.
- Insufficient sales to make dedicated channel profitable.
- Information and contacts that the intermediary provides.
- Experience that the intermediary has.

Kotler (1997, p. 530)

It was shown in the last chapter how electronic commerce can lower distribution and transaction costs. If so, some of the need for intermediaries may be reduced. As outlined in the previous chapter, e-commerce can significantly reduce the cost of distribution in many industries, particularly in the case of information-based products; these include products, such as software and news services, which can be digitized and distributed at much lower cost via the Internet than in a hard copy format. Many software and information providers now distribute updates via the Internet not only saving both reproduction and postage costs but also removing the need in many cases for intermediaries. There is less incentive to go to a software retailer for update diskettes or to go to a newsagent for the latest news when these can be downloaded straight from the Internet at lower cost.

Disintermediation may also occur in other businesses that do not sell information, but rely heavily on information, such as financial services and travel agents. For example, one study estimates that the distribution costs for a typical round trip airline ticket are $16 via Orbitz (an online booking system) compared with $26 via a travel agency (Global Aviation Associates, 2003). The threat to traditional travel agents is clear. Unless they can provide added value either to the airlines or to the customer to justify the additional cost, in addition to the traditional service of finding out which airline seats are available, they are unlikely to survive.

Although the scope for disintermediation is greater in the case of information products, it may also occur in the supply of physical goods. In this case the supplier may still have significant shipping and handling costs, so it will need to find significant cost savings elsewhere. For example, Dell has managed to do this successfully on the Internet by linking their online ordering with innovations in their supply chain, which allow reduced stockholding costs as well as customized assembly of PCs.

Mini-case study: Jane Brook Estate

The Jane Brook Estate (Figure 6.4) is located in the luscious Swan River Valley, home to more than 30 wineries, 20 km north-east of Perth in Western Australia. Table grapes were first planted at Jane Brook in 1913, and the Estate developed a reputation over the years for producing excellent red table wine.

In 1972 David and Beverley Atkinson purchased the property and changed to production of a wider range and higher quality wines. The vineyards have been replanted with premium grape varieties, a laboratory for grape and wine analysis has been set up and the winemaking facilities re-equipped with stainless steel tanks, refrigeration plants and new oak storage.

Jane Brook Estate Wines have traditionally sold their wines through distributors in western and eastern Australia and through wine importers in Japan, Singapore, Malaysia, the UK and the USA. However, keen to explore new technology and marketing channels, in June, 1995 Jane Brook became the first Australian winery to have a home page on the World Wide Web and now regularly takes orders online from customers in Australia, Japan, Malaysia, Singapore, France, the UK and the USA.

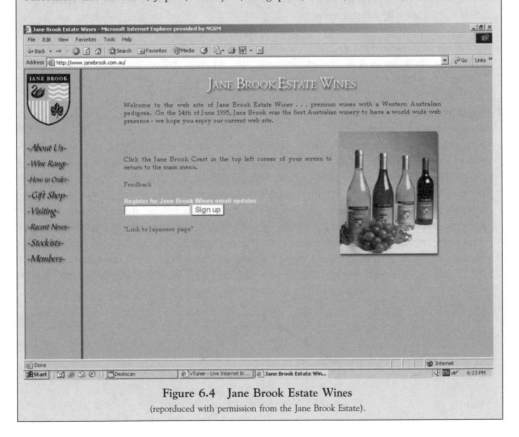

Figure 6.4   Jane Brook Estate Wines
(reporduced with permission from the Jane Brook Estate).

Transaction cost theory

Transaction cost theory was introduced in the last chapter, and arguments for disintermediation are often based on transaction costs. Lower transaction costs using a direct electronic link, it is argued, will favour direct marketing over transactions via an intermediary.

The disintermediation hypothesis (Figure 6.5) rests on two key assumptions (Sarkar et al., 1995). These are:

1. Electronic commerce will reduce all transaction costs to zero (i.e. become insignificant).
2. Transactions are atomic (i.e., unitary and not further decomposable into smaller units).

Assumption 1, that all transaction costs will tend to zero, is problematic, first of all from a practical viewpoint. There are still transaction costs incurred in ordering goods online, although lower in many cases than offline. Second, if the producer adopts a network organization, then it is quite likely that market co-ordination services, along with many other services, are likely to be outsourced and will result in more, rather than fewer intermediaries in the value system.

If this assumption is relaxed so that different classes of transactions are affected in different ways (assumption 1″), then a very different outcome is possible.

Disintermediation is only one of the possibilities predicted on the basis of assumption 1″. Other possibilities (Figure 6.6) are:

1. *Supplemented direct market* Existing direct marketers like Dell use the Internet to supplement their activities.
2. *Network-based transactions* These reinforce an existing channel structure when firms use electronic commerce to supplement the economies of scale, scope and knowledge that arise as a result of the physical technologies involved; this may also arise when the network permits existing intermediaries to create economies of scale, scope and knowledge which arise for supporting information or risk management services. Examples include credit card companies who might use the Internet to offer money back guarantees for purchases made over the network.
3. *Cybermediaries* These use the Internet to reduce the producer → intermediary or the intermediary → consumer transaction costs. Cybermediaries are simply intermediaries

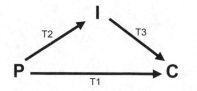

Figure 6.5 Disintermediation hypothesis
(I = intermediary; P = producer; C = customer; T1–T3 = transactions).

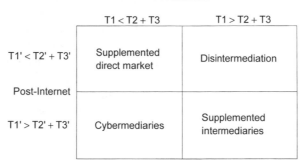

Figure 6.6 Other possibilities.

that take advantage of the Internet to create these economies of scale and scope by aggregating transactions.

Assumption 2, which characterizes intermediaries' roles generally as co-ordination, is also problematic as it underestimates the services provided by an intermediary. For example, intermediaries may benefit consumers by providing assistance in search and evaluation, needs assessment and product matching, risk reduction and product distribution/delivery. Intermediaries may also benefit producers by creating and disseminating product information and creating product awareness, influencing consumer purchases, providing customer information, reducing exposure to risk and reducing costs of distribution through economies of scale. Finally, another common intermediary function is to balance and integrate the sometimes-competing needs of producers and consumers.

In other words, it is likely that there will still be a place for intermediaries in electronic commerce, although they may be new ones. Some of the new intermediaries that are emerging include the following:

- *Portals* These provide a gateway to services on the Web (e.g., AOL).
- *Directories* Directory service intermediaries help consumers find producers by categorizing websites and providing structured menus to facilitate navigation (e.g., general directories like Yahoo!, specialized directories created by an individual interested in a topic).
- *Search services* In contrast to the directories, search sites (e.g., Lycos and Infoseek) provide users with the capabilities for conducting keyword searches of extensive databases of websites/pages.
- *Malls* The term "virtual mall", or "Internet mall", is often used to refer to any site that has more than two commercial sites linked to it. Hence, many of the commercial directories described above are also "malls". However, a key difference between a mall and a directory is the source of their income. A mall derives its income from its "tenants", whereas a directory will typically rely on advertising for sale.

- *Publishers*   Publishers become intermediaries when they offer links to producers through advertising or product listings related to their content.
- *Virtual resellers*   In contrast to malls, which provide cyber-infrastructure, but do not sell products directly, virtual resellers do. The classic example is Amazon.com, which claims to be the world's largest bookstore with a database of over a million titles, yet which has little of the costs associated with a traditional bricks-and-mortar retailer. Another is the auction site QXL, which in addition to auctioning items for sale by individuals or by firms also sells goods that it has bought cheaply from a manufacturer.
- *Website evaluators*   These provide some form of evaluation that may help to reduce some of the risk to consumers. Examples include ZD-Net, which includes regular reviews of computer hardware and software, and Bizrate, which publishes league tables of e-tailers rated by customers on price, quality and service, so customers can make their own choice.
- *Auditors*   Auditors perform a similar function. For example, Nielsen, which provides audience measurement services in other media, is quickly moving to capture a pre-eminent position in web measurement as well as through its Nielsen Interactive Services subsidiary.
- *Financial intermediaries*   Any form of electronic commerce will require some means of making or authorizing payments from buyer to seller; this requires intermediaries in the form of credit card companies (e.g., Visa or Mastercard), electronic equivalents to writing checks (e.g., Checkfree), paying in cash (e.g., Digicash) and sending secure electronic mail authorizing a payment (e.g., First Virtual).
- *Electronic market makers*   Several auction houses and exchanges have arisen to capitalize on the opportunity to link buyers and sellers worldwide. Sometimes goods may be exchanged rather than money. Examples include eBay, Barter Net and net Trader.
- *Intelligent software agents*   Price comparison agents were discussed earlier, but more advanced ones are being developed which may eventually take over the role of human buying agents. For example, Infospace provides a service that automatically searches the Web for a better offer every time you are considering a purchase of a flight, book or car.
- *Infomediary*   Unlike virtual retailers, such as Amazon, which make their money buying and selling products on the Internet, infomediaries make their money collecting and selling information. An example is moneyeXtra.co.uk, which provides information on financial products in the UK, and mortgagerate.com, which provides information on mortgages in the USA.

Some intermediaries combine a number of functions. For example, Autobytel, an online auto dealership, provides a one-stop shop for car purchasers, linking up dealerships in the USA, auto insurance, financing and other related services from its site. Depending on their strategy these new infomediaries could either be competitors or partners to traditional intermediaries. For example, search engines, such as Yahoo!, and ISPs, such as AOL, which possess valuable information on customers could either choose to compete with Internet retailers, such as Barnes & Noble and Amazon, or collaborate or both.

Mini-case study: TicketClic.com

TicketClic.com (Figure 6.7) allows online booking of tickets for events, cinemas, theatres, theme parks, water parks, museums, concert and sport venues in Belgium, France, Italy and the USA. It was developed by OmniTicket, a ticketing company formed in January, 1999 by the merger of two industry leaders in ticketing: VGS Systems Engineering, a multi-national company founded in 1986, is a pioneer in real-time ticketing and access control solutions for leisure and culture venues; and Access Control Technologies, Inc., a Canadian company founded in 1994, is a pioneer in sophisticated ticket reservation networks for theatres, sports and leisure venues.

OmniTicket's systems allow venues to maximize their reach and increase revenues via OmniTicket's Internet-based ticket distribution website or through OmniTicket's distribution partners including call centres, travel agencies and retail points of sale. However, the system also allows venues to maintain control over their real-time marketing, sales data and ticket inventory, critical if they are to maximize capacity utilization. Clients include Walt Disney Attractions (Florida and Paris), Paramount

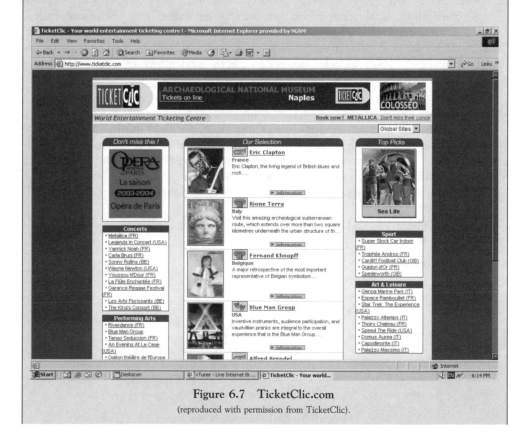

Figure 6.7   TicketClic.com
(reproduced with permission from TicketClic).

Parks of North America, Port Aventura, Tivoli, Universal Studios (Hollywood and Florida) and the Colosseum of Rome, the London Eye, the Louvre (Paris), the Metropolitan Museum of Art (New York), the Palais des Beaux Arts (Bruxelles), Topkapi Museum (Istanbul) and Ocean Park (China).

Disaggregation/Reaggregation

Whereas disintermediation changes the structure of the distribution chain external to the firm, disaggregation involves unbundling of activities within the firm; these include all activities in the value chain, including design, production, marketing, distribution and customer support. For most traditional businesses, a value chain usually refers to the flow of physical activities, such as the transfer of raw materials from suppliers to the factory, processing of materials into finished goods, transfer of the finished goods to sales and distribution, and then transfer to the customer. However, in many information-intensive businesses nowadays, it is not goods that are physically transported within the firm, but information. For example, in many manufacturing businesses nowadays, goods are not physically transported from one site to another; rather they are manufactured, assembled and distributed from the same site with information flowing from one department to the next. The main value is added in the information flows (e.g., in the design of the assembled product, in the market research, in the advertising and promotion).

Evans and Wurstner (2000) argue that electronic commerce will have a significant impact on many industries by changing the value of information flows in many industries, which have been built around conventional information channels. In many industries the trade-off has been between the richness and reach of information. For example, a firm may choose between a large salesforce in order to communicate with the customer in depth and a mass-advertising campaign in order to reach a wide market. The Internet changes the fundamental economic basis for the firm by providing both richness and reach (Figure 6.8)

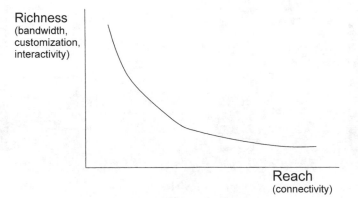

Figure 6.8   Richness versus reach.

and by increasing the power of the customer as well. Evans and Wurstner argue that firms will increasingly need to compete on both richness and reach as well as what they call "affiliation" – aligning more closely with the interests of the customer. As we saw in Chapter 4 some ways this can be achieved include the use of customer relationship management (CRM), personalization or other marketing techniques to better identify and serve customer needs.

Evans and Wurstner argue that this economic shift can lead to melting of the "glue" that holds the different activities of the firm together and "deconstruction" of the business.

Mini-case study: Deconstruction of the newspaper industry

Newspapers typically contain a bundle of different products, such as news articles, display advertisements, classified advertisements, share prices, features, columns, cartoons, TV listings and so forth. In order to produce this there is a complex organization of journalists, columnists, editors, subeditors, printers and an elaborate distribution system. This organization exists in order to make use of the economies of scale provided by the printing press. Writers cannot reach readers directly because they cannot cheaply print and distribute their work alone. Therefore, it makes economic sense for the newspaper to bundle multiple news articles together, along with the other material that newspapers provide.

As a result of the Internet and other e-business technologies changing the economics of reproducing and distributing information, the existing business model built on a bundling of news and information that makes up a newspaper can no longer be taken for granted (Figure 6.9). For example, using the Internet, journalists are able

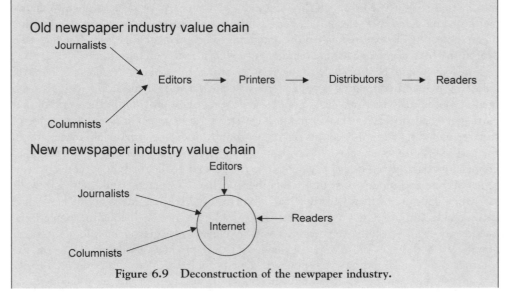

Figure 6.9 Deconstruction of the newpaper industry.

to directly publish material and reach readers around the world. Similarly, columnists or cartoonists can send their content directly to subscribers. At the same time, using search engines, readers are able to mix and match content from a wide range of sources on the Internet to suit their own needs. They are able to download news as and when desired as well as selecting movie reviews, travel features and recipes directly from their favourite movie critic, travel writer and master chef.

Downes and Mui (1998) take the argument of transaction cost theory to its extreme in their "law of diminishing firms": as transaction costs in the open market approach zero, so does the size of the firm; this follows logically from the theory of the firm first proposed by Coase, who argued the reason firms exist in the first place is to perform certain transactions at lower cost than in the open market. If Coase is right, it follows that if the cost of a transaction is reduced in the open market, there is no reason for the transaction to be performed internally; this can be observed in many industries.

Many of the less information-intensive activities, such as the assembly and distribution of items, are already being outsourced in many firms. For example, in the case of consumer electronics, although Sony may design the product in Japan, it outsources manufacture and assembly of many products to lower labour cost countries, such as China. With changes in the transaction costs brought about by e-commerce, this outsourcing trend is likely to accelerate and extend to other activities. For example, in the UK, telephone support is often outsourced to specialized call centres located in less expensive localities. Automated customer support systems enable most queries to be dealt with by less skilled and experienced operators, leaving the most difficult queries to be referred to in-house staff.

Extranets, in particular, can reduce the time needed for product design and order information to be passed through the supply chain from design or sales through to manufacturing and delivery. For example, Ford, Chrysler and General Motors are co-operating on an industry-wide extranet called the automotive network exchange, which will handle everything from computer-automated design (CAD) files to purchase forms.

Firms may also be forced to disaggreggate owing to market pressures. If costs of searching out and contacting suppliers are sufficiently reduced, instead of going to the nearest source customers may search out the cheapest or best provider in the world of that particular good or service. For example, high street banks typically provide a range of services including current accounts, savings accounts, mortgages, financial advice, and in the past many customers relied on one bank for all these needs. Information and access to financial products was less readily available to the general public, making it more costly in terms of time and money to switch to another supplier. Customers would rely on a well-known bank or one with which they had a long history. At the same time the banks had considerable information on each customer which was not available to competitors, making the bank–customer relationship very asymmetrical in terms of information and power. With the greater information and choice of products easily available on the Internet the balance of power has changed. One possible threat to the traditional banks is that customers will be less loyal and will choose the best provider for each product: one provider for the cheapest, best service current account, another for savings, another for mortgages, etc.

Reaggregation

Although disaggregation has occurred in some industries, reaggregation rather than disaggregation has occurred in other cases. For example, rather than focusing on just one activity as predicted, many banks integrate more services to their portfolio, using information systems to achieve economies of scope.

Timmers (1998) suggests there is trend toward increased integration of information flows and the addition of value-added activities. He classifies various types of e-businesses according to their functional integration and the degree of innovation (Figure 6.10). The degree of functional integration ranges from businesses performing a single function (e.g., shops that only provide marketing over the Internet) to businesses with fully integrated functions in the value chain. The degree of innovation ranges from essentially an electronic substitute for traditional ways of doing business to more innovative ways, such as offering functions that were not available before. Rather than leading to disaggregation, or unbundling of activities, both these trends could lead to further integration of activities.

However, the same theory can also be used to suggest that producers will disaggregate certain functions, resulting in a greater reliance on intermediaries. Reduced co-ordination costs imply an "unbundling" of functions, making it easier and more efficient to buy value chain functions rather than to make them in-house. For example, Malone et al. (1987) argue that electronic networks will favour free market transactions over hierarchies. First,

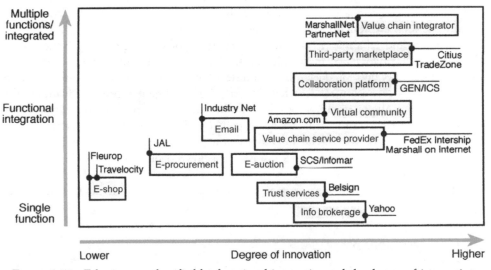

Figure 6.10   E-businesses classified by functional integration and the degree of innovation
(reproduced with permission from Taylor & Francis).

widespread use of information technology will decrease the costs of co-ordination involved in tasks, such as selecting suppliers, scheduling activities and budgeting resources. The second argument is based on the relative complexity of products and the specificity of assets required to produce them, factors that normally favour hierarchies. It is argued that as information technology develops, products and services that were previously considered complex will become lower in complexity relative to the technology available to process them. At the same time, flexible manufacturing technology is allowing rapid changeover of production lines and decreasing the specificity of firms' assets; these too will favour market transactions over hierarchies.

Digital convergence

Whereas disintermediation and disaggregation involve changes within an industry value chain, the third effect involves linking of value chains across industries. In previous chapters we looked at some of the key technologies used in electronic commerce and how many were "converging" to allow transfer of data between different devices and systems. This technological convergence has also led in some instances to breaking down of the traditional industry boundaries and convergence between the industries involved.

Whereas in the past the hardware and software for TV broadcasting did not allow interchange of data with PC hardware and software, now it is possible to view television programmes on a PC and some television sets have intelligent processing ability, making it unclear where the boundaries of the broadcasting and PC industries begin and end. A similar blurring of boundaries is occurring all the way along the digital value chain from the content source through to the customer.

Greenstein and Khanna (1997) identify two types of convergence: convergence in substitutes and convergence in complements. Convergence in substitutes occurs when different firms develop products with features that are similar to features of other products (e.g., a television set that has some of the intelligent processing features of a PC or a PC that allows reception of television broadcasts). In time, products that share increasingly common features will become interchangeable. Convergence in complements occurs when products work better in combination than separately (e.g., a television set that allows broadcast information to instantly be downloaded to a PC). The different kinds of convergence have very different economic effects and vary along the digital value chain from content provider to customer. For convenience we can divide this into three segments: content production, distribution and content retrieval.

Content production

Typical firms in this segment of the value chain include film studios, such as Disney, news providers, such as Reuters, and television broadcasters, such as the BBC. Convergence in production has been mainly complementary (as far as the author is aware). Recent years have seen the rise of global media conglomerates spanning film, television, music, news, information, games, business and educational software, such as Time Warner in the USA, Pearson in the UK, News Corporation in Australia and Bertelsmann in Germany. There are obvious benefits to controlling all these various types of content within the group, especially once the content is digitized, since they may use similar distribution media and may serve the same customers.

Distribution

Further along the value chain in the distribution stage, convergence has been mainly in substitutes. Typical companies here include telephone companies and cable companies. Here too there have been numerous joint ventures, mergers and acquisitions between companies in the cable/satellite TV, electricity and telephone businesses, as they seek to exploit their existing networks to deliver the increasing traffic in provision of various information, entertainment and educational content to consumers. For example, cable providers and telephone companies often now provide Internet access, competing with ISPs. Following the development of new technology that provides consumers with high-speed Internet access over electricity power lines, electricity companies could join them.

Content retrieval and processing

At the customer end of the chain, both convergence in substitutes and complements can be observed. For example, it is now possible to access the Internet using a variety of hardware including TVs, PCs, PDAs (personal digital assistants) and mobile phones; this has stimulated diversification into new industry sectors and joint ventures between firms in different industry sectors. Firms here include computing firms, such as IBM and Microsoft, and consumer electronics manufacturers, such as Sony and Matsushita. For example, Apple and Sony have worked on a joint venture to develop set-top boxes that allow access to the Internet and other services from the television. At the same time, the various devices are complementary in that data can be transferred between them (e.g., between a mobile phone and a PC). New complementary products are also being developed (e.g., digital cameras that allow photographs to be stored on a PC and displayed on a TV set).

Covell (2003) argues that digital convergence is about to enter a new phase based on rich media and mobile Internet access: first, with improvements in Internet infrastructure and increasing broadband adoption, rich media, such as Internet telephony, streaming media, videoconferencing, and Flash animation, are becoming common; and, second, as discussed in Chapter 2, several wireless network technologies are now available, such as wireless LANs, Wi-Fi, home networks and broadband satellite networks. Together with rich media technologies, these technologies promise to overcome many of the constraints of previous technologies and accelerate the convergence process.

Convergence around customers

As well as technological convergence, Deise et al. (2000), drawing on ideas from customer relationship management, argue that in future industry boundaries will be dictated by customer relationships. For example, many banks now have interests in media, telecommunications and travel, while many manufacturing companies, such as GM, now offer financial services. As seen in Chapter 4 e-business can be integrated with CRM systems, so leveraging the customer base.

Mini-case study: East Japan Railway

The East Japan Railway Company (EJR) (Figure 6.11) was established when the bankrupted railway public corporation was privatized and divided into seven regional companies in 1987. EJR has a network of 7,500 km of tracks in the eastern half of Japan including the Tokyo metropolitan area and serves more than 16 million passengers daily through 1,695 stations. In terms of passenger volume and operating revenue (¥166 trillion in the 2002 fiscal year), EJR is outstanding in comparison with other

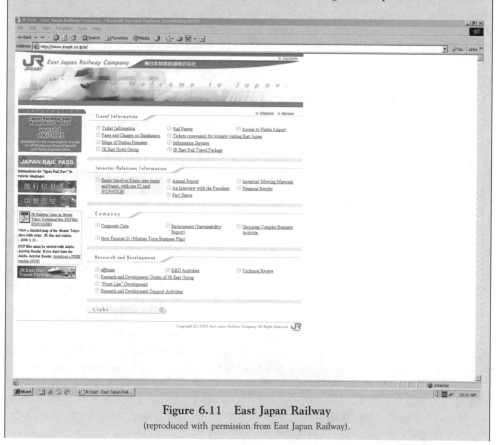

Figure 6.11   East Japan Railway

(reproduced with permission from East Japan Railway).

railway companies in the world. However, Japan's low birth rate and ageing population expected to result in a decrease in the total population from 2007, so the demand for railway services is not expected to grow significantly in the future. In order to grow it was, therefore, critical for the company to diversify into other businesses as well as to sustain the demand for railway.

The privatization enabled the company to diversify into other business areas. It currently operates shopping centres, hotels, restaurants, convenience stores, resorts, travel agencies, residential developments, advertising and credit card operations. The revenue from these diversified businesses now occupies around 30% of the consolidated revenue of the EJR group.

In March, 1996 the EJR established its home page on the Internet as a new means of information and advertisement media. In April, 2000 it launched an online shopping, reservation and information system. Now its home page has 850,000 hits per day. The website serves two purposes: to reinforce its existing operations and to create new business.

Reinforcement of its existing operations

Services provided include:

- *Railway* Online reservation of trains and package tours; information service about the railway and real-time train operations; and information service for foreigners.
- *Other businesses* Online advertisement and sales promotion; and hotel and car rental reservations.
- *Public relations activities* Investor relations activities; recruit information; and corporate citizenship

In these areas the Internet, with its on-demand availability and interactivity, has increased convenience to customers as it allows them to make reservations or to get information anytime from anywhere. In addition, the Internet's multimedia capabilities and digital representation allows improved quality and quantity of information.

New businesses

In April, 2000 the EJR established an online shopping mall that takes advantage of EJR's existing customer base and EJR's strong brand recognition, as well as the existing railway infrastructure. For example, EJR's website is advertised in the trains and stations. In addition, when customers purchase some products that are selected by retail companies in the EJR group, they can pay by using their EJR store card or other credit cards. The products are delivered by the group's logistics companies to either the customer's home, a kiosk or EJR stations for pickup by the customer. Providing pickup at stores in stations dramatically increases customer convenience for those customers who are unable to receive the products by home delivery, as they are away at work during the daytime.

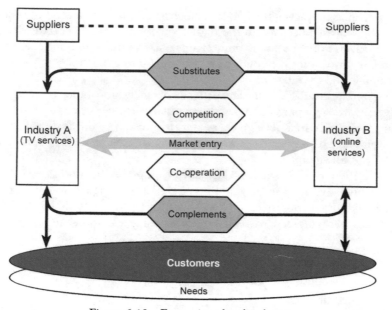

Figure 6.12   Forces in related industries
(reproduced with permission from Taylor & Francis).

In order to analyse the competition in converging industries, it is necessary to consider not only the competitive forces within your own industry, as in Porter's five-forces model, but also the forces in related industries. Dowling et al. (1998) suggest that this can be done by considering the relationships of each force with the forces in the converging industries centred around customer needs (Figure 6.12).

As shown above the effects of electronic commerce on industries is diverse and likely to depend on the interplay of several factors. However, a general statement can be made that the immediate competitive impact is that firms are facing an increasing number and a greater variety of competitors as new firms enter the market. Another significant change as a result of the converging technologies is that the scope of competition has changed. In the past, competition between firms was within part of the value chain (e.g., in the connection of customers to the telephone network). Increasingly, competition is along different parts of a value chain (e.g., in the content and delivery of information services) and across value chains (e.g., between telephone companies and cable TV companies); this requires firms to look at neighbouring or parallel value chains as well as traditional value chains. Instead of defining the business mission in terms of products or position in a value chain, the question in the future may be what function does the firm serve or what core competencies does the firm possess and what other products and services can the firm provide? If this trend continues, instead of the linear value chains we see in most industries in future in many industries we may see multiple and interlinked value chains or firms offering a variety of content over multiple media.

> **Mini-case study: Vizzavi**
>
> In May, 2000 VivendiNet (a joint venture between Vivendi and Canal+) and Vodafone AirTouch plc ("Vodafone") announced the creation of a 50/50 company to establish Europe's first multi-access Internet portal. This new company, Vizzavi (from the French "vis-à-vis", meaning "partner"), allows customers to:
>
> - Access personalized services, such as email, address book and calendar.
> - Search for information using a search engine, a directory and live help services.
> - View and listen to a variety of content, such as information, entertainment and music.
> - Conduct e-commerce transactions.
>
> The multi-access Internet portal will provide these services to Vivendi and Vodafone's 70 million customers throughout Europe in a consistent format, across different platforms, including mobile handsets, personal computers, televisions and PDAs.

The Internet could also threaten to replace traditional public-switched telephone networks (PSTNs). In Chapter 2 we saw how the Internet protocol (IP) allows the transfer of packets of digital data between computers in a network and how in theory the data could be voice, fax, video, text and so on in origin. Some companies, such as Nortek Networks and ADC Communications, are starting to offer IP telephony networks that are capable of high-speed and high-volume multimedia data transfer over long distances. Voice over IP (VoIP) telephony is simply a development to allow IP networks to integrate seamlessly with the PSTN; this is achieved using a gateway device between the IP network and the external telephone lines which compresses the voice signal and assembles it into packets together with header information. Some PBXs (private branch exchanges) such as Siemens, already feature built-in gateways as do some routers, such as Cisco's. Although things are changing rapidly, the advantage is much lower cost over long distances. At present, long-distance calls are relatively expensive compared with local calls: free in the USA and cheaper in Europe. Since Internet access is provided at local rate, using VoIP it costs the same to call someone across the other side of the world as it does to call someone next door.

Impact on global industries

As shown in Chapter 3, there are significant differences between countries both in terms of Internet penetration and usage. Therefore, the impact of e-business is likely to vary considerably worldwide. Coltman et al. (2000) suggest the different impacts internationally can be analysed by integrating the idea of transaction costs with the popular integration responsiveness framework of Prahalad and Doz (1987) and Bartlett and Ghoshal (1989). Thus, transaction cost reduction is another dimension in addition to

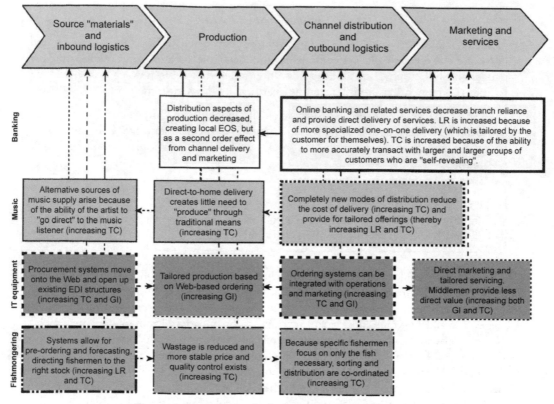

Figure 6.13 Impact of e-business on global industries.

EOS = economics of scales; LR = local responsiveness; TC = transaction cost; EDI = electronic data interchange; GI = global integration

the tension between global integration and local responsiveness in multinational enterprises. For example, although reductions in transaction costs may exert strong pressures in the banking industry, this needs to be balanced against strong pressures for local responsiveness. In the IT equipment industry, similar pressures result from reduction in transaction costs, but these need to be balanced against strong pressures for global integration in order to achieve economies of scale.

Coltman et al. suggest that, in order to determine the impact of e-business on global industries (Figure 6.13), the effect of each of these pressures for change needs to be examined at each stage of the value chain in order to identify "stress points". Thus, in banking the pressures for transaction cost reduction and local responsiveness would be expected to result in significant changes in the distribution and marketing. In the IT equipment industry, by contrast, the pressures resulting from transaction cost reductions and global integration would be expected to lead to changes in the inbound logistics part of the industry value chain. Corresponding stress points for music and fishing are also shown.

Luthje (2002) argues that the longer term impact of the Internet may be the emergence of contract manufacturers as "global supply chain facilitators", particularly in the procurement of electronics components and parts. Internet-based manufacturing promises to facilitate this function because it requires the definition of uniform interfaces between manufacturing procedures in different plants and locations. The economies of scale offered by use of Internet standards makes the Internet ideal for dealing with different types of customer relations, production cultures, and political and social regulations. The global electronics parts and components markets may also foster the delocalization of sourcing relationships. On the labour side, there may be substantial rationalization of engineering work, an increased separation of product and process engineering, and a diminished role for personalized co-operation between product and manufacturing engineers within local industry networks.

The internationalization is likely to vary depending on the type of industry. Kotha et al. (2001) examines the factors associated with the propensity of pure US-based Internet firms to enhance their international presence on the Internet by developing country-specific websites. Despite the assertion that all Internet firms are born global, they found that internationalization by Internet firms is positively related to two types of intangible assets – reputation and website traffic – and the levels of competitive and co-operative activity. This finding is also supported by Chen (2003), who found that US domination was strongest in markets for digital products that do not require a local physical distribution network and in markets for information products that require little local adaptation. Both studies suggest that the ability of Internet firms to internationalize depends on the type of firm-specific resource.

Non-economic factors

The discussion so far has concentrated on the impact of economic forces on industries where electronic commerce is introduced. However, there may also be other non-economic forces at work in a particular industry or market that may affect the outcome. In particular, four other forces need to be considered: organizational capabilities, customer relationships, institutional factors and public policy.

Organizational capabilities

As discussed above, intermediaries perform several functions, some of which may be difficult to replace. Even though it might lead to lower transaction costs, some firms may not wish to change the existing industry status quo because they lack the resources and skills to take over the functions of existing intermediaries. In many cases, therefore, existing intermediaries have an advantage in going online themselves. For example, Ingram Micro, an existing intermediary in the PC supply chain, has taken the initiative to form RosettaNet, a consortium of companies in the PC supply chain, to set electronic commerce standards for the industry. By agreeing to common terms and processes, the aim is to enhance the flow of information and compete effectively with Dell's direct model.

Supplier and customer relationships

Another factor often cited by firms under threat from electronic commerce is that, even if there are economic reasons that favour switching to another supplier, customers may not do so: first, because of lethargy and, second, because they may value long-term relationships with the supplier; this was the point made by Clemons et al. (1993) in their "move-to-the-middle hypothesis". They argue that increased co-ordination costs and increased risks of opportunistic behaviour will lead firms to increasing co-operation with trusted suppliers and customers rather than less; this is particularly the case where the firm has entered into long-term agreements with a supplier and has made significant investments in supplier specific systems, such as JIT systems. It may also be the case in personal services (e.g., legal or medical services). Many customers will prefer to rely on a solicitor or doctor who is familiar with their case and whom they trust despite higher fees.

Firms could also use e-business to improve their existing customer relationships and, far from leading to reconfiguration of the industry, it may actually reinforce the position of existing firms; this may be the case, for example, where the firm adopts CRM and utilizes customer information and customer databases to improve service to existing customers, as discussed in Chapter 4. An example is the use by publishing giant McGraw-Hill which needed to integrate several publishers within the group, each of which deals with different subjects and different customers. It solved this problem by creating a Web-based architecture that linked an off-the-shelf Java browser to the publisher's master product file and the company's data warehouse to provide a single, integrated view to the customer. The system now provides the platform for new applications, such as the electronic downloading of books for academics.

Institutionalization

Some sectors may also be affected differently by e-business where there are significant institutional factors. Selznick (1957) defines institutionalization as a process in which an organization is infused with value beyond the technical requirements at hand; this occurs, for example, where the organization performs some social function that is not purely commercial, as in the case of educational establishments and other public services. In these organizations the pursuit of economic goals is typically accompanied by non-economic goals, so actions cannot be fully understood without understanding the social context (Granovetter, 1992). Thus, although there may be valid economic arguments why a public institution may become disaggregated or be disintermediated, this may not occur if these are outweighed by institutional factors that support their continuance; this is particularly the case of non-profit sectors (e.g., in the world of art, which by its nature, is often driven by non-profit objectives).

Mini-case study: Adoption of electronic commerce in auction houses

Auctioneering internationally is dominated by the big four auction houses based in London, Sotheby's, Christie's, Phillips' and Bonham's, who have significant advantages in economies of scale, knowledge, superior reputation, trust, huge resources and upper class contacts. The big four have been quite active in their use of IT and e-commerce. For example, they initiated sophisticated experiments with auctions broadcast live on satellite television and are actively using the Internet in pre- and after-sales activities, such as price results and catalogues. An example is LotFinder, Christie's computerized service to make searching for a specific item at Christie's worldwide auctions easy. Sotheby's (Figure 6.14) has also entered in a joint venture with Amazon to provide an auction site; this disintermediates dealers to some extent, as the filtering roles of dealers are taken over by the auction houses. However, outside of the big four auction houses, the use of the Internet by smaller auction houses and dealers, who rely to a greater extent on private clients, has been negligible. Adelaar (2000) suggests that the reluctance of many auctioneers and dealers to use Web-based e-commerce can partly be explained by the degree of the social and cultural embeddedness of client relationships. Many auctioneers were reluctant to jeopardize their reputations by using a still insecure and unreliable technology.

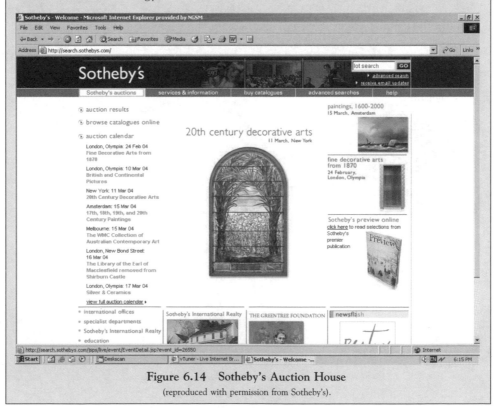

Figure 6.14 Sotheby's Auction House
(reproduced with permission from Sotheby's).

The question that needs to be considered in assessing how institutional environments will be affected is whether or not the organization provides some service beyond the purely economic function. Burt (1992) makes the observation that intermediaries may exist in situations that he terms *tertius gaudens* from the Latin meaning "the third party gains". For example, a third party may gain or be of value in a relationship where two parties are competing for the same thing or where two parties have conflicting demands. A classic example of the former listed by Burt is a woman with more than one suitor. An intermediary, such as a marriage broker, may perform a useful function by acting as an arbiter in competition; this is one of the functions that is performed, for example, by some auction sites on the Internet and one of the reasons for the existence of stock exchanges. A classic example of the latter is the mediator in diplomatic circles who aims to reconcile differences between parties who are unable or unwilling to deal directly with each other. An example in electronic commerce may be where a customer or seller is doubtful about the reliability of the other party in an electronic transaction and relies on an intermediary to validate the other party. Organizations that provide an equivalent service on the Internet are VeriSign and Escrow.com.

Mini-case study: VeriSign.com

VeriSign (Figure 6.15) maintains a database of millions of web addresses registered in .com and .net top-level domains and serves all of the world's domain name registrars

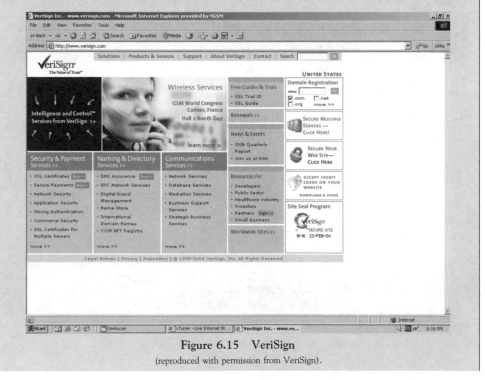

Figure 6.15   VeriSign

(reproduced with permission from VeriSign).

> that register .com and .net domain names. Using this infrastructure, VeriSign also offers services that allow companies to manage identities across disparate networks, devices and endpoints, and provides trust services for Internet users, including secure sockets layer (SSL) server IDs for website authentication and encryption, while VeriSign Payment Services enables customers to securely process and manage online payments.

Public policy issues

The industry changes that are forecast clearly raise a number of public policy issues, which will be dealt with in more detail in Chapter 9. Clearly, the role and scope of competition and regulatory bodies may need to be re-examined in the light of digital convergence between industries. At the same time, government policy may work against some of the economic forces highlighted earlier. For example, although economic forces may favour disaggregation or aggregation of certain firms, governments may intervene to prevent this happening.

The changes also raise a number of important questions for public policy makers. For example, should large companies, such as telcos, which already have a dominant market position in existing markets be allowed to become engaged in the provision of ISP and entertainment services and, if so, who will control them? Second, should proprietary standards be allowed for technologies that are crucial to the development of electronic commerce worldwide and, if so, what is an appropriate reward for innovating companies? (The latter is particularly relevant given the recent actions taken by the US government against Microsoft, discussed further in Chapter 9.)

Summary

Building on the analysis in the previous chapter, this chapter showed how e-business has changed the structure of many industries by changing the economic fundamentals of many businesses; this may be reflected in a shift in power of the various players in an industry or, more significantly, in a reconfiguration of the industry structure. The main effects can be summarized by the three Ds:

- Disintermediation/Reintermediation.
- Disaggregation/Aggregation.
- Digital convergence.

The main drivers of change in industry structures are changes in cost structures, although institutional pressures, national cultures and public policy also need to be considered.

References

Adelaar, T. (2000). Electronic commerce and the implications for market structure. *Journal of Computer-mediated Communication*, **5**(3), March. Available at *http://www.ascusc.org/jcmc/vol5/issue3/adelaar.htm*

Bartlett, C. and Ghoshal, S. (1989). *Managing across Borders: The Transnational Solution*. Harvard Business School Press, Boston.

Burt, R.S. (1992). The social structure of competition. In: N. Nohria and R. G. Eccles (eds), *Networks and Organizations* (pp. 57–91). Harvard Business School Press, Boston.

Chen, S. (2003). *Globalization of Internet sites* (Working paper). National Graduate School of Management, Australian National University, Canberra.

Clemons, E.K., Reddi, S.P. and Row, M.C. (1993). The impact of information technology on the organization of economic activity. *Journal of Management Information Systems*, **10**(2), Fall, 9–35.

Coase, R.H. (1937). The nature of the firm. *Economica*, **4**, 336–405.

Coltman, T., Devinney, T.M., Latukefu, A.S. and Midgley, D.F. (2000). International perspectives on the state of the e-business revolution. Available at *http://www.agsm.unsw.edu.au/~timdev/research/GLOBALEBIZ.PDF*

Covell, A. (2003). Digital convergence Phase 2. Available at *http://www.digital-convergence.com*

Deise, M.V., Nowikow, C., King, P. and Wright, A. (2000). *Executive's Guide to E-Business: From Tactics to Strategy*. John Wiley & Sons, New York.

Dowling, M., Lechner, C. and Thielmann, B. (1998). Convergence: Innovation and change of market structures between television and online services. *Electronic Markets*, **8**(4), 31–5.

Downes, L. and Mui, C. (1998). *Unleashing the Killer App: Digital Strategies for Market Dominance*. Harvard Business School Press, Boston.

Evans, P. and Wurstner, T.S. (2000). *Blown to Bits: How the New Economics of Information Transforms Strategy*. Harvard Business School Press, Boston.

Global Aviation Associates (2003). *An Analysis of Distribution Costs: Orbitz vs. Sabre-base*. GDS Travel Agency, Washington, DC.

Granovetter, M. (1992). The problems of explanation in economic sociology. In: N. Nohria and R.G. Eccles (eds), *Networks and Organizations* (pp. 25–56). Harvard Business School Press, Boston.

Greenstein, S. and Khanna, T. (1997). What does industry convergence mean? In: D.B. Yoffie (ed.), *Competing in the Age of Digital Convergence* (pp. 201–26). Harvard Business School Press, Boston.

Kotha, S., Rindova, V.P. and Rothaermel, F.T. (2001). Assets and actions: Firm-specific factors in the internationalization of U.S. Internet firms. *Journal of International Business Studies*, **32**(4), 769–91.

Kotler, P. (1997). *Marketing Management: Analysis, Planning, Implementation and Control* (9th edn). Prentice Hall, London.

Luthje, B. (2002). Electronics contract manufacturing: Global production and the international division of labor in the age of the Internet. *Industry and Innovation*, **9**(3), 227–49.

Malone, T.W., Yates, J. and Benjamin, R.I. (1987). Electronic markets and electronic hierarchies. *Communications of the ACM*. June, 484–97.

Porter, M.E. (1980). *Competitive Strategies: Techniques for Analysing Industries and Competitors*. Free Press, New York.

Porter, M.E. (1985). *Competitive Advantage: Creating and Sustaining Superior Performance*. Free Press, New York.

Porter, M.E. (2001). Strategy and the Internet. *Harvard Business Review*, March.

Prahalad, C.K. and Doz, Y. (1987). *The Multinational Mission: Balancing Global Demands and Local Vision*. Free Press, New York.

Sarkar, M.B., Butler, B. and Steinfeld, C. (1995). Intermediaries and cybermediaries: A continuing role for mediating players in the electronic marketplace. *Journal of Computer-mediated Communication*, 1(3), March. Available at *http://www.ascusc.org/jcmc/vol1/issue3/sarkar.htm*

Selznick, P. (1957). *Leadership in Administration*. Harper & Row, New York.

Tapscott, D. (2001). Rethinking strategy in a networked world (or why Michael Porter is wrong about the Internet). *Strategy + Business*, **24**. Available at *http://www.dontapscott.com/Strategy_Business.pdf* or *http://www.strategy-business.com*

Timmers, P. (1998). Business models for electronic markets. *Electronic Markets*, 8(2), 3–8.

Key concepts

- Clemon's move-to-the-middle hypothesis
- Customer relationship management (CRM)
- Cybermediation
- Deconstruction
- Digital convergence
- Disaggregation
- Disintermediation
- Factors determining substitutability of a product
- Five-forces model
- Five-forces analysis in a converging industry
- Informediary
- Institutionalization
- Law of diminishing firms
- Malone's electronic market hypothesis
- Reintermediation
- Transaction cost–integration–local responsiveness framework
- Value chain analysis
- Value system analysis

Self-assessment questions

1 Explain how the five forces in Porter's model may be changed by e-business.
2 How can Porter's model be adapted for a converging industry?
3 Give examples of changes to the value chain and the value system brought about by e-business.
4 Explain what is meant by disintermediation and reintermediation.
5 How can transaction costs help explain "deconstruction" of activities in an e-business?
6 Explain the law of diminishing firms.
7 Explain the different assumptions in Malone's electronic market hypothesis and Clemon's move-to-the-middle hypothesis.
8 Give some examples of digital convergence.
9 Apart from transaction costs what are some of the other factors that may affect how e-business impacts an industry?
10 How and why may the impact of e-business vary by industry and country?

Discussion questions

1 How is e-business changing the structure of your industry?

2 Given the advances in information technology that are likely in the future, is the position of infomediaries sustainable?

3 Are pressures for disaggregation increasing relative to pressures for consolidation?

4 Why is trust important in e-business and how can it be improved?

5 Can e-business ever replace face-to-face interaction?

6 Whose view about the impact of the Internet on strategy do you agree with: Michael Porter's or Don Tapscott's?

7 What will be the impact of the Internet on the location of business activities worldwide?

8 What will be the likely impact of new technologies, such as rich media and mobile communications, on industries?

DEVELOPING AN E-BUSINESS STRATEGY

Introduction

Traditional strategy textbooks generally prescribe an approach to strategy development like that in Figure 7.1; this consists of a series of steps:

- Define objectives.
- Assess external environment.
- Assess internal environment.
- Identify gaps.
- Develop a strategic plan.
- Implement the plan.

Although many companies attempt to do so, in practice few companies actually manage to follow such a process exactly. It is particularly difficult to do so in the case of e-businesses that have to contend with additional issues. The previous chapters have shown that there are significant differences in the markets and economics of e-businesses, much of it due to the underlying technology. This chapter discusses how some of these differences need to be taken into account when developing a strategy for an e-business. Five significant characteristics of e-markets are highlighted:

1. Some transactions are virtual.
2. The markets are unstable.
3. The markets are fast-moving.
4. Firms are highly interconnected.
5. There is high uncertainty in the markets.

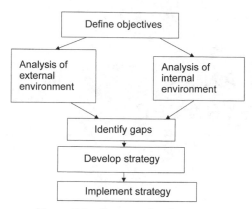

Figure 7.1   Strategy development.

Creating value virtually

The value chain model was introduced in Chapter 6. The most obvious difference when analysing an e-business is that one or more parts of its value chain is online. Rayport and Sviolka (1995) show this as a virtual value chain that runs parallel to the real value chain. Each stage of the virtual value chain offers many new opportunities to use information to create a new product or service. In order to do this, processes must be put in place at each stage to gather the information, organize it, select the valuable information, synthesize it and distribute it (Figure 7.2). For example, a consumer electronics company could exploit the matrix by using the Internet to gather information from customers around the world during the product development stage. The company could gather, organize, select, synthesize and distribute design information drawn from the R&D process to create a

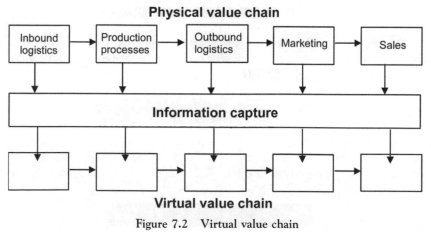

Figure 7.2   Virtual value chain
(reproduced with permission from Harvard Business School Press).

computer simulation for customers, who could then give feedback which in turn could be used to improve the product design.

The virtual matrix is of particular value when applied to information-based industries. For example, by creating a virtual value chain, a digital camera can offer value to its customers in a number of ways: first, the image captured on a digital camera saves costs by avoiding the need for chemical processing, provides a better image quality and economizes on storage; and, second, a digital photo can be manipulated and reused in several different ways (e.g., to create a colour copy for brochures, a still in a video clip or a gif file in CD-ROM catalogues or online services). This allows many more revenue streams to be developed.

E-commerce revenue streams

The personal finance site Motley Fool (Figure 7.2) summarizes some typical revenue streams from e-commerce in the five Cs:

- *Connection* Such sites as AOL and Freeserve obtain revenues from providing connection to the Internet. In the case of AOL this comes directly from users, while in the case of Freeserve some revenues are obtained from the telephone company and some from the next revenue stream.
- *Commercials* Many sites obtain revenues from advertisers who either pay a fixed fee to place an advertisement or pay according to the number of page impressions.
- *Commerce* Some sites obtain revenues from directly providing a service or selling a product; these can be either online retailers, such as Amazon, or manufacturers, such as Dell, selling directly online.
- *Content* Some sites obtain revenues from the content placed on the site (e.g., online news or databases).
- *Community* Some sites obtain revenues from membership fees. For example, subscribers to Compuserve not only get Internet access but also the option to take part in online discussion groups as part of the package.

Additional revenues may be obtained from activities not directly related to the site, but from making use of expertise gained:

- *Consulting* Some successful Internet start-ups have gone on to provide the benefit of their experience to other companies. For example, Jerry Yang a founder of Yahoo has set up a consulting company advising companies on setting up e-businesses.
- *Contracting* An extension of the above, this involves outsourcing of certain activities. For example, the personal finance site iii.co.uk provides a service building websites for other companies in addition to its primary service of providing financial information.
- *Controlling* This may eventually evolve into managing certain activities on behalf of other companies. For example, Inktomi not only builds websites for companies but also manages them on their behalf, taking care of the infrastructure.

(Fischer, 1999)

Internet companies should have at least one of these revenue streams, and some companies have revenues from all five. Typically, the more revenue streams that a company can tap into, the better, although one revenue stream may be sufficient if it is large enough and reliable. The question is which revenue stream (or streams) is likely to be greatest or the most profitable and the most reliable?

Connection

Connection is a highly capital-intensive business with most of the cash going toward technology, advertising and customer service, so this revenue stream is likely to have the lowest profitability margins. On the other hand, the revenue stream from connection is predictable and provides a recurring stream of payments earned from monthly subscriber fees. There are customer switching costs, such as those involved in switching an email account, so once customers are signed they are likely to stay with the same provider for a considerable time. However, the high set-up and marketing costs mean that, early in the company's life, profits are likely to be low. Furthermore, as competition increases, connection fees are likely to decline. There is also the threat of new high-speed connection services that will replace conventional telephone dial-up access.

Commercials

Apart from connection, online advertising was one of the Internet's first revenue streams and is still growing. While providing connection is typically a low-margin revenue stream due to high fixed costs, advertising is typically a high-margin revenue stream. It costs relatively little to run an advertisement on an established website. However, since revenues are usually linked to the number of page impressions, to be successful the website must be well known and popular.

Commerce

Online commerce represents the largest revenue stream for the entire Internet industry. However, it is worth bearing in mind that it still represents only a small percentage of sales compared with non-Internet sales. Its value and share of economic activity also varies considerably by economic sector. According to the US Department of Commerce (2004), the share was highest in manufacturing (19.6% in 2002) and lowest in the service sector (0.9% in 2002). As discussed in Chapter 3, there are also significant differences between business-to-consumer (B2C) and business-to-business (B2B) markets. Despite receiving the majority of media attention due to its recent rapid growth, B2C e-commerce represents only a small share of total e-commerce sales (7% compared with 93% for B2B in 2002) (US Department of Commerce, 2004) and, although B2C has grown more quickly initially, B2B is expected to as more firms switch from existing electronic data interchange (EDI) networks to the Internet.

Content

All sites offer content in some form, whether as an online catalogue or as an advertisement. However, some sites also charge a subscription fee for content, usually for specialist information; this may consist of editorials, specially commissioned work or consolidated content from other sources. At present this is mainly for financial information and news, but as multimedia technology improves other types of content, such as movies and music, will increasingly be available online.

Community

Community revenue is important because it is probably the one revenue stream that is difficult to replicate offline. As seen in Chapter 4, it also has a stimulating effect on the other revenue streams. Communities can be profitable once they achieve critical mass, as they are self-sustaining and require little additional spending.

Mini-case study: Peoplesound

Peoplesound (Figure 7.3) claims to be Europe's leading music download company with 200,000 registered users and 6.5 million page impressions a month. The company

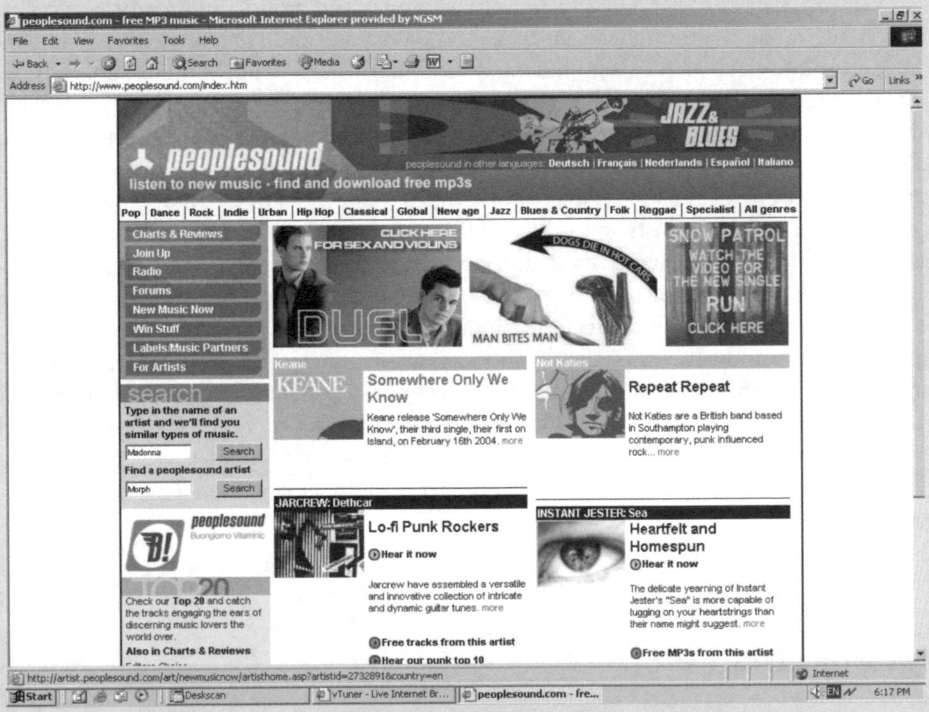

Figure 7.3   Peoplesound

(reproduced with permission from Peoplesound).

provides free music that can be played from the website or downloaded as files to a personal computer or MP3 player. However, the site concentrates on music from less well-known artists and so avoids copyright issues.

The company was founded in June, 1999 by 28-year-old Ernesto Schmitt (formerly with Boston Consulting Group), Bruno Heese and Paul Levett (Gemini Consulting) and Martin Turner (CompuServe). Peoplesound has more than 100 staff working in offices in London, Munich and Paris. The multilingual site covers the UK, France, Germany and the Netherlands and there are plans to expand into Italy, Spain and Asia.

Its business model relies on several revenue streams. As well as advertising and sponsorship, the site sells CDs, speakers, MP3 players and other music-related goods. It also has a B2B element in the licensing, publishing and provision of information to the music industry, and it makes money from talent scouts who sign artists from Peoplesound's books.

Value system analysis

As shown in Chapter 6, as well as examining revenues and profits in different parts of the value chain, value chain analysis can be extended beyond the company to include other firms in the industry, such as suppliers and customers, in a "value system" analysis. For example, to the above revenue streams for websites can also be added potentially profitable opportunities in support services, infrastructure provision, security software and venture capital (Cohan, 2000). This analysis is particularly useful in e-business as it can highlight one of the key strategic opportunities discussed in Chapter 6: restructuring an existing industry. Gadiesh and Gilbert (1998) suggest that an important part of such analysis should be examining costs at different stages of the value chain and market size. They suggest drawing up a profit pool map showing the share of industry revenue and operating margins of different parts of the industry value system. Figure 7.4 shows one such map for the PC industry; this clearly shows that personal computers and components represent the largest share of industry revenues, but the highest operating margins are in microprocessor and software production. Such diagrams can be used to highlight the choices available to firms. One approach is to take the profit pool as given and use it to decide where in the value chain to compete, taking into consideration the firm's capabilities.

Unstable markets

Another characteristic of e-commerce is the instability of the markets; this arises from two types of pressures. First, there are certain, long-term, macro trends that are driving change

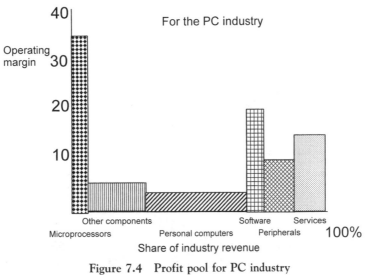

Figure 7.4 Profit pool for PC industry
(reproduced with permission from Harvard Business School Press).

across a number of industries. The three major ones common across a whole range of industry sectors are globalization, deregulation and digitization.

As discussed in Chapter 1, the improvement and cost reductions in digital technology have had significant impact in business for many years now. The Internet has simply accelerated much of what was already happening and spread it into other industries across the world. Second, the deregulation and liberalization of many markets has opened up new opportunities for many firms, and recent years have seen an increase in the number of related diversifications. For example, in the UK following privatization a number of companies in the energy sector have branched out into related markets, such as other forms of energy or telecommunications, making use of their physical distribution networks. Similarly, the media industry in recent years has seen a rash of takeovers and mergers as many firms are attempting to transform themselves into multimedia organizations. Finally, on an international level the globalization of many industries and the liberalization of many markets, such as Eastern Europe, have opened up new foreign markets for Western firms while bringing Western firms into competition with multinationals based in other countries. Such international competition is likely to accelerate following political moves, such as the signing of the General Agreement on Trade and Tariffs by the leading industrial nations which promises to reduce barriers to international trade.

Downes and Mui (1998) show this as three forces that must be added to Porter's five-forces model:

- Globalization.
- Digitization.
- Deregulation.

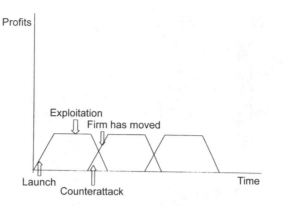

Figure 7.5 Hypercompetition.

Although this refined model can be useful for examining the impact on traditional industries, it still assumes that the new industry will be relatively stable after the change. Some researchers have challenged the validity of this assumption in the case of some technology-driven industries. An alternative model of competition drawn from observations in many dynamic industries is that of D'Aveni and Gunther (1994) who describes a scenario of ever-increasing competition and changing power between players (Figure 7.5). He calls this "hypercompetition". In such markets any competitive advantage is short-lived, and firms must take advantage of any small window of opportunity that arises. In such markets the aim should not be to attain a fit with the environment as in traditional markets, but to change the rules of competition or create disruptions during which temporary advantages can be exploited; this leads to a very different view of competition from traditional industries where the aim is to establish a strong position and defend it.

Mini-case: CDNow

Initially, the financial markets welcomed the arrival of online music sellers. However, that feeling has changed radically in just a short period of time. CDNow (Figure 7.6), a leading online music destination and one of the hottest webpages on the Internet, reached 4 million consumers and $77 million of sales in the first 6 months of 2000. CDNow added approximately 270,000 new costumers during the second quarter of 2000. Approximately 72% of sales in the quarter came from repeat purchases by existing customers, as compared with 66% in the first quarter of 2000. Nevertheless, CDNow was never able to make a profit and a drying cash flow forced it to look for a buyer. On July 19, 2000, BMG acquired all the outstanding capital stock of CDNow for just $3.00 per share or $117 million.

What went wrong? The book e-tailer Amazon decided to start selling CDs online and rapidly topped CDNow as the number one music e-tailer. Even a merger between CDNow and the No. 3 in the business, N2K, could not save the company. There were

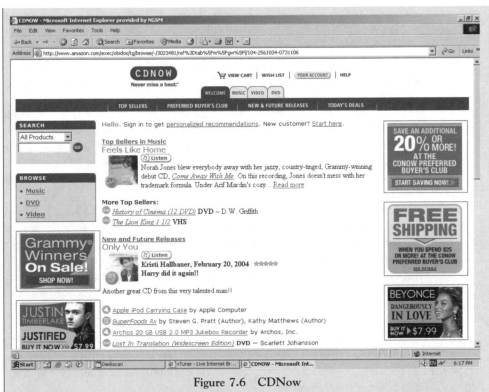

Figure 7.6 CDNow
(reproduced with permission from Amazon).

also weaknesses in the business model and management. Lavish marketing expenditure, slim margins and above all a failure to expand into higher margin markets doomed the company.

In addition, CDNow found that costs associated with the transport and fulfilment of product orders crippled the profits of the company. Like many e-tailing operations it started off with low inventory and distribution requirements, but it has found it necessary as the business expands to build large warehouses and distribution systems in order to provide an acceptable service to customers. One advantage Amazon had was that it did not have to bear all of that brand-building and infrastructure investment on the back of the music alone.

Value innovation

One of the most striking features of competition in e-business is that new entrants have often been able with limited resources to undermine existing competition in an industry through the use of new business models; this is similar to what Kim and Mauborgne (1997) call "value innovation", meaning that strategy is driven by what is valued by the customer without being constrained by existing industry rules. Conventional strategic logic and the logic of value innovation differ along five basic dimensions of strategy:

- *Industry assumptions*   Conventional strategic approaches take the industry conditions as given and set strategy accordingly; instead, value innovators challenge existing industry assumptions and look for quantum leaps in value.
- *Strategic focus*   In conventional approaches, companies set the parameters of their strategic thinking according to competitors. They compare their strengths and weaknesses with those of their competitors and focus on building advantages. Value innovators monitor competitors, but do not use them as benchmarks. They do not expend their resources to offer certain product and service features just because that is what their rivals are doing.
- *Customers*   Many companies seek growth through retaining and expanding their customer bases; this often leads to finer segmentation and greater customization of offerings to meet specialized needs. Value innovation follows a different logic; instead of focusing on the differences among customers, value innovators build on the powerful commonalities in the features that customers value. This enables these companies to capture the core of the market, even if it means that they lose some of their customers.
- *Assets and capabilities*   Many companies view business opportunities through the lens of their existing assets and capabilities. In contrast, value innovators start from a clean slate. This is not to say that value innovators do not leverage their existing assets and capabilities, but they do not let existing assets and capabilities constrain or bias their assessment of business opportunities.
- *Product and service offerings*   Conventional competition takes place within clearly established boundaries defined by the products and services the industry traditionally offers. Value innovators often cross those boundaries. They think in terms of the total solution buyers seek, and they try to overcome the chief compromises their industry forces customers to make.

Creating a new value curve

Kim and Mauborgne (1999) suggest that the key to discovering new value curves lies in answering four questions (Figure 7.7):

1. What factors can be reduced well below the industry standard?
2. What factors can be raised well above the industry standard?
3. What factors can be eliminated that the industry takes for granted?
4. What factors can be created that the industry has never offered?

For example, Amazon:

- Reduced cost.

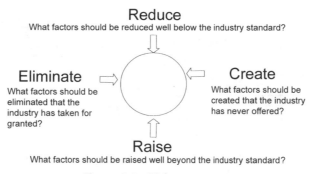

Figure 7.7   Value curve
(reproduced with permission from Harvard Business School Press).

- Raised the range of books available.
- Eliminated the need for stores.
- Created the ability to search for and order books online.

Mini-case study: Value innovation in the US car-retailing industry

Value innovation is never ending. Innovators in an industry will inevitably at some point be replaced by other firms, who come up with a new value curve. An example is the car-retailing industry in the USA, which went through three successive waves of value innovation. Prior to 1993 the car-retailing industry structure in the USA consisted of two segments: new car retailing (through licensed dealerships) and used car retailing. Within the used car-retailing industry, consumers had a choice of three channels:

- Newspaper advertisements, which offered the benefits of finding lowest price cars (but offered limited choice).
- Local used car dealers, which offered reasonable choice (but poor reliability and disappointing sales process).
- Exclusive car dealerships, which offered reliable quality, but limited choice.

CarMax saw an opportunity to create market space between these strategic groups which takes the benefits of the three groups – low price, variety and reliability, while eliminating the trade-offs – by creating a car superstore.

AutoNation then blurred the distinction between the new and used car industries by introducing a complementary value proposition not offered by CarMax: an inter-state service for the cars purchased at AutoNation. Finally, Autobytel (Figure 7.8) took competition to another level by electronically linking customers with dealers and manufacturers using the Internet. As shown in previous chapters, this allows access to a 24-h, 7-day week service globally, so eliminating barriers of distance and time.

Figure 7.8   Autobytel
(reproduced with permission of Autobytel).

Deise et al. (2000) suggest that the value offered by e-business can be expressed as two equations:

$$\text{Customer value} = \frac{(\text{Service})(\text{Quality})}{(\text{Price})(\text{Time})} \qquad (7.1)$$

$$\text{Competitive capability} = \frac{(\text{Agility})(\text{Reach})}{(\text{Time-to-market})} \qquad (7.2)$$

The e-business value for the customer consists of four variables: service, price, quality and fulfilment time:

- *Service*   E-business provides six capabilities that improve customer service: interactive and personalized customer communications; speed and accuracy; enhanced ability to track and measure capability; instantaneous, 24/7 communications; a customer-driven business model; and, finally, instantaneous customer communication.
- *Price*   E-business can sometimes reduce the price customers pay because such devices as volume aggregation, auctions, the decoupling of product offerings and pay-per-use payment models increase the transparency of company pricing.
- *Quality*   E-business improves and customizes the customer experience by providing the

customer better information on products and services and by enabling customers to form communities that provide useful feedback on quality of service.

- *Fulfilment time goes down*   E-business helps companies improve their internal business processes, thereby reducing fulfilment time. Methods include automated order to payment and streamlined purchase initiation processes, delaying product differentiation to a point as close to the customer as possible, just-in-time (JIT) production, networked and outsourced shipping.

The e-business value proposition for the company consists of three variables: agility, reach and time to market:

- *Agility*   Agility refers to the ease with which a company is able to change strategic direction quickly and smoothly, and to provide customers with what they want, even if that is not a standard product or configuration. E-business infrastructures provide the ability to add volume quickly and in turn leads to flexibility in mergers and acquisitions and quick reconfiguration of the virtual value chain.
- *Reach*   E-business enables a company to reach global markets while targeting new demographics within current markets. It also allows firms to leverage their brand across several dissimilar industries.
- *Time to market*   E-business enables firms to participate in collaborative product design with customers, collaborative R&D with supply chain partners, concurrent engineering and other methods to reduce the time to market.

Amit and Zott (2001) suggest that successful e-businesses create value through four primary ways: efficiency, lock-in, complementarity and novelty. As discussed in Chapter 5, efficiency can be realized in a number of ways, such as reducing customers' search costs, faster decision making, simplifying processing, etc. Complementarities can be either vertical (e.g., after-sales service) or horizontal (e.g., one-stop shopping). Lock-in arises through high switching costs (e.g., through learning requirements and personal relationships). Finally, novelty in e-businesses arises most commonly through creating new transaction structures, such as online auctions, reverse markets, etc.

Speed of change

Apart from the instability of the market, one of the greatest challenges for firms engaged in e-commerce is the sheer speed of change. If the market were unstable but changes occurred gradually, the problems would be less great. The problem is that changes occur much more quickly than most firms are accustomed to. Timescales that take years in most industries take place within months or weeks, a phenomenon many have called "Internet time". Speed is all the more critical in the case of Internet start-ups that need to match the "burn rate", the rate at which the firm uses up its initial financing, or where the company needs to capture a large share of the market quickly before competitors catch up.

Mini-case study: Freeserve

Freeserve (Figure 7.9), now the UK's largest ISP, grew from initial discussions in July, 1998 to a business worth over £1 billion just 1 year later. Set up by the electrical retailer Dixon's, the service was able to grow so quickly partly because of the preparation that preceded it. Dixon's had been looking since 1994 to set up an Internet service, but until the beginning of 1998 it had been solely focused on setting up a subscription service, similar to those of successful American operators. The initial plan was to charge £12 a month, with the software preloaded on some of the PCs, and the target was to attract 50,000 users. Then, a second idea was to set up Freeserve as a one-stop service supported by advertising, which would provide access to the World Wide Web, a search engine and its own portal, offering interesting sites to users and the opportunity for online merchants to trade over the site. The breakthrough came in July, 1998 when Planet Online, a fledgling telecommunications company, and later Energis, the energy and telecommunications group, became involved. They were prepared to allow

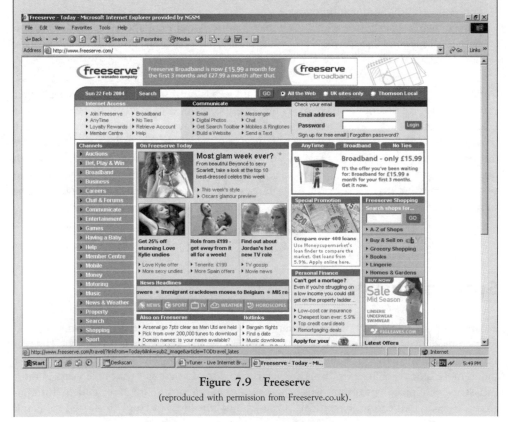

Figure 7.9   Freeserve
(reproduced with permission from Freeserve.co.uk).

> Freeserve to receive a slice of the income from each call, enabling Freeserve to offer a service that was free to users, yet profitable. On September 22, less than 2 months after the initial discussions, the service was launched. One of the reasons for the speed with which the deal was done was that Dixon's executives realized they only had 3 months before competitors reacted.

Speed to market is also important where products rapidly become obsolete. Figure 7.10 shows the relationship between profits and time of market introduction relative to competitors for consumer electronics (Clark and Wheelwright, 1993). If a firm is able to launch a product 6 months earlier than its rivals, this results in profits that are three times as large over its lifetime; however, a product that is 6 months later than its rivals earns negligible profits.

Eisenhardt and Brown (1998) in their study of firms in fast-changing environments found that a common practice was to introduce new products according to strict schedules rather than reacting to events, such as changes in customer demand or technology. They termed this practice "time pacing" as opposed to "event pacing". Time pacing creates a sense of urgency around meeting deadlines and focuses individuals and teams around common goals.

Two processes are critical in time pacing: the first is managing transitions, or shifts from one activity to the next; and the second is managing rhythm, or the pace at which organizations change. Transitions include entering or leaving markets, absorbing a new acquisition, launching new alliances and bringing production online. As a result of typically involving a large number of people, many of whom are not used to working with one another, and of occurring less frequently than other activities, transitions are often where many companies fail. Transitions are especially critical in fast-changing markets, where it is difficult to catch up after failure. Eisenhardt and Brown were unable to find any common practice for managing transitions. Each company had a different set of steps, different timing, different specifications about who should be

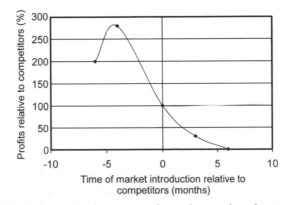

Figure 7.10 Relationship between profits and time of market introduction
(reproduced from Lambert and Slater, 1999, with permission from Elsevier).

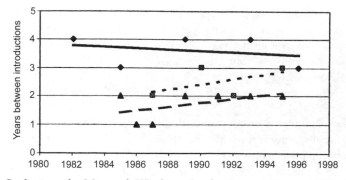

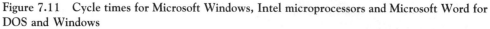

Figure 7.11 Cycle times for Microsoft Windows, Intel microprocessors and Microsoft Word for DOS and Windows

(reproduced from Lambert and Slater, 1999, with permission from Elsevier).

involved and when; but, both transition processes worked because in each case everyone followed a script.

The second critical dimension of time pacing is setting the right rhythms for change and synchronizing those rhythms both with the marketplace and with the organization's internal capabilities. Sources of rhythm for a company include customers, competitors, suppliers and complementors. For example, Intel's time-pacing strategy must synchronize with others; a new, powerful chip is of little value if computer manufacturers have not designed systems to use it. Bringing early to market a chip that is capable of processing multimedia applications quickly is of little use if there is not enough customer demand.

Eisenhardt and Brown's conclusions are supported by other research, which shows that there are limits to what customers need and can absorb (Lambert and Slater, 1999). Figure 7.11 illustrates the major introductions for Microsoft Windows, Intel micro-processors and Microsoft Word for DOS and Windows. As can be seen, if anything the cycle times are increasing rather than decreasing. One explanation could be that these companies synchronized their cycle times with the customer's ability to absorb new products and the customer's needed improvement cycles, instead of blindly pursuing speed.

Most of the arguments supporting a relationship between performance to schedule and financial performance are based on an "imposed market window", as shown in Figure 7.12. However, only a very small percentage of firms today actually operate within this strict definition of an imposed market window; these tend to be firms that face substantial barriers to market entry and cost impacts if they are slow to market, firms that are developing products with little or no room for differentiation or firms that are directly tied to the product development cycle of another supplier.

As the firm moves from the imposed market window toward the second type of market window, the controllable window, the less sensitive it is to schedule variance. A controllable market window is characterized by having significant room for differentiation within a specific market segment so that the firm can "own" that segment. The purest form

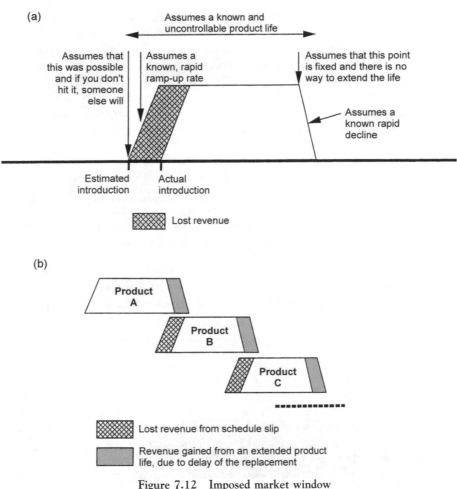

Figure 7.12 Imposed market window
(reproduced from Lambert and Slater, with permission from Elsevier).

of controllable market window would be a monopoly where there is a sole supplier and that supplier sets the standards for future products. Firms that operate within this type of window have nearly complete control over the beginning and end of the market window. Figure 7.12 shows the effect of schedule slips within the controllable market window. The lost revenue from product B's slippage is made up by the extension of product A's life. Intel's PC microprocessors and Microsoft Windows are examples of product lines operating within fairly controllable market windows.

Lambert and Slater propose that more important than just speed to market are the following three product development management principles:

- *First to mindshare* (FTM), instead of first to market. "First to mindshare" means that the firm and its products set the standard that other competitors are compared against. Bill

Gates of Microsoft is quoted as once having said "[when customers must upgrade to a new way of computing] the only questions are whose and when. Winning the 'whose' is far more important than winning the 'when'." First to mindshare considers how a stream of product introductions and associated services can create a dominant position in the customer's mind as opposed to focusing on individual products.

- *Effective market introduction timing* (EMIT), instead of fast cycle times. EMIT considers customer adoption rates, the firm's market position, the type of market window it faces, mind share strategy and competitive pressures to determine the optimal introduction cycle time for its products.

- *Managed responsiveness* (MR), instead of on-time schedule performance. MR assesses the firm's market position, competitive threats, customer needs, mind share development strategy, long-term business strategy and the type of market window the firm faces to determine which projects are schedule-sensitive and which are not. It also provides a framework for continuous scanning of the internal and market conditions in order to make project adjustments that are responsive to the emerging situation.

An implication is that while speed to market is important, it is also important to monitor suppliers, partners and customers and match their speed. In some cases this may require a slowing down of scedules.

Mini-case study: Boo.com

In May, 2000 the fashion retailer Boo.com (Figure 7.13) was declared bankrupt after reportedly burning through $120 million in 6 months. (The site has since been bought and relaunched as part of rival fashion site fashionmall.com.) Set up by three Swedes, Ernst Malmsten, Patrik Hedelin and former model Kajsa Leander, and with offices in London, Stockholm, Paris, New York and Munich, the company was launched with the goal of being the world's "first truly online retailer of sportswear and fashion". Boo had attempted to create the Web's first immersive retail environment with its own online guide (Miss Boo), its own online magazine (Boom) and some of the most fashionable clothing brands. However, critics say it was over-designed, difficult to navigate and completely out of touch with the needs of most web users. With big-name backers like Benetton and Bernard Arnault, the chairman of Louis Vuitton Moet Hennessy, Boo.com was one of the most highly publicized e-commerce sites.

Although the site was generating revenues, it could not generate enough revenues to make up for the vast sums already spent starting the company. Boo.com was plagued by troubles from the start. Its fashionable range of sports-oriented designer clothing was highly praised as was its technically sophisticated website. However, its initial launch was delayed for 6 months, and when it finally opened its website many shoppers were put off by the cartoon salespeople and difficulties in navigating the site. A large proportion of its potential market was unable to use the site because the website design was too advanced for most computers and the long download times were frustrating.

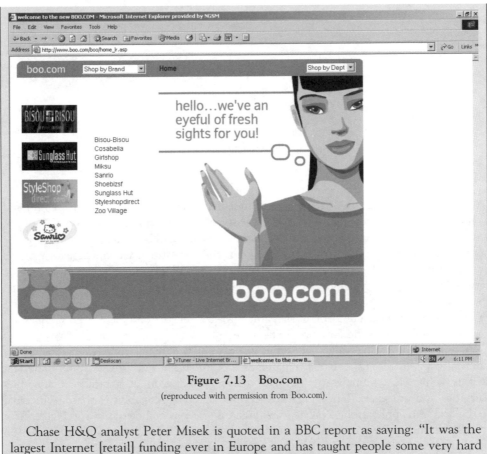

Figure 7.13 Boo.com
(reproduced with permission from Boo.com).

Chase H&Q analyst Peter Misek is quoted in a BBC report as saying: "It was the largest Internet [retail] funding ever in Europe and has taught people some very hard lessons about remembering the business plan."

Interconnectedness of individuals, groups and organizations

The fourth characteristic of e-commerce, which has been highlighted several times already, is the ability to connect individuals, groups and organizations worldwide, and one of the significant differences from traditional industries is the high degree of interconnectedness of the various parties. In particular, as was shown in Chapter 6, complementary product providers and allies play a significant role in determining success in the industry.

Figure 7.14 Value net
(reproduced with permission from Doubleday).

A useful model that shows the role of complementors is the value net by Nalebluff and Brandenburger (1996) shown in Figure 7.14; this shows relationships between the firm, customers, suppliers, competitors and complementors and can be used to examine how the actions of one group impact on other groups in the system. For example, growth of the market may be very dependent on the availability of complementary products. Multimedia services require the availability of networks capable of carrying that traffic. Conversely, the investment in broadband networks requires the availability of services on the network. By co-operating with competitors the firm may be able to provide better services for customers and reduce the power of suppliers, etc.

A refinement to the value net is the value web, which incorporates an analysis of internal capabilities and external requirements (Cartwright and Oliver, 2000). The first step is value cluster analysis (VCA), or the representation of a firm's value-adding activities and processes. These activities represent the core capabilities that are internal to the firm. An application of value cluster analysis to e-Bay is shown below in Figure 7.15; this shows that e-Bay conducts certain activities internally, such as building the action database, managing the auction process, billing, collecting payments and offering online community services. Other essential activities are done externally, such as shipping, payment, escrow services, hardware support and links to other online sites.

The second step is to identify the firm's customers, suppliers, competitors and complementors and to place these around the firm undergoing VCA (in this case e-Bay). In this case customers include both buyers and sellers of the auctions, although only sellers pay for the service because individuals can be both buyers and sellers. Allies include AOL for site traffic and iEscrow for escrow services. Complementors include search engines that provide the traffic, as well as credit card companies and shipping services because these are required to complete the service. Finally, competitors include other online auctions, traditional auctions and classified advertisements.

In the final step, lines are drawn to show key links or relationships between each group. For example, Figure 7.15 clearly shows that Yahoo is both a competitor and a complementor to e-Bay. It complements e-Bay by providing traffic to the site but also competes with e-Bay since it has its own auction site.

Applying analytical tools, such as the value net or value web, to any e-business or industry will soon show the complex web of interrelationships between firms. Four types of

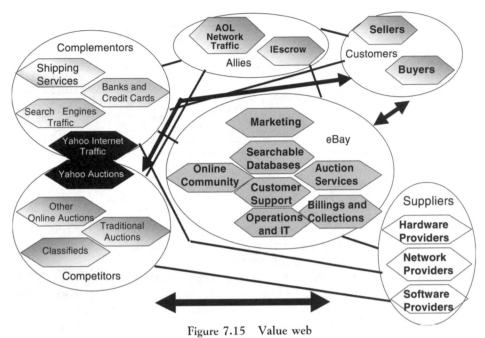

Figure 7.15   Value web

(*source:* Cartwright and Oliver, 2000, reproduced with permission from Emerald Publishing).

relationship are very common among web businesses. The first type is co-branding, sponsorship or linking of websites, which was covered in Chapter 4.

The second type of relationship is a resource-based alliance where two or more firms join forces for some mutually beneficial purpose. The commonest types of alliance relationship are joint R&D, sharing of customer information or integration along the supply chain. An example is the AOL-Time Warner merger in the edu-tainment industry in January, 2000.

The third type is standards agreements where firms agree to adopt a common standard to exchange information or to ensure compatibility of products, such as the WAP consortium in mobile telephones. The power of standards was demonstrated in Chapter 5, and this type of relationship is increasingly common.

The fourth type of relationship that will be very common is what Werbach (2000) terms "syndication"; this refers to the sale of the same good to many customers, who then integrate it with other offerings and redistribute it.

Syndication is common in the news and entertainment industries. For example, TV programmes, cartoons and newspaper articles are often syndicated. However, in other industries it has been very rare for three reasons. First, syndication only works with information goods, which are never "consumed". Millions of people can watch the same news programme over and over again, which is not true of physical goods, such as food or cars. Second, syndication requires modularity. A syndicated good usually needs to be combined with other products. Thus, a news programme is only part of a television

Table 7.1   Syndication network roles

Players	Originators	Syndicators	Distributors
Role	Create original content	Package content	Deliver content
Traditional examples	Journalists	Reuters	*Financial Times* CNN
Web examples	Inktomi Motley Fool	Linkshare Motley Fool	Yahoo! Motley Fool

station's programming. Third, syndication requires many independent distribution points; otherwise there is no point in syndication. The global infrastructure provided by the Internet makes it ideal for distributing information goods.

Within a syndication network, there are three roles that businesses can play (Table 7.1): originators create original content; syndicators package that content for distribution, often integrating it with content from other originators; and distributors deliver the content to customers. A company can play one role in a syndication network or it can play two or three roles simultaneously. It can also shift from one role to another over time.

Syndication has a number of important strategic consequences. First, it offers the ability to broaden the company's reach at low cost. Syndicated material can be reused many times throughout the world. Second, it can turn competitors into complementors. Syndicated news stories can be repackaged and sold to competitors. Third, it has implications for which capabilities and activities are considered core. Amazon now hosts several hundreds of small e-commerce providers on its site. The shops benefit not only from the Amazon name but also from the visitors to the Amazon site in return for a listing fee and commission on each sale. Apart from the additional revenues from the shops, Amazon benefits from additional trade resulting from the visitors to the shops who then buy something else from the Amazon site.

Mini-case study: Motley Fool

An example of a site that makes good use of syndication is the Motley Fool (*www.fool.com*, *www.fool.co.uk*) (Figure 7.16), a popular personal finance site. It originates the content it uses on its own website, on its America Online site and in its own publications. It also syndicates this material through syndicators like iSyndicate. It acts as a syndicator itself, providing stockmarket commentary in various formats to sites such as Yahoo!, as well as to newspapers and to radio stations. Finally, it distributes syndicated business stories from news wires, such as Reuters.

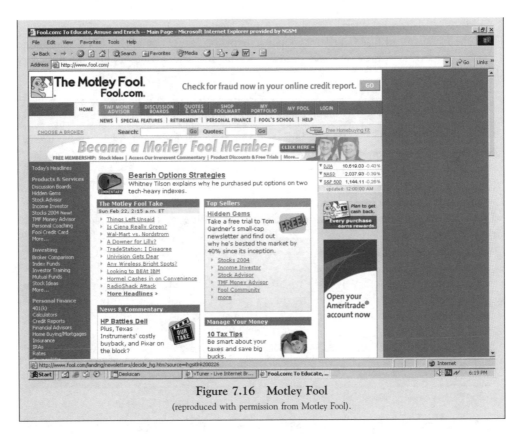

Figure 7.16 Motley Fool
(reproduced with permission from Motley Fool).

Uncertainty of market and technology

The final characteristic of e-commerce is the high uncertainty surrounding future markets and technologies. Courtney et al. (1997) identify three strategic postures that firms can adopt in the face of uncertainty: shaping the future, adapting to the future and reserving the right to play. A posture defines the intent of a strategy relative to the current and future state of an industry.

Shapers aim to play a leading role in shaping the industry, and their strategies are aimed at creating new opportunities in a market – either by shaking up relatively stable industries or by trying to control the direction of the market in industries with higher levels of uncertainty. Examples are Kodak, which is pursuing a shaping strategy in digital photography because this new technology supersedes chemical photography, and AOL, which is aiming to bring together the Internet and media industries. There are more opportunities for shapers in countries where the Internet market is less developed. In Japan, for example, the initial lack of interest in the Internet has allowed one entrepreneur, Masayoshi Son, to control the major companies in Internet sectors, including an Internet portal (Yahoo Japan), currency sales (Forexbank), insurance (Insweb), car retailing (CarPoint Japan), stockbroking (Etrade), stock exchange (Nasdaq Japan), a toy store (E-shopping Toys Japan) and a neighbourhood directory (Geocities Japan).

Mini-case study: Softbank

Softbank (Figure 7.17) is Japan's largest Internet-based firm and one of the largest Internet venture companies in the world. Softbank was established by Masayoshi Son, the son of Korean immigrants, in Japan. He left for the USA when still in high school and graduated from the University of California, Berkeley with an economics degree before returning to Japan to establish a string of ventures. By 1980, he had made his first million dollars by selling a design for an electronic translator to Sharp Corp., and he founded Softbank Corp. in Tokyo in 1981. By the mid-1990s, Softbank had achieved 40% domestic market shares in software distribution and 30% in software publishing.

Returning to the USA in 1995 with nearly a billion dollars to spend, Son lured a couple of Silicon Valley veterans to run Softbank Technology Ventures. In 1996, it invested $200 million in 55 companies in 4 months. Son has often talked of creating an

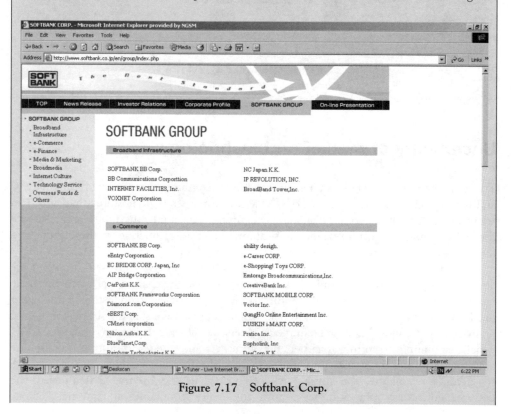

Figure 7.17   Softbank Corp.

> Internet zaibatsu, a reference to the pre-World War II Japanese corporate form better known as a keiretsu, or a vertically integrated manufacturing and trading conglomerate. However, since 1996, Son has concentrated less on empire building and more on betting. Son now prefers to invest about 30% of capital, rather than aiming for outright ownership of his targets. Softbank's basic strategy is to invest early and often and hope for a win from one of the many bets.
>
> The company suffered huge losses during the dot.com crash, but since then has bounced back with significant investment in broadband in Japan through its subsidiary Yahoo BB. Japan is now on the verge of overtaking the USA in the percentage of households with a high-speed Internet connection.

In contrast to shapers, adapters take the current industry structure and its future evolution as givens and try to take advantage of the opportunities the market offers. In environments with little uncertainty, this entails choices about strategic positioning in the current industry. At higher levels of uncertainty, this requires the ability to recognize and respond quickly to market developments. Examples are retail banks that have started up Internet operations after seeing the success of pioneers, such as Netbank in the USA.

The third strategic posture, reserving the right to play, involves making incremental investments now that will put a company in a position of advantage in the future; this allows the company to wait until the environment becomes less uncertain before formulating a strategy. Many firms have adopted this last posture in relation to e-commerce by making small investments in Internet ventures and waiting to see if they pay off. If the venture turns out well, the firm can invest more; if not, it can pull out without losing too much.

Internet strategy in practice

In a study of strategic decision making by e-commerce entrepreneurs (Chen, 2003a) one of the striking features was the high importance of the "fun" and excitement that the Internet offers and the chance to try out new ideas. For example, one entrepreneur described his enjoyment of the "buzz that comes from seeing the possibilities and seeing things work." It is, therefore, not surprising that the presence of a clear, self-generated vision came out as the strongest discriminating factor (Table 7.2).

This finding is consistent with the findings of other research, which has shown that successful entrepreneurs are more intuitive than the general population of managers. However, paradoxically, the survey also showed that although the entrepreneurs used their gut feeling more than managers, they also reported a relatively high degree of planning. The follow-up interviews provided some explanation for this apparent paradox. All the entrepreneurs reported a great deal of thinking before making important strategic decisions about the company. Much as professional sportsmen mentally rehearse activities before taking part in a tournament or race, what these

Table 7.2 Comparison of IT managers and Internet entrepreneurs

	IT managers' mean score	Internet entrepreneurs' mean score
Self-generated vision (1) versus relying on others' vision (10)	4.36	2.16
Gut feeling (1) versus planning in detail (10)	6.07	4.22
Planning (1) versus doing (10)	3.50	5.21
Not reliant on data (1) versus need for data (10)	5.79	4.36
Go with the flow (1) versus need clear deadlines (10)	5.86	5.86
Leader (1) versus worker (10)	4.71	6.93
Tough (1) versus sensitive to people (10)	4.71	5.50
Need for other people (1) versus work well alone (10)	6.43	7.29
Long-term (1) versus short-term interest in job (10)	3.07	3.30
Doing job for interest (1) versus doing it for the money (10)	4.07	3.86

entrepreneurs appeared to be doing was mentally running through possible scenarios and responses. In fact, one specifically described the process as scenario planning (Chapter 10).

Strategic options

Using the above techniques a variety of different strategic options can be generated, but often there may be so many that it may be useful to categorize them for further examination. In traditional strategy textbooks, probably the best known generic strategies framework is that of Porter (1980), who classifies strategies into three types: lowest cost, differentiation and focus. Porter argues that firms should clearly pursue one of the generic strategies and avoid "getting stuck in the middle". However, many have argued that this framework does not adequately represent competition in today's more technologically driven industries, where firms actively pursue low cost, differentiation and focus simultaneously. Hax and Wilde (1999) have proposed a new framework for generic strategies, which they believe more accurately reflects the new competition (Figure 7.18). They propose that the new strategies can be classified into three types: best product, customer solutions and system lock-in.

The best product strategic option is built on the classic forms of competition through

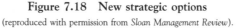

Figure 7.18 New strategic options

(reproduced with permission from *Sloan Management Review*).

low cost or differentiation. A company can achieve cost leadership by aggressively pursuing economies of scale, product and process simplification, and significant product market share, which allows it to exploit experience and learning effects. A company can differentiate by enhancing product attributes in a way that adds value for the customer. It can achieve this differentiation through technology, brand usage, additional features or special services. Through the best product option, companies create bonds with customers through the intrinsic superiority of their product or service. Important means for this purpose are introducing products rapidly and establishing a so-called dominant design.

The customer solutions strategic option is based on a wider offering of products and services which satisfies most, if not all, the customer's needs. The focus here is on the customer, rather than the product. A company might offer a broad bundle of products and services that is targeted and customized to a specific customer's needs. For example, by working closely with customers, the company can anticipate needs and create products that best meet their needs; this too creates strong bonds. Learning about customer needs increases the company's ability to satisfy the customers future requirements, while learning by the customer can also create switching costs.

The system lock-in strategic option has the widest possible scope. Instead of narrowly focusing on the product or the customer, the company considers all the players in the system which contribute to the creation of economic value. In this strategic position, bonding plays its most influential role. The company is particularly concerned with nurturing, attracting and retaining so-called "complementors" along with the normal industry participants. Typical examples include computer hardware and software producers, high-fidelity equipment manufacturers and CD disk providers; TV set, video recorder, and videocassette makers; and producers of telephone handsets and telecom networks. The epitome of this position is achieving a de facto proprietary standard, such as the Windows operating system.

These options are not mutually exclusive, but it is useful to differentiate the three alternatives in terms of their scope, scale and bonding (see Table 7.3).

Scope significantly increases as we move from best product to system lock-in. At the extreme end of the best product position, where a company often opts for low cost, the scope is cut to a minimum. The scope expands to include product features as a company moves to a differentiated, best product position. It then expands beyond the product to

Table 7.3 Characteristics of three options for strategic positioning

	Best product	Customer solutions	System lock-in
Scope	Defeatured/Fully featured • Low cost • Differentiated	Broad product range • Bundling • Joint development • Outsourcing	Nurturing complementors • Variety and number • Open architecture
Scale	Product • Market share	Customer • Customer share	System • Complementor state
Bonding	Link to product • First to market • Dominant design	Link to customers • Customer lock-in • Learning • Customization	Link to system • Competitor lock-out • Proprietary standards

include the customer's activities in the case of customer solutions. The company finally reaches the broadest possible scope as a system lock-in company when it includes complementors.

Scale, typically measured as market share, is critical when evaluating a best product position, while in the case of customer solutions a company must consider its share of a customer's purchases. For a system lock-in position, complementor share is the most critical consideration.

Ultimately, bonding deals with the forces that link the product or service with the customer. In the best product option, this is done through the characteristics of the product itself. The customer solutions position achieves this through learning and customization. In the system lock-in position, the bonding mechanism is the proprietary standard which is critical in achieving profitability and sustainability.

The real value of new business models

Mention has been made several times in this and earlier chapters of new e-business models. But, what exactly do we mean and how important are they? One definition is "an architecture for the product, service and information flows, including the various business actors and their roles; and a description of the potential benefits for the various business actors; and a description of the sources of revenues" (Timmers, 1998). Many schemes have been suggested for classifying different types of e-business models (Alt and Zimmerman, 2001). Depending on the classification scheme as many as 29 e-business models currently in use have been described. However, some key distinctions identified between various models are:

Table 7.4 Failure rates of different business models

	Survival rate (%)	Failure rate (%)
Portal	80.0	20.0
Marketplace	75.0	25.0
Free site	85.0	15.0
Pay site	91.5	8.5
Pure Internet	77.2	22.8
Clicks and mortar	97.4	2.6

Reproduced with permission from Business Horizons.

- The supply chain model.
- Whether the model serves the business or consumer market.
- Whether the model is a pure Internet or clicks-and-mortar model.
- The revenue model.

Mahadevan (2000); Weill and Vitale (2001)

To see how important the type of business model is, Chen (2003b) compared the odds of survival of businesses adopting different models. A sample of 453 US Internet businesses considered among the "best in their class" in existence in 1999 was drawn up from leading magazines and directories. Their survival or failure in 2002 was then compared according to the type of business model.

An initial analysis seemed to confirm the anecdotal reports from Internet entrepreneurs, investors and venture capitalists. Table 7.4 shows that failure rates are higher among:

- B2C versus B2B sites.
- Retail, portal and marketplaces versus direct sales.
- Free versus pay sites.
- Pure Internet versus clicks-and-mortar sites.

However, one problem with the preceding analysis is that it is difficult to distinguish the importance of the different factors and ignores the possible joint effects of two or more factors. For example, the direct sales model is more common in B2B sites than in B2C sites. How much of the increased survival rate among B2B sites is due to the higher use of the direct sales business model and how much is due to the fact that it operates in a B2B market? A statistical technique that allows the relative contributions of all the factors to be determined is binary logistic regression. When this is used a slightly different picture emerges. Table 7.5 shows that – although retail and portal sites are slightly less likely to survive compared with direct sales sites, marketplace models are more likely to survive compared with direct sales sites and free sites are slightly less likely to survive compared

Table 7.5   Odds of survival of different business models

Retail versus direct sale	0.93 : 1
Portal versus direct sale	0.97 : 1
Portal versus direct sale	0.97 : 1
Marketplace versus direct sale	1.3 : 1
Pay versus free	0.8 : 1
Pay versus free	0.8 : 1
Clicks and mortar versus pure Internet	11 : 1*

* Significant at <0.01 level.
Reproduced with permission from Business Horizons.

with pay sites – these differences were not statistically significant. In contrast, the effect of offline revenues was highly significant. Clicks-and-mortar sites are nearly *11 times more likely to survive* than pure Internet sites. This finding was confirmed by Day et al. (2003), who similarly found in their study of B2B exchanges, that there was a statistically significant difference in the proportion of independent start-ups versus exchanges linked to incumbents that ceased operations.

The finding is also consistent with other research that shows that firms that are part of a group are often at a strategic advantage compared with independent firms, since the parent company can provide support through utilization of common resources, such as brands, relationships with customers and suppliers, as well as cash; this is of particular significance given the high "burn rate" of Internet businesses.

The study also showed that it is important to consider the effect of payment in conjunction with other dimensions of the business model. Comparing the effect of payment in different supply models shows that the risk of failure decreases with payment in the case of retail and direct sales sites, but increases in the case of portals and marketplaces (Figure 7.19). One reason may be that, in the case of portals or marketplaces, it may be difficult to attract a critical mass of users unless the service is offered free, at least initially. The importance of scale in the success of virtual communities has been shown in other studies (Bughin and Zeisser, 2001). The point is that in deciding whether or not to charge for the service, different business models behave differently and different elements of the business model cannot be considered in isolation.

Payment is of particular significance given the high "burn rate" of Internet businesses. Like many new ventures, Internet businesses are under severe pressures to grow quickly to satisfy investors, so not only do Internet business models need to be flexible they also need to enable rapid growth. A common route that has been adopted by many Internet businesses has been to invest heavily in building a brand and customer base in order to generate more cash through an initial public offering (IPO) (Figure 7.20).

Successful businesses by definition are ones that have managed to match the stages of growth while working with a limited capital. If all goes well the company is able to make

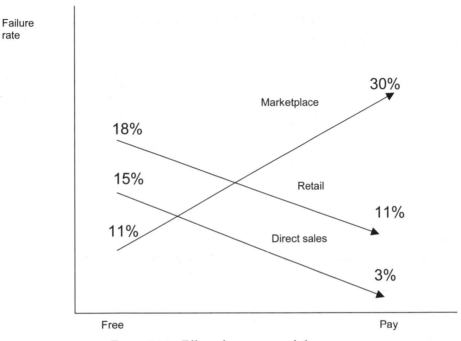

Figure 7.19 Effect of payment on failure rates.

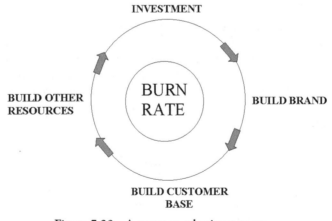

Figure 7.20 A common e-business route
(reproduced with permission from Business Horizons).

sufficient progress and access additional capital by the time it has used up its initial capital. However, if the timing is wrong, the "burn rate", or the rate at which it uses up its funds, may be too high and the company fails to generate additional funds by the time it has used up its start-up capital.

Evaluating e-business opportunities and e-business models

Valuing e-business opportunities, particularly those using a new business model, is difficult for a number of reasons. First, like many new businesses, they will typically have losses or very small profits for a few years, mainly owing to the high marketing costs required in order to attract new customers. This is compounded by the fact that there is often an absence of historical data and no or few comparable firms, since e-businesses are a relatively new phenomenon. Owing to the difficulties of precise valuations, many analysts have resorted to rough and ready methods such as the following:

Price–earnings ratio

P/E ratios are widely used in valuing businesses, even traditional businesses, the principle being to calculate the value of a share by multiplying earnings per share by the price/earnings ratio. The two most common ways to determine the P/E ratio are historical averages and industry-wide averages. Historical averages are usually not possible as most Internet companies have very short trading histories. Industry-wide P/Es are in principle a viable alternative, but, if the whole industry is overvalued, the industry-wide P/E will lead investors to overvalue the shares of individual companies.

Price-to-sales ratios

Although many Internet companies neither have earnings nor expect to have them in the foreseeable future, they do have sales; so, some analysts have suggested using price-to-sales ratios. This does give some advantages in valuing companies without earnings, but, as discussed above for P/E ratios, if the whole industry is overvalued, then industry-wide price-to-sales ratios will lead to inflated valuations of the individual companies within the industry. Also, this measure ignores profit margins, which are of course critical to determine profitability.

TEMA (theoretical earnings multiple analysis)

Some analysts have tried to obtain more accurate valuations by estimating revenue growth and profit margins. This solves, at least in principle, the problem that many Internet companies currently have no earnings. The problem it creates, of course, is how to come up with an accurate estimation of future revenue growth and operating margins.

Visitor count

Given the problems with the previous methods, some analysts prefer to use figures that do not have to be guessed, such as number of individuals that visit a website. The problem then is that it is difficult to place a value on a visitor.

LTV (lifetime value of a customer)

A similar idea for subscription websites is to value the number of subscribers. The LTV method is widely used in the publishing business to figure out how much a magazine can afford to spend in order to get new subscribers. As is well known, prices of new subscriptions typically do not cover their costs, but they generate two additional sources of revenue: subscription renewals and advertisement revenue. For example, assume an average subscriber sticks to a magazine for, say, 4 years, and brings in an annual revenue of, say, £100 (£20 for a subscription renewal and £80 for advertising), that works out at a value of £400 per subscriber over his or her lifetime.

Price-per-engineer

An alternative to valuing customers is to value the employees of the company. This method is mostly used to value companies that make Internet hardware and software, data-networking security products, semiconductor technologies, and e-commerce applications. The problem is, of course, that the profitability of a company is not just dependent on talented engineers.

These methods assume that these alternative measures provide a more reliable indication of long-term performance than earnings.

Adjusted discounted cash flow

A more precise way of valuing business opportunities than those listed above is to prepare an adjusted discounted cash flow forecast. There are a number of ways in which earnings can theoretically be normalized (Damodaran, 2002). With a firm that has a substantial earnings history and an underlying stability in terms of its business mix, two methods are:

1. Average the firm's dollar earnings over prior periods. The simplest way to normalize earnings is to use the average earnings over prior periods. This is best suited for firms that have a long history of earnings and that have not changed significantly in scale over the period. If it is applied to a firm that has become grown or downsized significantly over time, the estimate will be incorrect.
2. Average the firm's return on capital or equity (or profit margins) over prior periods. In this approach averaging is done on scaled earnings instead of dollar earnings. The advantage of the approach is that it allows the normalized earnings estimate to reflect the current scale of the firm.

Where the firm does not have a substantial earnings history and an underlying stability in terms of its business mix, an alternative approach is to use current return on capital or equity (or margin) of comparable firms. As with the use of alternative measures, this method assumes that return on capital or equity is a more reliable guide than forecasts based on current earnings.

Where the business does not have a cash flow history and there are no comparable firms, one approach that has been suggested is to work backwards to the present, combining this with probability-weighted scenarios and classic strategic analysis (Desmet et al., 2000). Instead of trying to forecast cash flow in a high-growth, unstable market, the approach relies on forecasting cash flow in a more stable, lower growth state in the future; and then extrapolating back to current performance.

Adjust for leverage

Finally, earnings in an e-business can be negative because the firm takes on a large debt for other than operational reasons. This may arise, for example, because of significant infrastructure investments or because it was the only way in which the acquirer could raise funds for the acquisition. In such a case, another approach is to adjust for this debt, assuming normal leverage.

Choosing between the different approaches

Which approach – using alternative measures, normalizing earnings or adjusting leverage – should be used depends on the main reason the earnings are negative (Figure 7.21):

1. If the earnings are negative simply due to excessive debt but otherwise the firm is operationally sound, adjusting margins over time toward those of the larger and more stable firms in the sector should yield the best estimates.
2. If the operations are not sound but the phenomenon is transient, normalizing earnings would normally be the best approach.
3. If the earnings are negative due to long-term operational problems in the firm or sector, then use of alternative measures should be considered.

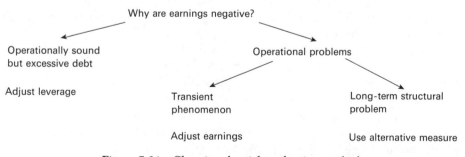

Figure 7.21 Choosing the right valuation method.

Gravity-free balance sheet

Some businesses need few, or even negative, net assets. The latter include some advertising agencies; some manufacturers who have re-engineered their balance sheets, such as

Dell; and journal publishers who are able to extract subscriptions from customers years ahead. Typically, these companies show negligible tangible fixed assets, either because they do not use them or because they lease them. The advantage of having negative net assets is that the company can use its balance sheet to generate cash and thus create value as it grows. Most companies need to invest cash to increase their assets as sales grow. These companies are able to get cash from customers well before they have to pay cash to their creditors and so enjoy a healthy working capital.

The "gravity-free" balance sheet has sometimes claimed to explain Internet valuations; for example, Mauboussin and Hiler (1999) write:

> We disagree with the consensus view that hype and hysteria drive the high flying valuations of internet stocks. ... Earnings for an internet company can substantially understate the company's total free cash flow ... (because) the balance sheet of a New Economy company can unveil an important source of cash. ... What is obvious is that many Internet companies are currently incurring losses as they spend millions on marketing, while their off-line competitors reap cash earnings. What is less obvious is that New Economy companies spend much less on their computers and office space than Old Economy companies spend on bricks-and-mortar and working capital.

Real options

An alternative method for valuing Internet companies is to take into account the future options that the firm has available. Many e-businesses are investments that are not likely to be profitable until some time in the future, but offer investors the possibility to participate in future market growth opportunities. An alternative approach to DCF valuation in such cases is to use real options. This technique has been applied to other uncertain and long-term investments, such as R&D (Trigeorgis, 1996), and more recently to IT systems (e.g., Benaroch and Kaufmann, 2000). The advantages of real options over traditional valuation methods is that they take into consideration the flexibility to take managerial actions that can change project outcomes over time. This flexibility can add value to the net present value (NPV) of a project. Some typical options that may be hidden in a project are options to abandon the project or to expand the project:

- *Abandon option* The project may contain an option to abandon it at some future date, if the return is not good, and direct resources to other uses.
- *Expansion option* The project may contain an option to increase investment at some point in the future if results are promising.

These options may not be available if an initial investment is not made, so they need to be factored into assessments of strategic options; this can be done by calculating the value of an equivalent financial derivative. For example, the option to expand can be considered as the equivalent of a call option that gives the holder the right to buy the asset for an agreed price at a future date. The option to abandon the project can be considered as the equivalent of a put option to sell the asset for an agreed price at a future date.

The value of the financial option can then be calculated using the Black–Scholes option pricing model:

$$P = SN(d_1) - X e^{-r_f T} \cdot N(d_2)$$

$$d_1 = \frac{\ln(S/X) + (r_f + \sigma^2/2)T}{\sigma \sqrt{T}}$$

$$d_2 = d_1 - \sigma \sqrt{T}$$

where P is the price of a call option, $N(\cdot)$ is the cumulative normal distribution function, S is the underlying asset, r is the volatility of S, X is the option's exercise price, T is the time to maturity and r_f is the risk-free rate.

Fortunately, it is not usually necessary to calculate real options values directly using the Black–Scholes equation, as tables have been prepared to simplify pricing (see, e.g., Luehrman, 1998). The difficulty is to identify the appropriate option that a project contains and to estimate the values in the equation: r_f can be estimated from the market interest rate on government bonds, r can be estimated from similar projects, while S, X and T can be estimated from conventional DCF analyses.

One of the key insights provided by a real options analysis is that it shows that the value of an option increases as volatility increases and it allows this factor to be considered in the valuation of projects; this may highlight the hidden potential of projects that would appear unprofitable using conventional DCF analysis. Luehrman (1998) uses the analogy of a tomato garden (Figure 7.22). Clearly, ripe tomatoes (projects whose value exceeds their cost and also have low volatility) should be invested in now. However, the graph also identifies other projects that may be worth investing in. For example, it may still be worth investing in a project whose value is less than cost according to conventional DCF analysis, but which has a high volatility (a green tomato) as there is a chance that the project will pay off in a big way.

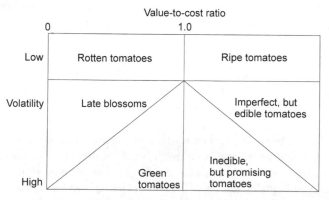

Figure 7.22 Tomato garden
(reproduced with permission from Harvard Business School Press).

Real options and game theory

A promising approach is to combine real options with game-theoretic models (Chen, 2003c). Game theory is a branch of mathematics that applies mathematical techniques to analyse the outcomes of interactions between players in games and has recently been applied with growing success and interest in the strategic management field. An example of how this might be applied is valuing the know-how in e-businesses.

One of the greatest problems with e-businesses, as with many other high-tech businesses, is that much of the value lies in know-how or trade secrets. Legally, this is defined as knowledge outside the public domain gained during the course of employment which may be advantageous to a competitor, and is normally protected as a legal obligation of employees either explicitly or implicitly in the contract of employment.

The simplest case is where the firm has no tangible assets and its value consists entirely of the skills of its workers and management. In this case the added value of the firm will be given by the sum of the contribution of the workforce and the contribution of the management and owners, with the split in compensation being determined by bargaining between the workforce and management. This bargaining can be modelled as a simple bargaining game in which each party exchanges offers (Baird et al., 1994). The most extreme option available to the employer is to sell off the assets of the firm, while the most extreme option available to the workers is to strike and shut the firm down.

The outcome of such a bargaining game would turn on such factors as how firm-specific the skills of the workers are, the economic conditions and availability of alternative employment, the availability of potential buyers, legal restraints in the event of a strike and legal restraints on any new owners. Thus, the credibility of the threat to sell off the firm depends on whether the employees have firm-specific skills doing their current jobs. The ability to sell assets is less credible when employees have developed firm-specific skills, since a new employer would be more likely to keep them than hire new workers. Similarly, if the workers can readily find work and transfer their skills elsewhere, it will also increase their bargaining position.

On the other hand, if the employer is free to hire new workers in the event of a strike, this will strengthen its bargaining position. Similarly, were new buyers free of existing obligations and free to restructure the firm as they wished, the employer has a much stronger threat in the bargaining game with its workforce. The presumed value of the firm thus depends on the agreements reached by the owner, legal restraints and the options available to owners.

Likewise, brands can be valued by treating them as a method of signalling quality and other product characteristics to consumers; this allows various models developed in game theory to be applied, such as Akerlof's (1970) classic "market for lemons" model in which price signals quality. In this model, Akerlof shows that relying on high prices as a signal of quality can lead to market failure if producers of low-quality goods can just as easily charge high prices as producers of high-quality goods. Brands may thus be a better signal of quality by virtue of the fact that they are costly investments for firms to make. Thus, the commitment of the firm as evidenced by its advertising for the brand can signal to the buyer that the seller has enough confidence in the product to invest in the brand. For example, Nalebluff and Brandenburger (1996) cite the example of Gillette, which spent more than $100 million on the launch of its Sensor shaving system in 1990, and argue that it was not only the information content in the advertisements about the technological superiority of the system that was responsible for the success of the campaign but also the obviously expensive nature of the advertisements which demonstrated Gillette's confidence in the new product. Such an analysis would suggest that, in determining the value of the brand, we should seek to include a measure of how much the brand increased consumer confidence in the product above and beyond the indication provided by the price. From an options perspective, additional value may also be derived from the strategic options made possible by that increased confidence. For example, investment in the Sensor brand might open up other markets, such as branded aftershave; this could be valued as a call option (an option to buy or make additional investments). Alternatively, a failure of test marketing might be of value in preventing additional losses in similar projects; this could be valued as a put option (the option to sell or cancel proposed investments).

Table 7.6 Checklist for developing an e-business strategy

Checklist questions	Possible frameworks
Industry analysis • What is the current state of the industry? • What are the possible effects of e-business on the industry • Where are profits to be made?	Five-forces analysis (Chapter 6) Value chain and value system analysis (Chapter 6) Three Ds analysis (Chapter 6) Richness–reach–affiliation (Chapter 6) Profit pool analysis Value net Value web Scenario analysis (Chapter 10)
E-business value proposition • What are the benefits that e-business can provide to the customer and to the firm? • What new value propositions can e-business provide?	Value curve E-business value drivers Delta model Eight Cs revenue streams
Timing • How quickly can this be achieved? • Is the market ready? • Is the technology ready?	Time pacing FTM, EMIT, MR
Strategic posture • What strategic posture do we adopt?	Shape–adapt–reserve the right to play
Checking the business case • What are the possible scenarios for how the industry will develop? • How robust is the e-business proposition? • Is it or could it be profitable?	Scenario analysis (Chapter 10) DCF modelling Real options

Summary

Developing an e-business strategy is unlike developing a strategy for a traditional business in several ways. This chapter highlighted five key characteristics of the market that need to be considered:

- Importance of virtual markets.
- Instability of the market.
- Speed of change.
- Interconnectedness of firms.
- High market uncertainty.

Each of these requires an adaptation of the traditional strategic management process and new or revised analytical frameworks. Several frameworks were described that are more appropriate in developing an e-business strategy. A checklist of questions to ask in developing an e-business strategy and some possible frameworks that can be used are shown in Table 7.6.

References

Akerlof, G. (1970). The market for lemons: quality uncertainty and the market mechanism. *Quarterly Journal of Economics*, **84**(3), 488–500.

Alt, R. and Zimmermann, H. (2001). Preface: Introduction to special section. *Business Models*, **11**(1), 3–9.

Amit, R. and Zott, C. (2001). Value creation in e-business. *Strategic Management Journal*, **22**, 493–520.

Baird, D.G., Gertner, R.H. and Picker, R.C. (1994). *Game Theory and the Law*. Harvard University Press, Cambridge, MA.

Benaroch, M. and Kaufmann, R.J. (2000). Justifying electronic banking network expansion using real options analysis. *MIS Quarterly*, **24**(2), 197–225.

Bughin, J. and Zeisser, M. (2000). The marketing scale effectiveness of virtual communities. *Electronic Markets*, **11**(4), 258–62.

Cartwright, S.D. and Oliver, R.W. (2000). Untangling the value web. *Journal of Business Strategy*, January/February, 22–7.

Chen, S. (2003a). Strategic decision-making by e-commerce entrepreneurs. *International Journal of Management and Decision-making*, **4**(2/3), 133–42.

Chen, S. (2003b). The real value of "e-business models". *Business Horizons*, **46**(6), 27–33.

Chen, S. (2003c). Valuing intellectual capital using game theory. *Journal of Intellectual Capital*, **4**(2), 191–201.

Cohan, P.S. (2000). *Net Profit: How to Invest and Compete in the World of Internet Business*. Jossey-Bass, San Francisco.

Courtney, H., Kirkland, J. and Viguerie, P. (1997). Strategy under uncertainty. *Harvard Business Review*, November/December, 66–79.

Damodaran, A. (2002). *The Dark Side of Valuation*. Financial Times/Prentice Hall, NJ.

Day, G.S., Fein, A.J. and Ruppersberger, G. (2003). Shakeouts in digital markets: Lessons from B2B exchanges. *California Management Review*, **45**(2), 131–50.

Deise, M., Nowikow, C., King, P. and Wright, A. (2000). *Executive's Guide to E-Business: From Tactics to Strategy*. John Wiley & Sons, New York.

Desmet, D., Francis, T., Hu, A., Koller, T.M. & Riedel, G.A. (2000). Valuing dot-coms. *McKinsey Quarterly*, 148–57.

Downes, L. and Mui, C. (1998). *Unleashing the Killer App: Digital Strategies for Market Dominance*. Harvard Business School Press, Boston.

Durfee, T. and Chen, G. (2002). Should we e-? *Journal of Business Strategy*, **23**(1), 14–17.

Eisenhardt, K.M. and Brown, S.L. (1998). Time pacing: Competing in markets that won't stand still. *Harvard Business Review*, **76**(2), March/April, 59–69.

Fischer, J. (1999). *Understanding the Internet Economy: A Companion Guide to The Motley Fool's Internet Report*. Motley Fool Inc., New York.

Gadiesh, O. and Gilbert, J.L. (1998). How to map your industry's profit pool. *Harvard Business Review*, May/June, 149–62.

Hax, A.C. and Wilde, D.L. (1999). The delta model: Adaptive management for a changing world. *Sloan Management Review*, Winter, 11–28.

Kim, W.C. and Mauborgne, R. (1997). Value innovation: The strategic logic of high growth. *Harvard Business Review*, 102–112.

Kim, W.C. and Mauborgne, R. (1999). Creating new market space. *Harvard Business Review*, **75**(1), January/February, 83–93.

Lambert, D. and Slater, S.F. (1999). First, fast and on time: The path to success. Or is it? *Journal of Product Innovation Management*, **16**(5), 427–38.

Luehrman, T.A. (1998). Strategy as a portfolio of real options. *Harvard Business Review*, **76**(5), September/October, 89–99.

Mahadevan, B. (2000). Business models for Internet-based e-commerce: An anatomy. *California Management Review*, **42**(4), 55–69.

Mauboussin, M. and Hiler, B. (1999). *Cashflow.com: Cash Economics in the New Economy*. Credit Suisse First Boston.

Nalebluff, B. and Brandenburger, A.M. (1996). *Co-opetition*. HarperCollins, London.

Porter, M.E. (1980). *Competitive Strategies: Techniques for Analyzing Industries and Competitors*. Free Press, New York.

Rayport, J. and Sviolka, J.J. (1995). Exploiting the virtual value chain. *Harvard Business Review*, **73**(6), November/December, 75–85.

Timmers, P. (1998). Business models for electronic commerce. *Electronic Markets*, **8**(2), 3–8.

Trigeorgis, L. (1996). *Real Options*. MIT Press, Cambridge, MA.

Weill, P. and Vitale, M.R. (2001). *Place to Space: Migrating to eBusiness Models*. Harvard Business School Press, Boston.

Werbach, K. (2000). Syndication: The emerging model for business in the Internet era. *Harvard Business Review*, May/June, 84–93.

D'Aveni, R.A. and Gunther, R. (1994). *Hypercompetition: Managing the Dynamics of Strategic Maneuvering*. Free Press, New York.

Clark, S.C. and Wheelwright, K.B. (1992). *Revolutionizing Product Development: Quantum Leaps in Speed, Efficiency and Quality*. Free Press, New York.

US Department of Commerce (2004). 2002 E-commerce multi-sector report. Available at *www.census.gov/estats*.

Key concepts

- Eight Cs revenue streams
- Burn rate
- Competitive capability equation
- Customer value equation
- DCF valuation
- Delta model
- Effective market introduction timing (EMIT)

- First-mover advantage
- First-to-mindshare (FTM)
- Gravity-free balance sheet
- Hypercompetition
- Managed responsiveness (MR)
- Profit pool
- Real options
- Scenario analysis

- Second-mover advantage
- Strategic postures
- Syndication
- Time pacing
- Value curve
- Value innovation
- Value net
- Value web
- Virtual value chain

Self-assessment questions

1 Explain how the virtual value matrix can be used to identify e-business opportunities.
2 Identify the various revenue streams that are possible in an e-business.
3 Explain the term "hypercompetition" and why this is relevant for e-business.
4 What are some of the key drivers of competitive advantage in e-business?
5 Sketch a diagram of the value net and the value web for your business.
6 What are the various roles that a business can adopt in syndication?
7 Describe and give examples for each of the generic strategies identified by Hax and Wilde.
8 List various ways for valuing an e-business and give their pros and cons.
9 Explain the term "gravity-free balance sheet".
10 Explain how real options can be used to value an e-business.

Discussion questions

1 Which traditional strategy frameworks are useful for e-business and which ones are less useful?
2 Is hypercompetition inconsistent with first-mover advantage?
3 Discuss the importance of time in e-business.
4 What are the key uncertainties in the e-business environment at present?
5 How should Internet businesses be valued?
6 What differences would you make in the strategic decision-making process in an e-business compared with an offline business?

IMPLEMENTING
AN E-BUSINESS STRATEGY

Introduction

Chapters 6 and 7 discussed e-business models and how to formulate an e-business strategy. This chapter discusses how to implement an e-business strategy. The importance of implementation is often overlooked; this was shown in a study conducted by Chen (2003). One of the surprising findings was that despite the emphasis given to business models by many Internet entrepreneurs, investors and researchers, failure rates did not vary much across business models, apart from clicks-and-mortar models having a distinct advantage over pure Internet business models (see p. 240: "The real value of new business models"). What was important was how the strategy was implemented.

The same five characteristics of e-business described in the last chapter which influence strategy formulation also influence how these strategies are implemented. Organizational structures, systems, processes and culture all need to be aligned with the strategy and take advantage of new technologies, while coping with the particular demands of competing in e-business.

Chapter 7 described Chen's (2003) study comparing successful versus failed Internet firms. The main finding was that clicks-and-mortar models had a significant advantage over pure play models. However, a second major finding was that, although the odds of failure did not differ much between models, the problems encountered did differ significantly. Table 8.1 shows the key problem areas by business model; this emphasizes that success or failure is less about the model than about how to implement that model.

Virtual organization

One of the most obvious issues that arises in e-businesses is that at least some parts of their operations are virtual. Venkateraman and Henderson (1998) suggest that virtual organizations can be built around three "vectors" (Figure 8.1):

- The customer interaction vector (virtual encounter) is concerned with opportunities for company-to-customer (C2C) interactions. As seen in Chapter 4, e-business offers a wide range of C2C interactions including interactive services, dynamic customization of products and virtual communities.
- The asset configuration vector (virtual sourcing) focuses on virtual integration in a business network, in sharp contrast to the vertically integrated model of the industrial economy. Using Internet firms can dynamically assemble and co-ordinate the assets required to deliver the product or service to customers.
- The knowledge leverage vector (virtual expertise) is concerned with using e-business technologies to leverage diverse sources of expertise within and across organizational boundaries. IT now enables knowledge and expertise to become drivers of value creation and organizational effectiveness.

Some of the virtual arrangements for the customer interaction vector have already been discussed in Chapter 4 on e-marketing, so this chapter will focus on the other two vectors.

Table 8.1 Key problem areas by business model

Business model		Key problem areas	Examples
Corporate structure	Pure Internet	Creating brand awareness Copycats	Wine.com
	Clicks and mortar	Channel conflict	Levi Strauss, Starbucks, Reebok
Revenue model	Free	Generating sufficient revenues elsewhere	The Globe, Cybergold, Alladvantage, Freeride
	Pay	Product/Price trade-offs	Iam, Arzoo
Supply model	Direct sales	Product/Service quality Cost of operations	Musicmaker
	Retailer	Shipping costs, speediness and reliability of delivery	Pets.com, Webvan, Kozmo, Furniture.com, eToys
	Portal	Attracting sufficient eyeballs Copycats	Go, Quepasa
	Marketplace	Gaining critical mass of buyers and sellers Copycats	Bizbuyer, LetsBuyIt, Bid.com, Metalsite, Chemdex
Market type	Consumer	Increasing consumer awareness, interest and access	PlanetRx, Mercata
	Business	Integrating with ERP systems of buyers	Rx.Zoho

ERP = enterprise resource planning

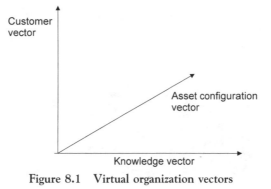

Figure 8.1 Virtual organization vectors
(reproduced with permission from *Sloan Management Review*).

Intranets and extranets were described in Chapter 2, and these can be used to provide significant benefits in the other two dimensions of virtuality.

Virtual knowledge/expertise

Groupware, such as Lotus Notes, has been used for several years now in business to facilitate teamwork over several locations and time periods. For example, consulting companies have used groupware to share knowledge and expertise among teams spread throughout the world, while pharmaceutical companies have used groupware to share knowledge among research teams in different parts of the world. However, corporate intranets can be used for the same purpose. As with the Internet, intranets have an advantage in that they use publicly available Internet standards and so are easy to install and use.

Mini-case study: Booz Allen Hamilton

In 1996 Booz Allen Hamilton (Figure 8.2) implemented one of the first global, Web-based intranets to support its knowledge management program. Called Knowledge Online, or KOL, the intranet has continued to thrive and now provides 3,500 Booz Allen Hamilton consultants access to the company's experts in all fields, including training, marketing documents, best practices, case studies and more. Today 83% of staff members in the company's worldwide commercial business sector access KOL on a monthly basis.

KOL offers today a range of applications from simple to sophisticated. Among them:

- A knowledge repository and expert skills database.
- A client information system.
- On-demand interactive training programs.

Figure 8.2   Booz Allen Hamilton
(reproduced with permission from Booz Allen Hamilton).

- An employee directory and human resources system.
- Recruiting and marketing applications.
- A time-reporting database and an automated digital library with links to outside private and public databases.

As well as its planned uses the company has found that by attaching author's names to documents the system has proved popular as a means of publicizing achievements within the company and that KOL has proved to be an invaluable training aid for new consultants.

Internet-based extranets have another significant advantage over previous software. They can also provide a link to other users, extending the range and usefulness of knowledge sharing; this allows specialist experts to be called on as and when required. For example, it allows physicians or other medical staff to get a second opinion on medical procedures by allowing other experts to view the patient records remotely. With webcams it is now even possible to make some visual diagnoses remotely.

Mini-case study: Hunter Area Telehealth Service, Australia

Hunter Area Telehealth Service (Figure 8.3) aims to provide better access to health services for rural and remote regions via telehealth initiatives. The service offers a full range of service and support for telehealth applications, including a fully integrated videoconferencing room and training facilities. Key advantages for patients include improved timeliness of diagnosis, increased access to specialist/professional opinion, reduction in travel time and improved availability of information for medical decisions regarding emergency transport decisions.

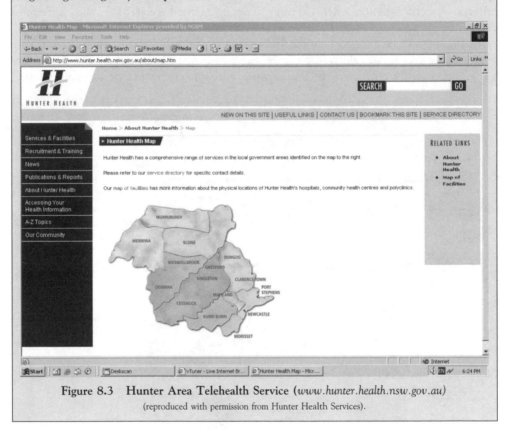

Figure 8.3   Hunter Area Telehealth Service (*www.hunter.health.nsw.gov.au*)
(reproduced with permission from Hunter Health Services).

The other main approach to corporate information management has been ERP software; this provides a centralized repository of information for the massive amount of transactional detail generated daily and allows the integration of business processes from planning to production, distribution and sales. Early versions of ERP software focused on internal networks and did not extend to external networks. Current efforts are aimed at integrating ERP and e-commerce applications. Three approaches that can be distinguished are the inside-out approach, outside-in approach and open electronic cart approach (Turban et al., 2000).

In the inside-out approach, leading ERP vendors, such as SAP, PeopleSoft, Oracle, Baan and J.D. Edwards, are attempting to extend their applications to users through a Web interface. For instance, SAP offers a B2B Internet commerce system to be used within the R13 system, while the strategic partner, Commerce One, provides additional commerce functionality to operate with SAP. The SAP business-to-business (B2B) procurement (BBP) solution provides a single entry screen to purchase goods and check pricing from multiple suppliers, availability and delivery times.

In the outside-in approach, multiple systems are integrated using software called an application server. Common application servers are Application Server (Netscape), Enterprise Server (Microsoft), Domino (Lotus), Websphere (IBM) and Enterprise Server (Sun).

In the open electronic cart approach, items from multiple sources can be tentatively selected and stored in an electronic cart or shopping basket on the buyer's PC. The e-cart has an open file format, so the ERP or any other legacy systems can be interfaced easily.

Mini-case study: Boots Healthcare International

The products of Boots' UK healthcare group (Figure 8.4) are sold around the world in over 130 countries. The product portfolio centres on three core categories, each with

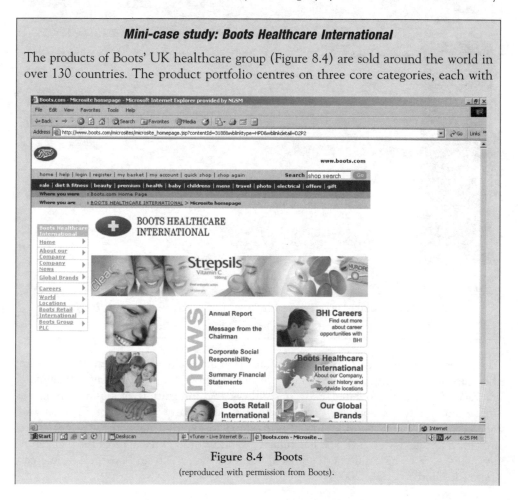

Figure 8.4   Boots

(reproduced with permission from Boots).

international market leading brands:

- Skincare – Balneum, E45, Lutsine, Onagrine, Curatoderm.
- Analgesics – Nurofen.
- Coughs and colds – Strepsils.

The products are sold directly to supermarkets, pharmacy chains and to individual pharmacy outlets (via wholesalers), with the major customers being major retailers, such as Boots the Chemist (BTC), Tesco, Sainsbury's and Safeway.

In June, 2003 Boots embarked on its biggest IT project to date, implementing wall-to-wall enterprise software from SAP across its 1,400 UK outlets and its sales and marketing company Boots Healthcare International. When completed it should be the biggest R/3 SAP implementation in retail. Boots will tightly integrate SAP with existing applications, such as its forecasting and replenishment engine and its tactical software for planning the location of goods in-store. Over time, the company will migrate its supply chain to SAP and use it for merchandising and supplier master data.

Many firms have created "business-to-employee", or B2E, portals. Among the advantages of B2E portals is the ability to personalize the interface to suit the user. With a B2E portal, as with many portals on the Internet, each user can choose what type of information will be accessible and how it is presented; this may not only be confined to work-related information, but to other daily information, such as company information and links to other sites relevant to activities and interests outside work.

Mini-case: Benefits of B2E portals
(source: Peoplesoft)

According to HR consultants PeopleSoft, by implementing an employee portal as opposed to maintaining its current intranet environment, a typical company can expect to achieve the following benefits:

- Cut administrative staff costs.
- Reduce the time needed to maintain Web-based content by up to 80%.
- Cut the time and effort needed to deploy and Web-enable applications by up to 55%.
- Reduce web developer training by 40%.
- Reduce application developer training by 75%.
- Reduce new hire set-up time by 54%.
- Eliminate the need to administer user job and profile changes manually.
- Reduce printing, distribution and storage costs.
- Lower helpdesk volume by 20%.

For an organization with 10,000 employees, 12 application developers and a 5% employee growth rate, implementing an enterprise portal at a cost of $1.7 million, they calculated that these savings add up to an internal rate of return of 87% and a payback period of 1.2 years. The above figures do not include increased productivity of employees and managers in non-administrative positions.

A portal greatly simplifies many regularly occurring activities and processes for the average user; this equates to an extra 15 hours per employee annually for productive work, with a manager gaining 30 hours. Other "soft" benefits not covered in the study included improved employee satisfaction, which is now known to be associated with enhanced customer loyalty.

As e-business technologies, coupled with continued advances in voice recognition and artificial intelligence, become more commonplace, even more radical changes in the use of information are expected. Just as there has been a paradigm shift in e-business strategy, Malhotra (2000) argues that this requires a shift from information management to knowledge management; this will require systems that move beyond simply capturing past experiences to using that information creatively. The emphasis will be on doing the right thing than simply doing the thing right.

Virtual sourcing

Extranets provide the technical driver for virtualizing along the third dimension of virtual sourcing. An organizational form that has been noted in many industries over the last decade and is particularly evident in e-business is the network organization. A classic, pre-Internet example is Benetton, which manages a complex network of suppliers near its base in Milan to provide just-in-time (JIT) garments to its shops. Using a model similar to the one Dell uses for PCs, Benetton holds its garments in an undyed state and only dyes them when it knows which colours are most in demand in their stores; this gives the company more flexibility over production and enables the company to better match supply to customer demand.

Moore (1997) has likened management of such networks to managing an ecosystem. The significance of an ecosystem is that organizations co-evolve. Co-evolution occurs any time two or more systems are linked in such a way that changes to one feedback into the other. Biologists have long been aware of co-evolution, which raises several questions about the traditional Darwinian view that species adapt to their environments. According to the co-evolutionary viewpoint, species co-create the environments with other species. Co-evolution also calls into question the idea that species evolve to fit some established niche in their environments, because the discovery of the niche will inevitably change everything surrounding it and even the niche itself.

In biology an example of a co-evolutionary relationship is the relationship between flowers and bees. Plants produce flowers in order to attract bees that in turn benefit the plant by distributing the pollen. Such relationships are called symbiotic. On the other hand, co-evolution can take the form of biological arms races that occur between predator and prey species. The prey may have to develop more elaborate defence mechanisms to

Table 8.2 Stages of co-evolutionary business development

Stage of development	Leadership challenges	Co-operative challenges	Competitive challenges
Pioneering	Value	Work with customers and suppliers to define new value proposition	Protect ideas from others
Expansion	Critical mass	Bring new offer to market by working with suppliers to increase supply	Establish dominant standard, tie lead customers, suppliers and channels
Authority	Lead co-evolution	Provide compelling vision for the future that encourages supplier and customers to work together	Maintain strong bargaining power
Renewal	Continuous performance improvement	Work with innovators to bring new ideas to market	Maintain high barriers to entry, customer-switching costs

predators, including thorns and poisons in plants, while predators counter these defences by developing resistance to certain poisons.

Similar types of relationships can be found among e-businesses. For example, there is competition between different channels, such as television, mobile telephones and PC networks. Symbiotic relationships can also be found. For example, search engines and websites have a mutual dependence. Yahoo could not survive without the advertising from websites. On the other hand, without search engines many websites could not attract enough traffic to survive. Instead of the conventional strategic management notion of fit to one's environment, a better image is that of co-evolving firms in an interconnected network.

Moore (1997) describes how these two aspects of co-evolution change in the four stages of business development (Table 8.2). Different stages of development present different management challenges.

As business ecosystems emerge, the traditional multi-divisional form, or the "M-form", organization is being replaced by the ecosystem form, or the "E-form", organization. The E-form organization integrates all the functions and the organizational networks needed to establish end-to-end business processes.

An E-form organization must manage the economics of the total ecosystem to its advantage, while satisfying other players in the system; this is easier where the firm has strong power relative to other players. For example, the strong power of Ford in Australia was crucial in building an electronic data interchange (EDI) network of suppliers (Ratnasingham, 1998).

Mini-case study: Blue Scope Steel

Blue Scope Steel (formerly BHP Steel) (Figure 8.5) is Australia's largest steel company with manufacturing operations in Australia, New Zealand, Asia, Oceania and the USA and sales offices in 15 countries worldwide.

Chan and Swatman (2000) compared the implementation issues at different stages of the process:

1. *Early implementation* Value-added network (VAN)-based EDI commenced in September, 1988 with a PC-based EDI pilot, which went live in January, 1989 and ended in 1993.
2. *Electronic trading gateway (ETG) and barcoding* A major e-commerce project, which brought EDI and e-commerce efforts in-house. This project commenced in 1989 and was fully integrated by 1994, although some components continued to be developed after that time.
3. *Internet e-commerce* This project started in 1996 and is ongoing.

They found that in the early stages of implementation, technological issues seemed to dominate the process, but, over time, management and business issues became

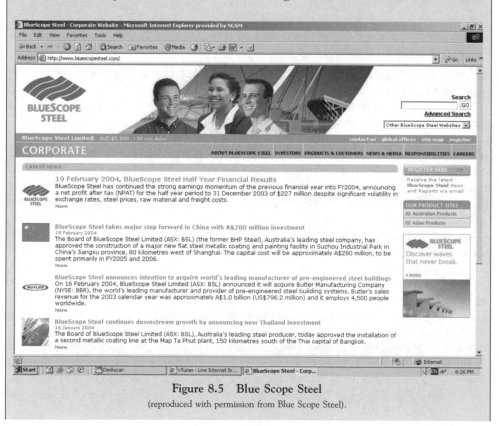

Figure 8.5 Blue Scope Steel
(reproduced with permission from Blue Scope Steel).

increasingly important. In the first phase technical and software problems were the main issues. In the second phase the main problem was getting customers involved. After 4 years BHP Steel only had three major customers trading electronically. The first phase was easier since suppliers had more incentive than customers to participate. With Internet-based e-commerce the technology is less of an issue: the main issue is serving the needs of trading partners at both ends of the value chain.

Internet-based systems are likely to be easier to implement than systems based on previous technologies, such as EDI. Reasons include the low cost and widespread availability of the technology, ease of use and familiarity of employees with the technology (Wells, 2000). Another factor that may be important in persuading customers to adopt the system is that the technology is based on an open standard, so customers would not be tied by the system to a particular supplier as would be the case in an EDI system.

Mini-case: Implementing an e-business logistics system at USCS

USCS (Figure 8.6) is a public, refrigerated warehousing company, operating 31 warehouses and an extensive food distribution programme, in eight states in the USA. In 1999, following the defection of a key client to a competitor that had a more developed IT infrastructure, USCS re-evaluated the firm's IT priorities based on the recognition of a rapid need for an e-commerce strategy that would help USCS to leapfrog the competition.

The project was launched at the start of November, 1999 with a project team consisting of the head of IT, the programming supervisor and a number of representatives from the business side. After 1 month, it was determined that the project should be broken down into the following component parts:

- An application needed to be written that would provide the information/services on the Web.
- A wide area network (WAN) was needed to link the remote AS400s.
- An Internet service provider (ISP) was needed to support the interface of the application with the Web.

It was agreed that the scope of the system would be to:

- Place everything that internal users could see on customers' screens.
- Provide online order entry.
- Provide carriers with a portal to update the status of orders (i.e., schedule and delivery status).

Because of the relative lack of e-commerce expertise at USCS, the company decided to rely on external resources for everything. The software production was outsourced to an offshore (India)-based company. However, owing to the complexity of the existing system and the tight time lines dictated by the project, the company outsourced the

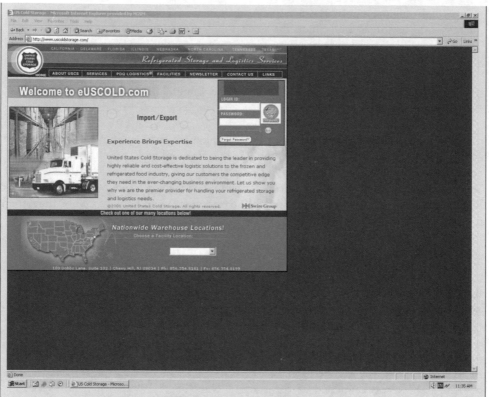

Figure 8.6   US Cold Storage

(reproduced with permission from US Cold Storage).

development of the WAN to existing contractors. Finally, following a pre-qualification process, the selection of an ISP was conducted on the basis of competitive bids.

Approximately a year after the launch, USCS conducted a post-implementation review with three key users; this identified lessons to be learned about: speed of development versus product; the importance of maintaining internal awareness; the target market; and staffing.

USCS made a decision not to consult with the future users of the system because the goal was to get the product out as quickly as possible. Accordingly, it was agreed that consulting future users to achieve a consensus on requirements and specifications ran the risk of being too lengthy a process. On reflection, given the size of the user's *post hoc* gap evaluations and the extensive amount of reprogramming that was necessary to fix the site, a more efficient approach may have been to involve customers in the more detailed design (phase 2, or 3 months into the project), rather than after the beta-testing phase.

As the primary aim of the system was to "help customers do their jobs better", in retrospect the company recognized that more effort should have been put into aggressively promoting the system's benefits and training plant managers and front line staff. The initial enthusiasm for the system was not capitalized on, and this made promotion at a later date harder.

At the outset of the project, it was perceived that the primary target market would be large companies that required real-time information on the status of their orders and inventories. However, it became apparent that many large companies were becoming increasingly reliant on the information resident in their own ERP systems. It also became evident that the system provided immense benefits for the smaller and medium-sized customers that did not have sophisticated inventory/order management systems. More effort should have been spent on identifying the needs of smaller users.

USCS had expected that the introduction of an online logistics service system would result in a reduction in back office personnel; this has not been the case so far, and a decrease in back office staffing levels is no longer expected. Although there has been a cut in the more mundane back office activities, like faxing and answering telephone calls, this has been replaced by a number of other activities that were never previously performed, but should have been.

Source: Rae-Smith and Ellinger (2002).

Changing to a virtual organization

Bringing about successful organizational change usually requires several things to be changed at the same time. For example, the McKinsey seven Ss model (Peters and Waterman, 1982) identifies seven things that need to be aligned in strategic change:

- Strategy.
- Systems.
- Structure.
- Style.
- Staff.
- Skills.
- Shared values.

Similarly, Johnson (1988) envisages a similar clustering of seven things around the organizational "paradigm", those things taken for granted in an organization (Figure 8.7).

In making the transition to an e-business all the above elements need to be balanced. For example, in the case of Marshall Industries, the company had to make parallel changes in a number of areas – structure, culture, processes and compensation systems (El-Sawy et al., 1999).

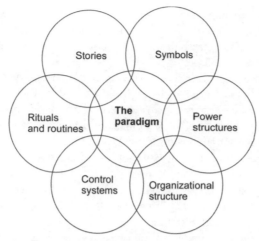

Figure 8.7 Organizational cultural web
(reproduced with permission from John Wiley & Sons).

Mini-case study: Reorganization at Marshall Industries

In 1991, when Rob Rodin took over as CEO, Marshall's processes and thinking were internally focused and customer needs were not given priority. All work was centred on meeting deadlines and short-term financial goals. For example, the company's 600 salespeople and branches operated independently in an MBO (management by objectives) incentive and promotion system. This system of incentives and promotions caused problems such as:

- 20% of total sales were shipped in the last 3 days of the month or quarter.
- Salespeople would ship ahead to make a quota, a number or win a prize, even if that was not best for the customer.
- Constant conflicts between departments about corporate cost allocations.
- Divisions hiding inventory from each other to keep for their own customers, resulting in shortages.
- Selling of products in inventory was pushed, even if it meant the customer not getting state-of-the-art products.

Rodin initiated a process of transformation to become a more customer-focused organization using e-business technology; this involved changes in organizational strategy, structure, systems and process to deliver quality, as well as building the necessary IT infrastructure (Figure 8.8).

The first step in aligning the organization and its processes with customer needs was to clearly state the goals in a way that all employees and customers could understand and aim to fulfil. Marshall came up with the slogan "Free, Perfect, Now" meaning products and services at the lowest possible cost, highest possible quality, greatest

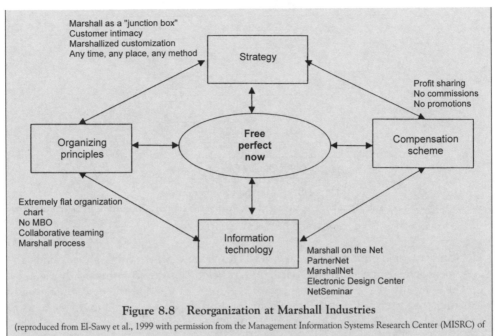

Figure 8.8   Reorganization at Marshall Industries

(reproduced from El-Sawy et al., 1999 with permission from the Management Information Systems Research Center (MISRC) of the University of Minnesota).

possible customization and fastest possible delivery time. "Free" was expanded to include the total cost of value-added services, such as inventory management and testing for customers as well as individual transactions. Similarly, "Perfect" was expanded from conformance to specifications and no defects to enhancements by features and benefits, customization and the anticipation of future needs. The "Now" aspect was also expanded to include increased accessibility (24/7), reduced delivery time and time to market for customers' products.

The new strategy called for conceptualizing Marshall as a junction box between customers and suppliers, focused on adding value, seeking to create a brand name by emphasizing the services through partnerships with customers and suppliers; this in turn was reflected in changes to the organizational structure. One of the most innovative changes was to invert the traditional organizational chart and place the customers at the top (Figure 8.9).

This emphasized that employees were more accountable to customers than any internal supervisor. Anyone in the organization could be the contact person for a particular customer, while others in the organization become the support functions for the contact person. Furthermore, the company has a chief quality officer instead of a president at the head. Every action taken and every decision made at Marshall, even the President's, is guided by quality goals set forth by the Chief Quality Officer.

There are no functions or departments in the organization, reflecting Marshall's surround strategy where work is organized around the needs of the customer rather than

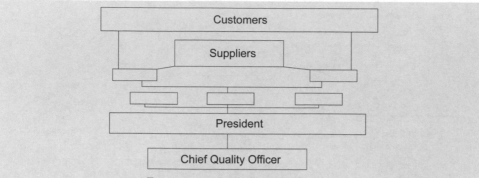

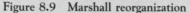

Figure 8.9   Marshall reorganization
(reproduced from El-Sawy et al., 1999 with permission from the Management Information Systems Research Center (MISRC) of the University of Minnesota).

according to rigid functional boundaries. This boundaryless philosophy extends to customers and suppliers, driving Marshall to develop close relationships with them.

The company also redesigned its compensation structure to fit the new strategy and structure. To foster collaboration, each employee at Marshall was paid in the same way and shared in a company-wide profit-sharing bonus pool, instead of getting paid by commissions. To reassure employees, educational seminars were run for months after the change and star earners under the old compensation structure were enlisted to promote the virtues of the new structure.

In addition to the new compensation scheme, a standard process, called the Marshall process (Figure 8.10), was instituted to provide a framework to orient all activities in the organization. Quality considerations and constant feedback were the

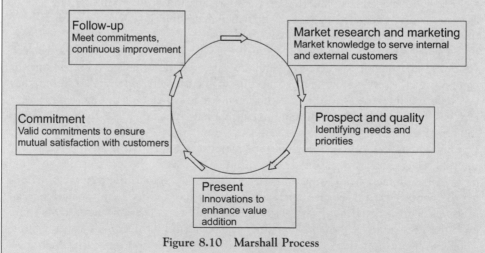

Figure 8.10   Marshall Process
(reproduced from El-Sawy et al., 1999 with permission from the Management Information Systems Research Center (MISRC) of the University of Minnesota).

cornerstones of all the internal activities whether they were marketing, operational, information systems-related, etc. The aim of the process was to satisfy customers rather than meeting internal financial goals. Furthermore, each employee was assessed in terms of their business skills, customer knowledge, supplier and product knowledge, system knowledge, and personal development and leadership. Roles were then assigned based on suitability of individual skills and knowledge for each phase of the Marshall process. (Marshall Industries was bought out by competitor Avnet in 1999, for reasons unrelated to its restructuring.)

Incremental change

In Chapter 7 one of the strategies mentioned for coping with the uncertainties in e-business was taking out options or making small investments in Internet ventures and waiting to see how the market develops before making larger commitments. Given the difficulty of bringing about such large-scale change, some organizations and consultants have applied the same principle in implementing e-business projects. Instead of automating mission-critical or overall internal processes first, they argue it is wiser to start with a non-mission-critical application that can be quickly implemented, that is highly visible and that can act as a springboard for larger projects (Lord, 2000). For example, automating an application, such as employee self-help, may not have a high impact on return on investment (ROI), but it will help getting employees accustomed to using Web-based applications and provide confidence in more critical applications.

Against this must be balanced the need for rapid and radical changes. While small projects can help instil confidence in the technology they can entrench existing structure and culture, which can be a problem if these need to change to meet the new demands of the e-business environment.

Separate e-business

Another approach some organizations have adopted to cope with the speed of change and uncertainty of e-business is to establish a separate e-business unit. Some arguments for this are that speed and flexibility are required to compete successfully in e-business, something that is difficult to achieve in a large organization.

Speed, which is the third characteristic of e-commerce competition, has many implications for organizations and requires particular management practices. Eisenhardt and Brown (1999) in their study of organizations in "high-velocity" environments, including many Silicon Valley companies, identify some practices that seem to be common among successful firms. Time pacing of product innovation was discussed in

Table 8.3 **Patching versus reorganization**

	Reorganization	Patching
Role of change	Change as a defensive reaction	Change as a proactive weapon
Scale of change	Changes are sweeping	Changes are mostly small, some are moderate, a few are large
Frequency	Changes are rare	Changes are ongoing
Formalization	Every change is unique	Change process is routine and follows standard patching routines
Driver of change	Get business focus right	Get business focus and size right
Precision of changes	Optimal restructuring at specific point in time	Roughly right realignments over time

Chapter 7. Another practice is the use of temporary structures, which Eisenhardt and Brown call "patching". While managers in traditional companies see structure as mostly stable, managers in companies that patch believe structure is inherently temporary.

Unlike large-scale restructuring, patching changes are usually small in scale and made frequently. The emphasis is on getting the patch roughly right and fixing problems later (see Table 8.3).

Patches can take several forms, the most common being splits and additions. For example, Dell Computer regularly uses splits to focus more closely on target markets. In 1994, Dell split into two segments: the transaction segment dealt with customers who bought equipment in small quantities; and the relationship segment catered to customers who bought in bulk. By 1996, Dell's managers had split the company into six segments. Since then, Dell has announced a new split almost quarterly. Commercial relationship accounts are now segmented into corporate and small business; government accounts are split into federal, state, and local; and other non-profits are divided into segments, such as education and medical.

While Dell has patched by splitting, Cisco Systems has grown from a small networking company into a broad-based telecommunications player by patching together a range of businesses as the Internet has developed. In the last 4 years it has added more than 20 businesses.

Successful patchers have often developed routines that the organization can follow without much thought. For example, Cisco has well-developed routines for selecting acquisition targets (its preference is for new companies about to launch their first product), for mobilizing special integration teams, for handling stock options and for tracking employee retention rates.

Patching routines also seem to have another benefit. While most patching changes are small, companies that patch also make large-scale changes and when they do they seem to be more successful at it. For example, Dell made a major shift in changing its Asian business from a country focus to a channel focus, while the acquisition of Stratacom was a major change for Cisco. As a result of both companies being used to making small changes these larger changes were more easily executed.

Patching relies on modular design principles. Modularity is a concept that will be familiar to computer programmers and systems designers, but works well with organizations as well. In systems design, modular design refers to a design in which the system is broken down into various modules that can be readily interchanged; this allows the system to be easily adapted to meet changing needs. For example, in an information system that is used worldwide, various modules could be developed for the user interface, allowing the system to be adapted to the local language.

Similar principles can be applied to organizational design. Business units need to be small enough for agility and large enough for efficiency. Successful firms are those that can quickly reconfigure resources to meet shifting market opportunities. They also need to be focused and discrete so that they can be combined seamlessly. Often, the modular structure is replicated within the business units of patching companies in the form of focused, semiautonomous teams. For example, managers at Sun Microsystems organize their company into discrete business units that they call planets and then into focused product teams within them.

Hybrid organizational arrangements

A couple of other organizational arrangements attempt to leverage the resources of large corporations while retaining the speed and flexibility of small firms: joint ventures between corporations and start-ups, and incubators.

Joint ventures with Internet start-ups

In an attempt to emulate some of the flexibility of smaller businesses, some large corporations have turned to Internet start-ups for advice on setting up their own Internet business; these provide advantages, such as allowing the corporation to capitalize on the experience of the start-ups and allowing them to attract management talent. At the same time, the corporation may find that the dot.com operations differ from their traditional operations and find it difficult to reconcile them. For example, a partnership between Toys 'R' Us and Benchmark Capital broke down over conflicts between the online and offline operations.

Mini-case study: Reflect.com

Procter & Gamble, the cosmetics and detergents group, independently established Reflect.com (Figure 8.11), an entirely new brand, available only online to allow women to order cosmetics manufactured according to their specifications. Initially,

Figure 8.11 Reflect.com
(reproduced with permission from Reflect).

the site ran into problems as a result of P&G's limited Internet experience, but the site has been a success following advice from Institutional Venture Partners, a group headed by Geoff Yang, one of the founders of Yahoo!

Incubators

The other type of organizational arrangement that has come to prominence is the "incubator"; these are companies set up to nurture and bring to market promising e-business ideas. By bringing together sources of support, such as finance, technical and marketing expertise, the aim is to kick-start e-businesses.

Many of these incubators have been established by venture capital firms, and this seems to signal a change in investment strategy. A basic investment principle is to diversify risk by investing in a variety of businesses. However, some of the leading venture capital firms have done the exact opposite by putting all their investments into one "basket" and focusing specifically on Internet ventures (e.g., @Ventures in the USA, Softbank TV in Japan and eVentures and Durlacher in the UK). Part of the attraction for venture capital firms is obviously the high stockmarket valuations for Internet businesses. However, incubators also provide significant benefits to Internet start-ups in sharing resources and passing on experience from other ventures. A classic example in the UK is Freeserve, which has itself gone on to offer an incubator service for other start-ups.

Mini-case study: Idealab!

Idealab! (Figure 8.12) is a US incubator founded in March, 1996 by entrepreneurs Bill and Larry Gross with about $3 million from movie mogul Steven Spielberg, Compaq Chairman Ben Rosen and others. It currently has approximately 50 businesses in various stages of development and has IPOed 5 of them. Idealab provides a full range of resources to help Internet start-up companies; these include financial and office space resources and the accompanying network infrastructure, advice and support services, such as development and technology, graphic design, marketing, competitive research, legal, accounting and business development support. Each company has at least one Idealab partner on its board. Companies that Idealab successfully brought to IPO include eToys, CitySearch, NetZero and Tickets.com:

- *eToys*   The leading Internet retailer of children's products, including toys, software, video games, music, videos and baby products (IPO May, 1999).

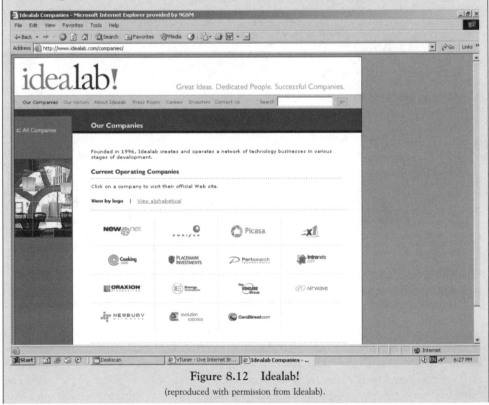

Figure 8.12   Idealab!

(reproduced with permission from Idealab).

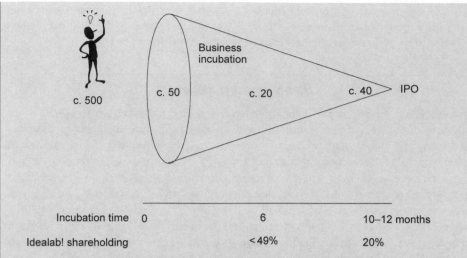

Incubation time   0   6   10–12 months

Idealab! shareholding   < 49%   20%

Figure 8.13   **Idealab's business development model**

- *Ticketmaster Online-CitySearch*   Guide to local content and services including live event ticketing, local auctions and online personals (IPO December, 1998).
- *NetZero*   An advertiser-supported ISP that offers free, full-service Internet access while delivering high-value advertising content according to user interests (IPO September, 1999).
- *Tickets.com*   A B2B ticketing solutions provider.

Other companies in the incubation stage include:

- *CarsDirect.com*   Complete online resource for researching, financing and purchasing new cars and related services.
- *Cooking.com*   Leading online retailer of cookware and specialty foods for cooking enthusiasts.
- *FirstLook.com*   The Web's premier preview marketing network, which enables consumers to discover and sample new products while offering advertisers an efficient, performance-based way to reach an active audience of targeted consumers.
- *PETsMART.com*   The most popular Internet destination for pet products, information and community.

Idealab's model for business development is shown in Figure 8.13. The aim is to bring successful businesses to market within 1 year.

Another benefit that incubators provide is networking. Personal networks are often essential in getting new businesses off the ground (Nohria, 1992), particularly so in the case of e-business start-ups. As we have seen in previous chapters the Internet economy is very much a network economy in which firms need to work with a variety of partners. The traditional way of networking in business is by joining business clubs, industry groups, etc.;

this is still used to large extent by Internet entrepreneurs. For example, one organization, First Tuesday, has been extremely successful in organizing events that bring together Internet start-ups and other parties, such as venture capitalists.

Mini-case study: First Tuesday

First Tuesday (Figure 8.14) provides networking for Internet start-ups. At First Tuesday events and on its website, Internet entrepreneurs can connect with providers they need for their business: capital, talent, technology, knowledge and services.

First Tuesday started in October, 1998 as an informal drinks party in a bar in Soho, London, when the founders brought together 80 friends interested in creating new media companies. Since then First Tuesday has attracted more than 70,000 registered users and expanded its monthly events into 17 European cities as well as holding regular events in over 80 cities globally. Since its launch it has helped entrepreneurs to raise over $100 million of seed capital and helped start hundreds of companies; these include Red Message, peoplesound.com, firebox.com, Moreover.com, Wildday.com, UPAQ, dipcard.com and Ihavemoved.com.

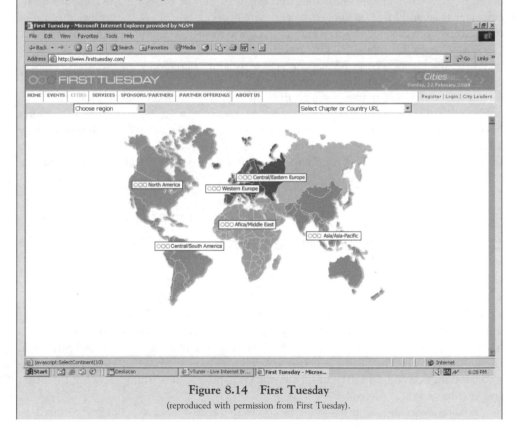

Figure 8.14   First Tuesday
(reproduced with permission from First Tuesday).

First Tuesday generates its revenue through sponsorship and licensing out its events across the world. In April, 2001 the company was bought out by a network including the majority of its licensees and private investors.

Incubators have a number of advantages over traditional venture capital firms and business clubs. First, networking is institutionalized, meaning that the incubator has mechanisms in place that foster networking (Hansen et al., 2000). The access and connections provided by incubators can help launch businesses quickly and increase cross-marketing opportunities. For example, the incubator Softbank was able to get the newly formed E-loan quickly off the ground worldwide by using its connections with partners worldwide. In the UK it was able to set up meetings with Yahoo!, and in France it was able to forge a marketing deal with the French television channel Canal Plus through its European incubator @Viso. By institutionalizing networking, an incubator achieves a scale of networking benefits that does not depend on the personal connections of a few people and that can be scaled up to benefit numerous companies.

The incubator model is being adopted not only by venture capitalists but also by major corporations. For example, Ford has established an incubator called ConsumerConnect to find new ways to leverage Ford's assets in the new economy, including the company's vast customer base and huge purchasing power. One of its early successes was Covisint, a new online B2B exchange for the auto industry that was formed as a joint venture among Ford, General Motors, Daimler-Chrysler, and Renault/Nissan. ConsumerConnect was able to kick-start the business by providing contacts with Ford's purchasing organization, responsible for purchasing $80 billion annually.

In other cases, a corporate incubator can help bring to market a technology that does not fit with the company's core businesses. At Lucent, for example, the New Ventures Group funds and incubates a variety of ventures that commercialize Bell Lab's technology which do not fit with the corporate strategy. Some of these ventures (e.g., Elemedia, which provides software for Internet telephony) have later turned out to be of such value that the company has reacquired them.

Choosing the governance mode

Venkateraman (2000) has identified two major categories of decision that influence the governance mode in e-businesses: operational decisions (production, sourcing, logistics, marketing and human resources) and financial decisions (investment logic, funding sources and performance criteria). The governance of dot.com business is best seen as a trade-off between these two categories: how firms differentiate and integrate operational and financial decisions. The basic governance choices can be arrayed along the diagonal as a continuum from subsidiary (spin-off) at one end and seamless (transparent) at the other end (Figure 8.15).

Venkateraman argues that, when faced with the fast pace of changes required in

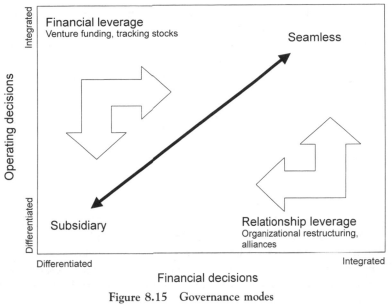

Figure 8.15 Governance modes
(reproduced with permission from TMS Reprints).

e-business, managers may benefit from differentiating the operations and decoupling the financial arrangements. An example is Nordstrom.com – the subsidiary of Nordstrom formed to accelerate the growth of its Internet and catalogue direct sales with minority funding from Benchmark Capital. The funding from the venture capital community allowed the subsidiary to invest in site development and to create the appropriate software as well as a distinct advertising campaign, without being handicapped by the need to use only internally generated resources. The subsidiary governance mode is appropriate under the following conditions:

1. The company is willing to explore new business models despite the constraints of current operations.
2. The subsidiary or spin-off can be created without being constrained by current technology and legacy operations.
3. The company allows the subsidiary freedom to form alliances, raise capital and attract new talent.

In other cases, differentiation of the dot.com operations may be inappropriate because the business requires a certain scale of operation or level of management attention to ensure success. For example, Cisco, which conducts much of its business online, cannot be segregated into dot.com and non-dot.com components. Intel is another company with more than 40% of sales conducted through the Net. The integrated governance mode is appropriate under the following conditions:

1. There is no meaningful way to separate digital and physical operations without creating confusion in the minds of customers.
2. Senior management is committed to embracing the opportunities and challenges of the Net to redefine the value proposition.
3. The entire organization can be mobilized to migrate to the dot.com world.

Chavez et al. (2000) identify three common ways to structure an e-business: integrate it into the core business, create a separate unit within the same parent or spin it off. When deciding between the various options, they suggest managers must determine which option optimizes the trade-offs between control, culture and currency:

- Control is the extent to which the parent company must co-ordinate and integrate the customer value proposition, strategies, operations, and assets of the online and offline businesses.
- Currency is the capital needed to fund the growth of the online business and offer the financial incentives to attract talent, strike alliances and make acquisitions.
- Culture is the ability to create an environment where people can experiment and learn, can make decisions fast, can be flexible and open to change, and can take an "options" approach to planning.

Integration

The integration option allows the established company to keep control of the venture, but provides the least number of currency options (e.g., it does not have dot.com stock to acquire people, strike alliances or make dot.com acquisitions) and the culture of the parent may dominate. In general, this structure allows the Internet venture the greatest opportunity to leverage parent company assets and systems, but gives it the least amount of flexibility.

Separate subsidiary

A separate subsidiary or division for its Internet business is again able to leverage parent company assets, while allowing the company to keep control, but offers little in the way of currency. However, as a separate business unit, it does allow the unit control over its own budget and day-to-day decision-making authority; it also allows the unit to create its own culture.

Mini-case study: Egg

The Prudential, founded in 1875, is one of the oldest insurance companies in the UK. In recent years the company has moved away from using its own salesforce to selling through independent financial advisers, but in October, 1998 it decided to launch an Internet business offering savings and loans direct to the public. The new business,

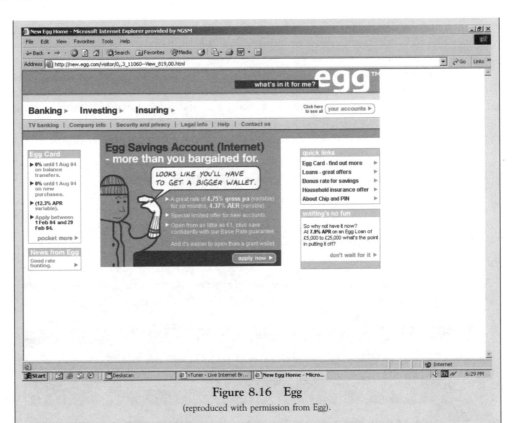

Figure 8.16 Egg

(reproduced with permission from Egg).

named Egg (Figure 8.16), was set up as a company within a company. As a separate entity Egg could pursue aggressive marketing and use the latest technology in its branded service without affecting the Prudential brand. Egg has a different business model from the rest of Prudential. Its marketing strategy was always to offer very attractive interest rates to savers with more tightly priced, more bundled products and to service that customer base with a low-cost structure. Egg used the Prudential's core banking systems that were launched in 1996, replaced the front office systems and installed an up-to-date customer relationship management system. The customer databases are kept completely separate and the two different brands are marketed independently. In 18 months Egg managed to build a customer base of over 1 million customers and the company was floated on the London Stock Exchange in June, 2000, netting £150 million for Egg and £50 million for the Prudential.

Spin-off

In the spin-off option, the parent loses some control. However, the business has a much higher level of currency. It can offer dot.com stock options to employees, strike alliances and acquisitions in return for stock, and go back to the capital markets to raise additional funding. The disadvantage is that the business has the least opportunity to leverage the parent company assets.

Another factor that also needs to be considered in the decision to integrate or not is the competence required to manage the two sets of operations; this is not only a challenge for established firms attempting e-business, but also for e-business start-ups that are aiming to grow. Often, it is not so much a case of developing new skills and systems, but whether existing skills and systems can be successfully adapted (Chen and Leteney, 2000).

Mini-case study: Developing competences for e-tail

Chen and Leteney (2000) compared three firms:

1. An Internet start-up retailing china and pottery, Small Island Trader (Figure 8.17).
2. An existing supplier of tools, Cooksons (Figure 8.18).
3. An existing store and direct mail retailer, the BBC shop.

As might be expected all three firms had to develop new competences in the virtual parts of the chain with which they had no experience (e.g., information, communication

Figure 8.17   smallislandtrader.com
(reproduced with permission from Small Island Trader).

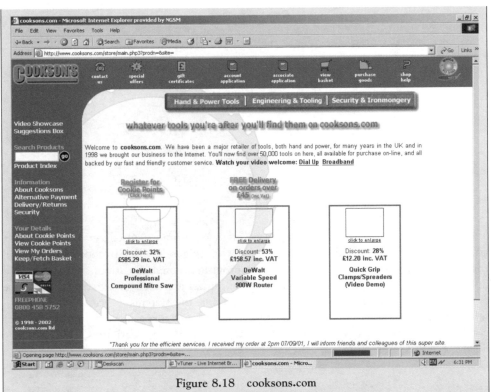

Figure 8.18 cooksons.com
(reproduced with permission from Cooksons).

and transaction capabilities). One of the benefits of Internet retail generally is the much wider range of products available compared with conventional stores, but selection and purchase is facilitated by the use of computer search facilities, email and online purchasing. As expected, all three companies studied found that they had to develop new systems and skills in each of these areas.

However, what was initially surprising in the cases examined was that the greatest problem areas reported were not in the areas listed above, where the firms lacked technical skills and experience, they were in the more routine areas – in the case of Cooksons and the BBC where they had existing skills and experience – supply, distribution and integration with existing systems.

A general lesson from many recent e-tailing failures seems to be that it is crucial to integrate front and back office operations. Even where Internet operations have been set up as a separate business, there is still a need to integrate the retail website to systems that manage the traditional "back office" activities of retail businesses, such as supply, inventory and delivery. It is how all the activities work together as a whole that is critical for success, rather than technical excellence in any one area.

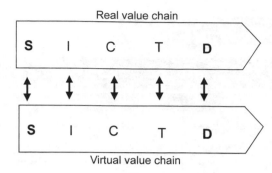

Real value chain

Virtual value chain

Figure 8.19 SICTD model
(reproduced with permission from Elsevier).

The operations for e-tailing firms can be analysed using a revised version of Rayport and Sviolka's (1995) virtual value chain framework (Figure 8.19); this shows activities in each of five processes – supply, information provision, communication, transaction and distribution – which are required in any retail business and each of which may either be done online or offline. This can be used to map out the systems, processes and competences that are required at each stage of the value chain. Some may cut across different parts of the chain, others will require integrating real and virtual activities. The challenge for firms will be how to manage the crossovers.

New organizational forms

New organizational arrangements are likely to emerge as new e-business technologies develop and e-business changes competition in industries. Two forms that have been suggested are organizations built around a digital function platform (Aldrich, 1999) and unbundled corporations (Hagel and Singer, 1999).

Digital function platform

A digital function platform (DFP) (Figure 8.20) is a business service or technology platform that supports business processes across multiple value chains. Using a DFP, previously disconnected and autonomous value chains are able to collaborate and combine their offerings more efficiently. Examples of such platforms that have already been tried for a number of years are ERP software packages, such as SAP, which integrate different processes within an organization. However, as in the case of conventional EDI systems, with the growing acceptance of Internet protocols it is likely that such packages will be replaced by newer systems based on open standards. With the development of newer platforms, such as Jini (which allows different devices to communicate with each

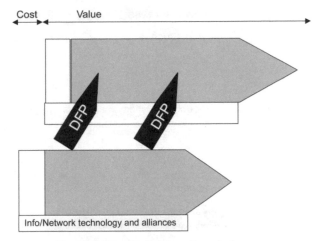

Figure 8.20 Digital function platform
(reproduced with permission from John Wiley & Sons).

other), the scope of DFPs is also likely to increase. The advantage of open systems is that it will make it much easier to communicate with other organizations in the value chain and make it easier to communicate across industries. For example, in the entertainment industry a common DFP would make it easier for firms in film, music, recording, television, Internet and computer games to share information and allow them to integrate their business processes more efficiently. These interlinked digital value chains form what is termed a digital value network (DVN).

Aldrich (1999) believes that such DVNs will lead to a new organizational structure built around the DVN, which he terms the "value-based organization" (VBO), similar to the E-form described by Moore (1996). The key feature of the VBO is that it focuses on activities where it has internal competences (value-added competences), while it harnesses the ability of partners in the network for activities where it has no specific competence.

Unbundling the business

Another form that could evolve is the unbundled corporation. In Chapter 6 it was shown that one of the possible effects of e-commerce is to disaggregate or aggregate activities in industries and firms. However, as well as economic implications, this has implications for how the firm organizes its activities. In this vein, Hagel and Singer (1999) argue that most companies can be deconstructed into three types of businesses: a customer relationship business, a product innovation business and an infrastructure business (Figure 8.21). Each of the businesses plays a unique role, employs different types of people and has different economic and competitive pressures.

The role of a customer relationship business is to find customers and build relationships with them. For example, at a retailer's the marketing personnel focus on drawing people

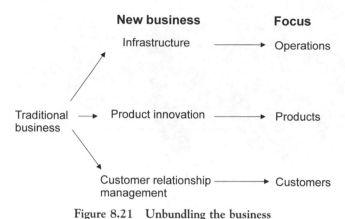

Figure 8.21   Unbundling the business
(reproduced with permission from John Wiley & Sons).

into their branches or stores. Other employees, such as salespeople, assist the customers and try to build personal relationships with them. Still other employees may be responsible for responding to customer questions and complaints, processing returns or collecting customer information.

The role of a product innovation business is to conceive of new products and services, and work out how to bring them to market. For example, at a retailer's both buyers and merchandisers search for interesting new products and effective ways to present them to shoppers.

The role of an infrastructure business is to build and manage facilities for operational tasks, such as logistics and storage, manufacturing, and communications. At a retailer's the infrastructure business is responsible for constructing new stores, maintaining existing outlets and managing the logistical network.

In most organizations these three businesses – customer relationship management, product innovation and infrastructure management – rarely map onto business units in the organizational structure of a corporation. For example, product innovation typically extends beyond the boundaries of a product development unit to include such activities as conducting market research, qualifying component suppliers, training sales and support people, and designing marketing materials.

Bundling the three businesses into a single corporation inevitably forces management to compromise the performance of each process. For example, finding and developing a relationship with a customer usually requires a large investment, and profitability requires achieving economies of scope by extending the relationship for as long as possible and generating as much revenue as possible from it. It is often in the interests of customer relationship businesses to create highly customized offerings to maximize sales; this leads to an intense service-oriented culture in which employees spend a lot of time interacting with customers and developing a feel for customers' requirements and preferences.

Product innovation businesses, on the other hand, are driven by speed considerations. The faster the business moves a new product from the research and development stage to the market, the more money the business makes; this leads to a culture that focuses on hiring and retaining talented employees, that rewards innovation and minimizes the administrative distractions that might slow down creativity. In contrast, infrastructure businesses are driven by scale. Such businesses generally require capital-intensive facilities, which entail high fixed costs. To keep costs as low as possible, they aim to make their activities and outputs as routine and predictable as possible, and focus on control of costs. A more efficient solution, which reduces these conflicts, might be to unbundle the three businesses.

Summary

This chapter examined how electronic commerce strategies can best be implemented and then identified the key features of new organizational forms that have developed, such as incubators, dot.coms and dot.corps. It also identified some new forms that might emerge in future as a result of changes in technology and industry reconfiguration. In order to implement e-business successfully, changes in business processes, organizational structure and culture may be required, and examples were given of how some organizations have implemented these changes. Table 8.4 shows a list of some issues to consider in implementing an e-business strategy and some frameworks discussed in this chapter that can be used to analyse each issue.

Table 8.4   Implementation checklist

Issue	Framework/Options
Governance mode • Do we integrate or spin off the e-business?	Operations versus finance Three Cs trade-off
Culture • What sort of culture do we build? • What do we need to change?	Seven Ss framework Cultural web
Knowledge management • How can we use information and the knowledge of our people better?	Intranets ERP
Industry deconstruction • How do we need to reorganize to fit with the new industry?	Process-based organization E-form organization
Real–virtual interface • How do we manage the interface between the e-business and the rest of the business?	Real SICTD model
Change management approach • What approach should we adopt in bringing about the transformation to e-business?	Escalating projects Patching Radical re-organization

References

Aldrich, D.F. (1999). *Mastering the Digital Marketplace*. John Wiley & Sons, Chichester, UK.

Chan, C. and Swatman, P.M.C. (2000). From EDI to Internet commerce: The BHP Steel experience. *Internet Research*, **10**(1), 72–82.

Chavez, R., Leiter, M. and Kiely, T. (2000). Should you spin off your Internet business? *Business Strategy Review*, **11**(2), 19–31.

Chen, S. (2003). The real value of "e-business models". *Business Horizons*, **46**(6), 27–33.

Chen, S. and Leteney, F. (2000). Get real! Managing the next stage of Internet retail. *European Management Journal*, **18**(5), October, 519–28.

Eisenhardt, S. and Brown, S.L. (1999). Patching: Restitching business portfolios in dynamic markets. *Harvard Business Review*, **77**(3), May/June, 72–82.

El-Sawy, O.A., Malhotra, A., Gosain, S. and Young, K.M. (1999). IT-intensive value innovation in the electronic economy: Insights from Marshall Industries. *MIS Quarterly*, **23**(3), 305–33.

Hagel, J. and Singer, M. (1999). Unbundling the corporation. *Harvard Business Review*, March/April, 133–41.

Hansen, M.T., Chesbrough, H.W., Nohria, N. and Sull, D.N. (2000). Networked incubators: Hothouses of the new economy. *Harvard Business Review*, September/October, 74–84.

Johnson, G. (1988). Rethinking incrementalism. *Strategic Management Journal*, **9**(1), 75–91.

Lord, C. (2000). The practicalities of developing a successful e-business strategy. *Journal of Business Strategy*, March/April, 40–3.

Malhotra, Y. (2000). Knowledge management for e-business performance. *Information Strategy: The Executive's Journal*, **16**(4), 5–16.

Moore, J. (1996). *The Death of Competition*. John Wiley & Sons, Chichester, UK.

Nohria, N. (1992). Information and search in the creation of new business ventures: The case of the 128 Venture Group. In: N. Nohria and R.G. Eccles (eds), *Networks and Organizations* (pp. 240–61). Harvard Business School Press, Boston.

Peoplesoft (2002). *Economic Benefits of the PeopleSoft Enterprise Portal* (PeopleSoft White Paper). Available at *http://www.peoplesoft.com.au/media/en/pdf/portal_roi_wp.pdf*

Peters, T.J. and Waterman, R.H. (1982). *In Search of Excellence*. Harper & Row, New York.

Rae-Smith, J.B. and Ellinger, A.E. (2002). Insight from the introduction of an online logistics service system. *Supply Chain Management*, **7**(1), 5–12.

Ratnasingham, P. (1998). The importance of trust in electronic commerce. *Internet Research – Electronic Network Applications and Policy*, **8**(4), 313–23.

Rayport, J. and Sviolka, J.J. (1995) Exploiting the virtual value chain. *Harvard Business Review*, **73**(6), November/December, 75–85.

Turban, E., Lee, J., King, D. and Chung, H.M. (2000). *Electronic Commerce: A Managerial Perspective*. Prentice Hall, Upper Saddle River, NJ.

Venkateraman, N. (2000). Five steps to a dot.com strategy: How to find your footing on the Web. *Sloan Management Review*, Spring, 15–28.

Venkateraman, N. and Henderson, J.C. (1998). Real strategies for virtual organizing. *Sloan Management Review*, Fall, 33–48.

Wells, M.G. (2000). Business process re-engineering implementations using Internet technology. *Business Process Management Journal*, **6**(2), 164–84.

Key concepts

- B2E portals
- Core processes
- Digital function platform
- Dot.com governance modes
- E-form
- ERP
- Groupware

- Incubators
- Knowledge management system
- Organizational co-evolution
- Patching changes
- Real–virtual SICTD model
- Unbundling of businesses
- Value-based organization

Self-assessment questions

1 Describe the different types of virtual organization.

2 What are some common problems in implementing e-business models?

3 Give examples of how e-business can help knowledge management.

4 Describe various dot.com governance modes and the pros and cons of each.

5 How are E-form organizations different from traditional organizations?

6 What are the different benefits of incubators?

7 Give examples of different types of patching.

8 What are the other things, apart from structure, that may need to be changed when converting to an e-business?

9 What is ERP software and how can it be integrated with Web-based applications?

10 What is a "digital function platform" and how does this affect e-business?

11 Explain how the following businesses may be unbundled in the e-business environment: a software developer, a construction company, a university.

Discussion questions

1 How relevant are the existing organizational forms for e-business?

2 Do incubators increase or reduce risk? For whom?

3 How does the stockmarket influence dot.corp structure?

4 What are barriers to adoption of e-business?

5 Why should there be problems in integrating real and virtual operations?

6 Does implementing an Internet-based business strategy create any particular problems compared with other IT-based strategies?

PUBLIC POLICY ISSUES

Introduction

A number of examples of the importance of public policy in the development of e-business have already been shown in previous chapters. For example, the Internet would not have been developed without public funding or government support. It is also doubtful that the Internet would have been commercialized without government backing. At the same time, the Internet has developed a life of its own, and the technological developments have in many cases overtaken the policy makers. As the volume and scope of transactions have increased so has the need for businesses to consider public policies relating to e-business.

As shown in previous chapters some of the characteristics of electronic transactions and more specifically Internet transactions are:

- Transactions can take place entirely virtually (i.e., without the need for a physical presence).
- Domain names have become crucial in marketing and branding.
- Data and information is easily copied and exchanged.
- Customer activity is easily tracked.
- The Internet creates a global market.
- The winner takes all in many electronic markets.

These characteristics of electronic transactions raise a number of challenges for existing public policy in a number of areas, such as recognition of legally binding contracts, rights to intellectual property, the right of individuals to privacy, disputes across jurisdictions and social exclusion.

Recognition of virtual transactions

The fact that much of e-commerce activity is virtual (i.e., not physical or tangible), sometimes has consequences for legal recognition of electronic business transactions. For example, traditional, non-electronic transactions are often completed by a written signature formalizing the agreement. Digital equivalents are an "electronic signature" or a "digital signature". An electronic signature is a generic term that refers to any signature created electronically (e.g., a name typed at the end of an email message by the sender, a digitized image of a handwritten signature that is attached to an electronic document, a secret code or PIN (like that used with ATM cards and credit cards to identify the sender to the recipient, a code or "handle" that the sender of a message uses to identify himself, a unique biometrics-based identifier like a fingerprint or a retinal scan). A digital signature is more specific and refers to a signature encrypted using the public key encryption method described in Chapter 2. For example, senders may encrypt their names. However, in order to decrypt the message the recipient will need the user's public key. There is the possibility that the senders are not who they purport to be; this is authenticated by a digital certificate issued by a trusted third party (TTP), such as the Post Office or other government agency, who acts as a certification authority (CA). Individuals or companies apply for digital certificates by sending the CA their public key and identifying information. The CA verifies the information and creates a certificate that contains the applicant's public key along with identifying information. The CA uses its private key to encrypt the certificate and sends the signed certificate to the applicant. The applicant can now send the digital certificate as proof of identification. The recipient can then use the CA's public key to decrypt the certificate and so be more confident of the true identity of the sender. Certificates now exist to authenticate websites (site certificates), individuals (personal certificates) and software companies (software publisher certificates). There are also a growing number of private third-party CAs. VeriSign (*www.verisign.com*) issues three classes of certificates: class 1 verifies that an email actually comes from the user's address; class 2 checks the user's identity against a commercial credit database; and class 3 requires notarized documents. Companies such as Netscape also offer systems and software that enable companies to issue their own private and in-house certificates. However, at present, there is no universal agreement about whether an electronic signature, which is a series of electronic impulses, constitutes "writing" and is an acceptable substitute.

The United Nations Council on International Trade Law (UNCITRAL) tried to establish an international standard in its Model Law in 1996 for Electronic Commerce, some of the key articles being the following:

Article 5. Legal recognition of data messages
Information shall not be denied legal effect, validity or enforceability solely on the grounds that it is in the form of a data message.

Article 6. Writing
(1) Where the law requires information to be in writing, that requirement is met by a

data message if the information contained therein is accessible so as to be usable for subsequent reference.

Article 7. Signature
(1) Where the law requires a signature of a person, that requirement is met in relation to a data message if:
  (a) a method is used to identify that person and to indicate that person's approval of the information contained in the data message; and
  (b) that method is as reliable as was appropriate for the purpose for which the data message was generated or communicated, in the light of all the circumstances, including any relevant agreement.

Article 8. Original
(1) Where the law requires information to be presented or retained in its original form, that requirement is met by a data message if:
  (a) there exists a reliable assurance as to the integrity of the information from the time when it was first generated in its final form, as a data message or otherwise; and
  (b) where it is required that information be presented, that information is capable of being displayed to the person to whom it is to be presented.

Article 9. Admissibility and evidential weight of data messages
(1) In any legal proceedings, nothing in the application of the rules of evidence shall apply so as to deny the admissibility of a data message in evidence:
  (a) on the sole ground that it is a data message; or,
  (b) if it is the best evidence that the person adducing it could reasonably be expected to obtain, on the grounds that it is not in its original form.

Article 10. Retention of data messages
(1) Where the law requires that certain documents, records or information be retained, that requirement is met by retaining data messages, provided that the following conditions are satisfied:
  (a) the information contained therein is accessible so as to be usable for subsequent reference; and
  (b) the data message is retained in the format in which it was generated, sent or received, or in a format which can be demonstrated to represent accurately the information generated, sent or received; and
  (c) such information, if any, is retained as enables the identification of the origin and destination of a data message and the date and time when it was sent or received.

Article 11. Formation and validity of contracts
(1) In the context of contract formation, unless otherwise agreed by the parties, an offer and the acceptance of an offer may be expressed by means of data messages. Where a

data message is used in the formation of a contract, that contract shall not be denied validity or enforceability on the sole ground that a data message was used for that purpose.

This law was followed by the Model Law on Electronic Signatures in 2001, intended to bring additional legal certainty regarding the use of electronic signatures. Building on the principle contained in article 7 of the UNCITRAL Model Law on Electronic Commerce, it establishes a presumption that, where they meet certain criteria of technical reliability, electronic signatures will be treated as equivalent to handwritten signatures. In establishing that presumption, the model law follows a technology-neutral approach and avoids favouring the use of any specific technical product. In addition, the model law establishes basic rules of conduct that may serve as guidelines for assessing possible responsibilities and liabilities that might bind upon the various parties involved in the electronic signature process: the signatory, the relying party and the TTPs that might intervene in the signature process. UNCITRAL aims to place electronic transactions on the same basis as non-electronic transactions. However, at the present time, there is still considerable variation worldwide in the implementation of the model law. For example, the postal authority in Hong Kong, Hong Kong Post, has already implemented digital certificates for millions of citizens, but other countries are not so advanced.

In Europe, requirements proposed by the EC for an "advanced electronic signature" conforming to the UNCITRAL model law are that:

- It is uniquely linked to the signatory.
- It is capable of identifying the signatory.
- It is created using means that the signatory can maintain under his sole control.
- It is linked to the data to which it relates in such a manner that any subsequent alteration of the data is revealed.

In 1999 the EU adopted the electronic signature directive which prohibits discrimination against an e-signature solely on the basis of its electronic nature. The main elements of the EC electronic signature directive are:

- *Legal recognition* The directive stipulates an electronic signature cannot be legally discriminated against solely on the grounds it is in electronic form. If a certificate and the service provider as well as the signature product used meet a set of specific requirements, there will be an automatic assumption that any resulting electronic signatures are as legally valid as a handwritten signature. Moreover, they can be used as evidence in legal proceedings.
- *Free circulation* All products and services related to electronic signatures can circulate freely and are only subject to the legislation of and control by the country of origin. Member states cannot make the provision of services related to electronic signatures subject to mandatory licensing.
- *Liability* It establishes minimum liability rules for service providers which would, in particular, be liable for the validity of a certificate's content. This approach ensures free

movement of certificates and certification services within the internal market, builds consumer trust and stimulates operators to develop secure systems and signatures without restrictive and inflexible regulation.

- *Technology-neutral framework* Given the pace of technological innovation, the legislation provides for legal recognition of electronic signatures irrespective of the technology used (such as digital signatures using asymmetric cryptography or biometrics).
- *Scope* The legislation covers the supply of certificates to the public and is aimed at identifying the sender of an electronic message. But, in accordance with the principles of party autonomy and contractual freedom, it does permit the operation of schemes governed by private law agreements, like corporate intranets or banking systems, where a relation of trust already exists and there is no obvious need for regulation.
- *International dimension* To promote a global market in electronic commerce the legislation includes mechanisms for co-operation with non-EU countries on the basis of mutual recognition of certificates and on bilateral and multilateral agreements.

In the USA the Electronic Signatures in Global and National Commerce Act became effective on October 1, 2000. The core of the E-Sign Act provides that a transaction in interstate or foreign commerce may not be denied legal effect just because it was created electronically or was consummated by an e-signature. The limited objective of the E-Sign Act, as with other electronic transaction legislation, is to ensure that an e-record or signature carries no less weight than a paper record or handwritten signature. The new law does not require that transactions be conducted by electronic means or consummated by e-signatures; instead, it merely facilitates transactions that parties choose to conduct electronically. At the state level, the most significant body of legislation currently in effect arises out of the Uniform Electronic Transactions Act (UETA); this formally legitimizes transactions arising out of an electronic communication between parties, be it a simple Internet sale and purchase or a more complicated electronic data interchange. Its key purpose is to accord e-records and e-signatures the same legal effect as written records and handwritten signatures and, in the limited cases where they are not the same, to spell out the effect of actions undertaken electronically.

Intellectual property rights

The other area of law that has been significantly affected by electronic commerce is intellectual property. Much of electronic commerce either deals in or relies on information, which brings it into confrontation with intellectual property law. Intellectual property rights have always been closely related to social and economic movements. Various intellectual property rights arose historically around the world as a means of ensuring that creators and inventors are able to profit from their intellectual endeavours. However, nowadays, although there are still conflicts between different countries regarding intellectual property rights, most countries have agreed to a set of internationally recognized rights. The World Intellectual Property Organization distinguishes two types of intellectual property rights that are commonly recognized in most countries: industrial property, protected by patents, trademarks and design rights, and literary and artistic works, protected by copyright (Cornish, 1996).

Industrial property laws deal principally with the protection of inventions, marks (trademarks and service marks) and industrial designs, and the repression of unfair competition. Inventions, marks and industrial designs give protection in the form of exclusive rights of exploitation. Repression of unfair competition protects against acts contrary to honest practices in industrial or commercial matters (e.g., in relation to undisclosed information, or trade secrets).

Certain intellectual property rights may be threatened by the nature of the Internet itself: first, with the increase in the number of websites, domain names have become essential to locating businesses on the Internet; and second, digital technologies make it very easy to copy and distribute information worldwide.

Trademarks

A trademark is a sign consisting of one or more distinctive words, letters, numbers, drawings, pictures, emblems, colours or any combination of the foregoing which identifies the capability of distinguishing the goods or services of one business from those of other businesses. In some countries and in some situations a mark may be protected without registration, but it is usual to register a trademark with a government office (usually the same office as that which grants patents). If a mark is registered, then no person or enterprise other than its owner may use it for goods or services identical with or similar to those for which the mark is registered. Any unauthorized use of a sign similar to the protected mark is also prohibited, if such use may lead to confusion in the minds of the public. The protection of a mark is generally not limited in time, provided its registration is periodically renewed (typically, every 10 years) and its use continues.

Threat to trademarks

As shown in previous chapters, domain names can act not only as unique addresses, but also as slogans, billboards or brand names. The business identity of many Internet firms, such as Yahoo!, Amazon.com and E-bay, is associated by the public with their domain names. Most non-Internet-based businesses also choose domain names that match or are easily derived from their corporate names, such as Dell.com, IBM.com or Microsoft.com.

Mueller (1999) identified four categories of domain name conflict:

- Infringement.
- Speculation.
- Character string conflicts.
- Parody and pre-emption.

Infringement

Infringement refers to domain name conflicts in which the original registrant intentionally attempts to trade off the resemblance between the domain name and another company's trademark. Also included under this category are so-called dilution cases in which the value of a mark would be tarnished or devalued by its association with the site of the domain name user. These are uses of a mark that would be illegal under existing trademark concepts, regardless of whether they occurred as Internet domain names or in any other context.

Speculation

Name speculation occurs when a domain name bearing a resemblance to a registered trademark is registered in the hope that the trademark owner will eventually buy it from the person who registered it. Name speculation is often treated as trademark infringement, although the most important criteria of trademark infringement – use in commerce, likelihood of confusion and dilution – are usually absent from speculation cases. Name speculators (commonly known as cybersquatters) do not usually pretend to be the company whose name they control. They simply traffic in the names themselves; this can sometimes be very profitable as some cases have shown. It is relatively inexpensive to reserve a name ($35–50 per year is the norm), and memorable names can fetch significantly in excess of the reservation price. In 1999 the domain name Business.com was sold for $7.5 million, more than twice the previous record of $3.3 million paid a year earlier by Compaq for the domain name altavista.com. Other domain names that have fetched large sums include wine.com, sold for $3 million, Wall Street.com for $1.03 million and drugs.com for $0.8 million.

Not all companies have been willing to pay such sums, and a number of well-publicized cases have ensued including the following:

In *Panavision International v. Toeppen* (CV 96-2384 DPP US Supreme Court), Toeppen had registered some 240 domain names of well-known companies, such as deltaairlines.com and britishairways.com, and attempted to sell the domain names to the companies for several thousand dollars. He did not actually offer to sell the trademarks to Panavision, but he offered to settle the matter if the company would pay him $13,000. Panavision subsequently filed an action for dilution of its trademarks. The court found Toeppen had made commercial use of Panavision's trademarks and agreed that his conduct diluted those marks. Accordingly, it found in favour of Panavision.

A similar situation arose in *Marks & Spencer v. One in a Million Limited and others*. One in a Million and others had registered a number of trademarks and domain names of well-known companies, such as Burger King.com, Cadburys.com, Marksandspencer.com, virgin.org and British Telecom.co.uk, and then attempted to sell the domain names concerned for varying sums of money. The companies filed suit alleging passing off and infringement of their trademarks. The court found in favour of the plaintiff and restrained One in a Million from using the Internet domain names and offering them for sale to any person other than the plaintiff.

Ironically, the World Intellectual Property Organization (WIPO) was also held to ransom by cybersquatters who had registered wipo.int and demanded $5,000 for its use.

Character string conflicts

"Character string" conflicts occur when there is more than one legitimate, non-speculative user of a given character string as a domain name, such as a non-trademarked company name, product name or personal name. An example was when the credit card company Visa tried to register its name in Australia they discovered that the domain name Visa.com.au was already owned by the Vomiting Infants Support Association.

One of the first and most commonly cited cases is that of *Hasbro, Inc. v. Internet Entertainment Group, Ltd*, No. C96-130WD (W.D. Wash. Feb. 9, 1995). In late 1995, Internet Entertainment Group (IEG) paid more than $20,000 to acquire the Internet domain name, candyland.com. It then spent a substantial amount of money on the site, including $150,000 for advertising in adult publications. But, at the beginning of 1996, it was sued by a leading toymaker, Hasbro, Inc., for infringing the trademark of a board game called Candy Land the company sells to young children. Hasbro wanted to offer an Internet version of Candy Land and claimed that "[IEG's] use of the CANDYLAND name in connection with a sexually explicit pornographic Internet site by its very nature tarnishes the pure, sweet, wholesome and fun imagery associated with Hasbro's CANDY LAND mark, and is certainly likely to undermine or damage the positive association evoked by the mark." In defence, IEG stated that it was not competing with Hasbro and noted that "[there are] third party uses of the candyland mark for a wide variety of goods and services, including food, dolls, childcare services, clothing, retail sales of groceries, vending machines, paper goods, wedding supplies and services, and real estate services." The Federal Court decided Hasbro had demonstrated a likelihood of prevailing on its claims and issued a preliminary injunction requiring IEG to stop using the CANDYLAND name and the Internet domain name candyland.com.

Parody, pre-emption and other

The last category involves uses of domain names for acts of parody, pre-emption or expression. In this type of conflict, the domain name deliberately invokes or resembles a company name or trademark in order to make a political or satirical point. For example, someone registered the name british-telecom.com in order to post information critical of that company. Another famous parody case is the peta.org conflict, in which the acronym for "People for the Ethical Treatment of Animals" (PETA) was registered by a critic who set up a satirical site for a fictitious organization called "People Eating Tasty Animals".

Sometimes, the aim is a deliberate "passing off", or attempt to confuse or deceive customers. On the Internet, a minor difference in a character in the domain name, which is difficult for users to notice, can point to a completely different address. Some businesses have taken advantage of this feature by registering domain names that are nearly the same as a famous name, but with one different character (e.g., amazon.com or micros0ft.com). All of these conflicts over domain name rights have resulted in litigation or threats of litigation under trademark law.

Trademark infringement can also arise for reasons other than domain name conflicts; these include deep-linking and meta-tagging.

In *Ticketmaster Corporation v. Microsoft Corporation* (No. 97-3055DDP C.D. Cal. 12 April, 1997) Ticketmaster filed a suit against Microsoft for what has become known as "deep-linking". Microsoft developed a site called "Seattle Sidewalk" that contained a hyperlink to a page deep within Ticketmaster's site. Ticketmaster complained that Microsoft was taking its content out of context and was depriving the company of income by bypassing banner advertisements on its home page, while benefiting from the use of Ticketmaster's trademarks. The case was settled out of court in January, 1999 after Microsoft agreed to stop deep-linking.

Another way trademark infringement can arise is through meta-tags; these are words in the HTML source that are not usually visible using a browser, but which help search engines or programmers to identify the content of the webpage. It has become popular practice to bury a well-known brand in the meta-tags in order to increase the strike rate using a search engine. The result is that a user searching for a product by a well-known brand name will find the site as well.

In *Playboy Enterprises Inc. v. Calvin Designer Label* (985 F. Supp. 1218 N.D. Cal. 1997), Playboy sued Calvin for allegedly including trademarked names in its domain name and meta-tags. Calvin operated websites with the domain names Playboyxxx.com and Playmatelive.com, and included references to Playboy in its meta-tags. Playboy demanded that Calvin change the domain names and remove the term "playboy" from its meta-tags. The US Federal judge ordered Calvin to refrain from "using in any manner the PLAYMATE or PLAYBOY trademarks ... in buried code of meta-tags on their home page or Web pages."

In the decision of *Brookfield Communications Inc. v. West Coast Entertainment Corp.*, West Coast, a national video rental chain, used the term "movie buff" in its meta-tags which is the trademark property of Brookfield's, a California-based provider of entertainment news on the Internet. One judge considered that "using another's trademark in a meta-tag is much like posting a sign with another's trademark in front of one's store" and the court decided that consumer "initial interest confusion" did exist. Accordingly, it decided in favour of Brookfield's.

In April, 1999 WIPO published its Report of the First WIPO Internet Domain Name Process, focusing on the problems caused by the conflict between trademarks and domain names. The WIPO recommendations have largely been implemented by the Internet Corporation for Assigned Names and Numbers (ICANN) and have resulted in implementation of a successful administrative system for resolving domain name disputes involving trademarks and a system of best practices for domain name registration authorities, designed to avoid such conflict. However, on June 28, 2000 WIPO received a letter of request from the Australian government and 19 of its other member governments to initiate a Second WIPO Process to address certain intellectual property issues relating to Internet domain names. The Second WIPO Process concerns a range of identifiers other than trademarks and is directed at examining bad faith, and the misleading registration and use of those identifiers as domain names. These other identifiers, which form the basis of naming systems used in the real or physical world, are:

- International non-proprietary names (INNs) for pharmaceutical substances, a consensus-based naming system used in the health sector to establish generic names for pharmaceutical substances that are free from private rights of property or control.
- The names and acronyms of international intergovernmental organizations (IGOs).
- Personal names.
- Geographical identifiers, such as indications of geographical source used on goods, geographical indications and other geographical terms.
- Trade names, which are the names used by enterprises to identify themselves.

At their meeting held from September 24 to October 3, 2001 WIPO member states decided to refer the report to the Standing Committee on the Law of Trademarks, Industrial Designs and Geographical Indications. Following this review, at their meeting from September 23 to October 1, 2002 WIPO member states took a decision based on the recommendations of the Standing Committee on the Law of Trademarks, Industrial Designs and Geographical Indications. This decision has been transmitted to ICANN.

Copyrighted works

Literary and artistic works (i.e., original creations in the fields of literature and arts) are protected by copyright. Practically all national copyright laws provide for the protection of the following types of works: literary works, including novels, short stories, poems, dramatic works and any other writings; musical works; choreographic works; artistic works; maps and technical drawings; photographic works and audio-visual works.

Some countries also provide for the protection of: derivative works (translations, adaptations); compilations of works that by reason of the selection and arrangement of the contents constitute intellectual creations; works of applied art (artistic jewellery, lamps, wallpaper, furniture, etc.) and computer programs.

Copyright protection generally means that certain uses of the work are lawful only if they are done with the authorization of the copyright owner. The most typical are the following: the right to copy or otherwise reproduce any kind of work; the right to distribute copies to the public; the right to rent copies of at least certain categories of works (such as computer programs and audio-visual works); the right to make sound recordings of the performances of literary and musical works; the right to perform in public, particularly musical, dramatic or audio-visual works; the right to communicate to the public by cable or otherwise the performances of such works and, particularly, to broadcast, by radio, television or other wireless means, any kind of work; the right to translate literary works; the right to rent, particularly, audio-visual works, works embodied in phonograms and computer programs; the right to adapt any kind of work, particularly the right to make audio-visual adaptations. Copyright protection is usually granted until

50 years (in some countries, 70 years) after the death of the author. However, in some countries, there are exceptions either for certain kinds of works (e.g., photographs, audio-visual works) or for certain uses (e.g., translations).

Under some national laws, some of these rights are merely "economic rights" (i.e., rights to remuneration). Other countries also recognize the "moral rights" of authors and creators, such as the right to demand that their names be indicated on the copies of the work and the right to oppose the mutilation or deformation of their works. Some strictly determined uses (e.g., quotations, the use of works by way of illustration for teaching or the use of articles on political or economic matters in other newspapers) require neither the authorization of, nor remuneration for, the owner of the copyright.

Copyright infringement

The ease with which files in digital format can be copied and distributed has led to several copyright disputes. As well as outright copying of text, images or soundtracks, this can also occur through hyperlinks.

Mini-case study: Shetland Times v. Wills

In *Shetland Times v. Wills* the Shetland Times obtained a preliminary injunction to prevent the Shetland News from offering links from its website to stories on subsidiary pages in the Shetland Times website. Shetland Times claimed that by linking a subsidiary story page in the Shetland Times website Shetland News created the appearance that the stories originated at the Shetland News website. The court stated in its decision that headlines could constitute literary works justifying copyright protection.

Music is an industry that has been plagued by copyright infringement, largely owing to the increasingly popular use of MP3 files. As discussed in Chapter 2, MP3 is a file compression format that allows songs to be readily stored and downloaded on the Internet, typically 1 MB per minute of music. To play an MP3 file requires special software on a PC or a portable MP3 player (for details see Chapter 10). A number of high-profile cases have been brought by the music industry in an attempt to stop the piracy of music on MP3 sites.

Mini-case study: RIAA v. Diamond Multimedia

In 1999 the Recording Industry Association of America (RIAA) filed a suit against Diamond Multimedia, the manufacturer of a portable MP3 player called the Rio. The RIAA might have accused Diamond of engaging in "contributory copyright infringement" on the grounds that it manufactured and sold a device whose principal use was to engage in copyright infringement. However, bearing in mind the defeat of the closely related argument in the 1984 case against Sony, they relied on an obscure provision of the Audio Home Recording Act of 1992 (AHRA), which makes it illegal to include in any "digital audio recording device" a "Serial Copy Management System" (SCMS) designed to prevent the device from making multiple copies from a single copyrighted work. The Court of Appeals found in favour of Diamond Multimedia, ruling that the AHRA did not apply to the Rio device, because the computer hard drive from which the Rio records the music cannot be considered either a digital audio recording device or a digital music recording within the meaning of the Act. Moreover, since MP3 files are not coded with generation status or other copyright information, and copies cannot be made of the files downloaded to the Rio, the SCMS would serve no useful function.

The second target of the recording industry has been websites on which unauthorized MP3 files have been posted. In November, 1999 the Justice Department secured the first conviction under the NET (no electronic theft) Anti-piracy Act against a student operating a pirate site on his university's server. In June, 2000 Time Warner and BMG settled a copyright infringement lawsuit against online music company MP3.com. According to executives familiar with the deal MP3.com agreed to pay between $15 million and $25 million (£9.9 million and £16.6 million) to each label and agreed to pay a royalty per unit as well.

Another target of the recording industry has been Internet intermediaries that help web surfers locate free MP3 files for downloading. The recording industry early on brought pressure to bear on the popular search engine Lycos, arguing that, by providing users with an indexed list of MP3 files available on the Internet, Lycos had infringed the Digital Millenium Copyright Act. Lycos backed down, and its MP3 index has since been considerably reduced.

Perhaps the best known target of the record industry has been Napster; this is not a traditional search engine, but a P2P (peer-to-peer) protocol that facilitates online communities of MP3 users by enabling individual computer users to share information concerning the contents of their hard drives. Using Napster a user interested in obtaining an MP3 copy of a particular song can search the drives of other members in the Napster community for the song in question and then, after locating a copy, to download it to their own drive. The service proved extraordinarily popular, especially among college students, and a high percentage of the traffic on many university networks now consists of Napster searches and downloads. Napster claimed it was not legally liable for copyright infringement since it neither stores nor caches any digital music (infringing or otherwise) on its servers and since it has published a copyright policy document in which it disclaims responsibility for the activities of its subscribers and insists that they promise not to violate the law. Nevertheless, in December, 1999 the RIAA filed suit, accusing Napster of both contributory and vicarious copyright infringement. In 2001, after much legal wrangling, Napster was forced to shut down. (In October, 2003 it was relaunched as a subscription service.)

A file-sharing site that still survives at the time of writing is Gnutella, a file-sharing protocol that is fully distributed, making it difficult to identify individual users.

Mini-case study: Gnutella

Gnutella (the name comes from GNU, a UNIX-like operating system offered by the Free Software Foundation, Nutella an Italian chocolate and hazelnut spread) (Figure 9.1) is fully distributed information-sharing software that allows users to make public information that they wish to share with others; this could be a file, a directory or even an entire disk drive. The software allows users to take data offline and add more information as and when desired.

Gnutella client software combines a mini search engine with a distributed file-serving system. When you search for something on the Gnutella Network, that search is transmitted to 10,000 other users in the Gnutella Network. This "horizon" may change over time and will be different each time you log on to the network. If anything is found in the files of the 10,000 users in your horizon, the software tells you.

Gnutella claim its system is designed to survive a nuclear war. Since the information is distributed, if some nodes in the network are removed the rest of the network can still function; this also gives it an advantage over Napster since it makes it difficult for authorities or marketing companies to link a query to a particular user.

Figure 9.1   Gnutella (*gnutella.wego.com*)
(reproduced with permission from Gnutella).

Inventions

An invention is defined as "a novel idea which permits in practice the solution of a specific problem in the field of technology" and can be protected by a patent. A patent is a document, issued by a government office, which describes the invention and creates a legal situation in which the patented invention can normally only be exploited (made, used, sold, imported) by or with the authorization of the patentee. The protection of inventions is limited in time (generally 20 years from the filing date of the application for the grant of a patent).

In most countries, the requirements for granting a patent are that:

1. The idea must be new in the sense that it has not already been published or publicly used.
2. It must be non-obvious ("involve an inventive step") in the sense that it would not have occurred to any specialist in the particular industrial field, had such a specialist been asked to find a solution to the particular problem.
3. It must be capable of industrial application in the sense that it can be industrially manufactured or used.

Patent infringement

Patent cases have been less common than trademark or copyright cases, but are on the increase as companies rely on so-called business method patents, increasingly popular among Internet entrepreneurs. Some high-profile cases include the following:

- *Priceline v. Microsoft Expedia* In October, 1999 Priceline filed a lawsuit against Microsoft Expedia for setting up a system allowing bidding for hotel rooms. Priceline has three patents covering its name-your-price auction system.
- *SBH v. Yahoo* In November, 1999 Yahoo was sued for allegedly infringing a patent for one-stop online shopping by SBH, a patent brokerage that helps market, sell and protect patents. SBH was acting on behalf of Juliette Harrington, an independent inventor living in New Zealand who had been granted a US patent for an "integrated interface for vendor/product oriented Internet Websites". SBH claimed Yahoo Shopping site, which allows consumers to shop at stores without ever leaving the Yahoo portal, instead of directing consumers to individual online stores to make a purchase, violated the patent. In 2001 the two sides reached an undisclosed settlement.
- *Amazon v. Barnes & Noble* In December, 1999 Amazon won a lawsuit against Barnes & Noble, who they claimed were infringing on Amazon's patented 1-click purchasing process.
- *InterTrust v. Microsoft* In July 2003, in a crucial preliminary hearing, Intertrust won a ruling against Microsoft on 144 counts of patent infringement, contending that Microsoft products ranging from the Windows operating system to the Xbox game system violated its digital rights management patents. Digital rights management

technology, more commonly known as "anti-piracy technology", is aimed at protecting content, such as songs and videos, from being illegally copied.

- *Pinpoint v. Amazon*   In July, 2003 Pinpoint Inc. sued Amazon and certain retail partners, including Borders Group, Toys 'R' Us, Virgin Group and Target, for allegedly violating its patents on software that assists online shoppers with their purchasing decisions. Pinpoint claimed Amazon and the other companies had violated several of its patents, which cover software that makes recommendations to Internet users, based on their past behaviour.

As discussed in Chapter 7, Internet business models are often easy to copy, and one argument in favour of business method patents is that without patent protection a start-up is at risk of being crushed by a larger company with more resources. On the other hand, it can also give an unfair advantage to companies. As seen in previous chapters, even a delay of a few months is crucial in a fast-growing market.

Content blocking

Another area where the Internet may run into conflict with the law is in the area of freedom of speech. Freedom of speech is enshrined in Article 19 of the United Nations Universal Declaration of Human Rights:

> Everyone has the right to freedom of opinion and expression; this right includes freedom to hold opinions without interference and to seek, receive and impart information and ideas through any media and regardless of frontiers.

As discussed in previous chapters one of the drivers behind the conception and design of the Internet was to allow the free sharing of information, and one of the cherished uses of the Internet has been to act as a public platform for free speech. However, different countries have different views on what restrictions should be applied to freedom of speech on the Internet.

The following are some common reasons and examples of restrictions on freedom of speech: material that would likely be considered offensive, such as child pornography, material harmful to children; excessively violent material; material that promotes, incites or instructs in matters of crime or violence.

In the USA the administration passed the Communications Decency Act in 1996, a bill that proposed restrictions on telecommunications in the USA, including the Internet. This prohibited any material that is judged to be indecent. Indecency according to the Act is "any comment, request, suggestion, proposal, image, or other communication that, in context, depicts or describes, in terms patently offensive as measured by contemporary standards, sexual or excretory activities or organs."

One of the main arguments of the supporters of the Act was that the Internet is easily accessible by children who may intentionally or otherwise be exposed to harmful material. However, opponents argued that this was not a valid reason and that existing laws, such as obscenity laws, are adequate. Unnecessary legislation could stifle the new medium. Children can be protected by other means. Unlike passive media, such as television, accessing the Internet requires active choice. Therefore, they argued parents should take responsibility for their own children's actions. Furthermore, they argued the Act was unconstitutional because it violated the First Amendment of the Bill of Rights in the American Constitution which states:

> Congress shall make no law respecting an establishment of religion, or prohibiting the free exercise thereof; or abridging the freedom of speech, or of the press; or the right of the people peaceably to assemble, and to petition the government for a redress of grievances.

After a judicial review the judges agreed the Act was unconstitutional since the language of the Communications Decency Act left open the possibility of restricting content that had artistic, educational and political merit.

In some countries, such as Denmark, South Korea and Afghanistan, schools, libraries and cybercafes are required to install filtering software to protect children who use their systems. In June, 2003 the US Supreme Court upheld the controversial Child Internet Protection Act passed in April, 2001 which requires schools and public libraries to install filtering software on all computers.

Mini-case study: Net Nanny

NETNANNY (Figure 9.2), developed by Net Nanny Ltd of Vancouver, British Columbia, is designed to prevent children from accessing areas on the Internet that a parent deems inappropriate and prevent children from giving their name, address, telephone number, credit card or other personal information to strangers via email or chat rooms. The program contains a dictionary in which the parent can enter the names of sites known to contain sexually explicit or other material. Parents may also enter such phrases as "what's your name?", "what's your phone number", "where do you live" or "are your parents at home?" If anyone attempts to ask these questions, NETNANNY will automatically log off the network or shut down the computer. NETNANNY can also be configured to block access to files on the PC's hard drive, floppy drive and CD-ROM, to prevent children from accessing and altering their parents' financial records, work-related files, and programs and files intended only for adults. Finally, the program keeps a log of all activity that occurs on the computer, allowing parents to monitor their children's use of the computer. By using this feature, parents can determine if their children are using the computer to access inappropriate material and can then augment the dictionary to prevent further access. The program is launched when the computer is started up and operates even when the parent is not present.

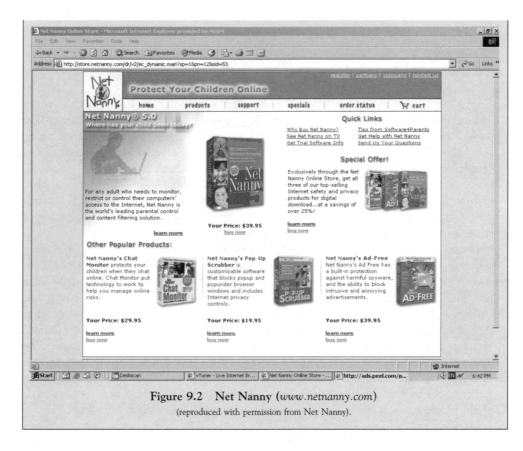

Figure 9.2   Net Nanny (*www.netnanny.com*)
(reproduced with permission from Net Nanny).

Material that vilifies people on the basis of race, gender, sexual preference or disability, or incites or promotes hatred on those bases

In January, 1996 Deutsche Telekom blocked access to Internet sites that were spreading anti-Semitic propaganda, a crime in Germany; this followed a request by Mannheim prosecutors who were investigating Ernst Zuendel, a German-born neo-Nazi living in Toronto. Deutsche Telekom also blocked access to a Californian company, Web Communications, because it provided access to Zuendel's site, the company maintaining that, although it did not agree with Zuendel, it was not its policy to censor users. Although Deutsche Telekom blocked access, the site was still available through CompuServe.

Material banned as contrary to the national or cultural interest

A number of countries including Burma, Bahrain, China, Saudi Arabia and United Arab Emirates filter overseas Internet sites to remove content that is banned as contrary to national or cultural interest.

Liability

In some cases the action of authorities has been not only to block the service but also to take action against the ISP:

- *Cubby Inc v. CompuServe Inc.* (1991) The first reported case involving an online service provider was *Cubby Inc. v CompuServe Inc.*; this decided whether an online service provider could be held liable for defamatory statements made by one of its subscribers. The decision rested on whether CompuServe was more akin to a "publisher", which is strictly liable, or a "distributor", which is not liable as long as they neither knew nor had reason to know of the defamation. It was found that CompuServe was more akin to a distributor as it had little or no editorial control over its subscribers. As CompuServe had no knowledge of the defamatory statements, no liability was imposed.
- *Stratton Oakmont Inc. v. Prodigy Services* (1995) In a more recent case, a slightly different approach was taken. In *Stratton Oakmont Inc. v Prodigy Services*, Prodigy, the service provider, was held to be a publisher of allegedly defamatory statements and therefore strictly liable for the statements of its subscribers, the reason being that Prodigy held itself out as having some kind of control over its bulletin boards such that it was suitable for families and therefore in theory exercised some kind of editorial control, even though Prodigy argued that it did no checking at all in practice. The Court found sufficient evidence of continuing editorial control to hold Prodigy to be a "publisher". This outcome was heavily criticized because it discouraged ISPs from policing content. An ISP could monitor content but risked increased liability or it could ignore content and risk prosecution for transmission of obscene material.
- *Local Court of Munich v. Felix Somm* (1998)   In May, 1998 a Bavarian court convicted Felix Somm, former head of the German division of the US online service provider CompuServe, of spreading child pornography and other illegal material by providing access to such information on the Internet. Germany's new multimedia law stipulated that access providers are not generally liable for Internet content, although they are required to take reasonable measures to block access to banned material. In November, 1999 the decision was overturned by the Regional Court on appeal.

Right to data privacy

Another area where businesses on the Internet may encounter legal restrictions is data privacy. As shown in Chapter 4 one of the most powerful applications of e-business technology is to collect information on customers. However, this needs to be balanced against individuals' right to privacy and the right to know what information has been collected on them.

One of the first attempts to legislate on this matter came in the late 1960s from the

Council of Europe, which sought to ensure that the European Convention on Human Rights conferred on individuals the right to protect personal information. Several member states of the EU subsequently passed legislation protecting the fundamental rights of individuals and in particular their right to privacy from abuses resulting from data processing (i.e., the collection, the use, the storage, etc. of personal information).

However, definitions of privacy vary according to context and environment. In many countries, privacy policy is either piecemeal or non-existent. Even in countries with similar cultures and linked histories, such as the USA, UK and Australia, privacy is defined differently:

- *USA*   "Privacy is the right to be left alone" – Justice Louis Brandeis.
- *UK*   "The right of individuals to be protected against intrusion into their personal life or affairs by direct physical means or by publication of information."
- *Australia*   "Privacy is a basic human right and the reasonable expectation of every person."

The privacy laws established by various countries can be classified into two types: comprehensive and sectoral.

Privacy law in the EU

The EU has adopted a comprehensive approach to privacy. In 1995 the Council of the EU approved the EU Data Protection Directive, which required member states to enact laws within 3 years which impose strict obligations limiting the processing of personal data.

The only reasons for which personal data may be processed include:

(a) the data subject has given his consent unambiguously;

(b) processing is necessary for the performance of a contract to which the data subject is a party or in order to take steps at the request of the data subject entering into a contract;

(c) processing is necessary for compliance with a legal obligation to which the controller is subject;

(d) processing is necessary in order to protect the vital interests of the data subject;

(e) processing is necessary for the performance of a task carried out in the public interest or in the exercise of official authority vested in the controller or in a third party to whom the data are disclosed; or

(f) processing is necessary for the purposes of the legitimate interests pursued by the controller or by the third party or parties to whom the data are disclosed, except where such interests are overridden by the interests or fundamental rights and freedoms of the data subject which require protection under Article 1(1).

All data collectors must register with the supervisory authority of each member state before processing information on data subjects and must also disclose how the information will be used.

In addition, the EU Data Protection Directive requires the following notification:

(a) the identity of the data controller and his representative, if any;
(b) the purpose of the processing of personal information;
(c) any other recipients of the data;
(d) whether replies to the questions are obligatory or voluntary;
(e) the possible consequences of the failure to reply to any questions asked by the controller; and
(f) the existence of the right of access to and the right to rectify the data concerning the individual.

It further requires that member states "shall guarantee for every data subject the right to obtain from the controller the following:

(a) confirmation of processing of data, the purposes of collection and the categories concerned;
(b) the correction of data; and
(c) notification to third parties of any corrections requested by the data subject to the information collected."

Finally, it requires that "no data be exported to a country with laws that do not give an "adequate level of protection' for data collection", except when the transfer of data is "necessary for the performance of a contract between the data subject and the controller" and the data subject has been informed of this. It should be noted that such legislation does not extend to other countries and currently there is a wide divergence of practices worldwide.

In 1998 the USA lobbied the EU and its member countries to convince them that the US system was adequate. It persuaded the EU to accept the "Safe Harbor Agreement" in which US companies would voluntarily self-certify to adhere to a set of privacy principles worked out by the US Department of Commerce and the Internal Market Directorate of the EC. Negotiations lasted 2 years and despite doubts the agreement was passed by the EC on July 26, 2000.

Privacy policy in the USA

In contrast, in the USA the approach has been to avoid general laws and, instead, focus on specific sectors. The Privacy Act 1974 regulates federal government record keeping. There are statutes that regulate specific personal data, such as credit reports, bank records and videotape rental records. However, the Clinton administration in its *Framework for Global Electronic Commerce* published in 1997 favoured a *laissez-faire*, market-driven approach to regulating the Internet. In general, self-regulation by the information industry along with technological privacy protection measures have been favoured. A number of information industry groups have issued voluntary codes of conduct and guidelines for fair information collection by their members. In some cases mandatory codes of conduct have recently been adopted. For example, in December, 1997 mandatory guidelines were issued by the Individual Reference Services Group (IRSG), which includes companies, such as LEXIS-NEXIS, which sell personal data via their online services; the three credit-reporting companies – Equifax, Experian and Trans Union; and other companies that sell personal information. The IRSG guidelines require that annual compliance audits be conducted by independent third parties. The guidelines prohibit members that are information suppliers from selling data to those found violating the guidelines.

The Privacy Act of 2003 (1) criminalizes the misuse, purchase, sale or disclosure of an individual's social security number without the individual's permission; (2) attempts to pre-empt identity theft and other types of theft by prohibiting the display and usage of social security numbers and their derivatives on federal documents by putting the responsibility on the commercial entities; (3) provides legal recourse to the Federal Trade Commission (FTC) on behalf of individuals for misuse, trafficking of personal, identifiable information in-between commercial entities and non-affiliated third parties.

Privacy policy in Canada

Canada has various regulations at the federal and provincial level regulating government information handling and has some sector-specific legislation as well. For example, Canada's Federal Bank Act requires that financial institutions adopt privacy codes, and most of the provinces have statutes regulating credit-reporting practices. As in the USA, industry groups have established model codes of conduct. For example, the Canadian Direct Marketing Association has compulsory guidelines that require members to ask permission before sending marketing email and to inform visitors to their websites as to what personal information is being collected and how it will be used. Meanwhile, the Standards Association has voluntary codes of practice for use by businesses. The Canadian Personal Information Protection and Electronic Documents Act also provides protection for certain personal data transferred from the EU to Canada. Canada was also the first government to make privacy impact assessments mandatory. All organizations/federal departments are held accountable for their information-handling practices, and a commissioner functions independently from other parts of the government when investigating. To ensure this independence the commissioner serves as an officer of the Canadian Parliament and reports directly to Canada's House of Commons and its Senate.

Privacy policy in Australia

In Australia, there is no constitutional right to the protection of privacy, although the Federal government enacted a Privacy Act as long ago as 1988, which regulates the handling of personal information by Federal government agencies and provides some protection for the use of credit information and tax file numbers by the private sector as well as the public sector. Under the Privacy Act, data users are required to develop and implement their own privacy regimes, which must be approved by the Australian Privacy Commissioner. Under the Privacy Act, personal data may not be transferred offshore, except where the transferee country has privacy legislation in place which is substantially similar to the Privacy Act or if, in the absence of such laws, the data subject concerned has consented to the transfer.

Other commonwealth laws contain privacy provisions that regulate the use of data matching, criminal convictions and Medicare information. Similar legislation was expected for the private sector. However, in March, 1997 the government announced its preference for voluntary self-regulation as in the USA to address private sector information-handling issues "because of concerns about the costs of compliance with a legislatively based scheme." In March, 2000 the Privacy Commissioner released a set of guidelines, known as the Guidelines on Workplace E-mail, Web Browsing and Privacy.

Most of the individual Australian states have to some extent issued their own guidelines regarding data privacy. There are also a number of other Federal laws that touch on the issue of data privacy, such as:

- The Crimes Act (1914).
- The National Health Act (1953).
- The Data Matching Program (Assistance and Tax) Act (1990).
- The Telecommunications Act (1997).

Privacy policy in Hong Kong

In Hong Kong, the Basic Law (i.e., Hong Kong's constitution, namely Articles 29 and 30) imposes obligations on the government to enact laws against intrusion of freedom and privacy of communications, except in the context of criminal investigations or if such instructions are in the interests of public security.

The Personal Data (Privacy) Ordinance enacted on December 20, 1996 protects: "any data relating to a living individual from which it is practicable for his or her identity to be ascertained." The data may be manually held or computerized. It may be collected by governmental or non-governmental organizations or by individuals. The Ordinance does not apply to personal data regarding corporations, governmental bodies or other entities. The Ordinance establishes the Office of the Privacy Commissioner, who is empowered to oversee the implementation of this regime, promote awareness of privacy rights, issue guidelines, consult the public for opinions and assess penalties for any contraventions.

Privacy policy in Japan

There is a constitutional right to privacy entrenched in Article 13 of the Japanese constitution, which states generally that both individuals and corporations have rights to privacy. In addition, there are various statutes that address privacy rights. The

Guidelines on the Protection of Personal Data in the Telecommunications Business (1988) provide fundamental rules regarding the confidentiality of communications and proper handling of personal data by telecommunications carriers and ISPs. The Guidelines regarding the Protection of Electronic Personal Data in the Private Sector (1997), issued by the Ministry of International Trade and Industry, provide guidance on the collection, storage and limitations as to the use of personal data.

Unsolicited email (spam)

As well as the right to see and correct personal data held by public and private sector organizations, one of the main concerns over use of personal data is controlling unsolicited advertising through email, often referred to on the Internet as "spamming". As seen in previous chapters it is relatively easy and cheap, given software such as LISTERV, to send copies of emails to thousands of people. Most online services prohibit mass email solicitations as well as the use of member names from public areas of their service. For example, MCI Telecommunications Corporation has a comprehensive policy against spamming, which it defines in part to be the sending of "unsolicited mass e-mailings to more than twenty-five e-mail users, if such unsolicited e-mailings provoke complaints from the recipients." However, such policies are voluntary on the part of service providers and are difficult to enforce. Hence, there have been some calls for such practices to be made compulsory through legislation.

The EU has legislation in the Distance Selling Directive (97/7/EC), which contains provisions requiring member states to enable consumers to register their objection to receiving unsolicited emails sent for the purpose of distance selling and to have their objections respected. However, the Distance Selling Directive does not apply to business-to-business (B2B) transactions and certain contracts are excluded including those relating to financial services.

Some alternatives to legislation are various technological solutions. The World Wide Web Consortium (*www.w3c.org*) has proposed the platform for privacy preferences (P3P), a platform that enables websites to express their privacy practices in a standard format that can be retrieved automatically and interpreted easily by software agents. P3P user agents will then automatically inform users of site practices, allowing them to decide whether or not to release personal information. However, at this time P3P has not been implemented and still has some gaps. For example, it does not provide a mechanism for making sure that sites act according to their policies nor does it guarantee securing personal data in transit or storage.

Other software allows users to remain anonymous while browsing the Web. For example, one ISP, Community Connexion, recently developed and released for free use and distribution a product called the Anonymizer (*www.anonymizer.com*) which allows individuals to surf the Internet without revealing transactional data to the websites they visit.

Encryption

The concern over data privacy needs to be balanced against the need for government agencies to be able to monitor certain activities of its citizens. For example, although encryption can ensure privacy of communications and make it much more difficult to commit fraud in Internet transactions, criminals can also use the technology to defeat law enforcement agencies. There have also been examples of terrorists using encryption as a means of concealing their activities. In 1996, several leading members of an Irish terrorist group were arrested and found to possess encrypted files that were eventually decrypted and found to contain information on potential terrorist targets. In the USA the FBI found that the laptop computer belonging to Ramzi Yousef (who masterminded the terrorist bombing of the World Trade Centre in 1994 and of a Manila airliner in late 1995) contained encrypted files concerning a terrorist plot to blow up 11 US-owned commercial airliners. In Japan the Aum Supreme Truth Cult, which was responsible for the release of sarin nerve gas in the Tokyo subway in March, 1995, killing 12 people and injuring some 6,000 more, stored its records on encrypted computer files. The authorities were able to decrypt the files, and the evidence they found was crucial to the investigation.

One solution that has been discussed is "key escrow" or the holding of encryption keys by trusted third parties (TTPs). However, many have criticized this scheme as being unworkable. An alternative to the use of TTPs and key escrow is the use of encryption products that support key recovery, also known as key encapsulation. Such encryption products, which are already commercially available and being used in the USA, can incorporate the public key of an agent (usually a company) known as a key recovery agent (KRA); this allows the user of such products to recover their (stored or communicated) data by approaching the KRA with an encrypted portion of the message. Lawful access to the keys can also be granted if a written authorization is served on the KRA. In both cases the KRA neither holds the user's private keys nor has access to the plain text of their message, so alleviating concerns about unauthorized reading of mail.

Multi-jurisdictional issues

Another set of social and legal issues arises from the global reach of the Internet, which by its nature crosses many jurisdictions; these may be federal, national or regional.

For example, in the USA, Internet retailers currently enjoy the same status as mail order retailers. They only collect sales tax from customers in areas where the companies have a physical presence, such as an office or warehouse. In October, 1998 the US Congress enacted the Internet Tax Freedom Act (ITFA), which immediately imposed a 3-year moratorium on any taxes on Internet access or discriminatory taxes on sales over the Internet while the issues were debated and resolved. In May, 2000 the House of Representatives voted to extend the ban on Internet taxes until October, 2003. At the time of writing a bill to make the moratorium permanent had stalled in the US Senate.

The bill does not apply directly to state and local sales taxes on Internet purchases. But there is growing concern among government circles that the growth of Internet sales could undermine the sales tax revenues used to finance public services including education, police and fire departments.

Traditional retailers are naturally also concerned about the advantage given to Internet retailers, but they face an additional problem. If they integrate their physical stores and their Internet operations (e.g., if the stores act as agents for the websites, by accepting merchandise returns in their stores for Internet purchases or by promoting their Internet sites within the bricks-and-mortar stores), they run the risk of causing a nexus or taxable place of operation in every state where they have a store. They would then have to collect a sales tax in that state, even for sales on the Internet.

The problem of taxation is more acute when sales operations are global. In October, 1998 ministers meeting in Ottawa at the OECD Ministerial Conference *A Borderless World – Realizing the Potential of Electronic Commerce* agreed that the same principles that governments apply to taxation of conventional commerce should equally apply to e-commerce, namely:

- *Efficiency* Compliance costs to business and administration costs for governments should be minimized as far as possible.
- *Certainty and simplicity* Tax policies should be clear and simple to understand, so that taxpayers know where they stand.
- *Effectiveness and fairness* Taxation should produce the right amount of tax at the right time, and the potential for evasion and avoidance should be minimized.
- *Flexibility* Taxation systems should be flexible and dynamic to ensure they keep pace with technological and commercial developments.
- *Neutrality* Taxation should seek to be neutral and equitable between forms of e-commerce and between conventional and electronic commerce, so avoiding double taxation or unintentional non-taxation.

Following on from the conference, a draft discussion paper was issued in March, 2000 for public comment on the application of the rules under tax treaties in the e-commerce context (OECD, 2000); this identified 26 different transactions and presented preliminary conclusions on how they should be characterized. However, there was disagreement regarding certain types of transactions, some members of the group believing that a distinction needs to be made between situations where the product is provided on a tangible medium (e.g., CD) or downloaded electronically, whereas others believed no distinction should be made. Examples of the disagreements are the different views requiring downloading of digital products and where content is acquired.

Transaction 2   Electronic ordering and downloading of digital products

This category of transaction stimulated much debate as it raised a fundamental character-ization issue (i.e., the distinction between the treaty definition of "royalties" and business profits). The majority considered that, in this type of transaction, the payments made by the customer would not constitute royalties but, rather, would fall within Article 7 as business profits. The members who share that position view this type of transaction as equivalent to the first category of transaction and consider that the mere fact that a digital product is delivered electronically should not change the treaty classification of the transaction. In their view, the act of copying the product onto the customer's hard disk or other non-temporary media is merely an incidental part of the transaction which is not important for classification purposes. The purpose of the transaction, for both the customer and the provider, is to deliver a digital product that the customer may use, not to allow the customer to use the copyright in that product, and the method of delivery is chosen by the provider and the customer merely to create distribution cost and time efficiencies.

A minority, however, considered that, in this type of transaction, the payment made by the customer falls within the treaty definition of "royalties". The members who put forward this view argue that the payment cannot be seen as being made in order to acquire a copy of the software or other digital product, since that copy does not exist until it is made by the customer by copying to the customer's hard disk or other non-temporary media. Since the customer makes the copy, the payment is made in order to acquire the right to make that copy and the payment must therefore be considered to be "for the use or the right to use a copyright ..." so as to constitute a royalty. They further argue that in this type of transaction there is no property or service, other than the right to make the copy, which is acquired by the customer from the provider. They conclude, therefore, that the payment is wholly for the right to copy and thus constitutes a royalty.

Transaction 25   Content acquisition transactions

The group agreed that two alternatives need to be distinguished. Where the site operator pays a content provider for the right to display copyrighted material, the payment would full under the definition of royalties to the extent that the public display of the content constitutes a right covered by the copyright of the owner of the content. Where the operator pays for the creation of new content and, as a result of the relevant contractual arrangements, becomes the owner of the copyright in the content created, the payment cannot be for royalties and falls under Article 7.

The Ottawa conference was followed by the Montreal conference in 2001 where the participants undertook to continue working to develop a framework that can accommodate established taxation principles that operate across a wide range of countries. At the time of writing discussions are still ongoing.

Dangers of winner takes all

Another set of public policy issues relating to e-business arises from the "winner takes all" phenomenon discussed in Chapter 5. The growing importance of global technological standards can lead, as we saw, to markets in which the "winner takes all".

This raises questions regarding competition law. The case brought by the Department of Justice against Microsoft (see inset box) is an example. This case and similar cases have both social and legal implications. While the case was brought against Microsoft on the specific question of whether or not the company broke the law, there are also wider questions for society. Do we want a society in which so much power is held in the hands of a single company or individual? Competition law is in place in many countries to ensure that this does not happen. But, as demonstrated in the Microsoft case, this concern must be balanced against the need to ensure that technological innovation is not stifled. At the same time, as competition laws are in place, intellectual property rights guarantee the rights of inventors and creators to profit from their endeavours. Without these laws, inventors and creators might be less ready to invest time and resources in their inventions or creations, and so society would be unable to benefit from these discoveries.

Mini-case study: US Department of Justice versus Microsoft

In May, 1998 the US Department of Justice and 19 other states filed an anti-trust suit against Microsoft, charging it with abusing its market power to thwart competition, including Netscape. A major turning point was reached in November, 1999 when presiding US District Court Judge Thomas Penfield Jackson published his Findings of Fact in the *Microsoft vs. US Department of Justice* case. In summary, the findings state that Microsoft has an effective monopoly of the PC operating system (OS) market, controlling some 95% of the market, and that Microsoft has used this market power to create barriers to entry. Furthermore, they state that Microsoft sidestepped the 1995 consent agreement not to preclude competition from products that could serve as alternative programming platforms. The methods they used to do this included market division, tying and coercive bundling, licence restrictions, intentional incompatibility, predatory distribution tactics and pricing, punitive OEM price increases, and delayed or incomplete disclosure of application program interfaces.

Overturning an earlier ruling that found Windows 98 and Internet Explorer to be inseparable products, the judge found that combining the OS and the Browser into one inseparable product had degraded the system's stability and security. Furthermore, the interlocking of the two products did not derive from any technological necessity. On more specific cases, the Judge found that Microsoft was guilty of:

- Retarding Netscape's ability to innovate by delaying access to new OS code.
- Hampering the development of Lotus SmartSuite by delaying access to new OS code.
- Preventing Intel from developing native signal processing (NSP) technology.
- Increasing the price of the preinstalled OS on computers by 200% in the past decade.
- Trying to stop Apple's QuickTime and RealNetwork's RealAudio technology.
- Violating Sun's licensing agreement by creating proprietary versions of Java.

Following the publishing of the Findings of Fact, the US Department of Justice filed a 70-page Conclusions of Law in December, 1999, proposing five possible punishments for Microsoft:

- Break Microsoft up into separate companies along product lines.
- Break Microsoft up into many identical smaller companies that are forced to compete with each other.
- Force Microsoft to allow competitors to sell their own versions of Windows, or to release the OS code as open-source.
- Force Microsoft to distribute competing products with Windows if it bundles its own.
- Force Microsoft to give equal prices to all the companies it sells to.

Microsoft's counter-arguments were that case law does not support the Department of Justice's claims and that, even if the Findings of Fact were true, Microsoft's actions still do not violate the Sherman Antitrust laws. They argued that by incorporating Internet Explorer into Windows they were merely adjusting their strategy in the light of the growing Internet-based economy. In doing so, they benefited consumers by offering them a superior product, for free, which encouraged consumers to get onto the Internet. In addition, Microsoft used intellectual property rights as a defence against anti-trust action. They argued that Internet Explorer and Windows 98 are now inseparable products, and as such are protected under federal copyright laws as one single product and should be exempt from anti-trust action. For this reason the claims against it by OEM's wishing to alter startup screens were unfounded, as it has the right against mutilation of its software product. Finally they argued that increased costs and problems would result from incompatibilities between fragmented operating systems and applications now monopolized by Microsoft products.

After a length legal process the Department of Justice finally reached a settlement with Microsoft in November, 2001. Under the terms of the agreement, Microsoft must license its operating system to key computer manufacturers for 5 years. The agreement also bans retaliation against manufacturers for 5 years. The agreement also bans retaliation against manufacturers electing to use non-Microsoft software. Microsoft must disclose its interface code – data used by software developers to write Windows-compatible code – and it must disclose its server protocols so non-Microsoft server software can work with Windows on a PC the same way that Microsoft software can. The settlement also bans exclusive agreements for support or development of certain Microsoft software.

The digital divide

The "winner takes all" phenomenon can also have more direct implications for individuals within a society. As well as positive externalities there may be negative externalites, and there is concern by some that electronic commerce may have undesirable distributive effects that affect individuals, small businesses and less developed nations. For example, many people have been concerned about a growing "digital divide" between poor and wealthy households. As seen in Chapter 2 a consistent finding across many countries is that intensive users of information technology tend to be well-educated and to have higher than average household incomes.

According to a report from the US Digital Divide Task Force (NTIA, 2000) groups that have traditionally been digital "have nots" are now making dramatic gains:

- The gap between households in rural areas and households nationwide that access the Internet has narrowed from 4.0 percentage points in 1998 to 2.6 percentage points in 2000. In rural areas this year, 38.9% of households had Internet access, compared with 41.5% nationally.
- Internet access among households earning $35,000 to $49,000 rose from 29.0% in December, 1998 to 46.1% in August, 2000 compared with 60.9% for households earning $50,000 to $74,999 and 77.7% for households earning above $75,000.
- Access to the Internet is also expanding across every education level, particularly for those with some high school or college education. Households headed by someone with "some college experience" showed the greatest expansion in Internet penetration of all education levels, rising from 30.2% in December, 1998 to 49.0% in August, 2000.
- Blacks and Hispanics still lag behind other groups, but have shown impressive gains in Internet access. Black households are now more than twice as likely to have home access than they were 20 months ago, rising from 11.2% to 23.5%. Hispanic households have also experienced a tremendous growth rate during this period, rising from 12.6% to 23.6%.
- The gap between men and women has largely disappeared. In December, 1998 34.2% of men and 31.4% of women were using the Internet. By August, 2000 44.6% of men and 44.2% of women were Internet users.
- Individuals 50 years of age and older – while still less likely than younger Americans to use the Internet – experienced the highest rate of growth in Internet usage of all age groups: 53% from December, 1998 to August, 2000 compared with a 35% growth rate for individual Internet usage nationwide.

Nonetheless, a digital divide remains or has expanded slightly in some cases. For example, divides still exist between those with different levels of income and education, different racial and ethnic groups, old and young, single- and dual-parent families, and those with and without disabilities:

- People with a disability are only half as likely to have access to the Internet as those without a disability: 21.6% compared with 42.1%. While just under 25% of people without a disability have never used a personal computer, close to 60% of people with a disability fall into that category.
- Among people with a disability, those who have impaired vision and problems with manual dexterity have even lower rates of Internet access and are less likely to use a

computer regularly than people with hearing difficulties. This difference holds in the aggregate, as well as across age groups.

- Large gaps also remain regarding Internet penetration rates among households of different races and ethnic origins. Asian Americans and Pacific Islanders have maintained the highest level of home Internet access at 56.8% but Blacks and Hispanics continue to have the lowest household Internet penetration rates at 23.5% and 23.6%, respectively.

Ethnic and racial origin is commonly associated with disparities in income and education, and there appears to be a similar correlation in use of information technology, the Internet and, by extension, electronic commerce. However, although the results showed that income and education levels were the most significant factors, the study concluded that, even after correcting for income, there were significant differences between the two groups.

Research on the effects of ethnicity on Internet usage is sparse, although Hoffman and Novak (1999) found that White users are more likely to report searching for product or service information than African Americans. One possibility is that general-purpose sites may not be perceived as an effective way to locate web content by African Americans; this might suggest, for example, the development of search engines targeted to the specific needs of ethnic groups.

Some researchers have suggested that public policy in the USA might have unintentionally actually widened the gap. For example, Cooper and Kimmelman (1999) argued that the Telecommunications Act of 1996 has had the unintended and unfortunate consequence of increasing the division between the telecommunications "haves" and "have-nots". As evidence, they point to:

- Increased concentration and less competition in the telecommunications and cable industries.
- Significant increases or flat prices, instead of declines, in cable, long distance and local phone rates.
- A growing disparity between those segments of the market employing heavy use of telecommunications networks, including the Internet, and those whose use is more modest.

It should be noted, however, that the Internet population undergoes considerable change, at least in the USA, according to research from the Pew Internet & American Life Project (*www.pewinternet.org*). A survey conducted in 2002 found that nearly one-quarter (24%) of Americans are completely disconnected from the Internet. The study identifies one group, "net evaders", as the 20% of non-Internet users who proudly reject the online world, yet they are comfortable having others pass Net-based information on to them. Another group are the "net dropouts", the 17% who once used the Internet, but quit after experiencing technical or ISP problems or lost interest. The most common reasons most cited for the lack of connection were that they don't want the Internet or they don't need it (52%), and concern about online pornography, credit card theft and fraud (43%), cost of access (30%), no time (29%), the Internet was too complicated (27%) and no computer (11%).

More stable has been the digital divide between developed countries and the rest of the world. As seen in Chapter 2 Internet access is also distinctly unequal between developed countries and the developing world. While growth in Internet usage has been astounding, it should be remembered that half the world's population has never made a telephone call, much less accessed the Internet. There have been concerns that without adequate actions to improve access in less developed countries, this is another digital divide that will grow.

Mini-case study: The G8 Dot Force

In July, 2000 at the Okinawa summit the G8 leaders agreed the outline of the Digital Opportunities Task Force, or "dot force", as they would like it to be known; this will comprise representatives from government, IT firms and NGOs from around the world. Its tasks will be to help bridge the digital divide by:

- Actively facilitating discussions with developing countries, international organizations and other stakeholders to promote international co-operation with a view to fostering policy, regulatory and network readiness; improving connectivity, increasing access and lowering cost; building human capacity; and encouraging participation in global e-commerce networks.
- Encouraging the G8's own efforts to co-operate on IT-related pilot programmes and projects.
- Promoting closer policy dialogue among partners and work to raise global public awareness of the challenges and opportunities.
- Examining inputs from the private sector and other interested groups, such as the Global Digital Divide Initiative's contributions.

In 2001 the G8 adopted an action plan consisting of nine action points to fulfil the aims agreed at the Okinawa summit:

- Help establish and support developing country and emerging economy national e-strategies.
- Improve connectivity, increase access and lower costs.
- Enhance human capacity development, knowledge creation and sharing.
- Foster enterprise and entrepreneurship for sustainable economic development.
- Establish and support universal participation in addressing new international policy and technical issues raised by the Internet and information and communication technology (ICT).
- Establish and support dedicated initiatives for ICT inclusion of the least developed countries.
- Promote ICT for health care and in support against HIV/AIDS and other infectious and communicable diseases.

- National and international effort to support local content and applications creation.
- Prioritize ICT in G8 and other development assistance policies and programmes, and enhance the co-ordination of multilateral initiatives.

In June, 2002 they adopted a plan aimed specifically at creating digital opportunities in Africa, where the digital divide is greatest in the world.

As Warschauer (2002) points out, the problem of the digital divide is complicated and not just a matter of technological development. Just as there are different types of literacy there are different types of computer literacy. Access to ICT cannot rest on provision of physical resources alone; rather, it must also encompass the provision of digital resources (such as relevant content), educational resources (such as training programmes) and social resources (such as community and institutional support).

Summary

This chapter showed how e-business is raising significant legal and social issues worldwide; this is to be expected, given the fundamental changes that the Internet and other e-business technologies are bringing about in many industries and economies. The nature and bases of competition in many industries are changing, and with that change comes challenges to the supporting legal regimes and social structures. Legal issues include the recognition and legal classification of electronic commerce transactions, use of personal information, freedom of speech, rights over intellectual property and jurisdiction on the Internet. A key social issue is the digital divide that is developing between some sectors of society and between the developed and less developed nations. These are issues that policy makers are still in the process of tackling and have yet to fully resolve.

References

Cooper, M. and Kimmelman, G. (1999). The digital divide confronts the Telecommunications Act of 1996: Economic reality versus public policy. Availability at: *http://www.consumersunion.org/other/telecom4-0299.htm*

Cornish, W.R. (1996). *Intellectual Property: Patents, Copyright, Trade Marks and Allied Rights* (3rd edn). Sweet & Maxwell, London.

G8 (2000). Okinawan Charter on the Global Information Society. Available at *http://www.g8kyushu-okinawa.go.jp/e/documents/it1.html*

Hoffman, D.L. and Novak, T.P. (1999). The growing digital divide: Implications for an open research agenda. In: B. Kahin and E. Brynjolffson (eds), *Understanding the Digital Economy:*

Data, Tools and Research. MIT Press, Cambridge. Available at *http://ecommerce.vanderbilt.edu/papers/pdf/Digital.Divide.chapter.nov9920.pdf*

Mueller, M. (1999). Trademarks and domain names: Property rights and institutional evolution in cyberspace. In: S.E. Gillett and I. Vogelsang (eds), *Competition, Deregulation, and Convergence: Proceedings of the 26th Annual Telecommunications Policy Research Conference*. Lawrence Erlbaum Associates, Mahwah, NJ. Available at *http://istweb.syr.edu/~mueller/studyhp.html*

NTIA (2000). Falling through the Net: Toward digital inclusion. Available at *http://search.ntia.doc.gov/pdf/fttn00.pdf*

OECD (2000). Report of the Technical Advisory Group on Treaty Characterization of E-commerce Payments. Available at *http://www.oecd.org/daf/fa/treaties/treatychar_4Sept.pdf*

Warschauer, M. (2002). Reconceptualizing the digital divide. Available at *http://firstmonday.org/issues/issue7_7/warschauer/index.html*

WIPO (1999). Report of the First WIPO Internet Domain Name Process. Available at *http://wipo2.wipo.int/process1/report/index.html*

WIPO (2001). Report of the Second WIPO Internet Domain Name Process. Available at *http://wipo2.wipo.int/process2/report/index.html*

Useful websites

Pew Internet & American Life Project *www.pewinternet.org*

Cyberspacelaw – learning materials on cyberlaw *http://www.cyberspacelaw.org*

Anonymizer *www.anonymizer.com*

Digital Divide *www.digitaldivide.gov*

Electronic taxation website *www.e-tax.org.uk*

Electronic Privacy Information Centre (general resource on data privacy issues) *www.epic.org*

Findlaw (general resource on cyberlaw) *www.findlaw.com*

World Intellectual Property Organization (general site on intellectual property) *www.wipo.org*

World Wide Web Consortium on P3P (technical solutions for data privacy) *www.w3c.org*

Key concepts

- Business model patent
- Copyright
- Cybersquatting
- Data privacy
- Deep linking
- Digital signiture
- Digital divide

- Domain name conflict
- Electronic signature
- Key escrow
- Meta-tags
- P2P
- P3P
- Passing off

- Patent
- Spam
- Tax nexus
- Trademark
- TTP

Self-assessment questions

1 Explain how digital signatures and digital certificates work.
2 Explain the difference between the various types of intellectual property and give examples of each in e-business.
3 Describe the types of conflict that can arise over domain names.
4 Explain how copyright infringement can arise without physically copying material from another website.
5 Explain the justification for business model patents.
6 What are some technical solutions to data privacy?
7 Explain arguments for and against stronger encryption policies.
8 What are some taxation problems that could arise in crossing jurisdictional boundaries?
9 Explain why competition law is a particular issue for e-business.
10 What are some social issues that are raised by the increase of e-business?

Discussion questions

1 Should business model patents be allowed?
2 Is the concept of copyright outdated given the widespread use of the Internet?
3 How should business on the Internet be regulated?
4 Which issues relevant to e-business should not be regulated by government?
5 What is your opinion about the OECD taxation proposals?
6 Why should businesses be concerned about the digital divide?
7 What can be done to overcome the digital divide?

FUTURE TRENDS

Introduction

A common theme running throughout this book is that changes in information and communications technologies have driven changes in the markets, economics and the strategies of firms engaged in e-business. This chapter examines some of the up-and-coming e-business technologies that are likely to have a significant impact in the future. It also examines two techniques used for forecasting: the relevance tree and scenario planning.

Technology forecasting

Trying to forecast the future of any technology is not easy. As we have seen in previous chapters some of the applications of the technologies currently being used were not foreseen at the time they were developed. For example, it was not clear until 1993–94 that the Internet would be the dominant means of networking people around the world. Going back further in time, Thomas Watson, the founder of IBM, is quoted as having originally forecast that there would be a market for just four computers in the world.

The problem in technological forecasting is that many factors are involved in determining which technology succeeds or/and how that technology is applied. However, a number of common patterns have been observed in many different technologies over the years (Twiss, 1992). The most common are:

- Steady growth.
- S-curve growth.
- Cyclical growth.
- Discontinuous growth.

Steady growth

The best known example of a steady growth pattern in information and communication technologies is the increase in processing power of microprocessors; this can be predicted reasonably accurately by Moore's law, articulated more than 30 years ago by an electrical engineer, Gordon Moore, the founder of Intel. Moore's law states that every 18 months processing power doubles while cost holds constant. Moore had observed that the size of semiconductors decreased with each succeeding generation of product and, as size decreases, the power increases geometrically both because circuits are closer together and because more of them can be placed on a chip. At the same time, the cost of producing a new chip was the same as the cost of producing its predecessor since improvements in manufacturing technology and increased volume minimized the cost of new facilities. So, older chips produced on equipment already depreciated would actually get cheaper.

Moore's law has operated with remarkable accuracy for 30 years and has been found to apply, for slightly different reasons, to other aspects of digital technology including computer memory, data storage and telecommunications bandwidth.

S-curve growth

This pattern of growth is less evident with the current technologies in electronic commerce owing to the relative newness of the market, although it can be seen to some extent with previous electronic data interchange (EDI) systems, which are increasingly being replaced by the Internet's business-to-business (B2B) system.

Cyclical growth

This pattern is also less evident in electronic commerce, although some commentators have argued that e-commerce technologies signal the beginning of a new cycle of industrial development rivalling the Industrial Revolution. Cyclical growth is also assumed in the industry and product life cycle models.

Discontinuous growth

The above patterns allow some extrapolation from past experience and can be used in planning and forecasting. Unfortunately, many of the technologies associated with electronic commerce do not appear to fit well with the above patterns, but exhibit discontinuous growth patterns; these are the most difficult to forecast by definition since the growth is different from past growth. One method sometimes used by R&D managers to identify discontinuous technologies is the relevance tree; this breaks down a technological system starting from the objectives into the contributing technologies. The hierarchical display of the tree shows the relationship between the technological choices at each level and how they relate to the system objectives. The tree could also be extended to show subobjectives, such as cost reduction and efficiency, and can be used

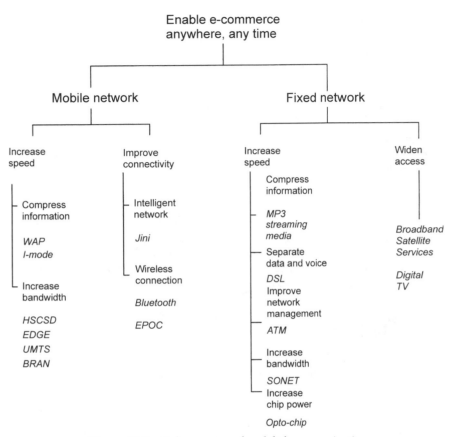

Figure 10.1   Relevance tree for global communications.

for planning R&D projects. An illustration of some of the key technologies for e-business is shown in Figure 10.1; these are examined in more detail below.

Data transmission

As the number of users and transmissions on the Internet increases a possible problem may arise if infrastructure development cannot keep up. Congestion was discussed in Chapter 5, when various pricing methods were discussed. An alternative is to develop faster networks and faster data transmission methods.

One such project that may reap rewards in new technologies and networks for data transmission is Internet2, a collaborative project involving more than 200 universities worldwide. Although its primary purpose is to develop new technologies to assist learning and research, the advanced networking technology and applications will undoubtedly have spin-off applications for business. Although Internet2 is not envisioned as a replacement for the Internet, it will include and further develop the National Science

Foundation's very high-speed Backbone Network Service (vBNS) which interconnects research supercomputers in the USA, and developments will eventually be shared with other networks, including the Internet.

Some of the applications currently being investigated include:

- Distributed learning modules, where students can take self-directed courses under the supervision of an educational system or teacher. Internet2 will also develop tools that will make it easy to create such software (called LearningWare) and will also help develop the Instructional Management System (IMS), a standard process for using the Internet in developing and delivering learning packages and tracking outcomes.
- New ways to envision and retrieve information (e.g., interactive multimedia information structures).
- Virtual environment sharing where participants in teleconferences can share the perception that everyone is in the same physical place, possibly with virtual models of shared work objects, such as architectural models or multimedia storyboards.
- Virtual laboratories where scientists in a number of different physical locations, each with unique expertise, resources and/or data, can collaborate on projects.

Connecting the home

We have already seen in previous chapters how several new technological standards are being developed to increase the connectivity between such devices as mobile telephones, televisions and PCs. In the future other household devices, such as refrigerators, cookers and entertainment centres, may be connected to the Internet. Three technological developments that will soon make such a scenario possible are the Open Services Gateway initiative (OSGi), HomePlug and SmartStack. OSG provides application programming interfaces (APIs) for applications that run on centralized computing platforms, such as residential gateways or even digital subscriber loop (DSL) modems. OSGi's API will be built on the Java platform, thus allowing portability between different platforms. OSGi will be compatible with Jini smart appliances and Bluetooth wireless devices as well as existing standards for home automation.

Possible applications include remote management of home appliances, security systems and patient monitoring. For example, the manufacturer of a Net-connected home appliance would be able to remotely diagnose problems and dispatch service personnel; security companies could use OSGi to inform of attempted burglaries; and outpatients could be monitored while they are at home and the hospital informed of any critical condition.

Use of OSGi will be complemented by other standards for home appliances, such as HomePlug and SmartStack. The HomePlug standard will allow direct connections to the Internet via standard electrical outlets, using the existing electrical wiring in the home. Combined with OSGi, HomePlug will enable consumers to place HomePlug-compliant Net devices virtually anywhere in the home.

SmartStack is a software-based modem that allows any "light Internet device" to access the Internet without the use of a PC. All required components for Internet connectivity (modem software, Internet protocols and a client application) are embedded on a single chip. With SmartStack, users will be able to connect any office or industrial equipment, consumer electronics device or household appliance or system to the Internet, to transmit and receive information, remotely access and interact with the equipment, and send and receive email; this includes vending machines, utility meters, point-of-sale devices, security or sprinkler systems, industrial machines and office equipment.

User-friendly software

Search agents and shopping agents were mentioned in earlier chapters, and some possible implications for how this might change buying behaviour were discussed. Although impressive these agents are still quite limited compared with a human user and are only capable of handling a small range of tasks or interacting with specified sites. As users of search agents will have noted, sometimes they return unexpected results, such as information on shipping agents or estate agents in response to a request to find information on software agents. They may also fail if the site searched changes the format of its data; this is because current agents are lacking in intelligence and flexibility. However, research currently under way at a number of institutions promises to deliver intelligent agents capable of handling a wide range of functions and able to adapt to different types of information.

For example, Autonomy (a company based in Cambridge, UK) has developed software that can automatically search for relevant material based on an analysis of users' text as they type it or read it. The system uses advanced pattern-matching techniques utilizing Bayesian inference and Claude Shannon's principles of information theory. By automatically forming an understanding of the concepts within the content of a piece of text or voice or by analysing an image or piece of video, the system is able to identify what the subject of the text is and what kind of information to retrieve. For example, it can be used to automatically search for related articles when the user reads an interesting article in a newspaper. It might also be used to locate other people within the organization who are working or have worked on similar projects. It might even be used to assist authors writing a book, such as this one, by automatically finding relevant sources of information.

Different software agents could be put together to offer a complete electronic commerce support system (ECSS). Wang (1999) identifies eight generic types of agents that would be required in such a system. Consider a system of software agents which assists a buyer in purchasing (Figure 10.2). The eight generic types are:

- *User interface* Interface descriptions specify the dialogue between the user and agents. In an object-oriented context there are two subclasses of a general interface object: one that requests input and one that presents information.
- *Goal* A central part of the ECSS is the provision of goal descriptions for the software agents. For example, if the negotiation has a goal of effective negotiation, how this will

Figure 10.2 Electronic purchasing system.

be measured and evaluated must be specified, including subgoals, such as satisfying time constraints and a high success rate.

- *Operational task* An agent can be employed to perform a basic operational task. For example, in Figure 10.2 the accounts payable agent can perform all the operations required in the accounts payable task and release the buyer from the paperwork.
- *Cognizance* In the above example the purchasing rule agent remembers all the rules and policies applied to the organization and provides guidelines for purchasing, while the negotiation agent may possess knowledge about the personal characteristics of negotiators, such as emotion, belief and culture.
- *Mnemonic instrument* A mnemonic instrument might be a sophisticated Internet search engine that finds a list of the most relevant suppliers.
- *Decision instrument* In the example the distributed inventory control agent might use inventory control models to support the buyer in making a purchase decision.
- *Work flow controller* A distribution inventory control agent might travel to the individual remote server mainframe computers located in corresponding warehouses to check inventory and bring inventory back to the buyer.
- *Learning instrument* A negotiation agent might learn negotiation skills from several buyers in dealing with various negotiators and under differing circumstances. When the agent faces an unfamiliar situation it would ask the buyer to give instructions and learn from the case.

One of the most promising areas of research with obvious applications for e-tailers and entertainment companies is research into synthetic characters that can mimic human behaviour. Animated characters in computer games have been extremely popular with some segments of the population, whether human-like characters, such as Lara Croft, or imaginary characters, such as Pokemon. Research is now being conducted at several institutions worldwide into giving such characters autonomous behaviour, complete with personality traits, such as sociability and friendliness. Several "virtual pets" are now available that exhibit the same behaviours as real life pets (e.g., wagging their tails and making facial expressions). These seem to be popular among Japanese consumers in particular where synthetic pets called "tamagotchis" have been a great hit. Software is also already available to create artificial human characters with limited behaviour. Ananova, the synthetic newsreader, is described below.

Other groups are working on software that will allow semi-independent avatars, or representations, of the user that can be used in virtual environments; this would allow, for example, users to take part in virtual meetings in which the avatar mimics the user's body posture and gestures. Such characters could be used in the future to create a more user-friendly interface for Web applications.

Mini-case study: Ananova

Ananova (*www.ananova.com*) (Figure 10.3) is a computer-generated newsreader designed to read news bulletins over the Web. News articles are coded into an extensible markup language (XML)-based format that includes tags describing the tone of the voice and facial expressions. The XML script is parsed into a text-to-speech engine, which produces an initial sound file and determines the melody of the sentence so that the voice sounds human. The voice output is also used to

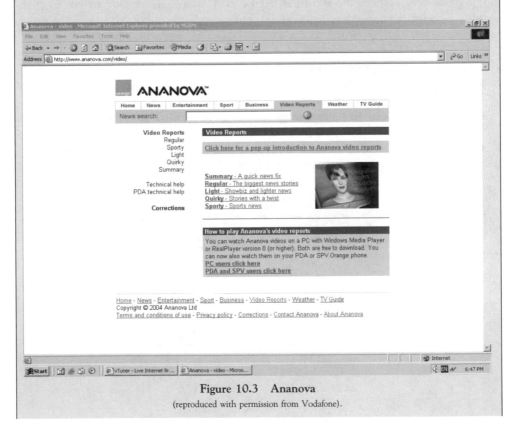

Figure 10.3 Ananova
(reproduced with permission from Vodafone).

direct a set of virtual "muscles" in the face so that the facial expression can be synchronized with the speech. Apart from national news, other applications that are envisaged include providing traffic news via in-car devices, early morning alarm calls, personalized entertainment schedules and current offers available in shops. (Ananova was bought by mobile phone company Orange in July, 2000.)

Synthetic actors have yet to reach the mass market and are unlikely to do so until virtual reality technology improves and becomes more widespread.

Security

Technological developments may also remove another stumbling block to e-commerce: fraud. One of the common reasons given for not using the Internet is the possibility of fraud either by the buyer or the purchaser. More widespread use of biometrics may significantly reduce the possibility of fraud. Biometrics is defined as "automated methods of identifying or authenticating the identity of a living person based on a physiological or behavioral characteristic" (International Biometrics Industry Association). The major biometric methods are shown in Figure 10.4. Many are already in use by high-security establishments, such as banks and defence installations, but have yet to be widely used for mass-market applications:

- *Fingerprints* Fingerprints have been established as a way to uniquely identify individuals for over a hundred years. The chance of two people, including twins, having the same fingerprint is estimated at less than 1 in a billion. Some biometric devices work by analysing the position of tiny points called minutiae, the end points and junctions of ridges. Others count the number of ridges between points. Others use image processing to identify the fingerprint. As might be expected, fingerprint devices are popular in military installations and financial institutions.

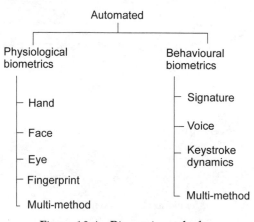

Figure 10.4 Biometric methods.

- *Eye patterns* Both the patterns of flecks on the iris and the pattern of blood vessels on the retina can be used to provide unique identification. Retinal scans have been available commercially since 1985, and most installations to date have been in military and bank facilities. Iris scan technology is newer and has the advantage that it does not require the user to focus on a target. In fact, a video image of the eye can be taken up to 3 feet away, making the technique easy to use.
- *Hand scans* Hand geometry is the oldest biometric technology and is widely deployed, including at airports, immigration facilities, hospitals, welfare agencies and day care centres.
- *Voice verification* Voice verification is also quite widely used because of its acceptability to users. It is being used in medium- and high-security situations, such as offices. It is also being increasingly applied in dial-up services, such as remote banking applications and terminal access.
- *Signature dynamics* Signature dynamics is of considerable interest as evidenced by the 100 or more patents in this area. Each company uses a slightly different technique to identify signatures, but generally relies on wired pens, sensitive tablets or a combination of both. Several devices can also capture the static image of the signature for reproduction and are becoming popular for bankcard, PC and delivery applications.
- *Keystroke dynamics* Keystroke dynamics identifies users by the way they type at a terminal. Studies by the US National Science Foundation have established that typing patterns are unique, but the technology has been difficult to commercialize because of difficulties in making adjustments for different keyboards.
- *Facial features* One of the fastest growing areas is facial recognition, stimulated by the increasing availability of multimedia video technology, which generally makes use of neural network technology and the statistical correlations of facial features to identify individuals; this is possibly the most promising of the biometric technologies for general application as it is the least obtrusive. For example, a webcam attached to the PC could be used to identify the user in restricted access applications.

Scenario planning and future mapping

As with any new technology there are three other key uncertainties that need to be considered: social, economic and political. One forecasting technique that companies have used successfully is scenario planning. For example, the oil company Shell claims that its use of scenario-planning techniques allowed it to foresee the potential impact of the two oil crises in the 1970s and to limit the consequent damage to its business. This approach aims to identify a range of plausible, self-consistent future scenarios and help executives identify risks and opportunities. The elements of a scenario include:

- A description of the current world.
- A description of the end state.

- A plot or story linking the current world to the end state.
- A set of logics underlying the plot.

There are several approaches to building scenarios, the most common being to project forward from current technological, social, political and economic trends and to imagine the outcomes, given certain events.

A technique that takes a different approach is future mapping (Mason, 1999); this has its origins in work at A. D. Little, Inc. during the mid-1970s (initially for IBM and later for Citibank) and is particularly suitable for a fast-changing field like e-commerce. In this approach participants build scenarios starting with a set of events and end states prepared in advance by knowledgeable experts; this gives participants a jump-start so that they can concentrate quickly on the logic and consequences of the scenarios. The purpose is to stimulate thinking about the key cause–effect relationships in the industry.

Mini-case: The Mobicom project

Mobicom (shorthand for evolution scenarios for emerging M-commerce services: new policy, market dynamics, methods of work and business models) is a project under the funding of the Information Society Technologies (IST) programme of the EC (DG XIII). The project is co-ordinated by the Athens University of Economics and Business (ELTRUN), and partners in the consortium include Sonera, Mannesmann/Vodafone, Stet Hellas, Lambrakis Research Foundation, Creditreform, ELTRUN, University of Cologne, University of Brighton, University of Jyväskylä.

The consortium used scenario-planning techniques to develop four different scenarios for how the industry may develop. Although it seemed that that mobile commerce is an industry with the characteristics of an unstable system, where there are many unpredictable factors, on further examination the group concluded that the system is more "controllable" than expected (i.e., there are some strong and predictable factors, such as interconnectivity and roaming, affecting the evolution of the consumer behaviour and industry). These factors are related to alternative channels of services from the customer perspective and to the battles of technologies and standards.

They concluded that it is likely that there will be no single, uniform platform for mobile services, as we have had so far in 2G cellular technology. Therefore, a factor of crucial importance is interconnectivity in order to provide access to the services; this will have significant implications on the size of the potential market and consequently increases the importance of roaming, integration, usability and pricing issues.

The four likely scenarios identified were:

- *Business as usual: slow growth in search of business models* (the trend scenario) By 2006 there has been a sloppy growth of mobile commerce and the market constellation resembles the situation of today. The economic downturn and aftermath of Universal Mobile Telecommunications System (UMTS) licensing rounds have stagnated the anticipated growth.

- *Consensus of institutions for controlled growth* According to our experts this is the most likely scenario. The big players have taken control over the development of infrastructure, standards and services for mobile commerce. Thanks to consensus, things are under control with few problems in technology, privacy, intellectual property rights (IPRs), etc. Some antagonists are seeing welfare losses as a consequence of operators holding back service integrators' innovations and common market competition.
- *Telecom is backing off* Telecom operators agreed to seamless roaming of mobile services all over Europe, as they see it in their interests to boost traffic on mobile networks. Competitively priced services on other technical platforms are pushing operators back to their traditional positions, specializing in data transmission and keeping up the infrastructure; this has opened up possibilities for new entrants on the service market. As a consequence, consumers face a growing number of options for getting access to the Internet, shopping and paying; hence, proprietary networks are losing ground. Simultaneously, IPR regulation is struggling for effectiveness and technical development seems to be constantly one step beyond.
- *Deregulated, liberalistic markets* The regulators were very active in creating and implementing a liberal mobile commerce policy, in order to boost competition on the common market. IPR regulation is effective, and seamless services are provided over various networks. Last-mile competition, portable subscriber addressing and transparent pricing of services have been introduced. The severe competition has boosted the innovation of services; however, few of them survive. This is causing problems in terms of using private and commercial data.

Source: Vrechopoulos et al. (2003).

Adoption of e-business in less developed countries (LDCs): The example of China

As mentioned in Chapter 3, one of the most significant developments in e-business markets has been the rapid adoption of e-business in the developing world. An example is China, now the second largest market of Internet users after the USA. Although this represents a tremendous business opportunity, the enormous economic and social implications are only just starting to be appreciated and studied. In the most extensive study on the use and impact of the Internet in China to date, the Chinese Academy of Social Sciences surveyed 12 cities and interviewed 4,100 users and non-users of the Internet (Liang, 2003). While previous research on Internet usage has mostly focused on the large cities, such as Beijing, Shanghai and Guangzhou, this research also examined usage in the small cities. Researchers surveyed three metropolises (Beijing, Shanghai and Guangzhou), four provincial capitals (Chengdu, Changsa, Xi'an and Shenyang) and five small cities with urban populations of less than 150,000 (Nanhai, Yima, Guangshui, Yimo and Fengnan). Unexpectedly, the researchers found that the proportion of Internet users in the small cities was close to, and in some cases even greater than, the proportion of users in capitals and metropolises. On average, the proportion of Internet users in relation to the urban population in the five small cities was 26.6%, higher than the 24% figure for provincial capitals and not far behind the 33% for metropolises. In fact, the city with the highest proportion of Internet users was Nanhai, in the booming Pearl River Delta, where 35.6% of the population are Internet users. Even in relatively poor cities, such as Yima, researchers observed that ordinary Chinese, especially the young, were prepared to pay to go online for news, interaction and entertainment. A key factor has been the springing up of low-cost Internet cafes, which charge as little as 1–2 yuan (10–20 cents) an hour for patrons to go online, making it affordable for many ordinary Chinese to go online. Another benefit has been that these cafes serve as "public schools", where many residents first learn to surf the Internet.

Mini-case: Booming Chinese market

The Chinese Internet sector is booming thanks to massive demand for short message service (SMS), online advertising and online games. The number of Internet users in China had reached 79.5 million by the end of 2003, second only to the USA, and leading Chinese websites reported rising profits for 2003. Sohu reported a profit of $26.4 million, Netease $39 million and Alibaba $12.09 million for 2003.

The booming market has attracted increasing foreign investment in the Chinese Internet sector:

- In June, 2003 the US-based eBay purchased a Chinese consumer-to-consumer (C2C) website named "eachnet".
- In October, 2003 Yahoo! purchased Internet research engine enterprise 3721 Hong Kong for $120 million.
- Toward the end of 2003 the US-based Tiger Fund injected $11 million into a leading Chinese online bookstore, Dangdang.
- In February, 2004 Alibaba, a leading B2B website in China, announced that it had secured $82 million of strategic investment from four overseas companies including SoftBank Corporation, Fidelity, Granite Global Ventures and Venture TDF China.

Other Chinese Internet firms have successfully raised funds in overseas listings. Ctrip, a travel information and booking service provider, raised $75.6 million through its initial public offering (IPO) on NASDAQ in December, 2003; others are planned.

However, the economic and social constraints on development in China should not be underestimated. Chen and Ning (2002) found that, although China has made significant progress in building the technical infrastructure and regulatory framework for e-commerce, it suffers still from poorly developed institutions and social networks; these are crucial in moving into the second phase of development of electronic commerce where the technologies are integrated into existing industries.

As discussed in Chapter 1, the Internet-based economy consists of several layers. The Internet infrastructure layer consists of the telecommunications companies, Internet service providers (ISPs), Internet backbone carriers and manufacturers of end-user networking equipment. The Internet applications layer produces software products and services necessary to facilitate Web transactions and transaction intermediaries, as well as consultants and service companies that design, build and maintain all types of websites, from portals to full e-commerce sites. The Internet intermediary layer consists of companies that do not directly generate revenues from transactions, but generate revenues through advertising, membership subscription fees and commissions from the Internet. Many layer 3 (intermediary layer) companies are purely Web content providers, while others are market makers or market intermediaries. This layer of the economy has so far failed to develop significantly in China.

A common problem with LDCs is that their institutional arrangements, while suitable for the early phase of partial industrialization, are not appropriate for the next phase of sustained industrialization, which requires closer co-ordination between industries. Thus, typically early industrialization is highly dependent on the supply of hard infrastructures. Continued industrialization increasingly depends on other types of collective goods and services (e.g., training, information, expertise, insurance), which are more specialized, less tangible and have a higher service content. In the case of China, two key supporting industries that are hindering the development of electronic commerce are finance and distribution. Internationally recognized credit cards are only available to those individuals and businesses with an account in foreign currency, typically with a minimum deposit of $200,000 to $300,000. Many retailers also still insist on some other form of identification even when a local card is presented. The use of credit is still regarded as dubious by some Chinese. Internet retailers in China usually require either cash on delivery, cash payment to the post office or establishment of a debit account. The poorly developed finance industry also limits investment in new electronic commerce firms. There are only 100 venture capital firms (mainly concentrated in the eastern cities of China) and the total funds amount to only $40 billion. Unlike Western countries, the bulk of the funding still comes from government sources and there is no secondary market for hi-tech stocks in China that companies can use to attract investment. The four leading ISP companies China.com, sina.com, netease.com, sohu.com have all had to rely on investment through the US NASDAQ market.

Another severe constraint on the development of electronic commerce is the lack of physical distribution systems. Although DHL provides a delivery service to 21 large cities, this represents only 2.6% of total stations in Asia Pacific; this has led some Chinese companies to establish their own distribution channels. For example, TCL Group (*www.tcl.com*), a manufacturer of domestic appliances, such as TV, DVD, telephones and air conditioners, has established a national network of 20,000 centres.

Apart from the more easily observable factors, electronic commerce in China is held back by other factors that are less easily observed; these include institutional structures that have been shown to be critical in industrial development. One of the key factors highlighted in the US government report *A Global Framework for Electronic Commerce* (Clinton and Gore, 1997) is the legal system. China has made some progress in this area. Following amendments to the Contract Law on October 1, 1999, contracts entered into on the Internet have been given the force of law. The Central Bank has also set up the

Finance Certification Policy Management Directorate, charged with helping to settle disputes arising from commerce. However, despite the introduction of tougher laws, the Chinese government is either unwilling or unable to enforce fully many of the e-commerce regulations it has instituted. Thus, software piracy is still very prevalent in China, as it is in many LDCs. In the Asia Pacific region as a whole the piracy rate is estimated to be 53% and in China it is reckoned to stand at 92%, according to the Business Software Association (2004); this, in turn, is slowing the development of a local Chinese software industry.

In addition to formal legal structures, studies of some of the most innovative regions in the world suggest that success is largely dependent on the presence of less formal institutions and networks; these include links between large companies, emerging companies, universities, support groups, local government, state government and federal government. Just as important as the institutions themselves are influencers, key individuals or bodies that are able to network with other influencers in each of the other segments as well as within each segment. For example, in Silicon Valley, leading figures in university engineering departments, venture capital firms, law firms and operating firms know one another, both formally and informally.

These informal entrepreneurial networks and formal links between institutions are either largely absent or poorly developed in China. For example, although the computer hardware industry is developing quickly in China, mechanisms for co-ordinating the activities of the hardware and software industries are lacking. Unlike the USA, where software development is closely linked with that of hardware manufacturers (e.g., the bundling of Microsoft Windows with Intel chips), in China this close co-ordination never happens. The result is that the software industry is lagging far behind. These constraints need to be overcome before e-commerce develops to the level it has reached in the developed economies.

The e-enterprise future

In conclusion, although the e-business revolution may have peaked in developed countries, it is only just beginning in many other countries. Even in the developed countries there are signs that a second wave of e-business development is under way. Therefore, there are likely to be yet more changes to come.

Throughout this book we have focused on some of the key differences between the strategic management of an e-business and that of a traditional business. However, looking forward another 10 years it is likely that many of the distinctions will be irrelevant because all businesses by that time will be e-businesses. The notion of a business that is not "e" in some aspect will be as alien as a business today without telephones or a home without a television.

References

Business Software Association (2004). Global software piracy study. Available at *http://www.bsa.org/globalstudy.htm*

Chen, S. and Ning, J. (2002). Constraints on e-commerce in less developed countries: The case of China. *Electronic Commerce Research*, **2**(1/2), 31–42.

Clinton, W. and Gore, A. (1997). *A Global Framework for Electronic Commerce*. White House, Washington, DC. Available at *http://www.technology.gov/digeconomy/framework.htm*

Liang, G. (2003). *Surveying Internet Usage and Impact in Twelve Chinese Cities*. Markle Foundation, New York.

Mason, D.H. (1999). Scenario planning: Mapping the paths to the desired future. In: L. Fahey, and R.M. Randall (eds), *Learning from the Future*. John Wiley & Sons, New York.

Twiss, B.C. (1992). *Forecasting for Technologists and Engineers: A Practical Guide for Better Decisions*. Peter Peregrinus, London.

Vrechopoulos, A., Constantiou, I., Mylonopoulos, N., Sideris, I. and Doukidis, G. (2003). The critical role of consumer behavior research in mobile commerce. *International Journal of Mobile Communications*, **1**(3), 329–40.

Wang, S. (1999). Analyzing agents for electronic commerce. *Information Systems Management*, Winter, 40–7.

Websites

The following websites provide news and information on the latest technological developments in e-business:

Internet.com *www.internet.com*
Red Herring *www.redherring.com*

Agents

Botspot *www.botspot.com*
Media Lab Agents Research Group *www.media.mit.edu/groups/agents*
MIT research on synthetic actors characters *www.media.mit.edu/groups/characters*
UMBC Agent Web *www.agents.umbc.edu*
NYU Media Lab *www.mrl.nyu.edu*
Microsoft research *microsoft.com/research*

Synthetic agents

Motion Factory *www.motion-factory.com*
Red3d *www.red3d.com*
Virtual Pet *www.virtualpet.com*
W-interactive *www.winteractive.fr*

Biometrics

International Biometrics Industry Association *www.ibia.org*
Association for Biometrics *www.afb.org.uk*

Key concepts

- Biometrics
- Cyclical growth
- Discontinuous growth
- Electronic commerce support system
- Future mapping

- HomePlug
- Internet2
- OSGi
- Relevance tree
- S-curve
- Scenario planning

- SmartStack
- Steady growth
- Synthetic agents
- vBNS

Self-assessment questions

1 Give examples of the different types of growth observed in industries.
2 Draw a relevance tree showing the key technological choices in providing intelligent, user-wearable devices, such as a wristwatch.
3 What will Internet2 provide?
4 Give examples of some of the applications in the home that will be made possible by OSGi.
5 Give examples of software under development that will make e-business more user-friendly.
6 What is biometrics?
7 What are the key elements of a scenario?
8 What is future mapping?
9 What are some constraints on the development of e-business?

Discussion questions

1 How will e-business develop in the next 5 years?
2 Which industries and businesses are most likely to be affected by the technologies in this chapter?
3 What are the consequences of technology developing faster along one or other of the routes shown in Figure 10.1?
4 What are some scenarios for e-business development in the developing world?
5 What are some of the key factors that will determine how e-business will develop in the future?

GLOSSARY

24/7/52 or 24/7 A business that is open 24 h a day, 7 days a week, 52 weeks a year.

ADSL *See* Asymmetric digital subscriber loop.

Affiliate networks A reciprocal arrangement between a company and third-party sites where traffic is directed to the company from third-party sites through banner advertisements and links and incentives.

Agents Software programs that assist people to perform such tasks as searching for information or comparing prices of products.

Animated banner advertisements (animated GIFs) Advertisements that display several different images in sequence.

Asymmetric digital subscriber loop (ADSL) A standard that allows large-sized files to be sent downstream at high speed while user responses are sent upstream at lower speed.

B2B Business to business.

B2C Business to consumer.

B2E Business to employee.

BBS *See* Bulletin Board Service.

Bandwidth The speed at which data can be transferred on a particular network. Usually measured in bits per second (bps).

Banner advertisement A typically rectangular graphic displayed on a webpage to advertise a brand.

Biometrics The science of using biological characteristics, such as fingerprints, retinal scans and voice recognition, to identify individuals.

Bluetooth Standard that allows devices in a network to sense each other.

Brick and mortar   Tangible physical assets, such as a factory, office building or warehouse.

Broadband technology   Technology that allows a high rate of data transmission.

Brochureware   An online version of a company's brochure designed to make visitors aware of and informed about a business's image or products.

Browser   The software interface between the Web content and the user. Examples include Internet Explorer and Netscape Navigator.

Bulletin Board Service (BBS)   A computerized meeting and announcement system that allows people to carry on discussions, upload and download files, and make announcements asynchronously.

Business model   A model showing how a business operates.

C2B   Consumer-to-business.

C2C   Consumer-to-consumer.

Certificate   A valid copy of a public key of an individual or organization together with identification information. It is issued by a trusted third party (TTP) or certification authority (CA).

Certification authority (CA)   An organization that issues certificates, or public keys and private keys, to individuals or organizations together with identification information.

Chat   A computer-mediated meeting where a number of individuals can send messages to each other over the Internet in real time or to a repository for later viewing.

Click-stream   A record of the path a user takes through a website.

Clickthrough   The action when a user clicks on a banner advertisement with the mouse to access the linked webpage.

Clickthrough rate   The proportion of users viewing an advertisement who click on it.

Co-branding   An arrangement between two or more companies who agree to jointly display content and perform joint promotion using brand logos or banner advertisements.

Collaborative software (or groupware)   Software that allows individuals to collaborate on projects by email, message lists and files.

Common Gateway Interface (CGI)   A method of processing information on a web server in response to a customer request.

Cookie   Small data file written to the user's hard disk that stores information that can be accessed the next time the user visits the site.

Customer relationship management system   Software and management practices to serve the customer from order through delivery and after-sales service.

GLOSSARY

Customer relationship marketing   *See* Relationship marketing.

Cybermediaries   Intermediaries who bring together buyers and sellers or those with particular information or service needs on the Internet.

Database marketing   The process of systematically collecting data about past, current and/or potential customers and using the data to formulate marketing strategy and foster personalized relationships with customers.

Decryption   The process of decoding (unscrambling) a message that has been encrypted.

Diffusion of innovation   The process by which an innovation spreads over time through a series of adopters.

Digital cash   An electronic version of cash (also referred to as virtual, electronic cash, or e-cash).

Digital certificates   Certificates consisting of keys made up of large numbers that are used to uniquely identify individuals.

Digital convergence   The technological trend in which different digital devices, such as televisions, computers and telephones, merge into a single device and where common software can be used across a range of devices.

Digital signatures   The electronic equivalent of written signatures that are used as an online method of identifying individuals or companies using public key encryption.

Digital television   Television images that are received and displayed on a digital television using binary code (0s and 1s).

Directories   Websites that provide a structured listing of registered websites in different categories. Yahoo! and Excite are the best known examples of directories.

Disintermediation   The process of eliminating the middleman from the exchange process.

Domain name   The web address that identifies a web server.

Domain name system   A method of representing Internet Protocol (IP) addresses as text-based names; these are used as web addresses.

Download   The process of retrieving electronic information, such as a webpage or email, from another remote location, such as a web server.

E-business (electronic business)   Business that is conducted using electronic networks or electronic media. Sometimes used synonymously with e-commerce and sometimes used more widely to include other business activities in addition to buying and selling.

E-commerce (electronic commerce)   The buying and selling of goods and services using electronic networks and electronic media.

Electronic data interchange (EDI) The exchange of standardized electronic business documents, such as purchase orders and invoices, between buyers and sellers.

Electronic mail (email) Messages or documents in electronic format.

Electronic mall *See* Virtual mall.

Electronic tokens Units of digital currency that are in standard electronic form and can be exchanged.

Encryption The scrambling of information into a form that cannot be read by unauthorized parties.

Extranet A network extending beyond a company to customers, suppliers, collaborators or even competitors. Usually, this is password-protected to prevent access by general Internet users.

File Transfer Protocol (FTP) A standard method for moving files across the Internet.

Filter Software that blocks unwanted material, such as pornography, from being downloaded from the Internet.

Firewall Specialized hardware and software application at the point where the company is connected to the Internet and designed to prevent unauthorized access into the company by outsiders.

Flow A state in which users have a positive experience from readily controlling their navigation and interaction on a website.

Frame A technique used to divide a webpage into different parts such as a menu and separate content.

Gbps One gigabit per second or 1,000,000,000 bps

General packet radio service (GPRS) A radio technology for GSM networks that adds packet-switching protocols, shorter set-up time for ISP connections, and offers the possibility to charge by amount of data sent rather than connect time.

GIF *See* Graphic interlaced file.

Global (or generic) top-level domain (gTLD) name The part of the domain name that refers to the category of site. The gTLD is usually the rightmost part of the domain name, such as *.co.uk* or *.com*.

Global System for Mobile Communications Originally called Groupe Spéciale Mobile, it is now the dominant 2G digital mobile phone standard for most of the world.

Gopher A directory-based structure containing information in certain categories.

GPRS *See* General Packet Radio Service.

Graphic interlaced file (GIF) A graphic format used to display images within webpages.

GLOSSARY

An interlaced GIF is displayed gradually on the screen, building up an image in several passes.

GSM *See* Global System for Mobile Communications.

Hackers Individuals who attempt to break through online firewalls for pleasure or profit.

Hit Each graphic or block of text requested from a web server.

Home page The main page (commonly the first page) that a visitor sees at a website, often linked to more pages.

Host Each server that is hooked up to the Internet is a host.

HTML (Hypertext Markup Language) A standard format used to define the text and layout of webpages.

HTTP (Hypertext Transfer Protocol) A standard that defines the way information is transmitted across the Internet.

Hyperlink A method of moving between one website page and another, indicated to the user by text highlighted by underlining and/or a different colour.

Infomediary A firm that specializes in the capture, collection or analysis of data. This service can be marketed to other businesses and can protect individual privacy.

Internet A global network of computer networks that use a common protocol (TCP/IP) for communication.

Internet access provider A company providing services to enable a company or individual to access the Internet. Internet access providers can be divided into Internet service providers (ISPs) and online service providers (OSPs).

Internet service providers (ISPs) Companies that provide home or business users with a connection to access the Internet. They can also host websites or provide a link from web servers to enable other companies and consumers access to a corporate website.

Interstitials Advertisements that are usually included within a "pop-up window".

Intranet A network within a single company that enables access to company information using the familiar tools of the Internet such as web browsers and Email.

IPO (initial public offering) The first offer of shares to the public.

Java A programming language standard supported by Sun Microsystems, which permits complex and graphical customer applications to be written and then accessed from a web browser.

Joint Photographic Experts Group (JPEG) A graphics standard specified by the JPEG. Used for graphic images typically requiring use of many colours, such as product photographs, where some loss of quality is acceptable.

Kbps Kilobit per second or 1,000 bps.

Lifetime value of a customer (LVC)   The sum of expected lifetime earnings minus the lifetime costs (acquisition costs, operating expenses, customer service) of a customer.

Loyalty schemes   Schemes where customers receive points for repeat purchases, which can be converted into offers, such as discounts, free products or cash (also known as online incentive schemes).

Marketspace   A virtual marketplace, such as the Internet, in which no direct contact occurs between buyers and sellers (also known as electronic marketspace).

Mass customization   The ability to provide tailored products or services for individual customers or a group of similar customers (a bespoke service), yet retain the economies of scale and the capacity of mass marketing or production.

Mbps   Megabit per second or 1,000,000 bps.

Meta-tags   Text within an HTML file summarizing the content of the site and relevant keywords that can be identified by a search engine.

Micro-payments   Digital cash systems that allow very small sums of money (less than 1 penny or cent) to be transferred.

Mirrored site   A copy of a website that can be used to reduce congestion and allows faster delivery of content.

Moore's law   A law that states that the power of microprocessors doubles every two years while costs decrease.

One-to-one marketing   A unique dialogue that occurs directly between a company and individual customers (or less strictly with groups of customers with similar needs).

Online communities   Groups of individuals who share common interests and use the Internet to foster their communities by accessing the same websites for communication.

Online service providers (OSPs)   An OSP is sometimes used to distinguish large Internet service providers (ISPs), such as AOL, from other access providers. Usually, they provide other services in addition to Internet access.

P2P   *See* Peer to peer.

Page impression   A count of each time a member of the audience views a webpage.

Peer to peer (P2P)   Electronic file-swapping systems that allow users to share files, computing capabilities, networks, bandwidth and storage.

Permission marketing   Marketing when the customer agrees to receive e-mail based on direct marketing.

Personalization   Delivering customized content for the individual through webpages, email or push technology.

PKI   *See* Public-key infrastructure

Plug-in   A program that must be downloaded to view particular content such as an animation.

Portal   A website that acts as a gateway to the information on the Internet by providing search engines, directories and other services, such as personalized news or free email.

Proxy server   A server that intercepts all requests from a web browser to the real server. If it can fulfil the requests itself, it will do so; if not, it forwards the request to the real server. The purpose is to improve performance and filter requests.

Psychographics (lifestyle criteria)   Profiling of individuals based on their preferred activities, interests and opinions.

Public key   A unique identifier of a buyer or a seller that is available to other parties to enable secure e-commerce using encryption based on digital certificates.

Public key encryption   An asymmetric form of encryption in which the keys, or digital certificates, used by the sender and receiver of information are different. The two keys are related in such a way that use of the pair of keys is the only means of encrypting and decrypting information.

Public key infrastructure (PKI)   Infrastructure of organizations and technology that allows public key encryption to be used.

Push technology   The delivery of Web-based content to the user's desktop without the need for the user to visit a site to download information.

Reach   The number of unique individuals who view an advertisement.

Reintermediation   The creation of new intermediaries between customers and suppliers providing services, such as supplier search and product evaluation.

Relationship marketing   Marketing practices designed to build and maintain long-term relationships with customers.

Rich media advertisements   Advertisements that are not static, but provide animation, sound or interactivity (e.g., to direct users to another site or perform some transaction).

Search engines   Specialized websites that use automatic software tools to locate webpages of registered sites that match the keywords typed in by the user.

Second-level domain name   Refers to the company name, also referred to as the enterprise name.

Secure electronic transaction (SET)   A standard for public key encryption intended to enable secure electronic commerce transactions (developed by Mastercard and Visa).

Secure sockets layer (SSL)   A commonly used encryption technique for scrambling data, such as credit card numbers as they are passed across the Internet from a web browser to a web server.

SET   *See* Secure electronic transaction.

Site "stickiness"   An indication of how long a visitor stays on a site.

Smartcards   Physical cards containing a memory chip that can be inserted into a smartcard reader before items can be purchased.

Software wallet   Software that credits or debits a user's account when a transaction is undertaken.

Spam   Unsolicited bulk mailing to a large number of individuals over the Internet.

Spider   Software that indexes webpages of registered sites on a regular basis.

Sponsorship   Payment to advertise on a website.

SSL   *See* Secure sockets layer.

Streaming   Transmission of digital content in small packets that are played as they come in; this allows large multimedia files to play without downloading the entire file at once.

Third-level, or subenterprise, domain name   Refers to an individual server within an organization.

Thumbnail   A quick sketch of a concept or an image reduced in size and detail.

Top-level domain name   That part of the domain name that refers to the category of site, such as *.com* or *.co.uk* (also known as global, or generic, top-level domain name, or gLTD).

Transfer Control Protocol/Internet Protocol (TCP/IP)   The standard for passing of data packets on the Internet.

Trusted third parties (TTPs)   Companies with which an agreement has been reached to share information.

Uniform (universal) resource locator (URL)   Text that indicates the web address of a site.

Upload   The transfer of files from a local computer to a server.

Value chain   A way of envisioning the collection of activities that a business undertakes to design, produce, market, deliver, and support products or services.

Vertical portals   Business-to-business sites that are designed to serve narrow niches within specific industries (e.g., by providing industry news, details of business techniques and product and service reviews); also known as vortals.

Viral marketing   Marketing in which a customer promotes something through use of a product or service, such as a website or email.

Virtual community   An Internet-based forum for special interest groups to communicate using a bulletin board to post messages.

Virtual mall   A website that brings together different electronic retailers at a single virtual (online) location (also known as electronic mall).

Virtual organization   An organization that uses information and communications technology to allow it to operate without clearly defined physical boundaries between different functions, some of which may be outsourced to third parties.

Virtual private network (VPN)   A network that connects two businesses, such as a franchise and its headquarters, using dedicated lines (communications lines that are not open to outside users) which are connected to ISPs.

VPN   *See* Virtual private network.

WAP (wireless application protocol)   A protocol that allows Internet access using a mobile phone.

Web servers   Computers that are used to store the web pages accessed by web browsers. They may also contain databases of customer or product information, which can be queried and retrieved using a browser.

Website   Content accessible on the World Wide Web that is created by a particular organization or individual.

Webcasting   The automatic delivery of content to many users.

Wi-Fi   *See* Wireless fidelity.

Wireless Fidelity (Wi-Fi)   Otherwise known as wireless networking, a standard that provides short-range, high-speed data connections between mobile data devices (such as laptops) and nearby Wi-Fi access points (special hardware connected to a wired network).

World Wide Web   A means for linking information on the Internet. Information on the World Wide Web is accessed using a browser.

WML (wireless markup language)   Markup language for mobile phones based on HTML.

XML (extensible markup language)   An advanced markup language that gives better control than HTML over format for structured information on webpages.

Author index

Lead authors in bold.

COMPANY AND PRODUCT INDEX

Mini-cases in bold.

SUBJECT INDEX

Tomato garden 248
TRADACOMS 35
Trademarks 296
Transaction cost 155
Transaction cost theory 190–4
Trusted third party 292
TTP 292

UMTS 63
Unbundling 287–8
UNCITRAL 294
Uniform Electronic Transaction Act 295
Uniform resource locator 46
United Arab Emirates 307
United Nations Universal Declaration of
    Human Rights 305
Unix 40
Unmetered Internet access 118–19
Unstable market 218–20
URL 46
USA 310
US Department of Justice v. Microsoft 317
USENET 40
User-friendly software 329–32
User interface 171
Utility 78

VADS 35
VALS 89
Valuation 245–50
Value-based organization 285
Value-added data service 35
Value-added network 35
Value chain 188
Value cluster analysis 232
Value curve 222
Value innovation 221–2
Value net 232
Value system analysis 186, 218
Value web 232
VAN 35
vBNS 325
VBO 285
Very small aperture terminal 69
Videoconferencing 25
Video on demand 74

Videotex 37
Viral marketing 137–8
Virtual community 132–8
Virtual machine 49
Virtual marketspace 107–9
Virtual organization 255–7
Virtual private networks 55
Virtual resellers 192
Virtual sourcing 262–3
Virtual transactions 292
Virtual value chain 214
Visitor count 244
VML 64
VOD 74
Voice activated markup language 64
Voice verification 333
VPN 55
VRML 71
VSAT 69

W-CDMA 61
WAP 60
Webcam 112
Website architectures 53
Website evaluators 192
Wi-Fi 66
Winner takes all 167, 316
Wireless devices 130
Wireless markup language 60
Wireless technologies 58
WML 60
World Wide Web 45
World Wide Web Consortium 313

X12 35
XML 71

Yield managers 159

.com 47
.gov 47
.int 47
.mil 47
.net 47
.org 47